T0245540

DÜNKIRCHEN 1940

OSPREY
PUBLISHING

DEDICATION

Dedicated to 'the Girls': Lynn, Chrissie, Jane and Shirley

ROBERT KERSHAW

DÜNKIRCHEN
1940

THE
GERMAN VIEW
OF DUNKIRK

OSPREY PUBLISHING
Bloomsbury Publishing Plc
Kemp House, Chawley Park, Cumnor Hill, Oxford OX2 9PH, UK
29 Earlsfort Terrace, Dublin 2, Ireland
1385 Broadway, 5th Floor, New York, NY 10018, USA
E-mail:info @ospreypublishing.com
www.ospreypublishing.com

OSPREY is a trademark of Osprey Publishing Ltd

First published in Great Britain in 2022

© Robert Kershaw, 2022

Robert Kershaw has asserted his right under the Copyright, Designs and Patents Act, 1988,
to be identified as Author of this work.

A catalogue record for this book is available from the British Library.

ISBN: HB 978 1 4728 5437 7; PB 978 1 4728 5439 1; eBook 978 1 4728 5438 4;
ePDF 978 1 4728 5440 7; XML 978 1 4728 5442 1

23 24 25 26   10 9 8 7 6 5

Image credits are given in full in the List of Illustrations (pp. 11–14).
Uncredited images form part of the author's collection.
Maps by Piernine Ltd
Index by Alan Rutter

Typeset by Deanta Global Publishing Services, Chennai, India
Printed and bound in Great Britain by CPI (Group) UK Ltd, Croydon CR0 4YY

Osprey Publishing supports the Woodland Trust, the UK's leading woodland conservation charity.

To find out more about our authors and books visit www.ospreypublishing.com. Here you will find
extracts, author interviews, details of forthcoming events and the option to sign up for our newsletter.

Contents

Prologue

Dunkerque, France

Eighty years after the Dunkirk evacuation, the plank walkway that was the East Mole no longer exists. There is a sign in bad English, supported by a photograph of British soldiers scrambling aboard a ship, to show where it once was. Two-thirds of the British Expeditionary Force (BEF) walked to safety along this fragile wooden platform, three abreast, but today there is simply a line of sea defence boulders next to a concrete walkway protruding into the harbour. Why couldn't the *Luftwaffe* collapse this flimsy wooden structure before? Off to the right is the seaside resort of Malo-les-Bains, with its crowds of holidaymakers relaxing on fine white sand with multi-coloured windbreaks and umbrellas. The backdrop is the sound of children playing, rising above the gentle surf. In May 1940 the French destroyer *L'Adroit* languished in shallow water offshore, like a beached grey whale, her back broken by Stuka bombs. There is no evidence of war here today.

Looking east, the gently shelving white-sand beach stretches 17½ miles into the distance, past the holiday resorts of Bray Dunes and De Panne in Belgium to Nieuport. On average 10,000 men per day queued here waiting to be picked up, despite being mercilessly bombed and machine gunned by the *Luftwaffe*. In total, an army three times the size of the present British Army passed across these beaches. Absolutely no trace of lorry piers covered with planking stretching out to sea or the abandoned vehicles, guns and military equipment remain. At especially low tide the dinosaur-like ribcage wrecks of the beached and bombed paddle steamers *Crested Eagle* and *Devonia* are still visible.

The former now hosts a mussel farm. Behind the red-brick Zuydcoote maritime hospital nearby, where columns of British troops waded out into the surf to be picked up, is the *Reserve Naturelle Dune Marchand*. This nature reserve of 83 acres preserves the original dune landscape into which British and French soldiers burrowed to avoid air attack. Apart from shrapnel and machine gun scars on the brickwork in some back streets, there is nothing to differentiate this scene from a popular holiday resort.

I stand on the hill at Cassel, the only high ground for miles around, with Dunkirk in line of sight 18 miles to the north. The panorama before me exudes history. Off the coast at Gravelines by Dunkirk port, the Spanish Armada was engaged in a running fight in the summer of 1588 with the combined British fleets of Drake and Howard. On 15 June 1658 the 'Battle of the Dunes' was fought just ahead, Dunkirk being under Spanish control in the morning, French by midday and British at the end of the afternoon. Indeed, Cassel was the hill where the 'Grand Old Duke of York' marched up and down again with 'ten thousand' during the French Revolutionary Wars. From my vantage point I can see virtually the whole of the Dunkirk perimeter as it was in May 1940, but there is little to suggest to the casual tourist that momentous events happened here. A huge black column of smoke boiled up from the burning refineries in 1940, a navigational guide for retreating British soldiers, aircraft from all sides and German infantry advancing on the port.

I was here to make sense of the plethora of documents I had amassed on the German view of Dunkirk. British narratives tend to be tinged with nostalgic patriotism, especially television documentaries. Few clues can be discerned from the landscape, except it is totally flat bordering the Dunkirk beaches, and there is an extensive canal and waterway system enclosing the former perimeter. At the back of my mind was the absence of fear within any British veteran accounts about Dunkirk that a panzer attack might reach the beaches. I knew about Hitler's Panzer Halt Order, and the prevailing opinion that, but for the stop, Dunkirk would have been captured before the BEF even got there. This forms part of the accepted Dunkirk myth. But contemporary German accounts reveal that, even before the halt was ordered, the French checked the lead panzer division in its tracks on the western outskirts of Dunkirk.

My own military experience suggested the approaches to Dunkirk port, deliberately flooded, and herringboned with drainage ditches, were completely unsuited for armoured operations. The Dunkirk evacuation took nine days, but the panzers were held back for only one of those nine. What really happened during the four days when the core fighting divisions – the seed corn of the future British army – were evacuated?

Dunkerque in May 1940 was a town of 31,000 inhabitants crammed behind old city walls, which from the 19th century had been at the heart of an expanding urban conurbation of around 100,000 people. It was the third largest port in France and a steel and shipbuilding centre. It was a lot greyer then, French poet Henri Damaye describing Dunkirk as 'an austere town with forbidding streets', filled with commercial bustle.[1]

There had been enormous relief in France when British Prime Minister Neville Chamberlain abandoned the Czechs and signed the Munich Agreement in the September of 1938. By early 1939, the grateful French felt they had dodged conflict and death at the last minute. War was, however, back on the agenda when the German *Wehrmacht* entered Prague. Danzig in Poland looked like it might be next, but the French did not seriously believe anyone would go to war over Danzig.

But crowds of Spanish Civil War refugees thronging southern France suggested democracy in Europe was indeed at risk. Rearmament and the arms race stepped up. An unprecedented military style parade on Bastille Day along the Champs-Élysées was conducted to reassure the French people of their army's invincibility and give Germany pause for thought. Up to 45% of people interviewed that July anticipated a war in 1939 and 76% of them now felt force ought to be used against Germany if it attempted to seize the free city of Danzig. Hitler's shocking announcement of a non-aggression pact with the Soviet Union took the breath out of diplomatic safeguards that stood in the way of war, as well as engendering a sense of acute betrayal among the Left. Stalin had, at a blow, left Hitler free to attack Western Europe. On 31 August the First French Army reservists were called up.[2]

Two days later Dunkerque railway station was congested with men leaving to rejoin units or steaming into the station to form up with the 310th and 73rd Infantry Regiments. There was no patriotic fervour like that of 1914. Grim expressionless faces peered out from trucks departing in streets watched by World War I widows, dressed once again in black. General mobilization was called when wireless reports announced the Germans had invaded Poland. On 3 September Britain declared war with Germany, and France later followed suit.

Nine months of the so-called *drôle de guerre* or Phoney War followed. Dunkerque's mayor, Alfred Dorp, drew up a list of 72 large cellars that could be converted into public air raid shelters. Public building walls were sandbagged for protection and private individuals strengthened their basement cellars and covered air vents to block out gas. Blackouts were instituted and street lighting converted to blue. Sirens wailed out at 5pm on the day war was declared but it was a false alarm. During the winter of 1939–40, 15 air raid warnings sounded, but none between January and 3 May, which encouraged a false sense of security. Thereafter sirens wailed each day when German *Luftwaffe* reconnaissance over flights stepped up.

Schoolgirl Paule Rogalin lived in Dunkerque with her mother. 'My father had been drafted', she recalled, 'and was stationed nearby.' Wartime measures were scary; she was 'petrified' having to take an old-fashioned World War I gas mask to school, because it was thought the Germans would once again use gas. 'Since so many French ships were coming through Dunkerque we saw soldiers all the time, and we knew something bad was going to happen soon. It was like living on dynamite.'[3]

Drôle de guerre was unreal. The border with Belgium was not today's relaxed demarcation line; it was strongly defended with bunkers. Belgium and Holland were neutral, so there were no military exchanges or cooperation of any consequence. Travel between France and Belgium along the fortified frontier to the east of Dunkirk was forbidden. A bizarre consequence of this was the slavish rule applied by zealous officials at a wedding, when the French bride and Belgian groom were obliged to exchange vows across a table positioned precisely, with legs either side of the frontier demarcation line.[4]

The command centre for French naval forces north, *Admiral Nord*, was at Bastion 32, one of the few old fortifications around the port that escaped demolition, situated between the outer harbour and the beach at Malo-les-Bains. The formidable coastal batteries defending the town all faced out to sea. Defence of the hinterland was the responsibility of the *Secteur Fortifié des Flandres* (SFF; Fortified Sector of Flanders), commanded by General Barthélémy. The 53rd French Infantry Division created and dug a network of concrete bunkers and field fortifications to protect it, with 400 installations for artillery and machine guns, screened by minefields with anti-tank guns. Simply put, Dunkerque was well defended. The 68th Infantry Division commanded by General Beaufrère, formed on 16 January 1940, had its infantry regiments inside the urban areas surrounding Dunkirk. The 22nd, 34th and the 225th Infantry Divisions were situated at Gravelines on the west side and the 59th at Sainte-Pole-sur-Mer to the east. They were in effect locals.

The morning of 10 May heralded a beautiful mild spring day. At 4am, the people of Dunkerque were woken again by the same irritating sirens that had whined every day for the past week. This time the noise included the dull thud of explosions and sharp cracks of anti-aircraft fire. These were not German reconnaissance flights or others laying magnetic sea mines. The *Luftwaffe* was dropping live bombs, plastering the airfield at Madyck as well as hitting the Dunes shunting yard. *Drôle de guerre* was over.

One twin-engine Heinkel III bomber crippled by anti-aircraft fire bellied onto a field in the Borre commune, near Hazebrouck south of the port. The German crew warned about the acute risk of an explosion, but a crowd of excited and curious onlookers pressed around the stricken bomber. French soldiers billeted in the local village set up a protective cordon, but at 6am the remaining 16 bombs on board were 'cooked off' in the heat from the burning aircraft and blew up, sweeping the crowd aside. Thirty civilians and 40 soldiers were killed and over 100 people injured; the true figure was never known.

It was an ominous sign of what was to come. Yet, ironically there was a palpable sense of relief that the shooting had finally started, with optimism that at last there may be a positive outcome. 'The government were telling us we had nothing to worry about,' remembered Gustave Vancoille with the First French Army. They faced an advance by the German Army Group B. 'We would be sure to win,' he recalled, 'What is there to worry about if you are told you are the stronger. We went happily to battle.' They advanced into Belgium along roads lined with cheering crowds, convinced, like in 1914, that they would stop the Germans.[5]

List of Illustrations

Hitler in conversation with his adjutants alongside his specially commissioned *Reichsbahn* train *Amerika*. The modern equivalent would be the US president's Air Force One. The *Führer's* supreme commander, *General* Walther von Brauchitsch, is conversing with *Generaloberst* Keitel, his chief of staff, to the left. (Photo by ullstein bild/ullstein bild via Getty Images)

Hitler's *Luftwaffe* adjutant, Nicolaus von Below, at the *Führer's* left shoulder as he converses with OKW Chief of Operations Jodl, checked the weather for the 10 May western offensive en route. (Photo by Keystone/Getty Images)

Hitler took advantage of the fine weather at the *Felsennest* (Crag's Nest) bunker headquarters. He was much taken with the natural beauty of the site. (NARA)

Inside the Spartan briefing hut at the *Felsennest* HQ outside the village of Rodert, overlooking the Belgian frontier. The *Führer's* intention was to make it a symbolic pilgrimage site after the war. (Photo by Henry Guttmann/Hulton Archive/Getty Images)

War correspondent Leo Leixner filmed this bitter Belgian holding action at the Ghent-Terneuzen canal, typical of the German infantry *Blitzkrieg* progress through Belgium, published in the German propaganda magazine *Signal*. The Germans regarded the Belgian Army with wary respect. (*Signal*, July 1940)

The impetuous panzer corps commander *schnelle* or 'speedy' Heinz Guderian in his armoured command half-track directing operations from the front, constantly pushing for greater freedom of action. (Bundesarchiv, Bild 101I-769-0229-15A, Fotograf(in): Borchert, Erich [Eric])

General von Brauchitsch, commander in chief of the German Army (right), closely conferring with his chief of staff at OKH, Franz Halder (left). They repeatedly clashed with Hitler about the pace of the panzer advance. (Photo by Heinrich Hoffmann/ullstein bild via Getty Images)

Generaloberst Fedor von Bock commanded Army Group B, which penetrated Holland and Belgium, taking on the main bulk of the Allied armies. (Photo by Heinrich Hoffmann/ullstein bild via Getty Images)

Hitler (left) confers with *Generaloberst* Gerd von Rundstedt, the commander of Army Group A, at Charlerville on 24 May. He seconded his desire to pause the panzer advance and censored Brauchitsch for over reaching his decision remit. (Bettmann via Getty Images)

The 1st Panzer Division's attack on Dunkirk was road bound, threading its way through villages encumbered by canal lines. It was fought to a standstill by the French 68th Division before the Panzer Halt Order was applied. (Bundesarchiv, Bild 1011-126-0321-03, Fotograf(in): Boesig, Heinz)

Hermann Göring, the commander in chief of the Luftwaffe, conversing with his senior officers. He flamboyantly assured the *Führer* that the *Luftwaffe* was all that was required to finish off the BEF in the Dunkirk pocket. (Photo by Keystone-France/Gamma-Keystone via Getty Images)

A German tank from the 2nd (Vienna) Panzer Division is knocked out at a village intersection as the von Prittwitz battle group battled its way into Boulogne from the south on 23 May.

Oberst Balck commanded one of the 1st Panzer Division's battle groups during the abortive advance on Dunkirk on 24 May, and was halted at the canal line on the western outskirts. (Photo by Heinrich Hoffmann/ ullstein bild via Getty Images)

Hauptmann Edwin Dwinger was with the 10 Panzer Division headquarters during the concentric attacks on Calais and observed the final attacks on the citadel.

Oberfeldwebel Langhammer and his Panzer Mark IV crew proudly display their turret victory tally for sinking a British destroyer in Boulogne harbour. (Photo by Atlantic-Press/ullstein bild via Getty Images)

The destroyer *Venetia* backs out of Boulogne harbour on fire with all guns blazing during the evening of 23 May – 'a magnificent sight', according to one eyewitness.

Generalleutnant Schaal's 10th Panzer Division commanders at Calais: *Oberst* Menny commanding the 69th Regiment battle group (second from

General Georg von Küchler commanding Eighteenth Army was appointed to coordinate and command the ten divisions tasked to reduce the Dunkirk pocket. The Germans failed to capitalize on the Belgian surrender by rolling up the beaches from the east. (Photo by Keystone/Hulton Archive/Getty Images)

German infantry trying to assemble for the attack in flooded landscape; the defenders dominated the exposed dry ground. (© Pierre Metsu)

A photograph showing the main attack axis of the German 18th Infantry Division towards Bergues and Dunkirk. The 51st Regiment attacked left and the 54th Regiment right of this road.

Final Stuka attacks against Bergues, which breached the town wall, the lynchpin of the French defense of the Dunkirk pocket to the south.

The only infantry recourse to advance over a half-dozen concentric canal lines was to assault the crossings in vulnerable dinghies, which was immensely clumsy and costly. (Photo by ullstein bild/ullstein bild via Getty Images)

The German dead from 192th Regiment laid out after their costly advance from the east of the Dunkirk pocket at Nieuport. The *Spiess* or sergeant major has the grim task of harvesting identity discs while soldiers look for missing friends.

German soldiers advance across a totally flat and fire-swept landscape. The axis of attack was always billowing clouds of smoke bubbling up from the blazing refineries at Dunkirk.

Dune positions held by the 8th Zouaves to the east of the perimeter, blocking attacks by the German 56th Division, which had to be withdrawn totally exhausted and 'fought-out' from the line.

Just one part of the 51st Regiment's haul of French prisoners once the 18th Division penetrated the harbour area of Dunkirk on 4 June. (Photo by ullstein bild/ullstein bild via Getty Images)

Generalleutnant Friedrich-Carl Cranz, the commander of the 18th Division, takes the final surrender of Dunkirk alongside his staff. The perimeter was held for a further three days after the last British had departed.

List of Maps

Chapter 1

Führer Weather

HOUR OF DECISION

Christa Schroeder was a 32-year-old secretary, who worked within Adolf Hitler's trusted inner circle, and had done so since 1933. She realized on 9 May 1940 'that something was going on'. There had been numerous military discussions the previous month, she recalled, but 'nothing had penetrated their military office'. The inner circle was informed, with little notice, 'that same evening they would be off on a trip'. Nothing was said about where to, or how long the journey would last. *Obergruppenführer* (Lieutenant General) Schaub, one of Hitler's SS aides, gently poked fun, 'it could be eight days, a fortnight, it could be a month, it could even last a year!' The staff did not find this helpful.[1]

After the successful conclusion of the Polish campaign in October 1939, Hitler, taken aback at the unexpected declaration of war by Britain and France, resolved to deal with them quickly. There was only a limited window of opportunity to strike in the west before Germany would be gradually overwhelmed by their combination of economic and military strength. Bad weather, unsatisfactory operational planning and the manifest disapproval of many of his most senior generals resulted in no less than 29 postponements during the extraordinarily harsh winter of 1939–40. *Sitzkrieg*, the German equivalent of Phoney War, was what resulted. It had indeed been 'all quiet on the Western Front' these past eight months.

Nicolaus von Below, Hitler's *Luftwaffe* adjutant since 1937, recalled Hitler finally set X-Day for 5 May 1940, but stable weather, vital for

Luftwaffe air support, still eluded him. The Army meanwhile kept almost two million men on high alert at 24 hours' notice to move. On 4 May, Hitler was obliged to delay until the 7th. He became increasingly agitated, according to *Oberst* (Colonel) Walter Warlimont commanding Section 'L' *Landesverteidigung* at the *Oberkommando der Wehrmacht* (OKW) supreme headquarters, 'because of the danger of a security leak'. This was ratcheted up when Göring, his *Luftwaffe* chief and confidant, extracted yet another postponement to 10 May 'against his better judgement', Warlimont heard Hitler insist, 'but not a day longer'.[2]

On the evening of the 9th, Christa Schroeder, accompanied by another secretary and Hitler's press chief Otto Dietrich, was driven out of Berlin towards Staaken airport. To their surprise they passed the airport and continued on to Berlin-Finkenberg railway station. Hitler had driven there unobtrusively escorted by an entourage of plain-clothes detectives and *Sicherheitsdienst* (SD; security service) men. The rest of the dispersed staff arrived surreptitiously in small groups.

The *Führer's* special train, *Amerika*, was waiting alongside the platform in the small station, gently hissing steam. It consisted of ten to 12 dark-green *Deutsche Reichsbahn* coaches lined up behind two powerful steam locomotives. Coupled behind these were two *Flakwagen* or anti-aircraft flatbed carriages. They were constructed in the same dark-green aerodynamic style as the coaches and mounted two quadruple 20mm *Flakvierling* guns at each end, four in all. The train was the equivalent of the present American president's Air Force One VIP flight. The train had defence and communications elements, with Hitler's personal passenger car, with sleeping and dining facilities, and baggage cars situated between them. *Amerika's* two locomotives were changed every 100 to 120 miles with another fully charged with coal on stand-by, so that there was always a fully fuelled alternative at any time. Decor inside was functional 'middle-class' art deco, a contrast to Göring's *Sonderzug* (special train), *Asien*, which was far more opulent. Hitler's coaches had heating and air conditioning, rare at the time. *Amerika* was named after Hitler's penchant for German writer Karl May's Winnetou and Old Shatterhand Wild West novels, rather than any special affinity with the United States. It was an ironic dig at American treatment of their Native Americans, which played out well to German propaganda. At 5pm the two locomotives puffed majestically out of Finkenberg station onto the main Hamburg line. Hitler's office announced he was to visit the troops in Denmark and Norway. Many on board guessed or knew differently. 'I doubt that anybody was taken in by this', von Below admitted, 'because everyone had his private source.'[3]

A humorous deception was kept up for Hitler's civilian secretaries. 'Have you all got your sea-sick pills?' Hitler's Army adjutant *Generalleutnant* (Lieutenant General) Rudolf Schmundt joked. Christa Schroeder assumed they were going to Norway because the *Chef* or 'boss', Hitler, was joining in with the fun. 'If you are good, you could bring home a sealskin memento,' he ventured.[4] 'During the journey Hitler was in a sparkling mood,' von Below remembered, 'completely confident of victory and devoid of any niggling doubts.' The good-natured banter continued, 'the atmosphere at dinner in the buffet car was lively', he observed.[5]

Hitler had used the train during the Polish campaign. Its command and communications car or *Befehlswagen* was equipped with modern communications equipment and a conference room, with teleprinters and encryption devices. A complete telephone exchange and radio room with the enigma encoding machine had been installed, able to decode encrypted messages. Short-wave radio enabled voice transmission along the train, but the other more specialized appliances could only be operated at train halts, having to be plugged in at various stations in order to work. This was generally where the locomotives were changed over. A long stop was made at Hagenow-Land to take telephone messages on board. At half-past midnight the train switched points, to head due west to Hannover, 'only noticed by those paying attention', Christa Schroeder remembered.[6] At Burgdorf near Hannover, von Below used the stop, 'where I collected the latest weather forecast. It was satisfactory.' The operation was on.[7]

Hitler was preoccupied during the journey by the outcome of the revolutionary new glider assault he had supported to be flown against the key Belgian military fortress at Eban-Emael. It had been discussed in great detail the week before. The huge modern fort blocked panzer entry onto the north Belgian plain. The glider-borne force would have flown over further north, as the sky began to lighten in the east behind it. Nine German DFS230 gliders transporting 77 soldiers landed directly on top of the seemingly impregnable concrete fortress and bottled up the 1,200-strong garrison below ground, in hardened gun chambers. It had taken 60,000 German troops 11 days to batter the Belgian border forts into submission in August 1914 at tremendous cost. That could not be repeated.

'It was twilight', Schroeder remembered, when *Amerika* hissed and squeaked to a standstill at the nondescript station of Euskirchen, situated between Bonn and Aachen, next to the Belgian border. Station platform name shields had been removed and all local signposts; military route markers now indicated the direction. Hitler and his entourage boarded six-wheeled Mercedes cross-country automobiles and set off, passing shadowy nameless villages in the growing light as they gradually climbed into the hilly wooded Eifel mountain region. They halted at a command bunker dug into the side of a slope. This was the *Felsennest* or 'crags nest' headquarters established 1,200 feet high on a hill about 430 yards from the nearby village of Rodert. Secured by a series of wooden watchtowers along a chain link enclosure, it housed a small bunker at the top for the *Führer*. Everybody ate in the dining bunker and a barracks situated a short way off down the slope. The constricted nature of the site meant much of the headquarters and staff were dispersed and billeted in Rodert. 'As we stood before the bunker in the gathering dawn we heard heavy artillery impacts in the distance,' Christa Schroeder remembered. Hitler gestured at the direction of noise and formally announced '*Meine Herren* [gentlemen], the offensive against the western powers has just begun.'[8]

'Soldiers of the Westfront!' Hitler announced in his special communiqué to the troops that morning, 'the hour for the decisive battle for the future of the German people has arrived'. He maintained, 'The battle beginning today will decide the fate of the German nation for the next thousand years. Do your duty! The German people are alongside you, with their blessing.'

'It was the most scenic of all the headquarters,' Schroeder recalled, 'freshly leafed trees were alive with birdsong.' The commanding view overlooking the Belgian border, less than 20 miles distant, was impressive. 'A bird paradise', Hitler called it. This rocky eyrie was a metaphorical perch from which Germany would soar above Western Europe and snatch power. Over the next three weeks so-called '*Führer* weather' was to grace the campaign with beautiful springtime conditions. Thereafter, successful future operations, in the Balkans and during the early days in Russia, would be labelled '*Führer* weather', when victories and fine campaigning conditions coincided.

The weather decision governing X-Day was fundamental. Alfred-Ingemar Berndt, serving with *Panzerjäger Abteilung* (Anti-tank Battalion) 605, a self-propelled gun unit, remembered, 'the month of March did not bring spring. The first day of spring brought only snow and ice.'[9] On 9 January 1940 the weather forecast had predicted 12 to 14 consecutive days of clear winter weather, bringing with it temperatures of minus 10° to minus 15°C across the European mainland, auguring well for a campaign launch. However, the next day a copy of the deployment plan for the forthcoming western offensive was compromised when a German pilot accidently force-landed on the Belgian side of the border near Mechelen with papers containing all the details. The enforced delay caused by the blunder made the winter seem endless.

'Spring came at the beginning of April', Berndt noted, ironically observing, 'we confirmed that brown soil was under the white blanket of snow'. *Sitzkrieg*, was, however, maintained; an almost emotional reluctance to commence hostilities. The spectre of former slaughter on the Western Front during 1914–18 war was lodged in the memories of both sides. 'We won't shoot unless you shoot first', proclaimed banners hung on the wire along the Rhine and Siegfried Line. *Oberst* Ulrich Liss, an Intelligence Chief at OKH Army Headquarters, recalled that 'if a shot rang out in the German Seventh Army sector, a report followed to Army Supreme Headquarters'. By the beginning of May Berndt noticed the 'seeds were turning green, although winter and slush persisted'. Even so, 'the ground was drying and filled us with hope we could start soon'.[10]

Until February 1940, before the plan was compromised, a three-pronged operational attack against the West had been the favoured military option of the German General Staff. Hitler preferred not to stake all on one card, aiming to reinforce success where it emerged. *General* Erich von Manstein's *Sichelschnitt* or sickle-cut plan emerged as a creative operational proposal, which broke the planning deadlock, and was enthusiastically embraced by Hitler. Unlike the former scheme, an adaptation of the 1914 Schlieffen Plan, by going through neutral Belgium, von Manstein proposed massing the panzer and motorized forces against a previously unnoticed weak point in the French fortified lines. This would involve switching the *Schwerpunkt* or main point of effort to the southern wing of the German armies lined up for the attack. Army Group A under *Generaloberst* (Colonel General) von Rundstedt would tear apart the front between Liège and Sedan and encircle from the south, including everything that the enemy threw into Belgium – as had happened in 1914 – and wipe it out. This would be in combination with Army Group B led by *Generaloberst* von Bock attacking north of Liège. Von Bock would swiftly occupy neutral Holland, drawing against himself as many of the Allied armies as possible into central Belgium. These he would bind with a swift and aggressive attack spearheaded by three panzer divisions and the as-yet untested and unseen revolutionary *Fallschirmjäger* (paratrooper) arm. The aim was to deceive and promote uncertainty as to where the *Schwerpunkt* or actual main German thrust was emerging. It was a huge operational gamble, designed to distract attention from the inner encircling wing of the panzer-heavy Army Group A. It was to advance through the seemingly impassable forested and craggy Ardennes region of Belgium and Luxembourg, unsuited to vehicles.

Von Bock was to attack with over 29 divisions from the anticipated Belgian direction supported by *General der Flieger* (Air Force General) Albert Kesselring's *Luftflotte* (Air Fleet) 2. This Air Fleet had two flying corps, a Flak (anti-aircraft) corps and the German airborne 7th *Flieger* Division, reinforced by specialized flying support assets. All this would cloak the movement of Army Group A: seven panzer and three to four motorized infantry divisions, with up to 46 infantry divisions marching on behind. Army Group C with 19 divisions under von Leeb was to pin French forces up against the Maginot Line. Army Groups A and C were supported by Hugo Sperrle's *Luftflotte* 3, with three flying and one Flak corps.

In comparative terms the two assailants facing each other across the Western Front were about equal, ten panzer divisions versus 11 Allied tank or partially armoured divisions. Both sides fielded seven motorized infantry divisions and Germany had 117 against 119 infantry divisions, as well as an airborne and a cavalry division. Infantry strengths were about equal; the Allies had more tanks and artillery, but the superior numbers and modern aircraft types of the *Luftwaffe* offset the advantage.[11]

The German intention was to separate the Allied powers, in particular the French from the British, and annihilate each in battle. In strategic and tactical terms the German plan was revolutionary.

Even since World War I, the hills and deep valleys of the Ardennes countryside had been regarded unsuitable for mass operations or deployment. Tactically the Germans were ignoring the sacred principle that a breakthrough without flank protection was traditionally doomed to failure. Speed and surprise were to be the imperatives applied to negate this truism. So long as the bulk of the Allied armies in northern France was pinned inside Belgium, a panzer formation could unexpectedly emerge from the Ardennes forests and race for the Atlantic coast. On reaching the Somme River estuary, this scythe-like movement would sever enemy forces committed to Belgium from their resupply bases.

The Germans had not wasted the long winter months. *Hauptmann* (Captain) Hans-Georg von Altenstadt with the Silesian 18th Infantry Division remembered: 'Never before had we so many opportunities to practise our assault pioneers in rapid river crossings. We never had a winter in Silesia where we had shot off so much exercise ammunition as this one.'[12]

The winter proved harsh, so much so that the vehicle columns of the *SS-Leibstandarte Adolf Hitler* (LAH) Regiment were pressed into service during January 1940 to deliver coal to bakers in the Bad Ems area. Local authorities ran short of fuel for bakeries to bake the local population's bread. Tactical training for the regiment's officers and NCOs continued throughout the bleak winter as did tactical exercises and war games with their parent formation: *General* Guderian's XIX Panzer Corps. Combat training graduated from individual to unit level with an increased emphasis on night manoeuvres. Von Altenstadt remembered 'digging trenches and marking out dummy bunkers and field defences, which we attacked from every conceivable direction, cleared and then blew up'. They hurled live grenades and practised live field firing so often that 'when flamethrowers mouthed their fiery greeting right next to us, we were not bothered by it'. Four months of concentrated and intense live-fire training brought the division 'up to a high level' of assessment. March training exercises covering 25 to 30 miles per day were 'no longer special achievements'. In between there were opportunities to walk and bicycle and mix with the locals, in particular the female populace. Limited free time was seldom wasted; von Altenstadt recalled, 'many gold rings were exchanged between Rhine maidens and our Silesian fighters'.[13]

Alfred-Ingemar Berndt with *Panzerjäger Abteilung* 605 recalled, 'the bet that the attack would begin on May 1st was lost'. Berndt, a committed National Socialist like many of his zealous comrades, had yet to see action, and was 'burning to meet the enemy, to show him how German soldiers fight'. His *Feldwebel* (Sergeant) had won the bottle of Sekt wagered on the start date, yet shortly before midnight, nine days later, the alarm sounded. 'In 15 minutes the company had to be at their vehicles with pack and sack.' Motors were turned over and the self-propelled guns rolled with accompanying trucks to form march packets and columns ready for the off. He remembered, 'the night was noticeably cool… Streams of fog floated in the river valley. Over the roads leading to the border was a light blue glow, clouds of dust and the dimmed lights of motor transport.'[14]

Local villages woke to the sounds of bustling activity in side streets, as the steady stream of vehicle packets emerged onto the main roads. 'Suppressed calls reached our ears over the noise of engines. Tight columns, batteries, tank companies were getting ready to march to follow our advance.' Small arms magazines were loaded ready for action, machine guns and main tank armaments would be made ready just before crossing the frontier. Unsurprisingly, following so many false alarms, Berndt's company chief and platoon commander happened to be still absent on leave. Despite the frustration 'they reached the company on the other side of the border on the first day of the war'. 'You have to be lucky,' he recalled.[15]

Hauptmann von Altenstadt with the 18th Division saw 'a glowing fresh young spring day broke on the 10th May'. '*Führer* weather,' he pronounced. Tension rose 'slowly but remorselessly as the clock hand neared H-Hour, when we were to break in across the border'. His division had lost more than 2,000 casualties from a strength of about 14,800 during their 27-day fight for Poland, more than any other division in the *Wehrmacht*. Polish veterans had a good idea what to expect once they were over that frontier. Veterans bonded, recalling 'the serious moments they felt at the outbreak of war' the previous September. 'This is a new war we are about to enter,' von Altenstadt recalled, and it would be a lot more difficult than Poland: 'A few of us, and many at home had told us about the grim struggles during the World War, the courage of the French, the chivalrous tenacity of the English, and their artillery, flyers and tanks.'[16]

Post-war historians have tended to underestimate the extent to which von Bock's Army Group B, despite facing the bulk of the Allied armies, aggressively tore into the defences of the Low Countries with its Eighteenth and Sixth Armies. The prevailing narrative generally concentrates on the epic dash by Army Group A to the Atlantic coast. Von Bock's, being the lesser of two powerful thrust lines, is often described as a feint. Deception there was, but the overall configuration of the advance was more a massive double offensive. Von Bock's force with 29 divisions was about two-thirds the size of von Rundstedt's 46 divisions with Army Group A, a force to be reckoned with.

Luftwaffe bomber corps *Kampfgeschwader* (squadrons) took off between 2.45 and 3.56am on 10 May. Many aircraft flew out to sea along the Dutch coastline to aid deception before turning inland. *General* Kesselring's *Luftflotte* 2 supported von Bock's jab to the right of the operational advance to the west, diverting the enemy until Army Group A's left hook to the south threw him off balance. The bomber *Kampf* and *Stuka* (dive-bomber) *Gruppen* (Wings) flew 3,000 sorties on the first day alone, supported by 2,000 *Jagd* (fighter) and *Zerstörergruppen* (Me 110s). The Allies could only muster 44 bomber and 541 fighter sorties in response.[17]

'The Dutch fought poorly at the frontier,' von Bock wrote in his diary that day. The operation unfolded smoothly: 'the Dutch population is friendly and nice' and 'the prisoners of war appear satisfied with their lot'. Even so the opening rounds were a tense affair. 'Reports about the success of our airborne landings in Holland are unclear,' he recalled, 'apparently not a complete success.' Their insertion was aimed at unravelling the Dutch defensive 'Fortress Holland' philosophy, opening up the interior by flying over rather than trying to force terrain crisscrossed with rivers, waterways and canals. Von Bock was aware 'two parachute battalions have succeeded in seizing the Moerdijk bridge [over the Meuse River], that is the main thing,' he accepted, 'for the moment.' Mirroring Hitler's former concern, he sought an opening for his panzers, followed by the slower foot-marching infantry. Link-ups between the airborne and ground advance were achieved south of Maastricht, despite blown bridges. 'Fort Eban-Emael is silent!' he wrote in his diary, 'the airborne landing there was therefore a success!'[18]

The Dutch strategic concept of retiring behind a moat created by blown bridges into the 'Keep' area inside 'Fortress Holland' was unhinged by the first major airborne landings in modern history. Some 4,500 paratroopers jumped and 500 landed by glider to capture key objectives. A further 12,000 light infantry were air-landed at airfields to interdict the political heart of Holland inside The Hague. The fleeing civilian population emerged to fill the roads, but where to? Amid confusion and panic Germans appeared everywhere. The bridges at Moerdijk and Doordrecht were secured and hotly contested, forming an enclave to link up with the German Sixth Army advancing from the east, and begin to break into the urban conurbation of Rotterdam. Nevertheless, it was a pyrrhic airborne achievement. An attempted political *coup de main* conducted by the air land division at The Hague was repelled. One in four officers and 28% of the committed units became casualties inside five days. An airborne corridor was established between Rotterdam and Doordrecht to the south, a seven- by ten-mile perimeter bordered by the waterways of the Old and New Maas Rivers.

On the first day of the offensive alone, *Generalleutnant* Friedrich-Karl Cranz's veteran 18th Division with Army Group B had to attack over four separate waterways into Holland. It would reach Dunkirk three weeks later. As the minute hand struck H-Hour, *Hauptmann* von Altenstadt recalled 'a roaring overhead... With beating hearts we could detect 10, 20, 50 German aircraft in the still dark starry sky. They were heading westward towards Maastricht and Eban-Emael.'[19]

The concentrated bridge building and assault dinghy crossing exercises, laboriously conducted throughout the winter, paid off. 'The bridges at Stein were built faster than in any peacetime exercises,' he maintained. By the following day they were across the Juliana Canal, the Maas River, Hertogenbosch Canal and Albert Canal. Anti-tank gunner *Unteroffizier* (Lance Corporal) Haakert recalled seeing 'a few wounded on the empty streets and shocked faces' and little else, 'because no Dutchman had expected to see German soldiers here already'. At the first brief halt: 'It was clear the Dutch did not want this war. They stood anxiously and distraught on the roads, but a cigarette and a friendly greeting soon broke the tension between the Dutch population and us.'

Haakert saw that the Dutch troops on the opposite bank of the Juliana Canal did not seem particularly hostile. Any small pockets of resistance were in any case smothered by overwhelming firepower.

'Left from me the first gun fired shot after shot into an enemy bunker.' No counter-attacks came in from an enemy 'attacked too quickly and hard to reciprocate', he remembered. A fighting reconnaissance painstakingly picked its way across the destroyed superstructure of the bridge, 'one hand grenade and 35 men raised their hands', he recalled. The advance was rapidly continued. 'Generally the Dutch army, used to peacetime soldiering were satisfied once they had blown their bridges', *Hauptmann* von Altenstadt recalled, 'and then go smilingly into captivity'. German soldiers approved of the clean and tidy villages they overran, 'and we were convinced there were no grounds for hostility between us'. Political neutrality of course had been studiously ignored.[20]

Infantryman Karl Schonfeldt, who advanced over the same ground, recorded in his diary:

> Whit Monday. At the edge of the Albert Canal stand black smoke-stained bunkers, gliders and the graves of fallen *Fallschirmjäger*, showing how the fight developed here. It was hard going. Where flamethrowers were used, the grass is no longer growing. A pretty young woman sat amid the ruined houses, staring defiantly ahead. Fear and terror from the past few days still etched across her beautiful face. This pretty face, so full of fear, remained with me for a long time.

The advance was going well. One *Gefreiter* (Corporal) with Army Group B's Sixth Army recalled that 'not a shot rang out, they still seemed to be asleep'. 'The whole thing was going like an exercise,' he jubilantly wrote home, 'or like a *Luftwaffe*-led May-Day fly-pass.'[21]

By 4am on 10 May Belgium had appealed to France for help. There had been no military agreements or collaboration between the Allies and neutral Belgium and Holland. Two and a half hours later both the Belgian and Dutch governments were asking General Gamelin's Headquarters at Vincennes for military assistance, which was passed onto First Army Group. They initiated the *Dyle* and *Breda* operations secretly set up the previous March. Inside an hour the advance units of the French Seventh Army and the BEF began crossing the frontier into Belgium. Nineteen-year-old Clive Tonry, a signaller with the BEF, remembered 'we packed up all our kit and loaded it onto the trucks and went off to war'. Gunner James Bradley, ten years his senior, also recalled a pell-mell sudden departure:

> We took everything out on the ground, our guns, Bren-gun carriers and everything we had, and dashed into Belgium, where there were no prepared positions for us. It was a mobile war after that, it was fight and move – fight and move.[22]

Army Group B faced an Allied line-up of the Seventh French Army on the north coast, with the Belgians in between, and the BEF, First French Army and Ninth French Army bordering the Maginot Line to the south. The whole line aimed to swing east like a door hinged on Sedan, to slam on the German westward advance. The continuous front would have the Belgians left of the BEF along the River Dyle or Escaut River. The French Seventh Army was to operate on the far-left flank and cross the mouth of the Rhine to link with the Dutch. Speed was of the essence. Belgian and Dutch neutrality had predicated some delay by necessity, so the move by Army Group 1 into Belgium had to be conducted with some urgency, which was precisely what the Germans wanted.

Both opposing sides accelerated forward to extract the maximum tactical advantage. Nineteen-year-old Coldstream Guardsman Bill Weeks with the British 1st Division remembered how, 'The Germans really moved fast. We weren't ready, not for this. We had five rounds of ammo for each rifle, which was ludicrous really, but that's the way it was.'[23]

If anything, the Allies in the north had the advantage of being motorized; virtually all the BEF was vehicle-borne. Most of the opposing Army Group B force, apart from the three reduced panzer divisions and the airborne *Fallschirmjäger*, were foot-borne infantry supported by horse-drawn artillery. They were not dissimilar to the Kaiser's invasion force that had attacked through the same territory following the 1914 Schlieffen Plan. German infantryman Berndt Messerschmidt summed up what these ceaseless forced marches entailed:

> Pace was naturally dependent day by day on endurance and staying power. Blisters were the outcome of going and gait, with running foot sores – but that was not particularly onerous. Naturally it didn't put any smiles on faces. Daily march objectives were set, and known. You just had to get going.[24]

TO THE SEA

It was anticipated the *Sichelschnitt* manoeuvre wielded by Army Group A would cut off the Allied armies at the knee, isolating the northern armies from their base of operations on the Channel coast. The American *Time* magazine appears to have been the first to coin the term *Blitzkrieg* or Lightning War to describe the September 1939 campaign in Poland; not describing it as an occupation, 'but a war of quick penetration and obliteration'. The outcome in Poland was not, however, the result of novel operational or strategic planning. The German panzers were not employed independently within a division framework. *General* Guderian's XIX Motorized Corps with Army Group North was the only formation that had handled its two panzer and two light divisions as a single entity. Army Group South, commanded by *Generaloberst* von Rundstedt, had split its armour among the various armies and corps. Guderian had emerged from the campaign clear about the need for combined action by tanks, artillery and infantry on wheels and tracks within panzer divisions, to work closely with air support. Army Group A in this campaign was to radically employ the panzer force at the operational level; subscribing to *General* von Manstein's creative *Sichelschnitt* concept relied upon *Schnelletruppen*, fast-moving mobile units, to freely range ahead of the marching foot-borne infantry. This had never been attempted before on such a scale. Poland had very nearly prematurely ended with a logistic disaster, because the *Wehrmacht* and *Luftwaffe* almost ran out of ammunition. For this campaign, the motorized columns would carry their own integral fuel and ammunition. This produced a fleet of 41,140 vehicles, including 1,222 battle tanks and 134,370 men. Nothing quite like this had ever been fielded in the history of warfare.[25]

It was not a 'lightning war' at the start. 'I can remember the traffic jam very well,' *Unteroffizier* Gerd Ahlschwede with the 1st Panzer Division recalled, 'it was like one endless military worm.' Each division had maps issued showing the advance routes along roads and tracks in different colours. Supply routes were kept open for the passage of reinforcements. The clearly marked roads and paths were plotted beforehand on maps up to the Meuse River. Panzer and infantry columns marched along every road and track across very rugged country. *General* Reinhardt commanding the 6th and 8th Panzer Divisions with XLI Panzer Corps recalled the march planning conducted by Army Group A 'collapsed quickly, like a house of cards' on the very first day. The gigantic armada of 41,140 tracked and wheeled vehicles had a theoretical length of 960 miles. Each panzer division column was over 90 miles in length and took about ten hours to pass. Mixed panzer and motorized divisions were 80 miles long and took eight and a half hours to move by. By midday on 10 May Guderian's three panzer divisions were already fighting on Belgian territory, but the main body of the next corps, Reinhardt's, was still east of the Rhine. Behind them the third echelon, von Wietersheim's XIV Motorized Corps, had yet to leave its assembly areas around Marburg and Giessen in the *Reich*. Gerd Ahlschwede remembered achieving some dexterity, overtaking units out of line, 'but when we left the borders of the *Reich* the traffic jam eased off, because different groups went on different but parallel roads heading in the same direction'.[26]

Hauptmann Carganico recalled the cloying congestion at the Luxembourg border:

The sight of the yellow road signs has clearly perked up our tank drivers, after sitting for five hours in this terrific heat behind their gear levers; changing gear – steering uphill and downhill – stopping and starting.

'It seemed to me that the whole road had a life of its own,' C.C. Christophé, an embedded war correspondent with the 2nd Panzer Division recalled, 'rolling along beneath a huge dust cloud.' *Leutnant* (Lieutenant) Hans Steinbecher, the youngest officer in the division, had already served in Poland and wrote in his diary about 'a day I never thought possible. It seemed as though there were only panzers in the world.'[27]

Guderian's lead corps quickly cleared the traffic snarl-ups, but chaos piled up behind them. On 11 May there were miles-long traffic jams in the Ardennes. Engineers were called forward with blowtorches and sledgehammers to demolish roadblocks, shown later in *Wochenschau* newsreels. Again and again narrow gorges were blocked with huge enemy demolition craters, 15 to 20 metres across and 6 to 8 metres deep. These had to be bridged or filled in. The Belgian Ardennes Rifle Division supported at times by advancing French cavalry fought bruising and delaying rearguards. Resistance was stiffer on the Belgian rather than Luxembourg frontier. Ironically Luxembourg police even helped to regulate the German traffic flowing through. By 12 May there was a virtual gridlock of movement on the right wing of the advance. Infantry division vehicle convoys barged onto the wider roads set aside for the panzer divisions. Hans P.*, a radio operator with 6th Machine Gun Battalion, a motorized infantry unit, remembered rising tension as they crossed the Belgian border at Losheim; helmets were put on and rifles loaded. It was Whit Sunday, and they were greeted amiably enough by civilians as they passed Malmedy and St Vith: 'But the further we penetrated into Belgium, the more seldom we received signs of friendship, until finally we no longer got a sound out of anybody… The countryside made an empty and dead impression,' he recalled. They were, however, increasingly buoyed by the appearance of 'innumerable German columns moving through all the villages and small towns, heading in one direction – forward against the enemy!' Momentum created problems:

> Impelled by sheer exuberance, all the previous carefully and precisely calculated rules, such as anti-aircraft spacing and regulations forbidding overtaking, were all cast to the wind. Now it was columns close up and get forward quickly, which soon led to excited altercations between column commanders, who had the same firm intention – get forward and close with the enemy!

As his battalion pressed forward, 'it was impossible, other troops tried the same, so the two columns became interwoven and nobody could overtake'.

Ironically, the primary difficulty was less Belgian and French rearguards, but instead an anti-panzer prejudice directed by foot-marching infantry columns at the priorities afforded to armoured columns. Army Group A created the biggest traffic jam ever experienced on European roads. On 12 May, convoys on the right wing or northern sector of the advance were clogged up for over 150 miles from the

---

*The use of initials rather than full name is a very common feature within German sources, as families may not wish in such accounts to be associated with the discredited German *Reich*.

Meuse River, across French, Belgian and Luxembourg territory all the way back to the River Rhine in Germany. Hans P. was caught up in this endless column:

> We went along in dribs and drabs only so far as the panzers freed up the road ahead of us. A couple of hours at snail's pace – halt for an hour, 200 metres forward – a three-hour pause, then a 10-kilometre rush – and again a few hours waiting. This went on throughout the whole of Whit Sunday, the following night and again until midday on Monday.[28]

Radio operator Erich Kuby with *Nachrichten* (Signals) *Abteilung* 3 recalled how in time 'fatigue began to overhaul the tension' at impending action. The day before the advance he had sat in his open BMW 'taking photographs and drinking tea'. On X-Day he remained 'sitting in the car and waiting – we're all waiting'. The sun shone down, it was beautiful weather, plenty of time to write home, but 'nope, we're off again, helmet on! Start the motor!' They drove through the night with dimmed headlights and by early morning were crossing the Luxembourg border. His troop was in action up front, but he remained bored. 'Lots of animals about,' he remembered, 'who was the enemy – Belgians, French, English?'[29]

March columns were only flowing in the centre, behind the advancing 1st Panzer Division spearhead. Allied air cover was nowhere to be seen over the heads of panzer crewmen, starting to feel vulnerable in the narrow forest rides. 'Again and again I cast a worried look up at the bright blue sky,' remembered *Major* Johann Graf von Kielmansegg: 'My division now presents an ideal attack target because it is not deployed and it is forced to move slowly forward on a single road. But we could not spot a single French reconnaissance aircraft.'[30]

Gerd Ahlschwede enjoyed the striking Ardennes scenery they passed through; 'we were very well camouflaged,' he remembered. 'It was very wooded, so we were hard to detect from the air.' All the time the pace of the advance was perceptibly increasing. 'We were told to finish this war as soon as possible,' panzer crewman Hans Becker with the 7th Panzer Division recalled, 'this is what Rommel [our commander] tried to do.'[31]

French aerial reconnaissance was kept at bay by von Bülow-Bothkamp's *Jägergeschwader* 2 (fighter squadron), with 43 *Luftwaffe* Flak batteries deployed along the line of march. The French lost two aircraft but spotted and photographed the motorized horde, passing the material to French Ninth Army Headquarters at Sedan. Like the 1916 German Verdun offensive, the French refused to believe the evidence. What was going on was neither conceivable nor credible, it had never happened before. Late on 12 May, German spearheads began to close up on the River Meuse. The only air raid they had experienced was a 'blue on blue' (German) attack the day before by 25 dive-bombers from *Stukageschwader* 1.

General der Kavallerie (General of the Cavalry) von Kleist's vanguards assembled at the river approaches, with *Generalleutnant* Reinhardt's XLI Corps on the right at Montherme and Guderian's XIX Corps to the left at Sedan. On 13 May extraordinarily heavy Stuka attacks started with an eight-hour rolling programme from 8am, which carried on into dusk. 'They came in swarms,' Ahlschwede recalled; 310 bombers, 200 dive-bombers and 300 fighters flew 1,215 sorties along a 27-mile stretch of the river around Sedan. Even watching German soldiers felt uneasy, observing this unprecedented concentration of airpower at work. 'All hell seems to have broken loose,' remembered light anti-aircraft gunner Hugo Novak, 'A sulpherous yellowish-grey wall rises on the other bank; it keeps growing. The enormous air pressure causes glass panes to rattle and crack.'

Defending French infantry were completely deafened by the howl of diving aircraft and sharp ear-splitting cracks from explosions. The psychological impact was greater than the physical damage. 'Twice I had acoustic hallucinations', recalled 1st Lieutenant Michard with the 55th French Infantry Division. He was bombed into a virtual stupor:

> All you feel is the nightmare noise of the bombs, whose whistling becomes louder and louder the closer they get. You have the feeling that they are zeroed in precisely on you; you wait with tense muscles. The explosion comes like a relief. But then there is another one, then there are two more and ten more … the whistling sounds are superimposed and crisscrossed like a fabric without gaps; the explosions blend in a ceaseless thunder.[32]

Ahlschwede watched fascinated as Stukas tipped over onto one wing. 'As they went down they switched on a howling siren, which had a great effect on the morale of the enemy.' They appeared to concentrate on a bunker or pocket of resistance, 'dropped their bombs, then went up again – it sounded like this – *whuumm!*' During the morning of 14 May German engineers threw bridges across the Meuse under fire and, as reinforcements flowed across, von Kleist expanded the bridgeheads on the far bank. Despite the real need to rest, Guderian impulsively pressed on. The Meuse had been crossed inside 24 hours between Charleville and Sedan with relatively light casualties, despite bitter fighting at other points.[33]

General von Kleist had wanted to confine Guderian to the small bridgehead he created at Sedan. Guderian obtained permission for 24 hours' freedom of action to enlarge the bridgehead to take reinforcing infantry. *Oberst* Walther K. Nehring, his Chief of Staff, recalled 'with characteristic boldness, Guderian used his permitted 24 hours to smash resistance and penetrate deep into enemy territory'. By 17 May his advance forces reached the bridge across the River Oise at Ribemont east of St Quentin.

Confidence in the competence of the senior chain of command by panzer generals was seriously compromised by the near debacle of traffic jams in the Ardennes. It had turned into an infantry versus panzer progress competition. It might have been a 'panzer graveyard' if the Allied air forces had been more effective. The *Sichelschnitt* thrust to the Atlantic coast, the whole point of Army Group A's *Schwerpunkt*, or main point of effort, was leading the panzer generals to gloss over seemingly 'reactionary' instructions from their superiors. They adopted a more freewheeling phase-by-phase approach, more in keeping with von Manstein's radical intent. *Auftragstaktik* or mission-orientated tactics was taught at the Prussian General Staff College. Command was devolved to initiative which, after identifying the mission, was about producing the appropriate resources for the subordinate commander to achieve the task, not painstakingly taking direction at every stage on how he should do it. *Oberstleutnant* (Lieutenant Colonel) Hermann Balck with the 1st Panzer Division for example had run water obstacle crossing exercises for his *Schützen* regiment to practise the Meuse crossing. They were conducted with minimum control. Such 'uninhibited' manoeuvres, he explained, were designed 'to allow everybody to get used to independent thinking and acting'. The overall plan imperative was to reach the coast. The second-tier leadership of panzer corps ruthlessly committed themselves to this objective.[34]

The bulk of the Allied armies were still moving into Belgium to meet the more conventional threat posed by von Bock's Army Group B. Virtually unopposed on crossing the Meuse, the panzer spearheads led by Guderian swiftly motored ahead. The French, assuming Paris was the target, moved all available forces to block that avenue, whereas the panzers were speeding towards the Atlantic coast. They broadly followed the line of the north bank of the River Somme, scene of some of the most murderous fighting of World War I, which resonated in the minds of many corps commanders who had fought there. Panzer crewmen recognized place names that had been grimly told them by their fathers. This time the advance was not running from the north, against the grain of the French landscape; the panzers were winding their way along valley bottom roads in, offering the least line of resistance. It was not, however, all glory and cost free. One excited signals *Unteroffizier* with Corps *Nachrichten Abteilung* 427 wrote home after crossing the German frontier, that 'column after column is moving forward along the march routes – impressive'. His ears buzzed with the roar of returning *Luftwaffe* bomber and reconnaissance sorties, but then he saw 'the first wounded being brought back in medical convoys':

> They groaned and writhed with pain, the poor fellows ... one or two were missing an arm or a foot, others had shrapnel in the face, having lost a nose and then another shot in the head. It's awful when people so young are crippled. The first time you see it, it's depressing, because in a quiet moment you wonder if *you* are going to get back home healthy and whole.[35]

The German columns ground on. French heavy tanks with the 2nd and 3rd French Light Mechanized Divisions (DLMs) clashed with the 3rd and 4th Panzer Divisions of the *Gruppe* Hoth in the first major tank battle in history, at the Gembloux Gap in Belgium. This was north of Guderian's thrust line. Vastly superior French tank types were fought to a standstill by packs of panzer platoons, which with the aid of radios in each tank were able to engage from multiple directions. As the fighting petered out to a successful German conclusion Guderian and Reinhardt's panzer corps had already passed them by to the south. *General* Erwin Rommel's 7th Panzer Division caught the French 1st DLM in the act of refuelling opposite Dinant and destroyed it; only 17 of 175 French tanks made it back to their own frontier. Time and again *Luftwaffe* close air support blocked mobile French advances, destroying fuel bowsers, which meant fully serviceable tanks had often to be abandoned. The French 2nd Division was shattered by the 6th Panzer Division, again unexpectedly caught strung out on the move. Many French tanks were surprised unloading at a railway station. By the morning of 16 May the 2nd Division had been split in two and scattered. A gap more than 40 miles wide was torn in the French defences, through which the panzer divisions began to motor to the coast. There was no Allied armour of any consequence able to stop them. *Hauptmann* Hans von Luck, Rommel's *Aufklärungs* (Recce) Battalion commander was told 'keep going, don't look to left or right, only forward'. 'The enemy is confused', Rommel insisted, 'we must take advantage of it.'[36]

By now *Gefreiter* Möllmann following up behind the lead tanks recalled, 'we have been on the move for five days and five nights … How long since we had any sleep? Our eyes are burning and stinging. It is as though the eyelids were inflamed.'[37]

Von Luck remembered, 'we suffered from the dust' in the fine weather, 'which covered the vehicles and gave us the feeling of chewing dry biscuits all the time'. Möllmann recalled,

> the drivers are the silent heroes of this march… They clench their teeth. Stay awake at all costs! Roads, roads, roads – always the same. The men at their side talk to them, telling them anything that comes into their heads. Anything to stay awake!

They drove two columns abreast, filling the roads on both sides, as 'the sun burns relentlessly down'.[38]

German progress was remorseless and indefatigable. French counter-measures often found the Germans already on the objective, or they had already passed. Recent research has ascribed the pace of success to artificial stimulants. The drug Pervitin was already widely used in German civil society by the late 1930s. It was a methylamphetamine marketed in a distinctive red, white and blue tube or box. The stimulant banished sleep and hunger while inducing a gratifying form of euphoria, not dissimilar to the widespread use of LSD by American soldiers serving in Vietnam during the 1960s and '70s. The user suddenly feels wide-awake, with an energy surge. Self-confidence increased and thought processes speeded up amid a gratifying sense of well-being. The pills proved 'a sensation' for students preparing for exams and switchboard operators and nurses seeking to get through the night shift. It could enhance performance for difficult physical or mental labour or simply provide a 'high' for young people about town. Gunner Heinrich Böll was an enthusiastic early user of the drug and frequently asked his parents to send more, claiming on duty, 'I only slept for two hours, and tonight again I won't have more than three hours sleep, but I've just got to stay awake.' Military duties and, in particular, operations are characterized by lack of sleep. While Böll was writing about administrative duty in Germany, his craving may have been about substance abuse. Pervitin, like LSD in Vietnam, heightened aggression and reduced personal inhibitions, a tangible part of live operations.[39]

Although many officers and soldiers in the *Wehrmacht* used Pervitin, its distribution was random. The Army and *Luftwaffe* had ordered 35 million tablets prior to the western campaign. Graf von Kielmansegg, the Supply Officer for the 1st Panzer Division had ordered 20,000 tablets. His division formed the vanguard for *schnelle* ('speedy') Heinz Guderian's XIX Panzer Corps. Troops took them en masse during the night of 10–11 May. The recommended dosage was one tablet per day, two at night in close sequence and, if necessary, one or two tablets after three to four hours. This sharpened perception with a heightened state of alertness, raising blood pressure some 25% and putting soldiers into a more combative mood, all the prerequisites for aggressive attack. It is claimed Guderian's panzer crews were using two to five Pervitin each day to keep the drivers going. Some veterans later reported concerns that they may never sleep properly again.

Side effects were pronounced, apparent from the Polish campaign, where the 8th Panzer Division had assessed 'very favourable' results. The drug increased the thirst for action, blunted hunger and switched off personal inhibitions, valuable prerequisites for combat. Vertigo and headaches could, however, come from raised blood pressure and, like all 'highs', they were followed by 'lows'. The sobering hangover produced a creeping deterioration of physical and mental performance and belligerent mood swings. Officers over 40 reported heart impacts; one colonel in the 12th Panzer Division died of a heart attack after taking a victory dip in the Atlantic. More and more cases of cardiac arrest were detected as well as chronic fatigue resulting in collapse. One staff officer was declared unfit for duty with 'chronic high blood pressure' having taken four Pervitin tablets each day in action for 33 days in six weeks of combat.[40]

Recent TV documentaries and associated articles have suggested the drug fuelled *Blitzkrieg* success. It certainly promoted endurance by keeping panzer and *Luftwaffe* crewmen and technical specialists awake. There were combat positives: an aggressive lack of inhibition is useful in the ruthless attainment of demanding goals. Pervitin did not, however, make soldiers cleverer or necessarily more capable. If anything, the side effects, such as low drive and depression, part of the post 'hangover' phase, tended to cloud mission focus. In the late 1930s young army medical officers anticipated genuine miracles from the performance-enhancing substance many overdosed on, but they unfortunately transitioned to so-called 'Pervitin corpses' as one Munich university described them. Addicted students at the Military Medical Academy produced 'extraordinarily poor' examination results. Neither was the drug a convincing panacea for combat capability. Arguably this was more a factor of euphoric nationalist cum ideological motivation, stemming from an apparently 'miraculous' military plan authored by a revered *Führer*. Gerd Ahlschwede with the 1st Panzer Division remembered, '*General* von Kleist said we would not get any sleep for three nights, but in reality we did not get any proper sleep for five or six nights, but this didn't matter.' He did not mention Pervitin. 'The operation was on track' and the pace of the advance remorseless, 'everybody was giving his best,' he emphasized.[41]

It took three anxious days for the forward elements of the 9th Panzer Division to relieve the beleaguered *Fallschirmjäger* holding the bridge spanning the Meuse at Moerdijk. *SS-Hauptsturmführer* (Captain) Kurt Meyer commanding the LAH reconnaissance motorcycle company recalled the discarded parachutes in the meadows around the bridge and 'many a brave paratrooper killed in front of the numerous pillboxes'. *General* von Küchler's Eighteenth Army held up at the approaches to Rotterdam appealed for *Luftwaffe* support 'by any means' to keep his men moving. *Kampfgeschwader 54* arrived over the embattled city with one hundred *Heinkel III* bombers even as surrender negotiations began. The talks were interrupted by the sudden appearance of the relieving SS who, seeing Dutch soldiers, immediately opened fire. *General* Student commanding the paratrooper 7th *Flieger* Division engaged in the negotiations and was near fatally wounded in the head. Despite attempts to wave off the bombers a concentrated deluge of high explosive rained down on the city centre and docks, igniting vegetable oil tanks and setting off the first fire-storm raid of the war. Eight hundred civilians perished and 78,000 were made homeless creating a ripple of refugee migration that transitioned to a bow wave, radiating out from the rapid German advance. Holland capitulated the same day.

Meyer's SS motorcycle troops seeking to bypass the centre and reach Delft 'looked at the raging fire in horror' and sought to avoid 'an impenetrable wall' of flame. They wound their way through a maze of blocked backstreets 'with our faces covered'. Meyer recalled, 'My motorcyclists were moving through the narrow streets as if possessed by the devil. Shop windows exploded about our ears. Burning decorations and clothed mannequins presented an unearthly picture.' Finally, 'soot-caked, with singed hair but laughing faces,' they emerged from the conflagration. The regiment spent 15 May rounding up 163 officers and 7,080 Dutch soldiers as part of the disarmament process, before moving off into northern France.[42]

On 17 May *General* Reichenau's Sixth Army entered Brussels, which had been declared an open city. Allied forces in Belgium, realizing their right flank was turned, began to retreat. By this stage of the campaign advancing German infantry units had captured sufficient vehicles to create 'flying columns', or motorized vanguards to carry the lead companies. This aided and accelerated the impetus of the advance. *Gefreiter* Helmut Pohl, an anti-tank gunner, entered Brussels in a vehicle-borne lead unit:

> As vanguard we received the task to secure important papers in the Foreign Ministry. We drove into the city as fast as possible, where they were still running the trams. The people were clueless. When they realized we were Germans, they immediately put their hands over their heads.

Private Reg Rymer, a machine gunner with the Cheshire Regiment, was driving in the opposite direction. 'We came into Brussels,' he recalled, amid a confusion of 'toing and froing'. This time 'they were throwing bricks, never mind sweets at us'. The irony of a swift advance followed by immediate retreat was not lost on the crowds, they were 'booing us something terrible!' he remembered.[43]

The weather in Dunkirk on 18 May was superb. There had been a couple of air raid warnings that Saturday morning but the preoccupation of the locals was less the *Luftwaffe*, more the seeming biblical influx of refugees. They had poured across the Belgian border to the east over the previous five days, completely overwhelming the civic authorities, who had no instructions to deal with the influx. The migrants arrived with lurid stories of destruction wrought by air raids and a 'spy fever' psychosis. There was apparently a 'fifth column', disguised nuns and priests who allegedly carried red blankets on the carriers of their bicycles.

Dunkirk's significance varied between the nations. The Belgians saw it as a potential jumping off point that could be resupplied, to mount a counter-offensive. The French viewed it as a fortified base, which could support an attack to the south across extended German thrust lines threatening the capital, Paris. The British saw it as a transit camp on the potential sea route to home and safety. As the Germans neared the coast the Channel ports were seen as potential enemy resupply and reinforcement nodal points. Indeed the French 224th Infantry Regiment had been shipped out of the port as early as 10 May to assist the Dutch on the island of Walcheren to the north-east.

During that evening of the 18th, between 10.15pm and 2.35am, 15 waves of *Luftwaffe* aircraft unloaded over the town and port. Disembarking Belgian and Dutch troops were caught on ships and bombed at the quaysides. The locks controlling the water levels in the basin were especially hit, as were warehouses and the hydraulic sub-station. The tugboats of the Rhine flotilla were sunk in the *Bassin du Commerce* and a British cargo ship alongside Mole Number 1.

Schoolgirl Paule Rogalin was with her mother visiting friends who lived in a barge anchored in Dunkirk port. 'We started to hear these loud explosions,' she remembered, but not hearing any air raid warnings 'we didn't know what it was':

Suddenly we were surrounded by fire. The big ships in the harbour were on fire, and men were jumping off them – some men were on fire as well. We were shocked, but we ran off the barge, and jumped into a ditch shelter nearby.

Bombs continued to fall and the shelter verged on collapse: 'I was almost up to my nose in dirt. I was getting buried alive, and my mother was trying to get me out, but she couldn't move her arms.'

Three young men came to the rescue; grasping her hands they pulled her out. 'It was terrible – something I cannot forget.' They ran terror stricken into town. 'Houses were collapsing and we could hear people down in the basement, who were screaming, because they were drowning in the water from burst pipes.'[44]

The refinery to the west of the port at Saint-Pol-sur-Mer was hit by incendiaries, which ignited 68,000 tons of fuel. Huge bulbous clouds of black smoke boiled up into the sky to create the primary navigation marker for all flyers for weeks. The Guillemont barracks were hit, killing 42 and injuring 200. By morning the Dunkirk fire brigade was overwhelmed, 60 people had died and several hundred more were injured. Most towns in northern France were experiencing similarly relentless air attacks, which created a mass exodus of refugees, who poured onto the roads. They came against Allied troops as they fell back and German columns as they advanced. More air raids came over Dunkirk the next day coinciding with 100,000 Belgian refugees coming across the frontier close by at Ghyvelde, east of the port.

'Dunkirk was totally overrun,' recalled local eyewitness Robert Béthegrues, 'the streets were filled with these unfortunate people looking for a place to stay overnight.' Belgian and Dutch police were overwhelmed attempting to control the influx of cars that were followed by horse-drawn carts. 'Hotel keepers were ordered to allow refugees to stay for only twenty-four hours,' he remembered. Many local inhabitants took in families who had lost everything, exhausted, hungry and dehydrated by the relentless pressure. 'Where ever you looked,' Béthegrues recalled, 'there were similar sad scenes.' The exodus streamed on towards Paris, as yet relatively unscathed, by road and rail. Dunkirk was becoming an exceedingly dangerous place.[45]

DOUBTS

Hitler's *Felsennest* headquarters back at the Eifel was divided in two parts: Army staff in HQ Area 2 (*Oberkommando des Heeres*, OKH), and the *Wehrmacht* Supreme Command (*Oberkommando der Wehrmacht*, OKW) in HQ Area 1. OKH was housed in a large farmhouse inside the sand track, half-timbered village of Rodert. Hitler's HQ Area was reached by a 200-yard sand track that traversed scrubland, the way indicated by phosphorous strips hanging in the trees. The core part of OKW was a fenced-in high barbed-wire enclosure. Civilian staff were quartered around the farmhouse in Rodert below. A concrete pillbox housed the mess, where a long wooden table could seat 20 people. Hitler's personal briefing room was at the centre of the enclosure, nine by 12 feet square, with a relief map of Flanders on the wall and a single wicker chair. 'Because room in the bunker was so limited,' secretary Christa Schroeder remembered, 'most of the discussions were held in the open,' benefitting from very fine May weather. Hitler was totally enamoured by the beauty of his surroundings and its majestic views, suggesting to the staff that they should return one day for a commemorative visit.

Generaloberst Jodl, the OKW Chief of Staff, prepared a daily situation brief at midday after assimilating the reports from the respective army, navy and air force aides. Over the next two hours Hitler developed his ideas and made his views for future operations known. He rarely gave a direct order; 'his preferred method was persuasion,' von Below his *Luftwaffe* aide explained, 'so that his generals put his ideas into effect from conviction'. Hitler, the World War I ranker, thought he best knew his soldiers. He was mistrustful of General Staff officers with their distinctive red-striped trousers, and made inroads into their authority and independence at every opportunity. The 200-yard dirt track wending its way between the two headquarter areas was a tangible manifestation of latent divisions within the command organization.[46]

Auftragstaktik was the mission-command philosophy used by the German General Staff. OKW defined missions, which Army OKH physically executed. OKW allocated appropriate resources to achieve these tasks, which was left to OKH initiative to carry out. The process, however, was not working well because of inherent personal and philosophical differences between the two staffs. *Generaloberst* von Brauchitsch, the head of the army, was not assured in his dealings with Hitler, a personality defect that meant army leaders were often presented with ready-made decisions they had not contributed to. During his stay the *Führer* only visited the OKH staff once in HQ Area 2, and that was on the first day of the campaign. Von Brauchitsch's right-hand man was Chief of Staff *Generalleutnant* Franz Halder, who did not fight the tensions. Halder, comfortably secure with the superiority of his command organization, was ever confident that polished execution would ultimately prove itself. This did not endear him to Hitler. 'As usual, he receives me in a cool almost hostile manner', he remembered at one typical conference. Von Below presciently observed before the campaign that, unlike the Navy and *Luftwaffe*, 'under Brauchitsch the Army continued to follow its own path, and this Hitler wanted to change'. Both prevaricated over the adoption of the *Sichelschnitt* plan proposed by von Manstein despite it being enthusiastically received by Hitler, adding to the *Führer's* irritation. 'He made no secret that Brauchitsch and Halder would have to be replaced,' von Below remembered, 'but it could not be done now, shortly before a new offensive.'[47]

'Hitler made great play of his experience as a soldier of the First World War', *Oberst* Walter Warlimont at OKW recalled. He believed the Kaiser's army had been 'stabbed in the back' in 1918, which obliged the generals to surrender undefeated. Since 1935 Hitler had achieved a string of political successes, three bloodless military occupations and two military victories. All this had been in the face of opposing generals and apparently discerning politicians, who had all got the *Führer's* personal predictions wrong. Hitler never felt the need to win the confidence of the officers around him. On the contrary, he eyed strong points and weaknesses, having made it clear to the military hierarchy in a speech on 23 November 1939 that 'I will stop at nothing and I shall crush anyone who opposes me.'[48]

The two elements making up the *Felsennest* headquarters mirrored opposite poles. *Generaloberst* Alfred Jodl likened the headquarters to 'a cross between a cloister and a concentration camp,' claiming 'it was not a military headquarters at all, it was a civilian one'. This was because many of the inner circle were civilian Nazi political men. 'Most of them', Warlimont observed, 'had decked themselves out in some sort of field-grey uniform, often with badges of their own choosing.' OKH by contrast was run on traditional military lines and regarded longingly by some of the OKW army officers who liked to associate 'among their own sort'. When a senior aide introduced the initiative of inviting officers from HQ Area 2 to dine at Hitler's bunker table at OKW the idea quickly proved unpopular. Enthusiasm among – at first – welcoming junior officers waned, and they had to be 'detailed' to attend when volunteers were not forthcoming. They much preferred to consort with their own when off duty rather than listen to Hitler's boring 'table talk'.

Information-gathering at staff level was as much about impressions derived from visiting friends and colleagues at front headquarters as reading signals and dispatches. Jodl showed little interest in visit impressions and both he and Hitler frowned upon senior OKW officers who maintained social contact with their army colleagues just 200 yards down the track. Jodl had won Hitler's confidence due to his handling of crises during the Norwegian campaign, and felt it his duty to uphold the '*Führer*'s genius' against 'undisciplined generals'. He was a 'yes man', like *General* Keitel, the OKW Chief of Staff, who according to Warlimont 'always considered his sole duty to be to support Hitler and smooth down any objections to Hitler's wishes'.[49]

Latent divisions inside the staff came to a head on 17 May, when the main body of the panzer formations had crossed the Meuse, and were clattering along the line of the River Somme. They went faster than anyone expected. Halder could hardly conceal his pride, having written in his diary the day before that 'the breakthrough is developing on almost classical lines'. Hitler, however, did not see it that way, increasingly obsessed with the vulnerability of the southern flank. He countenanced 'a pearl necklace' of infantry divisions, coming up slowly on foot with horse-drawn artillery and logistics, which needed to be firmly in position before the armoured thrust should be allowed to speed away. Von Brauchitsch was told at the midday conference that 'the principal danger' was in the south. Halder laconically wrote in his diary 'I can see no danger whatsoever at the moment'. Hitler on the other hand promptly travelled to von Rundstedt's Army Group A headquarters at Bastogne to share this concern. Halder appreciated the tension was ramping up at OKW, observing after the evening conference: 'A most unfortunate day. The *Führer* is terribly nervous. He is frightened by his own success, is unwilling to take any risks and is trying to rein us in.'[50]

Hitler was generally a late riser; the next morning conference was uncharacteristically held earlier at 10am not midday. Jodl noted 'a day of high tension' in his diary, because 'OKH has not carried out the instruction to build up the southern flank as rapidly as possible'. Von Brauchitsch and Halder were summoned by an intensely annoyed Hitler 'and ordered in the sharpest manner,' according to Jodl, 'to carry out the order'. Keitel, the Chief of Staff, immediately flew off to von

Rundstedt's headquarters to impress on the staff there to carry out the instruction at once, without waiting for OKH to issue the order. Halder described the interview as a 'most unpleasant discussion'. Exasperated at 'a completely different conception in the Führer's headquarters,' he wrote in some frustration that night:

> The *Führer* is full of incomprehensible fear about the southern flank. He rages and shouts that we are going about it the right way to ruin the entire operation and are running the risk of defeat... He entirely refuses to carry on with the operation westwards.[51]

General Guderian's XIX Panzer Corps was way out in front and acting practically autonomously. He commanded from his armoured half-track, flanked by key officers who motored alongside in motorcycle combinations. By ignoring his flanks, he was going faster than any enemy who might come at him from the side. Well aware of the inhibitions of his superior commanders, he felt the imperative was to keep going. If the tanks faltered, he suspected his panzer group would end up being absorbed and subordinated within the Army Group structure as a whole. They had already conquered more French territory in days than the German Army had done over four years in World War I. On 17 May, as the row about the speed and extent of the advance developed at the *Felsennest*, Guderian was summoned to report to his superior von Kleist and halt his armoured drive. Anticipating a congratulatory meeting after von Kleist flew to his command post at Soize, 'he was in for a bitter disappointment', his Chief of Staff Nehring recalled. 'Instead of an objective discussion and some praise for his men, there was bitter reproach for the extent of his advance.' 'When the first storm was passed,' Guderian later wrote, 'and he had stopped to draw breath, I asked that I might be relieved of my command.' Von Kleist was taken aback, but accepted.[52]

Oberstleutnant Hermann Balck with the 1st Panzer Division recalled how Guderian 'was very hard to get along with' and had a tendency to be 'constantly involved in battles with everybody else'. Guderian immediately radioed von Rundstedt to explain what had happened. He was instructed to rescind his resignation because the order had come from OKH. He was, however, allowed to continue with a 'reconnaissance in force'. 'A man like Guderian knew what to do with such an opportunity,' Nehring recalled, 'even if his command post did have to remain back at Soize', where he could be reached with instructions. 'It's a tribute to the German Army, as well as to Guderian's own remarkable abilities, that he was able to rise as high as he did', Balck later commented. Meanwhile at the *Felsennest* the storm had blown over. At 6pm Hitler was talked round by Halder and permission was given to resume the advance.[53]

Meanwhile to the north, Rommel's 7th Panzer Division with the *Gruppe* Hoth had reached the River Sambre, where bridges were captured intact. 'We had no information about the situation either in the individual sectors of the front, or as a whole', his *Aufklärungs* Battalion commander *Hauptmann* Hans von Luck remembered. 'We had the feeling of being alone at the head of a division advancing tempestuously.' Momentum was picking up: 'Forward! was the cry'. French resistance was collapsing ahead of them, 'caught completely unawares by our impetuous advance,' he recalled. *'La guerre est finie'* French prisoners shouted out as they passed them on the roads. 'Rommel's unorthodox tactics horrified the General Staff,' von Luck claimed. 'Our opponents are beginning to fall back and must not be allowed to find a foothold again,' Rommel insisted. Balck with the 1st Panzer Division vanguard echoed this philosophy. In such circumstances 'attack is the least costly operation' because 'what was easy today could cost a lot of blood tomorrow'.[54]

War correspondent C.C. Christophé, caught up in the exuberance of Guderian's advance and embedded with the 2nd Panzer Division, reported 'they're running, and see how they run!' They were through Belgium, where he observed, 'the further the armoured fighting vehicles penetrated the Belgian countryside, the greater the surprise from the enemy'. *Leutnant* Hans Steinbrecher recalled 'a huge panzer battle lies behind us, tank on tank, it was simply monstrous what men have to endure!' They were beginning to think 'soon an awful battle would blaze up ahead of us'. On 15 May they reached Cambrai: 'finally the English!' he observed. 'For the first time today we came up against British tanks.' His diary account claimed three tanks were knocked out by his crew; 'like wild hunters we were let off the leash to chase after the English'. It was his last recorded diary entry. 'I have just received a new task, to pick up the wounded Gerhard with the armoured recce vehicle,' he wrote. His patriotic entries were typical of the 'derring-do' accounts that flooded German bookshops immediately after the campaign. As the youngest officer in the regiment, he was proud to be entrusted with such a responsible mission. 'Strong enemy forces are reported out to the southwest', the final entry read. He never returned from the mission.[55]

Further north the 3rd Panzer Division was traversing Belgium as part of Hoth's XVI Panzer Corps. One officer with its 75th Panzer Artillery Regiment recalled 'during this period practically all our existence is spent on or beside the roads'. Each day they passed the same monotonous scenery. 'One sees before and behind, a long column of grey vehicles, the dust rising in yellowish-white clouds.' Everything was coated in a layer of dust and grime:

> Faces look as if powdered and the stubble on one's face resembles ripened grass. The heat is intense and the sun is almost too well meaning. Every man's face begins to peel and burn like fire. Many coloured neckties are soon worn by all, as neck and chin have been chafed sore by the rough field blouse.[56]

By night the columns were shrouded in darkness: 'Fewer details are seen, yet fires and the glow of fires are in great evidence. Reddish patches can invariably be detected on the horizon, and in all directions searchlights extend their long groping arms.' They drove with no lights. Only on moving off or halting could green or red lights be seen 'dancing along the dark silhouettes of the vehicles'. The Pervitin stimulus came into its own during the concentration needed for such night moves:

> For navigators, first or second drivers, these are the worst and most harassing hours of the day. The longest distances are covered by night and those in the driving seat have continuously to peer into uncertainty, in which danger lurks like an evil monster. Often the darkness stands like a black wall before the radiator. One foot on the accelerator or the brake pedal, so it goes on through the night until suddenly a tiny red light flares up ahead. Woe to the driver who from sheer weariness fails to see it and does not brake!

Journeys were conducted in silence, 'only the engine sings its monotonous song,' and at halts 'every driver sinks down over the steering wheel'.[57]

Luftwaffe air attacks kept the momentum going. *Generalmajor* (Major General) von Richthofen, supporting the *Gruppe* Kleist, flew over Guderian's march route in a Fiesler Storch light monoplane on 18 May. Looking down he saw:

> The roads are full of prisoners, abandoned guns and ammunition columns. What fantastic pictures of war destruction! We had not anticipated this in France. Overall good bomb strikes with amazing effect. Everything seems to suggest the complete collapse of the enemy.

Von Richthofen conferred with Guderian, 'who complains he is too spread out'. 'He wants to immediately push forward with weak forces on Amiens and Abbeville.'

Guderian advanced slowly on 18 and 19 May due to the succession of restraining instructions from above, but reached the old battlefields of the Great War on a line running through Cambrai, Péronne and Ham. He received complete freedom of action on the second day, and on 20 May was ordered to attack at Amiens. The 2nd Panzer Division was tasked to strike beyond to Abbeville at the mouth of the Somme River. Fuel shortages obliged the tanks to halt just in front of the town, which was, nevertheless, taken by a mixed force of infantry, sappers and artillery in the face of light resistance. According to Guderian's Chief of Staff, Nehring, 'a British battery was captured on a parade ground, armed only with blanks, because they had been carrying out a practice'. Large numbers of prisoners were taken. 'Nobody had expected the Germans quite so soon – we had hardly expected to arrive so soon ourselves.'[58]

As night descended Guderian's men pulled off the *pièce de résistance* of the campaign thus far. Pushing further along the Somme River from Abbeville, Austrians from *Oberstleutnant* Spitta's battalion with the 2nd Panzer reached Noyelles-sur-Mer on the Atlantic coast. This was in the vicinity of the Hundred Years War battlefield of Crécy. It was a total surprise. Panzer *Oberleutnant* (Lieutenant) Dietz recalled, 'a French Colonel is prepared to believe anything – that we came by sea, perhaps, or from the air – but cannot get it into his head that we marched overland.' 'Right now', Christophé with the 2nd Panzer remembered, 'they tasted the salty breath of the Channel, that has been called "English" for a long time'.[59]

Private Charles Waite with the British 2/7th Queen's Royal Regiment thought they were safely ensconced in the British rear at Abbeville.

> I looked across this field and there must have been, I would say, three or four hundred German troops coming in that direction [points] on the road. There was say about up to a dozen German tanks – terrifying. For ten minutes to a quarter of an hour there was nothing but firing, so I just threw myself down, dropped me rifle and just lay there. There was just 80 of us, and within 5 or 10 minutes, most of them were either dead or dying. We were in a terrible mess.[60]

Guardsman Bill Weeks, a regular with the 1st British Division, recalled the shock of learning the Germans had got behind them on the flank. 'Everybody was safeguarding the Maginot Line, never get past that,' he assumed. 'And what do they do?' he rhetorically asked, 'they went round it and attacked us!'[61]

Charles Waite assumed it was all over. 'I wanted to get it over quick', he remembered:

> To me it was obvious. This was our duty and we were not going to see any more. Suddenly on the road, there was a huge German standing there. He looked like a giant to us. He was an officer. He was pointing a revolver at us and calling out: 'Up Tommy! Up Tommy! *Hande Hoch!* [Hands up]'[62]

Back at the *Felsennest* OKH and OKW were equally taken aback. There were scenes of rejoicing; 'unusual,' Warlimont remembered, for such a traditionally sober headquarters. 'The *Führer* is beside himself with joy', Jodl wrote in his diary, 'talks in words of highest appreciation of the German Army and its leadership'. 'Is working on the peace treaty', he satisfactorily noted, 'first negotiations in the Forest of Compiègne like in 1918'.[63] Revenge would be sweet.

In 11 days Guderian penetrated over 200 miles through Luxembourg, Belgium and France in a scything sickle stroke that dismembered the Allied force structure. British Captain James Hill, working with Lord Gort's BEF HQ, remembered, 'we hadn't quite envisaged them going right through the north and going around our flank like that, we hadn't imagined that at all'.[64] Nearly a million Allied troops were trapped in a pocket north of the panzer corridor. Nine British divisions, 45 French and the whole of the Belgian Army were backed up west of the Scheldt River. If von Rundstedt turned north, the Allied forces would be encircled. The soldiers sensed they were verging on a momentous victory. Hans P., a radio operator with 6th Machine Gun Battalion, wrote in his diary:

> We voiced our amazement at the astounding progress of this campaign. None of us could have imagined the war in the west would go faster, easier forward than in Poland. Was this the traditionally renowned French Army we had so highly rated? It was a puzzle. Some suspected the *Führer* had a magic wand available for use by our commanders.[65]

Another *Feldwebel* triumphantly wrote home:

> The complete picture will become apparent in a few years, because at present we are standing on the verge of a change in the world order. *Ja* – you beloved wives and all who remain at home, you can be proud of your menfolk out here.[66]

The Allies were now staring total defeat in the face.

Chapter 2

Landser[*]

'What has happened here is totally unimaginable,' German *Landser* Ernst Kleist wrote home. 'One can only comprehend that it is going forward in a tempo never seen before, not far behind Poland.' 'How to compare?' he asked, 'like being part of Napoleon's onrush or Ghengis Khan's storm?' Kleist writing home thought less about battle or death, more an uneasy feeling that 'the rush forwards might subside'.[1] Hitler at the *Felsennest* HQ likewise went from an emotional high to confiding 'unease' to Jodl, his operations chief, 'that the infantry divisions are not pushing forward fast enough'. The main body was days behind the obvious trail of destruction left by the panzers. Infantryman Karl Schönfeld remembered:

> Dead cattle overlaid the fields, emitting a noxious smell. Time and again cows' legs stuck up in the air here, or the bloated carcass of a horse there ... [while] deeply compressed tank tracks led through freshly sowed fields.[2]

Jodl regarded the solitary figure of the *Führer* sitting in the small wooden briefing hut with some unease. On the night of the 21st/22nd he recalled 'he remained in the map room up to 1.30 in the morning'.[3]

---

[*]*Landser* can be loosely translated as the nickname of the typical German soldier, like 'Tommy' is to the British.

Gefreiter Felix Klaus described a typical march day for the 51st Regiment, with the 18th Infantry Division, having already marched more than 30 miles per day for the past three. They were woken up at 3am for another brutal day. The dispatch rider who brought the readiness order was met 'with sleepy faces'. 'Nobody could believe it possible that today, after so many fatiguing march days, they were called upon to do another.'

The announcement of the day's objective was always accompanied by a sinking feeling when they calculated how far it was. Curses sounded as they got ready:

> Excruciating pain showed on their faces as they pulled on boots over swollen feet once again. Shoulders ached from carrying machine guns all day long and hip bones smartly burned with the weight of heavily loaded belt orders. And we were going to do it again today?[4]

At the appointed time, battalions marched to their respective assembly areas. *Hauptmann* Siegfried Knappe remembered the routine for his horse-drawn 24th Artillery Regiment. It began with a 4.30am reveille for a 6am move: 'At that early hour it was still dark. It was always cold, and it was usually wet with early morning dew.'

Being the adjutant, he was lucky; 'a hot cup of tea usually helped me fight off the chill'. Batteries began to stir, 'grunts and slow-motion movements bringing the area alive'. Breakfast was coffee or tea to wash down bread with butter and jam, quickly crammed into the mouth alongside an occasional can of liverwurst or sausage meat. The mobile soup kitchen or *Gulaschkanon* (goulash cannon), on account of its gun-shaped chimney, soon gave off clouds of steam and the welcome smell of thick stew, prepared in large kettles. This, the main meal of the day, was ladled into personal mess tins after four hours marching.[5]

Sonderführer (special NCO) Neu with the 98th Infantry Division, part of Army Group A, recalled, 'The first 15 kilometres were a walk in the park, the next 10 strenuous and the rest slave labour'.[6]

Gefreiter Klaus, with the 51st Regiment, remembered before the sun rose 'fresh air had completely woken up the cosy heads' at which point companies would begin to sing. 'But by the time of the midday intense heat, tired steps along dusty streets meant nobody sang, throats were dried out by heat and dust.' Weary jokes promoted 'nervous and somewhat forced laughter' which stopped when stones bruised feet and uneven surfaces were wrenching ankles. Feet burned from the blisters rubbed by hard asphalt roads in Western Europe, not like the softer sandy dirt tracks experienced in Poland.[7]

'The sun burned down from the sky and opened up all our sweat pores', recalled *Hauptmann* Bönsch with the 18th Division artillery:

> Dust eddied high into the sky from tracks ground to powder by our wheels and horses' hooves. Faces and uniforms were covered in a grey layer of dust, so that we hardly recognized each other.[8]

Wochenschau German newsreels showed Luxembourg civilians spraying appreciative columns of smiling German infantry with garden hoses, offering a brief respite from the prickly heat. Perspiration ran into eyes and dripped from noses, saturating sticky hair beneath itchy helmets. Chafing rubbed uncomfortably between the legs, under arms and around neck collars; faces and hands were burned a dark brown. Glazed eyes peered out scanning the endless column ahead, willing it to halt. Little or no attention was paid to passing scenery as the sun burned down. Soldiers focused instead on feet dragging through the dust before them, or were dreamily transfixed at the end of the weapon carried by the soldier in front. 'Finally midday came', Klaus with the 51st Regiment recalled, and 'the battalion moved off the road'.[9]

The *Gulaschkanon* rolled up with the stew, most times tastefully prepared, 'but nobody wanted it, the day's effort had been too much, and tired men retired into the shadows', Bönsch recalled. They wanted peace and quiet, and not to think. Field breaks varied; Klaus got two hours, maybe time to recover an appetite. Siegfried Knappe remembered 'we had 45 minutes to eat' and 'after lunch, we would march until 5 or 6 pm, or until we reached our objective for the day'. They were steadily falling behind the panzers. 'We could not hear the battles that were being fought ahead of us', he recalled, 'because we were now two days behind the invasion force.' *Gefreiter* Klaus recalled the relief gained from a long stop with hot food. Cold wet helmets were put on again and the weight pulling at the belt seemed more acceptable. Stiff limbs were massaged and they got moving. With shouted commands the battalions assembled on the roads again: 'Hour after hour it went on, kilometre after kilometre was put behind. Again and again it was always the case: "only" another kilometre.'[10]

On 16 May *Gefreiter* Wied with the 54th Regiment from the 18th Division remembered: 'At about midday during a short rest, we noticed a memorial in our vicinity, a pyramid with a lion on top. We were at the battlefield of Waterloo where Blücher had defeated Napoleon.'

A General Staff officer paused his vehicle beside his battalion commander and grandly announced: 'Herr Major, your battalion is at the head of the German Army!' This raised spirits; 'forwards, only forwards,' the impressed Wied recalled. Ernst Kleist traversed the same ground: 'Yesterday we paused not far from Nivelles and went through the historical landscape of Waterloo. If the rumours are confirmed, there are seven French divisions, completely encircled, in front of us.'

It was likely the high point of the campaign, but inside five weeks Kleist would be dead. They had penetrated the Allied Dyle Line.[11]

In Belgium, the 21 infantry divisions of the Eighteenth and Sixth Armies took the brunt of the fighting. Army Group B's 29 or so divisions were on a subsidiary thrust, paralleling the main effort by Army Group A's more than 46 divisions, moving rapidly along the line of the River Somme. Von Bock had defeated the ten divisions of the Dutch Army and was now taking on the Belgian Army, the BEF and the First French Army. These 35 divisions represented the cream of the Allied defence. The advance by Eighteenth Army to the north and Sixth Army on their left was eerily reminiscent of the same German drive through Belgian territory during World War I. It was conducted with gritty and aggressive determination, crossing a latticework of canals and river lines, under constant artillery fire and prey to ambush and snipers. *Luftwaffe* support was generally haphazard.

Generalleutnant Friedrich-Carl Cranz commanding the 18th Division claimed in his post-campaign assessment that German infantry were superior to all their opponents. Offensive success came from 'infantry fire superiority'. His infantry sections were better equipped than their enemy counterparts. In particular: 'The MG 34, due to its high rate of fire, simple handling and light weight, and effectiveness on target ... is regarded by the troops as the best machine gun in the world.'

So effective, he argued, that the conventional German infantry section should be increased to 12 men and two MG 34s. 'Infantry fire superiority was decisive in the attack', he claimed in his after-action report, and 'had a detrimental effect on enemy morale'. *Wehrmacht* infantry were well supported with a menu of support weapons: light artillery pieces, 37mm anti-tank guns and heavy mortars. The mortar, 'light and mobile with a high accuracy and shrapnel effect on target', Cranz maintained, was the mainstay of the infantry battalions. In his view the effectiveness of the infantry *Blitzkrieg* was much aided by the technical excellence of its equipment and the quantity and lethal effect of its firepower.[12]

On 16 May the numerically superior Allied armies began a series of tactical withdrawals to the west, away from the Dyle Line, to avoid being outflanked by the panzer drive in the south. Screening their departure with light tanks and machine gun covered demolitions, rearguards fought tenacious local actions to fend off the German advance, so as to break clean to reach successive lines of withdrawal. These bitterly fought skirmishes encapsulated the experience of the Army Group B foot soldier. The *Luftwaffe* sowed confusion ahead at all road bridges and major road intersections, while both sides were perpetually advancing against flows of refugee misery, radiating outward and pushed along by fast-moving and unpredictable conflict zones.

Gefreiter Frey, bicycle borne with the 7th Company of the 192nd Regiment with the 56th Infantry Division, remembered 'every hour, *Ja*, every minute is costly' when trying to deny the enemy a chance to reform. 'German victory is not just about weapon effects,' he claimed, 'on the contrary, on countless occasions it was about the speed of the advance.' At Mecheln they carried bicycles on their backs across the ruined structure of the partially demolished bridge, in the stifling midday heat, utilizing engineer-laid wooden planks: 'Sweat ran in rivulets down their backs, creating light pathways through the crust of dust that covered faces, weapons and clothing.'[13]

They pushed on further, 'pistols gripped in fists and with rifles slung ready for action'. Up ahead came the dull thumps of demolitions as the vanguard blew road obstacles. Overhead from balconies and windows was an audience of 'civilians shyly leaning out of windows to watch the German soldiers pass by'. Frey was incredulous at the destruction wrought by the blown bridge, 'frightful', he remembered. Only the bridge piles remained standing at the centre of a huge circle of ground littered with chunks of stone and pieces of metal. Frey indulged in some good National Socialist rhetoric: 'Whole house facades had been blown away, freeing up a view of the furniture and belongings of peaceful citizens. Everything they owned had fallen victim to the criminal politics of the nonsensical ruling cliques.'[14]

On the far side of the waterway the company formed into a bicycle column and set off to secure the next canal crossing at Chapelle au Bois. They had just crossed the Dyle Line between Antwerp and Brussels, passing by the debris of Belgian retreat, piled high on cleared roads. On leaving the town they came across a number of 280mm heavy mortars abandoned in the streets. The inscriptions on their armoured gun shields showcased the battles they had participated in during World War I, reading '1916, 1917, 1918' and finally, Frey ironically recalled, '1940'.

The houses at Chapelle au Bois gradually rose from the shimmering heat haze as they approached. It was peaceful, 'unholy still' the corporal remembered. As the lead troop of cyclists rode down the dead streets 'suddenly whip like cracks against the house facades' sounded out. 'On the road surface', there was a 'whirring and whining from shots ricocheting into the air'. Bikes were dropped in the street amid the mad scramble for cover in the houses, where they began to move forward through both floors to locate the enemy. 'The town entrance is free of enemy. Outside the town it became dead-still again. Where is the enemy?'[15]

These short sharp, often brutal skirmishes were a characteristic feature of infantry advances through countless Belgian villages. Leo Leixner, a war correspondent with the Eighteenth Army recalled a Belgian holding action at the Ghent-Terneuzen Canal on 22 May.

> The enemy is defending the canal with all his might and all hell is breaking loose... The dead lie where they fell; tree branches are splintered as though in the aftermath of a hurricane; the ground is dotted with shell craters; the walls of the buildings still standing are pockmarked with machine-gun bursts.[16]

Leixner snapped a series of dramatic photographs of the engagement, for the German propaganda *Signal* magazine, which had a two and a half million circulation in the *Reich*. They show German motorcycle infantry in trouble sheltering behind trees. Two 37mm anti-tank guns have been manhandled forward, one either side of the street. 'We see two tanks coming around the bend 300 metres ahead of us,' he described. Both guns engage. One of the tanks retreats back down the road while the other seeks shelter behind a farmhouse. As it backs out into the road it takes a direct hit just at the corner of the building and bursts into flames. The whole fight is sequentially recorded with a camera. 'Nothing moves,' Leixner later wrote, 'the crew has escaped or is burning to death.' German soldiers peer out from behind the base of thick trees lining the Antwerp road. They are wary. The skirmish cost time. 'We keep a respectful distance from the dying steel dragon,' the reporter recalled, because the ammunition inside the burning hulk could detonate at any time.[17]

Frey's 7th Company eventually discovered, after clambering over back gardens behind the houses, that they were being faced off by a Belgian tank, with an infantry-manned machine gun, on the canal embankment off to their flank. Two 37mm guns were manhandled forward coming under intense fire. The company commander came up the main village street to investigate and began to spot and accurately lay the guns onto their targets. Enemy fire intensified, two tanks now and machine guns. German casualties lay vulnerable in the street. 'A sharp bang,' Frey recalled, and 'over there one of the tanks loudly exploded, struck at right angles, thick smoke poured from the hatches.' They intently observed, 'it remained silent'.[18]

Every bang and explosion reverberated around the houses and echoed throughout the streets. The big problem with urban ambushes was to track, amid conflicting reports and explosions, where the fire was actually coming from. Sharp cracks of passing bullets breaking the sound barrier could not be associated with the thump from the firing weapon, amid such disorientating sights and sounds. The only certainty of detection was to pick out the muzzle flash from the opposing weapon. Control was the biggest problem. Soldiers rushed into the nearest houses to seek cover; nobody knew for certain where they had gone until they identified themselves. Junior commanders had the most difficult task, to get men moving under fire. Immediate action drills had been practised, but it took courage and experience to manoeuvre effectively with fire support. Urban fighting often degenerated into one-on-one scraps with an unseen foe.

Frey's company engagement widened to a larger battle. Three German dead were lost overrunning the Belgian machine gun on the embankment. Further casualties were incurred trying to recover wounded lying in the main street. Incoming fire became so intense that the company commander and the anti-tank crews were forced off the street to shelter in a building. Once inside, soldiers venturing out 'immediately attracted a hail of fire against the house walls, windows and doors'. They found themselves trapped in their haven, pinned down by fire from three directions. 'There was no other option remaining', Frey recalled, 'except reinforcements and support from our own artillery'. That would have to wait until the main body of the battalion closed up. The regimental commander, meanwhile, made his way across the house rooftops to assess the situation. At that moment there were urgent cries from the besieged house: 'Hallo boys! Get out the house has started to burn – the dogs have set the roof alight with tracer!'

The only escape route was a frantic hammer and bayonet demolition of intervening stone walls. Zeroed in by enemy fire, the only way out was through rather than outside the blazing building. Only gradually did the walls crumble as men laboured in the stifling heat radiating down from the burning roof. Small holes were enlarged by the desperate expedient of blasting masonry clear with hand grenades. As dusk descended they managed to scramble out, just as German artillery shrieked overhead to bracket the enemy-held canal embankment. In the course of the day, what had begun as a company skirmish meeting engagement expanded into a deliberate battalion assault supported by the regiment's artillery. A process that cost time.[19]

These hotly contested village fights exacted a cumulative psychological toll. Hans P. with 6th Machine Gun Battalion recalled the first serious engagement of their advance through Belgium on 18 May:

Suddenly the report came through; *Point platoon has hit French tanks; Oberleutnant Arnim has fallen, several dead and seriously wounded.* For the first time the war had become apparent to us once again, in its true form, like the first Sunday in Poland.

Von Arnim had been a popular and well-liked officer. 'We were paralysed with sadness, reinforced by concern for our own lives,' he remembered, 'for now we would be committed to the same carnage'.[20]

There was a particularly hard fight for a village barn 2½ miles short of Le Quesnoy, south-east of Valenciennes. The farm building was held by tough French Colonial Moroccan troops. 'Several of our riflemen, sticking their heads up to engage the machine gun firing at them, fell with a bullet to the head.' Another machine gun opened up from the first house of the village, on the Valenciennes road. The new threat was only 100 yards away and Hans, a radio operator, had to sprint across an open street with the groups of riflemen attempting to get within striking distance. Despite the scary gauntlet of fire they lost just one wounded soldier, because 'the enemy fire was always a few split seconds too late'. More soldiers made it to the ditch on the other side of the road and after a sharp firefight the barn was captured. 'Seldom in my life was I so happy as at that moment,' Hans P. recalled. 'It was a sense of my complicated life being handed back to me again.' This intense relief was visibly shared by the men with him. 'I thought on the comrades, who were no longer fit and healthy, able to greet this beautiful sunny day like me':

> Being able to overcome the storm against my nerves and put the need for instinctive self-preservation behind me; and to calmly maintain radio communications during an uncomfortable night, in a dangerous situation – I put down as a gift from God – to whom I had so often prayed.[21]

He had survived another day.

LANDSER PORTRAIT

'The front is deep into Belgium,' *Gefreiter* L.M. with the 25th Infantry Division wrote home, 'weather is very hot, marching performance enormous, hardly slept, morale good'.[22] Field post letters like these and diaries during these weeks offer a barometer of the German *Landser*'s thoughts and opinions. A glimpse at their beliefs and concerns gives some clue to the motivation that propelled the rapid German advance through the Low Countries in May 1940, which so dismayed the Allied opposition. *Sieg im Westen,* the epic German propaganda film account of 'Victory in the West', typified the idealistic outpouring of national patriotism that appeared in dozens of soldier and regimental accounts released in the *Reich*'s bookshops soon after the campaign. Most appeared in the spring of 1941, before the invasion of Russia.

The German armies that invaded the west thought themselves Germany's finest historically to date. They represented the best concentration of idealized and technically proficient fighting power yet fielded. The emotional impact was not dissimilar to that of the Israeli Defense Force, lionized by its population for its unprecedented success during the 1967 'Six-Day War'. Although Germany prosecuted an aggressive pre-emptive strike against neutral countries, it was as yet broadly untarnished, relative to the *Wehrmacht*'s later conduct in Russia. Few soldiers in the ranks had witnessed the horrors that followed in the wake of the German occupation of Poland. The *Landser* invading Belgium, Holland and France held their heads high with pride, not shame. Soldiers anticipated an attack, welcoming the chance to reduce tension and settle the *Sitzkrieg* stand-off. Ironically the Japanese attack at Pearl Harbor was to have a greater emotional impact than the equally criminal assault on neutral Belgian and Dutch soil, a partial revisiting of 1914.

'An inner national enthusiasm emerged during these days,' soldier Hans P. recalled, 'even stronger than before the Polish campaign'.[23] The force that entered Russia the next year was to be far more worldly and hard-bitten. Like the 1967 Israeli war analogy, the panzers or tanks were regarded as the 'sword' and the air forces the 'hammer'. This surge of national unity was shared by the Kaiser's royalists, Weimar socialists and democrats; all subsumed in Hitler's National Socialism. They were united in the conviction that, having taken the plunge, Germany should never again be subjected to the humiliation of national defeat. Graf Spanocchi recalled his old traditional cavalry regiment were 'professional soldiers, who had in a sense established themselves as an island in the brown sea' of brown-shirted Nazis. 'We were ignorant 22-year-olds, living normal lives as robust young Lieutenants, amid the schizophrenics.' The injustice of the Versailles Treaty, after World War I, was felt by all, as was acute dislike of the French, who had exploited war repayments to the full. Soldier Rolf Müllender claimed disapproval had been 'passed on by my parents and also as a Rhinelander'. The French had occupied the Rhine in pursuit of reparations, he explained: 'We certainly had a certain desire for revenge – that I must openly admit – due to the French occupation of the Aachen area, and also against the Belgians. And there was another element – *Ja* – revenge for Versailles.'[24]

The make-up of German infantry divisions was variable, depending on individual conscription call-up 'waves'. Conscription had started in 1935, which meant three or four intakes before the war began. In terms of size the German Field Army in spring 1940 was half as large again as it had been at the outbreak of war, when it numbered 106 divisions. Since then, five new waves of recruits and reserves were mobilized to April 1940 to create 44 new infantry divisions. Including *Waffen SS* increments there were 155 German division formations at the outset of the invasion of the Low Countries and France, close to 3,000,000 men in army uniform. Twenty of the recently formed divisions had yet to be trained. By spring, however, there were over 100 infantry divisions with at least six months' training, which included 50-odd regular 'peacetime' divisions. These held the motorized, mountain and panzer troops, the most battle hardened, fully equipped with excellent training and morale.

The youngest were aged between 18 and 22, while reservists were older. A typical example was the 216th Infantry Division, destined to be committed at Dunkirk, which formed one month before the war started in August 1939. About one-third of its soldiers had fought in World War I, another third had been conscripted into the fledgling *Wehrmacht*, while the final third were so-called 'eight-week soldiers' called up at the last moment. Most of the reasonably trained active divisions formed a quarter of the western offensive first wave, peacetime regulars reinforced by trained reservists. The second main element was mostly fully trained reservists and the rest only cursorily trained. Something like half the offensive force had a few weeks' training under their belts, while the premier 25% had more than 40 weeks' training experience.[25]

Part of the euphoria felt by the swiftly advancing invasion force was that they were being successful against technically competent foes from economically advanced countries, on par with their own. Poland had been a brutal experience for some divisions, whereas this 'champagne' campaign was swiftly racing through Europe's advanced road network. Unlike the ideological and ethnic war waged later against 'subhuman' Bolshevik Russia, like Poland a landscape of dirt roads between agrarian communities and occasional cities, Western Europe was different. German tanks paused during the advance to fill up at French roadside Esso petrol pumps. Otto W. wrote home: 'We had everything we could ask for, living like royalty. Chocolate and coffee beans in generous amounts, swimming in wine and liquor. Every day a clean shirt and underwear. In other words brilliant!'

The rich farmland of France was a land of 'milk and honey'. German soldiers posted there during the occupation recalled 'living like God in France', an oasis of peace for four years amid bloody campaigns all around.[26]

War with France was seen as 'just' by the typical *Landser*. He was righting the wrongs of the post-1918 settlement and slaying the Versailles

Treaty dragon. Hitler Youth schoolboy Alfons Heck declared, 'to me the Fatherland was a somewhat mystical yet real concept of a nation which was infinitely dear and threatened by unrelenting enemies'. There was agreement that they were in the right. Even Heck's grandmother, a staunch traditional Catholic and not a natural Nazi supporter, was to later admit: 'You got to hand it to Adolf, he finally paid them back.'[27]

There are very few gritty soldier accounts of the war in the west on par with post-war veteran accounts of Russia. None are in any way comparable to the searing indictments of conflict, written by American soldiers, in the later Vietnam War. The primary reason for this literary shortfall, apart from the stirring tales of derring-do written by embedded National Socialist journalists during 1940–1, was that so few of these men survived the war. Survival mathematic averages were against them. In organizational terms the normal structure of an infantry combat division was 64% 'teeth', those fighting forward in platoons, companies and regimental battalions, against the remaining 36% logistics and resupply 'tail'; services that kept men in action. The panzer and motorized formations' imbalance was even greater. About half was teeth, the rest tail.

Many of the units that invaded France in 1940 went on to participate in as many as five or six campaigns in Europe, the Balkans, the Desert, Russia and the Mediterranean. Each deployment took its toll of the 'teeth' element, so that by 1945 very few panzer crew fighting in the dying days of the *Reich* had been in France at the beginning. The determined stubble-faced German soldier casting a stick grenade in Russia, portrayed under the dramatic headline of *Ich – Oder du!* (It's me – or you!) on the cover of a *Wehrmacht* propaganda magazine in 1941, was already likely dead. By the end of the Soviet winter counter-offensive that broke the German grip on Moscow in December 1941, about one-third of the veteran element of the German armies had perished.[28]

One memorable aspect of the *Blitzkrieg* campaign for *Landser* was that their war of movement was conducted rather like a form of 'military tourism'. They witnessed sights and landmarks never seen before. When ordinary people in Europe went anywhere in the 1930s, they did so on foot or riding a bicycle. As a consequence, they were fitter than the present generation. During the years of economic depression people rarely ventured beyond more than walking distance from their towns or villages. Assault Pioneer Wolfgang Döring, moving through Belgium after crossing the Meuse, excitedly wrote home that 'every day there is something new'. Rudolf Gschöpf, the 45th Infantry Division padre, noticed the shops were still open as they passed through Luxembourg. 'I used the opportunity,' he later wrote, 'to visit and tour this stimulating and beautiful town.' Likewise, infantry officer Werner L. wrote to his 'dearest' wife describing his 'tour' through Holland and Belgium: 'We move even further through changeable countryside; from Holland, where everything is prosperous and clean to Belgium, more densely populated, but with poor people.' His unit passed through Antwerp at night, 'completely silent and at its core an old stylish city'. He remarked on the 'huge and wonderful early gothic church buildings' in the area, many of which had been damaged by artillery or air attack. His descriptions resemble a tourist travel log: 'the rhododendrons bloom wonderfully in the old parks, many in this fertile country, and the gorse – like a golden memory from the Eifel'. Soldier Lutz Niethammer waxed lyrical: 'the region is simply beautiful' and 'the Belgian countryside is lovelier than France'. 'You could see real palm trees,' he recalled, 'a wonderful area.'[29]

This idyllic landscape, however, had to be fought over, as in 1914–18. *Landser* letters and diary accounts are permeated with references to World War I, which their fathers had fought. Something like 3¾ million German soldiers had fought in the West during that war and probably more than half the German soldiers in this campaign were born before it. The average birth year of most surviving *Feldpost* (military post) letter writers is 1913. Virtually all the soldiers in the invasion had near family, a father or brother, who had fought between 1914 and 1918. Revenge for this defeat features in many letters. War correspondent Dr Manfeld wrote in stirring terms 'the sons do not only fight over the graves of their fathers'. His nationalistic article proclaimed 'the hour of fulfilling [the World War] has come, the sons have stormed across their father's graves to victory'. These lofty words reflected the gradual change in the presentation of German war memorials by the end of the 1920s. Poignant grief for soldiers killed in battle changed in atmosphere to monuments about the mystique of brave fighters, who had fought on the front lines, in keeping with National Socialist philosophy. The political and military leadership of the Third *Reich* after Hitler came to power sought to inculcate military values within the general populace. The *Volk* as part of the 'community of destiny' had to be made fit for battle.[30]

World War I veteran *Gefreiter* A.M. with the 87th Infantry Division wrote home reminding his family 'now I have been summoned to France for a second time as a soldier, and find myself not far from my old battle position from 1918'. *Gefreiter* H.B. had gone into position at Chemin des Dames with the 5th Division, 'a historical area', which saw the final abortive German offensive in 1918. 'The ground is soaked through with the blood of our fathers from the World War,' he remembered. 'One crater after the other clearly shows the evidence. It must have been awful then, and here we are today, two huge armies up against each other.' *Landser* Rolf Müllender was wary of French artillery, 'because the fathers had always pointed out "French artillery barrages were the worst ever",' but 'despite that we were in good heart'.[31]

Even at the height of *Blitzkrieg* success, the shadow of 1914–18 raised uneasy doubts that there might be a repetition of the reverse at the Marne. The original Schlieffen Plan had come to grief against Joffre's unexpected French 1914 counter-offensive, which saved Paris. Assault Pioneer Wolfgang Döring was particularly worried at a tense moment along the River Somme that 'perhaps a second Marne fate would occur'. Likewise, signaller Erich Kuby with Army Group A suspected on 18 May they had 'reached a critical moment in the campaign'. Surely it could not keep going so well. He wrote in his diary: 'the French appeared to have something up their sleeve – their tanks ought to be attacking.'[32]

Powering momentum was idealistic zeal. Since 1935 German soldiers on joining up had sworn allegiance to Adolf Hitler, who personified the national Socialist state, as British soldiers did to their king. His person had transcended the depression years of the Weimar Republic, with its political schisms between the last vestiges of Kaiser *Reich* royalism, social democracy, communism and nationalism. The average age of those writing surviving *Feldpost* letters, born around 1913, meant many had been schooled in the years of the Weimar Republic and maybe one-third had served in 1914–18. The introduction of conscription in 1935 and later meant increasing numbers were educated under National Socialism in the new Third *Reich*. These men had joined the Hitler Youth at boy scout age and then served a brief period of *Reichsarbeitsdienst*, Labour Service, before being drafted, or volunteering for their preferred branch of the *Wehrmacht*. German rearmament and modernization of the *Luftwaffe* and panzer forces attracted many youngsters, completely immersed in enthusiasm for the regime. Essentially, the younger the soldier, the more likely he was to be visibly influenced by Nazi ideals.

Hitler appealed to both sides of the age spectrum by influence or persuasion. He had after all achieved two miracles. When the Nazis took power in 1933 there were six million unemployed and the army numbered 100,000 poorly armed soldiers. By 1936 and in the face of global economic crises, full employment reigned and the *Wehrmacht* had emerged ostensibly as one of the most powerful military forces in Europe. 'Germany awake!' the Nazis proclaimed, instituting revolutionary social change. One *had* to be a part of this process; suspicion was aroused if you did not participate. Nazi foreign policy triumphs had been in tandem with the economic 'miracle'.

Every conscript army reflects the society from which it is drawn. Older age groups in the army had lived through stark social contrasts from the Weimar Republic years. Economic improvements and enhanced feelings of security and orderliness appealed to these older soldiers. World War I veterans had been convinced they had been 'stabbed in the back' by social democrat politicians who had agreed a humiliating peace behind the backs of an undefeated army. These types strongly identified with the *Führer*, who had regained their national pride. Younger soldiers were enthused by the 'new' and 'better' age dawning. 'Unlike our elders,' remembered Alfons Heck, 'we the children of the '30s, knew nothing of the turmoil or freedom of the Weimar republic.' Young people had been 'getting off the streets' imbued with a sense of *Volk* and community. Most had personalities moulded by the Hitler Youth, where as Heck explained they 'received an almost daily dose of nationalistic instruction, which we swallowed as naturally as our morning milk'. 'Things were moving forward' and it was this unity of aspiration that affected the German invasion army of 1940. Both the military and political leadership placed emphasis on anchoring military values within the general population. The *Volk* had to be made fit for battle. The army, in a sense, therefore recognized the 'community of destiny' that victory over France and Britain would bring. 'The Wehrmacht always strove for cordial relations with the Hitler Youth,' Alfons Heck remembered, 'for the obvious reason that we were its pool of future manpower.'[33]

Time spent with the Hitler Youth and *Reichsarbeitdienst* meant German recruits were already exposed to military life on joining.

'Purposely,' Heck recalled, because 'the Hitler Youth was organized similar to the Wehrmacht in squads, platoons, companies, battalions and so on'. This 'community of boys' held regular tests of strength and endurance and physically fought each other in war games. 'They taught us to be tough,' soldier Johannes Köppen recalled. 'What did Hitler say a German boy must be? Swift as a greyhound, tough as leather and hard as Krupp steel.' Aggression was encouraged; 'nobody wanted to be a Mummy's boy, myself included,' remembered another soldier, Günther Damaske, 'so we cut the apron strings.' Training included vocational skills; motor engineering benefited the motorized and panzer forces, gliding the *Luftwaffe*. Henry Metelmann recalled they practised 'considerable military training, which meant the army was able to train us more speedily'. He became a tank driver, claiming, 'when we were finally let loose on the panzers, we knew what it was all about'. As later SS soldier Bernard Heisig explained, 'when the war broke out we were all mentally prepared'.[34]

They needed to be, because basic training in the *Wehrmacht* was as harsh as it was thorough, and pursued with draconian discipline. Older reservists had learned through practice with the Kaiser's Imperial Army and the *Reichswehr**, 'don't stick your neck out – never volunteer'. Younger soldiers learned. 'Everywhere there was a certain regimentation,' recalled infantryman Roland Kiemig from his days with the Hitler Youth. 'You didn't just walk around uselessly, you marched.' Soldiers were run around in circles, frog-jumped, hopped about and sprinted up and down on whistle blasts. 'Whenever I see a man in uniform now', panzer crewman Hans Becker later wrote, 'I picture him lying on his face waiting for permission to take his nose out of the mud.'[35]

This army was still, however, borne along on a wave of euphoric nationalism. 'You are nothing, the Volk – the People – is everything', National Socialist slogans intoned, demanding 'courage, preparedness to sacrifice and toughness'. Soldiers storming the citadel at Brest Litovsk, with casualties dropping all round during the 1939 Polish campaign, did so allegedly while singing the national anthem. Infantryman Hans Olte under training during the French *Blitzkrieg* wrote home, 'I must say, truthfully, this soldiering malarkey is great fun.' His brother Horst was

*The official name of the German Armed Forces from 1919 until 1935.

fighting in France. 'Horst is now one of the luckiest ones,' Hans wrote to his mother, '*Ach* how I would like to have gone with the soldiers.' 'Shame that I could not be with him,' he wrote in the next letter.[36]

Front-line combat had an impact on ideological zeal, but training and previous military experience combined to make the *Landser* formidable adversaries. The succession of foreign policy crises prior to the war benefited the campaign's logistics and operational mobility. Re-occupying the Rhineland in 1936 had involved 25 of the fledgling *Wehrmacht's* divisions; 22 moved into the region and three crossed the Rhine to the west bank. The March 1938 Sudetenland occupation exercised the German staff moving large numbers of troops by road and in March 1939 five armies moved from the Sudetenland to Prague and occupied Bohemia and Moravia. Sixty German divisions participated in the invasion and occupation of Poland in September 1939 while 23 deployed to a blocking position in the west. The practical experience was invaluable: rapid alerts, formations assembling, large-scale road moves, the selection of assembly areas and multiple road routes. Efficient orders of march had to be sorted out to reflect operational plans, to include artillery and logistics. Poland had taught the need for effective air liaison with artillery and sowed the germ of an idea for mobile vehicle-borne advance guards to precede marching infantry; panzers had been combat trained in forming all-arms mobile formations. All these developments predated any comprehensive French or British training or experience. The *Wehrmacht* had an active-service practised edge.

Soldiers had begun to accept the value of automated drills, a substitute for courage in confused combat situations. A. Stöhr explained: 'One did what was practised a hundred times before: Take cover – you give covering fire – I will attack. Get up – Go! Go!'[37]

Physical action often overcame psychological reserve. Peer pressure had an insidious influence, such as *Hals-schmerz*, the so-called 'sore throat' award, the *Ritterkreuz* or Knight's Cross (which was worn at the neck). Bravery awards were lionized by press and newsreels, providing an imperative to act in dangerous situations in itself. Certain soldiers were identified as having 'a calling', the iconic brave men who could be relied upon to save a situation. They became the renowned bunker and tank 'busters', men who led the assault or a risky patrol. Such men were called forward or volunteered immediately when the situation so demanded. 'Their names were known throughout their units,' one soldier remembered. Seeking danger and the cool skills required to deal with it is a recognizable aspect of modern sporting prowess. National Socialist wartime propaganda played upon these characteristics. Joseph Goebbels, the *Reichsminister* for Propaganda, declared 'whoever fears an honourable death, dies in disgrace'. Patriotism alongside effective military training and practical combat experience was the characteristic hallmark of the *Landser* who invaded the Low Countries in May 1940. The scale of competency varied from sensible mature men who overcame their fears to those with few feelings or apparent concerns, with little imagination. Having lived mundane depression-filled years, they were now part of momentous events. The sheer impetus of this invasion carried all before it at ever greater pace, sweeping the hopes, beliefs and concerns of soldiers remorselessly along with it. The coast beckoned, and that meant a likely end to the conflict.

But what of the enemy they faced?

DER FEIND – THE ENEMY

The 18th Infantry Division, which fought its way to Dunkirk, opposed Belgians, British and Frenchmen to get there. *Generalleutnant* Friedrich Cranz, its commander, commented in his after-action report that they did not differ fundamentally in performance, except maybe the Belgians on one occasion were the better soldiers, he conceded. He was convinced his own soldiers were the best in close combat, aided by superior firepower and light combat equipment. The enemy appeared to be deficient in weapon-handling skills, unlike his own men, and their leaders were not creative; passive rather than aggressive. Enemy officers, he observed, tended not to dig their own foxholes. Signaller Erich Kuby with *Nachrichten Abteilung 3* had an uncluttered *Landser* view. Most times they did not even know *what* nationality they were facing, or indeed what the general situation was. Nevertheless, German soldiers held certain opinions about the Dutch, Belgians, French, or British opponents they faced.[38]

Oberst Ulrich Liss, the Intelligence Chief of *Abteilung Fremde Heere* (enemy forces), assessed Dutch Army combat capability as 'low'. They were in the midst of reorganizing about ten weak divisions and some brigades. Having not fought for 135 years the Dutch would only momentarily resist, because they depended on Allied reinforcements and their ability to swiftly retire behind the canals and flooded watercourses of 'Fortress Holland'. They had not fought in Europe since Waterloo in 1815. German soldiers were not anticipating particular problems with the Dutch. Infantry officer Werner L., writing to his wife, thought the Belgians less friendly than the Dutch. Nazi ideology ranked the Dutch 'purer' in racial terms than Belgians and Frenchmen, who were further down the ethnic hierarchical scale.[39]

Motorcycle infantryman Karl Schönfeld's impressions riding through Holland were typical. Dutch civilians looked at them with 'sweet-sour expressions, standing alongside the roads'. Hostility was understated. He remembered pausing at a prosperous manor house, where the owner's daughter confronted him, saying Holland was being hostilely annexed. She referred to Denmark's experience, stating 'if Denmark had only three soldiers, they should resist until all three fell'. She could not comprehend that the Dutch queen would ever consider fleeing the country. Most German soldiers regarded Holland as the place they marched through to reach Belgium and France. Hard fighting only occurred when panzer vanguards tried to relieve their hard-pressed *Fallschirmjäger* at Rotterdam and The Hague. With the collapse of Dutch resistance, von Küchler's Eighteenth Army's thrust into Holland turned southwest on 14 May and became the right wing of the advance into Belgium.[40]

The Belgian declaration of neutrality in 1936 was as equally unwelcome for the Allies as Dutch non-cooperation. At a stroke the diplomatic announcement outflanked all the French effort that had gone into constructing the Maginot Line. French planning had now to contemplate possibly fighting in Belgium as well, creating future potential fodder for von Manstein's *Sichelschnitt* strategy. *Oberst* Liss assessed the Belgians 'as living fully in the shadow of the French', meaning positional defence was superior to attack. Helmet and uniform styles were even the same. Belgium's ten divisions deployed behind fortress lines had increased their training more recently, but infantry shooting and field craft skills were poor. Although regarded as one of the premier small European armies, it had its limitations according to one German intelligence assessment in 1939:

> The Belgian soldier is of variable quality, depending whether he is a Walloon or Fleming. The Walloons are similar to their French neighbours, similarly dressed, intelligent, but not as tough. The

Fleming is more like the Dutch, clumsy but braver. Both ethnic groups are not especially physically robust. Alcoholism is rife, and the Belgian soldier little inclined to be disciplined.[41]

The Belgians fought well but were constantly outmanoeuvred by the speed of the advance, and quickly cleared from the Scheldt River area. The outflanking movement by the panzer spearheads of Army Group A was matched with severe pressure from the German Sixth Army on the French First Army right of the BEF. Further south Ninth French Army had already collapsed. The Belgian Army to the left of the British had to fall back from the Dyle River position across intermediate stop lines from the Dendre to the Escaut on 19 May. German Eighteenth Army pressure increased even more on the Belgians after the Dutch capitulation, pushing them further west of Antwerp and the BEF beyond Brussels.

Lack of Allied coordination caused the British to have a low opinion of Belgian performance, not necessarily shared by the Germans, who had to force them back. The Belgians had local knowledge and were fighting for their own land. There was stiff resistance at countless water courses during the retreat. By the time they reached the Lys River they were fighting hard, compressed by the German Eighteenth Army with little space to manoeuvre. Alfred-Ingemar Berndt with the self-propelled guns of *Panzerjäger Abteilung* 605 grudgingly conceded 'the Belgians fought boldly, we give that to them'. Infantryman Helmut Neelsen nearing the line of the Lys remembered 'boarding dinghies and getting on the other bank where the Belgians fought bitterly from excellently laid-out trench systems'. Berndt, an ardent Nazi, considered 'the Flemish as friends. We are bound by ties of blood and language. They are German like us.'

So far as he was concerned 'we want to make the war as painless for them as possible. The Flemish didn't want war.' His men were sympathetic because '*Platt-Deutsch* was related to their own language, which is similar to Flemish', whereas 'the French-speaking Walloons with their *parlez-vous* were tiresome'.[42]

Unteroffizier Dittert with the 18th Division was subjected to a hotly contested assault river crossing of the Lys under intense Belgian fire. 'The machine gunner number 1 had his MG mounted on the prow [of the assault boat] and fired for all he was worth', he recalled, 'while the others powered with paddles and steered, with what their arms were able to give.' Before them was a burning factory on the far bank, with

Belgians dug in to its front. All they could detect was muzzle flash from rifles and machine guns. 'Here and there a comrade was lying on the ground.' They rushed the factory wall and threw the defenders out after vicious hand-to-hand fighting. Belgians emerged from fox holes, hands raised, 'with doubt written across their faces'. 'These were elite Belgian troops', he added, 'who had covered the withdrawing English, and had to pay their price, going into German captivity.'[43]

The main enemy was regarded as the French. Many senior German commanders with World War I experience thought Hitler's decision to swiftly mount a western offensive was rash. Very soon, as *Oberst* Liss explained, 'the former 1918 German veterans realized the offensive spirit of the French Army was no longer as it had been'. 'All the reserve officers we talked to who had experienced trench warfare during the World War I were very concerned about what was going to happen,' *Hauptmann* Siegfried Knappe with the 24th Artillery Regiment recalled. 'All the young officers on the other hand assumed that the invasion of France would be similar to the invasion of Poland.' Hitler's political antennae had correctly perceived the French were morally weak.[44]

Unteroffizier Max Lachner manned a bunker opposite the French on the upper Rhine during the *Sitzkrieg*, Phoney War, period. Despite the attack on Poland 'our weeks flowed by quietly', he recalled. Then, unexpectedly they were subjected to a sharp artillery barrage from the other side. 'My people emerged naked and half-naked from the water and bushes nearby, donned their uniforms and occupied their positions.' After a quarter of an hour a French soldier apologetically emerged waving a white sheet, pointing rearwards. It became apparent that a delegation of French senior officers had visited, demanding fire be opened up on the *Boche*.

> This happened to us practically every third or fourth day. If the French hung out the white sheet, we took cover, expecting a barrage, then waited until the man came out again and gave us the all clear. We knew those on the other side were people our age – probably soldiers from Alsace, who had sung the same songs at school we had learned.[45]

Only 23 German divisions faced 110 French and British divisions as Germany invaded Poland in September 1939. 'The French could have beaten the hell out of us when we were busy in Poland,' Alfons Heck's Uncle Franz, a police commissioner, insisted. 'Our victory in Poland must have scared the hell out of them,' Heck maintained; 'No, they missed their boat for good.'[46]

Hans Habe, a Foreign Legionary with the French Twelfth Army Corps, remembered 'months of waiting' during the *drôle de guerre*; it 'had worn down our nerves'. Not wanting a war, when the invasion occurred 'this is the real thing we thought'. There was momentary relief it had actually started; even so, the dramatic news on 10 May was not sufficient to encourage Parisians to change their plans for the forthcoming bank holiday weekend. They were soon shocked into reality by the violence of the assault. Massed airborne landings, highly mobile panzer attacks closely supported by pulverizing *Luftwaffe* air raids had never been experienced before. The average French soldier had resigned himself to years of static warfare along a trench line somewhere in France or Belgium. What had happened in the summer of 1914 on the Marne suggested there was little cause to worry.

Hitler had chosen the optimum psychological moment to shatter the Phoney War inertia. Years of political turbulence between the French left and right had convinced him the French would have no heart for conflict. French Sergeant Roux recalled 'during the first eight months the war was not tangible, and for many not even there, which made the reality on the people so much harder'. Schoolboy Stephen Grady living near the Channel coast remembered one conversation with an old soldier from the 208th Infantry Regiment who had sardonically admitted 'I signed up for a pension, not a war.' 'Who wants to get killed fighting our neighbours,' declared a companion. 'It is not as if the Germans are evil. I've got friends in the Alsace, and they say they're just the same as us.'[47]

Oberst Liss shrewdly assessed French Army potential for the OKW staff, concluding they were not in the same mould as in the 1914–18 war. French tactics would be orientated towards positional warfare, like on the Western Front. Twenty per cent of its infantry were in the Maginot Line, which organizationally, tactically and psychologically dominated French military thinking. The whole nation felt the line of fortifications safeguarded their future. Tanks would be used as infantry support weapons, not ones of opportunity. Liss came up with an intelligent estimate for the typical *Poilu*, who:

> is physically tough, intelligent, agile and very patriotic. Easily motivated, he is capable of achieving a lot. He will fight harder in his

own country than on enemy territory, and will be better in defence than offence. He does not readily accept discipline, but the army would impose draconian measures.

The French he noted were poorly trained and new equipment was well behind schedule. Senior staff command chains were not independently minded and would display poor initiative. In essence he felt the French Army remained 1914–18 orientated and this experience suggested the most combat effective formations would be those in north-west France, precisely where the German advance was heading.[48] The OKH view of the French was convincing up to a point, but insufficiently weighted, especially as German combat commanders sensed a collapse might well be in the offing. This accounted for the dichotomy of views and opinion between the OKH and OKW staff, who could hardly believe what was happening. They were losing control attempting to rein in energetic commanders who sensed opportunities too good to miss. *Oberstleutnant* Hermann Balck with the vanguard of the 1st Panzer Division was taking increasingly risky decisions to maintain momentum. On occasion he sensed 'the attack was dragging'. Moving rapidly forward was clearly unnerving the French. 'What was easy today could cost a lot of blood tomorrow,' he calculated, in attempts 'to reach the dominating terrain'. OKH and OKW seemed not to appreciate the immense tactical and operational opportunities opened up by their forward commanders. They sought instead to de-accelerate a momentum that appeared increasingly out of control.[49]

Hauptsturmführer Kurt Meyer with the LAH motorcycle recce company had reached France through Holland. He passed piles of discarded French helmets by the roadside in a large field 'as if arrayed for a parade': 'The neatly arranged helmets, so it seemed to me, expressed the hopelessness and weariness of the French Army. It was an army without spirit and drive. It no longer consisted of Verdun soldiers.'[50] Hermann Balck agreed: 'the French fought extremely poorly,' he claimed. 'Why fight?' the prisoners were asked: 'Because England wants us to; the rich want us to. We are not waging war; war is being waged with us.'[51]

Oberst Liss highlighted the respect that French General Gamelin had aroused during a high-ranking German delegation visit to Paris in 1937. Balck, writing post-campaign, dismissed him as 'only a second stringer', pointing out 'in 1939 there was no tough military leader at the helm of the French Army'.

French soldiers began to echo this sentiment. The complete and chaotic breakdown of communications suggested something was very wrong. 'What made us really downhearted,' recalled Gustave Vancoille, with the First French Army, 'was the moment that we realized that the government, that General Gamelin, had so misunderstood the German strategy'. 'Vague and unclear,' Balck insisted, 'the French Army was administered, but not led'. Stymied by a Maginot 'defence at any cost' mindset, the French failed to follow Marshal Foch's dictum 'always attack'.

Foreign Legionary Hans Habe would have agreed, recalling 'our march to the front was like a flight forward'.[52]

Newly appointed British Prime Minister Winston Churchill flew to Paris on 16 May to discuss the deteriorating situation with his French counterpart, Édouard Daladier, the minister for war, and General Gamelin. He was told the Germans had pushed 90 miles into northern France, scattering the French Ninth and First Armies in the process. 'Where is the strategic reserve?' Churchill asked, '*Acune*,' Gamelin responded – none. General de Gaulle's 4th Armoured Division counter-attack at Montcornet failed the next day, after some illusory gains. Gamelin by then had lost his nerve and was removed from command, and replaced by General Maxime Weygand, abruptly recalled from Syria. Weygand, aged 73, took up a poisoned chalice, a completely unknown situation in a different theatre of war. After the long flight from Syria he retired to bed, putting off any decisions for 24 hours in the midst of a crisis; meanwhile Guderian's panzers had reached the Atlantic coast.

French Sergeant Roux, writing in his diary, at this time suspected collapse was coming. He had marched for 13½ hours through the night, passing many destroyed houses:

The news was always worse. The Germans are on the march westwards. Brussels is in their hands. I'm depressed like never before. I have not seen a single train at any station. Does this mean the end of France?[53]

Schoolboy Stephen Grady living near the Channel coast likewise recalled the atmosphere of crisis:

Lorry-loads of British troops come roaring down the main road, but we have no idea where they are heading. Conflicting reports on the radio do not help. No one seems to know what is happening, or how close the German advance has come.

'By the 20th May, it is obvious things are going wrong,' he remembered, 'French troops start pouring down the road from Belgium. They look haunted and hungry, their carts loaded not just with military equipment but with looted civilian goods.'[54]

This was an army in retreat. Jean Murray, a gunner in a French infantry regiment, recalled, 'we marched incessantly, with a surprising continuity for two long hours'. The column was suddenly halted and illuminated by a powerful light. It was dark, and the men settled down and sat by the side of the road:

> A quarter of an hour passed, when an officer came to the back of the column, to announce that we were prisoners and that we must throw away our arms. The commander had already been taken away by the Germans.

'I threw my rifle away in a ditch,' he dismally recalled; 'How simple this had all been!'[55]

The ten divisions of the BEF represented less than 10% of the Allied effort, but they held a narrow sector in the centre of the front, with the Belgian Army to their left and First French Army on their right. They were directly in the path of the German Sixth Army, the left of the two 'drawing attack' armies with von Bock's Army Group B. Von Küchler's Eighteenth Army changed direction after the capitulation of Holland, putting the Belgians under increased pressure to the British left. By 18 May the threat of the panzer move by Army Group A on the flank to the south obliged a British retreat to the next line in depth on the Escaut, to conform with Allied withdrawals left and right.

German vanguards regarded the British with wary anticipation. Their fathers spoke of them as formidable opponents during World War I. Anticipation transitioned to a form of impatient contempt, when they found the British were skilfully withdrawing in contact. *Generalleutnant* Cranz's 18th Division found itself mining a seam during the advance, between the right wing of the British and the increasingly parlous situation within First French Army. Cranz dramatically announced in his division order of 16 May: 'the English into the sea, the French back to France!' 'When this is successful,' he claimed, splitting the two armies facing them, 'it will mean the end of the war in Belgium'. *Hauptmann* Hans-Georg von Altenstadt with his division staff recalled that 'repeated local sightings confirmed the enemy – mostly English and a few French – were only 1½ hours ahead, hurriedly marching westwards'. Cranz's division, apart from captured vehicle-borne company vanguards, was following up on foot, whereas the retiring British were largely vehicle-borne. One of the 54th Regiment battalion doctors recalled the excitement of the closing contact: 'the fact that the enemy ahead was the English had an electrifying effect'. Soldiers passing by on the march called out 'Tommy is the enemy! Get stuck in!' Quite often they found withdrawals covered by French or Belgian rearguards, raising the sardonic comment that 'Tommy was fighting to the last Frenchman.'[56]

The British, like the French Army, still lived in the shadow of the Great War. *Oberst* Liss assessed British combat capabilities as considerable, practised in British Empire bush wars and the military, financial, scientific and propaganda strengths that came from dominating a quarter of the world's land mass. Liss was an anglophile, having spent a pleasant military exchange in 1937 with the Royal Artillery's 7th Field Brigade on Salisbury Plain. The British Army's considerable 1914–18 reputation, enhanced by his own observations in England, led Liss to conclude 'British regular troops are assessed as being of high worth.' He wrote:

> The regular British soldier is courageous and disciplined. Tactical field training is impressive and his marksmanship skills are good. Older soldiers by virtue of their colonial experience are used to live active service. The ethnic character of the English enables them to accept casualties and setbacks with some equanimity. Territorial soldiers are highly motivated, but not well trained or led.

Liss thought highly of the experienced NCO corps but found the quality of their leaders – the officer corps – not to be uniform. They tended to be schematic, slow and lacking initiative. He noted British divisions were only partly motorized, only able to lift one-third of their soldiers, but they would likely be formidable opponents. In essence the British were an enigmatic opponent, they might cause problems, but there were not many of them: just ten divisions, five regular and five Territorial Army. In fact there were 13, but three of them were poorly armed line-of-communication troops.[57]

The British were not zealously motivated like the Germans and inter-war pacifism meant that although signing up in 1939 had been vigorous, it did not match the patriotic enthusiasm of 1914. Soldiers, moreover, had a less trusting and more cynical regard to authority than their 1914–18 forebears. British cinemas had portrayed a steady denigration of the British military leadership during the Great War, in anti-war films like the *Life and Death of Colonel Blimp* and *Dawn Patrol*. They were far less tolerant of the 'bullshit' that had featured during Phoney War training activity in France, a contrast to the tough live-fire training conducted by the *Wehrmacht*. The entire winter had been a dreary period of pointless digging and wiring with very little practical training activity. Morale had been poor. Soldiers were more discerning about officer shortcomings among leaders who remained their social superiors, but social deference was waning.

Senior and intermediate command levels were permeated with 1914–18 veterans, who, unlike their *Wehrmacht* counterparts, were not mentally prepared for modern mobile warfare. Training between digging was quite often the 1914–18 veterans lecturing the troops about their Great War experiences. Second Lieutenant Julian Fane with the territorial 48th Division remembered:

> They were busy teaching us to dig trenches and build barbed wire, which I rather thought was not quite the sort of training I was expecting for a modern war. Seemed to me to be based upon the old 1914–18 war.[58]

Unlike the reverence accorded uniforms in the *Reich*, British soldiers had low status during the inter-war period. 'Hundreds of boys just like me came from the hard times,' admitted Coldstream Guardsman Bill Weeks with the 1st Division. 'The Depression. There was nothing about – no work, terrible really, I think so. They talk about the "good old days", I don't think they were, bloody awful really.' Little enthusiasm accompanied conscription, more a desire to get the war over as soon as possible. 'I joined in February 1939, like so many young people of my age,' remembered signaller Private Wilf Saunders, 'we were getting pretty fed up with Hitler's antics.' They were psychologically unprepared for what they would face. Artillery gunner James Bradley 'believed there was going to be a war, but hoped there wouldn't be'; he wished to be properly trained 'and fulfil my obligations to my country'. Others like 19-year-old signaller Clive Tonry remembered 'it was all rather marvellous actually – the adventure – skylarking schoolboys!' 'You probably can't imagine the associations that France had for youngsters in this country', Wilf Saunders recalled, 'who had never been abroad at all, it all happened there, it was so romantic'.[59]

The prospect of war brought fear and trepidation for some. 'I was 20 then, I didn't mind going,' ex-greengrocer Charles Waite with the Queen's Royal Regiment admitted, 'but I really and truly wanted *not* to go into anything, where I was going to have to go out and kill anybody'. This was an unrealistic expectation, but their training did not prepare them for the rigours of combat. Waite 'didn't think this [killing] was right; it could be somebody who's got family and children, and it didn't seem right for me to have to go out and kill somebody like that'. Vernon Scannell with the 70th Argylls was told to bayonet straw dummies in training as if they were Hun soldiers out to rape his sister and mother. 'It wasn't proper preparation for the real thing,' he insisted, 'that was a total shock to my entire being.' *Oberst* Liss was broadly accurate in his assessment of the British; leadership would be wanting, but they would fight if their backs were up against the wall. Staff Captain James Hill serving in Gort's BEF Headquarters believed 'you had two things to fight for, you had your king and your country, and you were very proud of them,' he insisted, 'and you had the greatest empire the world had ever seen.'[60]

THE ENEMY'S CIVILIANS

Modern warfare blurred the previous distinction between soldiers and non-combatants. Enemy civilian populations were caught up because mass migration of refugees got in the way of the pace of *Blitzkrieg* advance. Dutch, Belgian and French refugees were targeted directly or indirectly by the *Luftwaffe* or became ensnared in the panzer advance. RAF fighter Pilot Officer Dennis David with 87 Squadron explained:

The Germans would strafe the roads full of refugees on purpose to cause congestion. Their tanks would then scoot around it. It stopped our troops from coming forward to meet them. It was a carefully organized plan, brilliant in concept. It was something we weren't used to. It put a new dimension into war. They bombed helpless people and used the shambles to move their forces forward.

The majority of people on the roads were women and children, because the older age groups, husbands and fathers had been called up for the army. Up to a third to a quarter were children. Hurried departures at the fear of approaching Germans created their own dynamic; neighbours influenced to stay would be foolhardy. Crowd pressure on the roads dispersed family groups, adding to the chaos. Fear of air attack provided a further terrifying imperative to flee, while intense bombing of rail links increased the mayhem on the roads. Authorities provided little or no centralized direction. Refugee road channels were set up to enable Allied military traffic to move forward but were generally ineffective, because state-sponsored evacuation preparation had been largely left to individual discretion. No one anticipated the massive numbers on the move. Evacuation schemes were designed to cater for positional warfare, clearing civilians from a clearly demarcated front line. There were no front lines in this *Blitzkrieg* war of movement. Signposted evacuation routes tended to direct crowds in huge circles, which were overrun and surrounded by the German advance. Allied soldiers marching on the same roads became inextricably mixed with refugee columns and attracted *Luftwaffe* attention like a magnet. German aircraft swooped down to bomb and strafe the columns, whatever their content. Machine Gunner Reg Rymer with the Cheshire regiment saw Stukas approaching their column, describing how 'they do their normal circle around, and one after another they dive down'. They appeared not to have spotted the army element:

And I thought they must be blind, they're not going after us. The next thing is they let their things go in among the refugees. Now these old people, young people, babies – to see them blown to pieces and not one bomb anywhere along the army convoy. You tell me who could be that cruel? We were there and being paid and supposed to be doing a job, so you expect it. But that? You see babies' legs and all kinds being thrown up in the air.[61]

Generalmajor Wolfram von Richthofen, a cousin of the legendary Great War 'Red Baron' flying ace, commanded the VIII *Fliegerkorps*, which covered the panzer thrust to the coast. As commander of the *Legion Condor*, he had pioneered the development of *Luftwaffe* aviation tactics during the Spanish Civil War. He had sanctioned the first 'terror bombing' of a city at Guernica. Rotterdam was punitively fire bombed, in error, to encourage Dutch capitulation. The *Luftwaffe* was the one arm of the *Wehrmacht* conceived and developed after Hitler's assumption of power in 1933. As the progeny of the Third *Reich*, it owed primary allegiance to the Nazi regime. It was as equally remorseless in its pursuit of technological objectives as Hitler's pursuit of political power. German fighter pilot Johannes Steinhoff recalled attending the first mass passing out of *Luftwaffe* cadet officers at Berlin in 1936. *Reichsmarshall* Göring addressed them in a huge amphitheatre, where he harangued the newly appointed lieutenants for an hour. He spoke of the disgrace and humiliation of the Treaty of Versailles that had banned Germany from having an air force. On closing, Steinhoff remembered him saying 'you will one day be my corps of vengeance'. The hall erupted and 'there probably wasn't a single person in attendance who wasn't totally motivated to give his utmost in support of this regime'.[62]

In May 1940 this support produced pitiless focus. RAF Fighter pilot Dennis David remembered:

Once, six of us ran into 40 Ju 87s [Stukas] dive-bombing a stream of refugees. We shot down 14 of them and broke up that raid. As we were going back to our base, another 150 German aircraft came in, but we were out of ammunition. It was hopeless.[63]

Interviews of captured German aircrew illuminated the casual way they had inflicted violence on Polish civilians and soldiers exposed on the roads the year before. One pilot admitted:

On the third day I did not care a hoot, and on the fourth day I was enjoying it. It was our pre-breakfast amusement to chase single soldiers over the fields with machine-gun fire and to leave them lying there with a few bullets in the back.

Similar eavesdropped conversations spoke of strafing attacks during nuisance raids on civilians at Norwich in England two years later.

Luftwaffe pilot Küster recalled with glee how: 'We shot up the town ... we fired at the trams and everything; it's great fun. There was no AA there.'[64]

Unemotive clinical killing at distance was perhaps akin to modern digital video games. It caused real anger. Staff Captain James Hill was tasked with clearing roads of refugees leading out of Brussels 'to let the British army up and secondly, unfortunately, to let it get back again'. Parks were set up to siphon off the refugee flow:

Of course the Germans very quickly spotted what was happening. They knew perfectly well the people in those parks were all civilians. So they made hay. They suddenly realized what was happening and they mercilessly bombed those parks when they were full of women and screaming children. Horses were going mad, galloping everywhere, breaking loose. It was really one of those horrible things you never really want to see in your life.[65]

One crew of a Heinkel III bomber crash-landed near Vimy in northern France. Three of the surviving crew from *Kampfgeschwader* 54, the pilot and two NCOs, were allegedly lynched by French civilians. Three civilians were shot as retribution following a trial at the end of June. Another 5th Panzer Division court martial investigated an incident of four German airmen severely beaten by a mob of 50 armed farmers and police, after they bellied in a field. Two farmers were executed for this after a brief hearing at Brest on 23 June.

The high-pitched whine from Stuka dive-bombers could be heard before and during a raid. Strafing runs from low-flying German fighter aircraft, which might suddenly appear, could not. The first sign was the ground erupting all around with ricochet splats and multiple detonations from explosive canon fire; this would be split seconds before the sight and sound of the aircraft roaring overhead. Refugees, as one French eyewitness recalled, took whatever action they could to protect themselves:

People lie in the ditches, hide in the woods, and glue themselves to trees in the courtyard. Children hang on to their mother's skirts. Women go round the trees and hid their faces in their arms, like a child who fends off a slap.[66]

Numerous German soldier diary and letter accounts about the 1940 French *Blitzkrieg* campaign have scant reference to *Luftwaffe* air attacks on civilians. There was often passing mention of poignant scenes of dead women and children among wrecked Allied vehicles on the roads. There was universal sympathy for the plight of the refugees, but expressed generally as unavoidable: *C'est la Guerre.* Ludwig Thalmaier, marching with 63rd Infantry Regiment, recalled in his diary 'meeting refugees' near St Quentin on 20 May:

> They tow everything they have in every possible conceivable vehicle: two-wheeled carriages harnessed to a single horse and bicycles stacked high. Many are in their slippers; old people were being pushed in prams. Children have a favourite toy under their arm ...[67]

Those in the vanguard of the march saw few civilians. 'Manoeuvres had not prepared us for the refugees and the empty houses,' artillery *Hauptmann* Siegfried Knappe with the 24th Regiment remembered. 'The population here in northern France had almost 100% fled,' Chaplain Rudolf Gschöpf with the 45th Infantry Division observed, 'leaving behind only thirsty stray cattle, bellowing among the smoking destruction of villages and wandering about the fields.' Amid all the desolation 'cows, calves or pigs lay around, having perished with no one able to feed or milk them or enable them to drink'. Domestic rabbits, reared for meat, were hopping everywhere, 'free as hares' because their owners had left the hutches open on fleeing. Knappe appreciated: 'They had left their homes when they heard the sounds of battle coming towards them. They had panicked and run away because they did not know what else to do.'[68]

Gschöpf came across one 86-year-old man, 'his fate accepted in a rocking chair, regarding us with huge terrified eyes, as if we were from another world'. They attempted to reassure him, by saying they were only bivouacking for the night. But there was worse: 'We went into a side room, and were rooted to the ground in shock. Two old ladies had hanged themselves because life had not been worth living.'[69]

Frenchman Georges Adrey saw that the refugee flow arrival order appeared governed by a certain social hierarchy, based on wealth. 'In the first days we saw the sumptuous and fast American cars go by, driven by uniformed chauffeurs' with 'elegant women clutching their jewellery boxes'. Following these were 'less fancy older cars', carrying primarily 'middle-class families', then after a gap of one or two days came 'the most incredible bangers'. Behind them were cyclists, 'mostly young people' and then whole families of pedestrians. Bringing up the rear 'came the heavy carts belonging to the peasants of the Nord Department'. Quite often the procession was 'a village undertaking a collective move, with the mayor, the priest, the elderly schoolmaster, and the local policeman'. Collective grief and suffering created a form of social levelling. Enforced detours by the military got people lost, expensive cars ran out of fuel, which was no longer available. Petrol pumps had been sucked dry by the retreating Allies or advancing German panzers. Strafing, demoralization and exhaustion slowed the directionless masses until the Germans caught up, by which time they presented a poignant spectacle. Infantryman Hans S. with the 12th Division wrote home to his parents: 'The suffering of the population is awful, worse than Poland. You can't picture thousands of refugees, with feet *kaputt*, making their tortured way home with inadequate footwear. *C'est la Guerre.*'[70]

'Maybe I ought to change my hatred of the French,' he admitted, 'because the people themselves certainly did not want this war.' Siegfried Knappe 'felt sorry that we had to do this to them'. 'The best thing they could have done,' he pointed out, 'was to go into their cellars and wait for the battle to pass them by.' Hans P. with 6th Machine Gun Battalion overtook 'endless columns of refugees' moving with every conceivable vehicle: 'They go totally directionless through the area. Nobody says to them whether they can return home, go further, or where to.'

Their company commander reprimanded them for offering food. 'Irresponsible,' he scolded, 'when our own logistics are not yet secure, and we ourselves may soon not have enough supplies'. German units had somehow to navigate their way through this mass of humanity. Signaller Erich Kuby recalled 'they feared us, but still pushed against us as they went by, climbing over dead horses to make their way'. He wondered how oddly 'the dead people are always taken away by someone', pondering 'whether we had a unit doing it, in case of any atrocities tribunal?'[71]

Alfred-Ingemar Berndt, fitfully trundling along roads with the self-propelled guns of *Panzerjäger Abteilung* 605, remembered: 'Sometimes we cannot advance, on account of double rows of hurrying refugee columns, occupying the narrow roads.' They presented an incongruously pathetic sight:

> They arrive with every type of vehicle, loaded grotesquely with the bulk of their possessions: a tall hall mirror, a palm tree floor stand, a corridor wardrobe and other objects not exactly necessary to sustain life. They must have lost their heads.[72]

German soldiers, like the retreating enemy, were disturbed by the sights because these people – but for a twist of fate – could be their own families. '*Ja* – I found this awful,' admitted panzer crewman Hans Becker with the 7th Panzer Division:

> I thought to myself, what if you had to leave your house and farm, and didn't know when you would return, and ended up looking like this. This had an effect on me. *C'est la Guerre*, this was war as the French would say. But the sadness was if someone returned later and saw that his house was destroyed, what must this person be thinking? He must be really angry with the Germans![73]

The war was becoming personal. RAF fighter pilot Flight Lieutenant Gerry Edge saw the people pushing wheelbarrows and the horse-drawn carts and trucks festooned with children as he flew towards the column on the road. He observed 'a Stuka above them, with its rear gunner machine gunning those refugees'. He was incensed, 'just hosing them down':

> That was the only time I remember deliberately firing at somebody rather than an object. I thought it might be a trap for me. I looked around carefully and closed in quickly, ready to break if someone got on my tail. I was not far behind that Stuka when he saw me and started to swing his guns around. I pressed the trigger and he went straight down in flames. I felt a savage delight in killing the two bastards in that plane who'd been murdering the refugees.[74]

Chapter 3

The Sea

THE SEA — WHAT NEXT?

On 21 May, *Führer* weather, the combination of German good fortune and fine spring weather, shone down on Abbeville, near the French Atlantic coast. The motorized 'Spitta' battalion from the 2nd Panzer Division had reached the sea at Noyelles the day before. A British artillery battery had been captured at Albert on the same day, 'drawn up on the barrack square and equipped only with training ammunition', remembered Guderian the XIX Panzer Corps commander, 'since nobody had reckoned on our appearance that day'.[1] *Oberst* Walther K. Nehring, his Chief of Staff, recalled:

> On the evening of that remarkable day when our tank divisions reached the sea and cut France in two, we had no idea where we were going next. Nor were our superiors, the Panzer *Gruppe* von Kleist, able to enlighten us.[2]

General Guderian's mood, clattering through the battered town of Abbeville in his armoured half-track, in no way reflected the weather. He generally moved with a small skeleton staff in an armoured command car, with his adjutant and a signals officer maintaining his radio equipment. He was frustrated: 'the 21st May was wasted while we waited for orders,' he complained. The half-track, packed with signals equipment and housing his enigma code deciphering machine, accompanied the group, escorted by two motorcycle dispatch riders.

He passed armoured vehicles tucked away in the side streets, while crewmembers laboured, servicing engines, tightening and greasing tracks and check-zeroing weapons. Some of the soldiers echoed Guderian's misgivings. 'We wasted two whole days,' men with the 2nd Vienna Panzer Division complained. Success would dissipate with time. Most took the opportunity to snatch some sleep, slumped over steering wheels and across seats. They were on stand-by to move out of the side streets and converge on the main thoroughfares as soon as they got the word to advance. 'What would our opponents do?' the Chief of Staff considered. 'They could hardly overlook the corridor running right through their land, and would surely pull themselves together and act.'[3]

OKW and OKH faced the same conundrum at Hitler's *Felsennest* headquarters back at the Eifel. Guderian contemplated a 10th Panzer Division advance on Dunkirk by way of Hesdin and St Omer, while the 1st Panzer Division should move against Calais and the 2nd Panzer on Boulogne. Geography dictated the logical course of action: deny the Channel ports to the Allies to prevent reinforcement or possible evacuation. 'After the exhilaration of the actual arrival on the coast,' Nehring recalled, 'tension increased hour by hour':

> Were we to stay here to stop a breakthrough by the main Allied force from the north – or go south towards Paris to halt the forces being brought up from there? Or were we to turn north to seal off the ports of Boulogne, Calais and Dunkirk?[4]

Oberstleutnant Balck with the 1st Panzer Division had always admired Guderian's particular contribution to panzer warfare communications. It was he who had insisted on the inclusion of a fifth panzer crewman, the radio operator, with a set in each tank. He moreover 'gave the panzer division a signals organization that allowed the division commander to command from any point within the division'. Guderian could likewise direct the Panzer Corps, because his skeletal tactical command group 'was in constant radio contact with me while travelling,' Nehring remembered. 'On his return in the evenings there was always a thorough discussion to assess the situation.' But, for the moment, Guderian's enigma machine remained immobile. Orders were not forthcoming. Impatiently he set off in the glorious weather to check 'our crossings and bridgeheads over the Somme' and talk to his men.[5]

Hitler at the *Felsennest* mirrored Guderian's uneasiness. The extent of the panzer successes in achieving such a penetration in an amazingly short time was incomprehensible. There was a real dilemma about the next move. Even Halder, the confident OKH Chief of Staff, confided in his diary that 21 May 'began in a rather tense atmosphere'. There appeared to be 'serious pressure' on the north flank of Fourth Army, north of the corridor near Arras. 'Only when we have seized the high ground of Arras shall we have won the battle,' he reckoned. Hitler had spent the night before gazing morosely at the situation map until 1.30 in the morning, in the briefing hut. The panzer forces had crashed into the military vacuum of the rear combat zone of the British and French armies. The whole campaign hinged on the decisions that would have to be taken next. Hitler was worried; his political antennae had detected French moral weakness, but nobody's had tuned into the potential consequences of the next move. The French appeared to be teetering, as the *Führer* had unbelievably predicted they would, but his political career was on the line if he got the next move wrong. Indeed, his communiqué on day one had pointed out Germany's fate 'for the next thousand years' was at stake. Senior generals had argued forcefully that a decisive success in the west was unlikely, yet here it was, but seemingly out of control.

Nevertheless, Guderian's signallers began to decipher enigma directions from OKH that afternoon sanctioning an advance by the panzer vanguard on Calais and Boulogne. 'I received orders to continue the advance in a northerly direction,' Guderian remembered, 'with the capture of the Channel ports as objective.'[6]

The first *Luftwaffe* daylight raids had hit Dunkirk the day before. The disabled port lock gates had just been repaired, allowing large warships moored along the quays to get away on the morning tide, missing the worst of subsequent attacks. One thousand tons of wheat caught fire and the burning oil at Saint-Pol-sur-Mer continued to send up huge bulbous clouds of black smoke into the sky, a beacon for all airmen. The smoke spread along and smudged the coastline. Six Belgian trains crammed with soldiers and civilians standing on Quay Number 10 at Freycinet were straddled by *Luftwaffe* bombs; hundreds were killed and injured. All this coincided with a massive exodus of civilians after it was announced by poster that protected professions had now been called up and young people aged 16 had to evacuate to the Loire-et-cher department. As the *Luftwaffe* had already cut the rail link between Albert and Amiens, the hastily packed refugees converged on the roads. Policemen and civil servants began to abandon their posts in the mounting panic of rumour and mass departures. Admiral Abrial, responsible for the defence of the port, strengthened the coastal defence batteries and ordered the opening of the Moëres canal seawater sluices. This began a six-day inundation of the flat land around Dunkirk from Bergues to Bray Dunes on the one side and Watten on the other.

Paule Rogalin, whose father was away with the army, returned to her house after the first night's bombing. 'It was still standing up,' she recalled, 'but we could see the drapes flying out of the windows.' A bomb had exploded inside, so they joined the exodus on the roads, 'bringing with us a few things that we carried on our backs'. Unable to find their friends amid the crowds, they walked on:

> We saw a lot of dead people, old men with half their heads blown off, children who were badly maimed. I remember seeing one man who had burned up inside his truck, and he was still at the wheel.

It was not long before 'the enemy started shooting at us from their aeroplanes, even though we were mostly just women, children and old people'. Constantly strafed by low-flying aircraft, they escaped by scrambling down canal embankments.[7]

Several French ships were hit by the *Luftwaffe* trying to leave port on the evening tide. One merchant ship, the *Pavon*, was hit and the blazing tanker *Niger* was run aground on the Mardyck sandbar. Just after midnight the French destroyer *Adroit* was struck by four bombs and beached at the holiday resort of Malo-les-Bains alongside the port. Having just replenished with a fresh consignment of 300 shells, she was torn in two by a series of spectacular explosions to become one of the most photographed propaganda icons left on the beaches of Dunkirk.

Across the Channel Admiral Bertram Ramsay conducted the first secret conference in the electric 'Dynamo' generator room, in his headquarters tunnel, deep beneath Dover castle. The subject was: *The urgent evacuation of large-scale units across the Channel.* The Channel ports of Calais, Boulogne and Dunkirk had become enormously militarily significant. It was assessed that perhaps 10,000 per day might be embarked from these ports *in extremis*.

Even as Guderian was visiting his troops along the Somme during that wasted afternoon of 21 May, 50 miles to the north-east, and on the other side of the panzer corridor, Hoth's *Panzergruppe* XVI Corps was preparing to cross the Scarpe River south of Arras. They formed the northern outer layer of the panzer wedge forcing its way to the coast, thickening Guderian's insertion that had already reached Noyelles. Von Rundstedt's armour was a long way ahead of its marching infantry, of which Hitler was anxiously aware. His vastly extended flanks were vulnerable to counter-attack from north or south. *Generalmajor* Rommel commanding the 7th Panzer Division was aware of this, but having consistently sliced through the rear of surprised Allied units, he intended to continue to advance that day. This was despite reports of stiff enemy resistance on the outskirts of Arras to the right of his route. His lead units were tired and somewhat disorganized because of the rapidity of the advance, but characteristically he disregarded advice to pause for rest and consolidation. He decided to press on. H-Hour for the continuation of the attack, aiming to skirt the south-west corner of Arras, was set for 2pm.

During the entire western campaign in 1940 only 15 counter-attacks were ever planned and only 11 of them actually took place. Just one substantial counter-move had happened thus far and what was approaching was the second. Although 43% of the 60% of actually conducted attacks took their objectives, none had any impact on the German advance. Roads clogged by refugees and *Luftwaffe* air interdiction were the primary reasons. Delays caused the French 1st Armoured Division to run out of petrol and it was badly mauled by Rommel's division, caught in the act of refuelling. Skirting Arras was an entirely acceptable risk, based on previous experience.[8]

Within an hour Rommel's 25th Panzer Regiment was well ahead of the 6th and 7th Rifle Regiments, following behind with the *SS Totenkopf* Division. At about 3.30pm Rommel's division staff received an urgent radio message from 6th Regiment: 'Powerful tank attack from Arras direction. Help. Help.' The division log reported 'the main body of the division was surprised by very strong armoured forces supported by infantry which attacked the division in the flank'. This developed into 'an extremely fierce fight between hundreds of enemy tanks and their supporting infantry'. Normally imperturbable, Rommel was shocked; 'we tried to create order' he recalled:

> The enemy tank fire had created chaos and confusion among our troops in the village and they were jamming up the roads and yards with their vehicles, instead of going into action with every available weapon to fight off the oncoming enemy.

The main body of 7th Panzer was hit full in the flank. British tanks ploughed through the 6th *Schützen* Regiment and attacked the *SS Totenkopf* Division west of Wailly, scattering its panicked screen of motorized infantry. *Panzerjäger Abteilung* 42 was shattered. 'Our own *Paks* [anti-tank guns] are not effective against British heavy tanks at close quarters,' the division bleakly reported: 'Established defensive fronts were broken through by the enemy, guns shot up or run over, and most of their crews killed.'[9] It was an alarming development; Rommel's headquarters map subsequently showed symbols of an attack launched by five British divisions. The Germans had no idea how insubstantial the attack actually was.

It had been a critical and confusing day for Allied high command on 20 May. The BEF had just completed its withdrawal from the Dyle line. Lord Gort commanding the BEF was unaware of the disastrous situation of the French Ninth Army to the south but had, nevertheless, dispatched two ad hoc forces to secure his right flank and hold Arras. General Ironside, the British Chief of the Imperial General Staff (CIGS) visiting France, had secured agreement that the French should attack north towards Cambrai, while Gort instructed the 5th and 50th Divisions supported by the First Army Tank Brigade to attack south of Arras. The pincer movement was designed to sever the panzer corridor. The French thrust failed to materialize through a lack of resolve and hesitant decision-making. General Gamelin had been sacked, but his successor Weygand was still in the process of taking over. Gort argued that with seven of nine divisions already locked in contact with the enemy, the plan made little sense. Even so, he attempted to commit elements from the uncommitted 5th and 50th Divisions.

The ensuing attack was limited and clumsily improvised. The committed force was robbed for various detached tasks and reserves and materialized at barely brigade-plus strength: 151 Infantry Brigade and two regiments from the Army Tank Brigade. All the units were in poor condition. Only two Territorial Army (TA) infantry battalions were earmarked for the attack, weakened and exhausted from marching the previous ten days in extremely hot weather. They badly needed rest. The territorial soldiers were infantry trained, but had no experience of all-arms cooperation and many had not even seen a British tank. Their supporting tanks had driven 120 miles over the previous five days, toing and froing between changes of position, labouring at 3mph, stopping and starting behind refugee columns and all the time harassed by air attack. Some 25% of their strength had fallen out due to track and other mechanical failures. Only 58 Mark I Matildas and 16 Mark IIs were in running order. The infantry commanding officers were in charge of the attack and no tank officers had arrived in time for the hastily convened orders group, neither was there any air support. Once they set off it was found the infantry could not keep up with the tanks, who agreed to continue alone.

The assault was launched by two parallel columns, 4 Royal Tank Regiment (RTR) to the east and 7 RTR to their right. The start was chaotic; the west 7 RTR column hit the Germans before they had even reached the planned start line. They then took a wrong turn and became entangled with the rear of the 4 RTR column. None of the radio sets were working and the commanding officer of 7 RTR was killed early on alongside his adjutant. French light tanks attacking in support to their rear mistakenly engaged a line of British anti-tank guns, which vigorously responded.

'Suddenly at the top in front of us was a whole stream of German lorries and trucks and half-tracks and motorcyclists,' Second Lieutenant Peter Vaux with 4 RTR remembered as the enemy came into view. He was riding a light Mark VI tank up front. 'No tanks,' he observed, 'and they were as astounded as we were.' The next one and a half hours was the all too brief 'happy time' of the attack:

I don't know how many Germans we killed and I don't know how many lorries and other vehicles we set on fire – it really was most successful and we really didn't see why we shouldn't go all the way to Berlin at the rate we were going.

This was more the sort of armoured romp against minimal opposition that German motorized troops had become accustomed to. Peter Vaux recalled:

> There was a German motorcyclist just in front of me and he was kicking away at his bike to make it start, and it wouldn't start and there was a vein standing on his forehead and my gunner was laughing so much he couldn't aim the gun and shoot him.[10]

Rommel managed to restore the situation. 25th Panzer Regiment up ahead was ordered to double back and take on the advancing British armour in the flanks and rear. Emergency measures were employed, 88mm flak guns were depressed and levelled at the advancing British tanks. Only they had sufficient velocity to penetrate the Matilda's 60 to 80mm armour. By nightfall nearly 300 Stuka sorties had been flown in support and 20 British tanks were knocked out by 105mm artillery pieces firing over open sights. Even so, when 25th Panzer Regiment got back to the battlefield, they were themselves confronted by a screen of British 2-pounder anti-tank guns, which accounted for about 20 panzers, Rommel's greatest loss by far in this campaign. It was a sobering experience for the panzer crewmen. Hans Becker with the division recalled:

> When you are involved in combat and the banging starts around you to right and left, it's as if the human mechanism is switched off. All you can think of is you are a goner, and you have no more feelings. You only look, think, and watch out – your life is in danger – and shoot.[11]

It was a painful day for the 7th Panzer Division, the worst yet. Reported casualties were 12 officers, 67 NCOs and 299 men; possibly an underestimate, as the British took some 400 POWs as against the 148 declared missing when the battle closed. Rommel lost his personal aide *Leutnant* Most, killed at his side, with as many as 30 tanks and armoured vehicles destroyed, including three heavy Panzer Mark IVs and six Panzer III medium tanks. The enemy count was 43 tanks, 25 of which were knocked out by artillery alone, and maybe 200 dead and about 50 POWs. It took five hours' fierce fighting to restore the situation.[12]

The engagement stalled Hoth's XVI Panzer Corps. Its 8th Panzer Division deployed elements eastward from Hesdin and the 6th had also to cover the rear, to screen off the flank of the British attack. *SS Totenkopf* went temporarily over to the defensive and elements of the 5th Panzer Division were thrown into confusion. Infantry reinforcements from the 12th Division were urgently force-marched forward to seal off the area and counter-attack the flanks of the incursion. Its war diary noted that this was the first time it received an order to go on the defensive in the campaign. Orders that night from Army Group A redeployed some 15 divisions both east and west of Arras to deal with the perceived threat. *General* von Kluge commanding Fourth Army became anxious about the vulnerable flanks of the panzer corridor driving for the Channel, because the British counter-attack had been in his area. *General* Halder at OKH Headquarters was unperturbed, once he appreciated the setback had been dealt with.[13]

Major Johann Graf von Kielmansegg, the logistics officer with the 1st Panzer Division, meanwhile relaxed on a comfortable settee at the Château Beaucort l'Hallue north-west of Amiens. It was the first château where they had grandly overnighted thus far in the advance. 'It was a virtual castle,' he recalled, 'set in very pretty parkland with beautiful old trees.' It provided welcome respite from the hot sun and an opportunity to mull over events, 'the first time the division had no enemy action throughout the day, apart from reconnaissance activity, since crossing the frontier'. He had time to reflect on 'what happened and what was coming': 'A turn to the south and the Lower Seine toward Rouen or what? Or northward, where the three Channel ports of Boulogne, Calais and Dunkirk beckoned?'

'It is absolutely impossible,' he concluded, 'even to roughly guess what was going to happen now.' The *Kampfgruppe* Kleist, to which they belonged, had sufficient resources to counter any moves coming from the pocket penned ahead. 'But how far forward had the German armies attacking frontally through Belgium come?' There had been unsubstantiated rumours: 'at Arras, the French had made a despairing southwards break-out attempt,' he heard. He acknowledged it was a weak point, 'and only about 30 miles away, not far for motorized troops'. Even so, von Kielmansegg speculated the French leadership had lost armies they were not even aware of. Languishing on his settee, he noted 'the Paris newspapers have reported a few German motorcycle units trying to reach the coast, acting like "confused children" desperate for resupply'. 'That several German panzer divisions standing on the coast could be described as such,' he caustically observed, 'we found somewhat amusing.' The irony was they were sitting on top of the British Army's logistic base and 'had everything we needed, fuel, English cigarettes, blankets, tea, medical supplies and vehicles'. Only the captured ammunition was incompatible with their needs. That evening they were warned the advance would continue early the next day. 'The alarming reports about a French armoured breakthrough at Arras set off the nerves in the high command, but had no effect on the soldiers.' He did not even consider the British. It became apparent that only local successes had been achieved at Arras; there was no breakthrough.[14]

THE CHANNEL PORTS

Since early on 22 May Guderian had edged northward towards the line of the River Canche, anticipating release. At last the order arrived and in the villages between Amiens and Abbeville the armoured vehicles of the 1st and 2nd Panzer Divisions started up. Belching exhaust fumes and clattering out of side streets and squares, and from woodland near towns and villages, they converged onto the main thoroughfares and formed into columns which began to drive north. Frustrated by his enforced inactivity, Guderian had characteristically set his men off 40 minutes before von Kleist's appointed H-Hour. 'We set off to the north,' his Chief of Staff Walther Nehring recalled, 'more sober and anxious now.'

Guderian had to revise his objectives. His leading vanguard, the 1st Division, was ordered to capture Calais and the 2nd to invest Boulogne. The 10th was told to advance on the line of the Aa River and take Dunkirk. Von Kleist's staff, however, jittery at recent events, directed that 10th Panzer should remain as *Gruppe* reserve at Doullens. Guderian, unexpectedly shorn of a third of his force, opted to advance up the coast and take Boulogne and Calais. The apparent close call at Arras had not steadied the high command's obsession with flanks. 'It was with a heavy heart that I changed my plan,' Guderian admitted. The columns were further reduced by other tasks. 'Neither the 1st nor 2nd Panzer Divisions could move at full strength,' Guderian complained, 'since units of both divisions, particularly the 2nd, had to be left behind to secure our Somme bridgeheads.' The infantry had still to arrive.

94

He was, however, rejoined at 9am by the motorized and excellently equipped infantry regiment *Grossdeutschland*, which had been moved forward from the Sedan bridgehead and came under command.[15]

The 2nd Panzer drove up the N1 road towards Montreuil and Samur, heading for Boulogne beyond. As they did so, two battalions of British infantry, the Irish and Welsh Guards, from the 20th Guards Brigade were landed by the destroyers HMS *Vimiera* and *Whitshed* in Boulogne harbour. Both battalions had been recalled from Whitsun leave in England on 11 May, alerted in the middle of an energetic night exercise near Camberley the day before. The pause at the mouth of the Somme was to prove costly for Guderian's XIX Panzer Corps. At the same time the leading elements of the British 30th Brigade, two regular and one TA infantry battalions with 50 tanks from 3 RTR, had begun unloading at Calais the night before. Piecemeal arrivals would come ashore throughout this and the next day. The *Luftwaffe* had already identified the increase of shipping around the Channel ports, with especially large numbers of transports leaving Dunkirk and Boulogne. This did not particularly alarm intelligence staffs, who saw the comings and goings as resupply and reinforcements, not evacuation. *Generalmajor* von Richthofen's VIII *Fliegerkorps* covering Guderian's move forward did, however, raise concerns, reporting on 23 May: 'Afternoon – Alarm! The English are landing troops from transporters and destroyers north and south of Boulogne.'[16]

By then it was too late.

The 10th Panzer Division staff, more used to receiving breakthrough and pursuit orders, greeted its flurry of contradictory instructions with disbelief. 'Halt, clear, secure, regroup,' the division's official historian noted, 'what had suddenly happened in the operations staffs?' Commanders and senior staffs shook their heads, but 'the troops did not see the order as a tragedy', as for them it represented a break in the pace of operations: 'Instead, they welcomed it as an opportunity to finally assemble, rest, sleep, wash and shave, and also carry out needed repairs to weapons, vehicles and equipment.'

Guderian pushed his command envelope out as far as he dared. At daybreak on 22 May the entire 10th Division was lined up ready to advance on receipt of a codeword. Instead, they were unexpectedly placed as *Panzergruppe* reserve west of Doullens. Having been assigned Dunkirk by Guderian as the next objective 70 miles away, they were diverted to a reserve assembly area only 18 miles distant. *General* Ferdinand Schaal, the division commander, was nevertheless ordered to proceed north by Guderian, seeking to exploit the convention that 'the last order is the only one that counts'. He moved the division out onto two assigned march roads. They covered 4 miles and 7½ miles respectively north-west of Doullens before Guderian was instructed again by von Kleist to halt. The original order remained in effect; 10th Panzer remained immobile for another administrative 'catch-up' day.[17]

Major von Kielmansegg's first 30 miles moving with the 1st Panzer northward early on 22 May was completely uneventful. They were the corps' lead division and secured the right flank of the 2nd Panzer Division marching parallel to the coast towards Montreuil. They passed the popular Parisian holiday resort at Le Touquet, and ascended the high ground, where they 'could see the sea shimmering over there, with our sister division advancing in between'. Strong French resistance was encountered at Maninghem, where the tanks soon broke through and were by evening approaching Desvres, where they came up against 'a new and bitter enemy'. Von Kielmansegg remembered that 'it was on this day that for the first time, enemy aircraft, primarily British, began to make life uncomfortable'.[18]

Nearer the coast the 2nd Panzer Division under *Generalleutnant* Rudolf Veiel diverged into two columns. One under *Oberst* von Prittwitz, the brigade commander of 2nd Panzer, approached up the coast via Étaples, to attack the southern suburbs of Boulogne west of the River Liane, which divided and flowed through the port town. On his right the *Gruppe* von Vaerst, the 2nd *Schützen* (infantry) Brigade commander, coming up the main N1 from Montreuil and through Samer, would approach Boulogne from the village of Baincthun on the east side of the Liane, to complete an encirclement of the town from the east and north-east.

Hauptmann Freiherr von Susskind-Schwendi commanding *Panzerjäger Abteilung* 38 drove with his staff and the bulk of his battalion with this column. They paused near Samer, having heard fighting on the road ahead. 'Abandoned French, Belgian and Dutch military vehicles of all kinds were packed together' on this road, he recalled, 'with civilian cars jammed between'. Von Susskind-Schwendi mounted a motorcycle combination to go forward to investigate whether his guns would be needed to clear the obstacle. 'Some kilometres off I saw a close formation of planes flying in the direction of our advance', he recalled. Not especially significant, because overwhelming *Luftwaffe* superiority until now suggested they ought to be 'friendly'. Another commander overtook him and told him his staff had been hit by air attack. The situation forward had been resolved.

I immediately returned and found it was pretty bad. A lot of motor vehicles, including my command car, were still burning. Enemy vehicles standing at the roadside were also hit by the bombs, where ammunition and fuel set on fire partly exploded. Casualties were awful. The staff and signals platoon lost 15 dead and 13 wounded. The wounded were already being tended on my return, and men were there digging graves for their fallen comrades.[19]

It was a major setback; his second company had also suffered serious losses.

Throughout the rest of the day both columns advancing on Boulogne were harassed by British air attacks. German soldiers, so used to an overwhelming *Luftwaffe* presence, found this acutely uncomfortable. 'There can be no question of repeating yesterday's surprise,' panzer *Oberleutnant* Dietz remembered, on the road to Boulogne, 'because enemy reconnaissance and fighter planes are continuously circling over the area, and enemy bombers constantly dropping their deadly gifts on the rear columns, tearing painful gaps in them.'[20]

The air situation was changing. Helmuth Spaeter, Guderian's aide for a while, recalled the impact on the *Grossdeutschland* Division, closing up to rejoin the advance. 'Increasing levels of air activity, especially by British and Canadian aircraft from England, demanded increased vigilance,' he remembered. 'Fierce air battles took place, while repeated low-level attacks often hampered the advance.'[21]

The German Army was becoming increasingly precocious about its air support. *Generalmajor* von Richthofen supporting von Kleist's *Gruppe* complained: 'All over the *Luftwaffe* has to fight the enemy at the same time. Our own infantry contributes little and our artillery even less. Flyers have to do it all, everybody is shrieking for their assistance.'[22]

Von Kielmansegg with the 1st Panzer Division appreciated the RAF was using 'its secure airbases in England,' exploiting gaps in the *Luftwaffe*'s coverage when they had to concentrate elsewhere, or waiting for ground staffs to catch up with the air strips leap-frogging forward. Nevertheless, the enemy's limited air forays:

Make it absolutely clear that such daring and repeated new operations like ours, can only be successfully executed if our own air superiority is available. The best and most vital cooperation for ground motors is flying motors. Infantry rarely help us out at serious moments – the flyers – every time![23]

RAF Fighter Command's UK-based 11 Group accounted for 25% of the *Luftwaffe*'s aircraft losses over the next four days, while RAF 2 Group's Blenheim light bombers flew 258 sorties against the *Gruppe* Kleist alone, losing 13 aircraft in the process. 'Kleist complained for the first time about enemy air superiority,' *Generalleutnant* Halder noted in his diary on 24 May. The panzer columns had to be wary and move dispersed to guard against air attack, which was a drag on tempo. The RAF had retreated, defeated, from France the day before, having lost 386 Hurricanes, mainly abandoned, with 56 pilots killed and 18 captured. 11 Group in England now took up the fight with 21 squadrons, five of which were retained for home defence, leaving 16 squadrons with 200 fighters to range over the Allied armies trapped up against the Channel coast. German soldiers were concerned less about air superiority, more about diminution to air parity, which in some local situations suggested an unwelcome inferiority. New aircraft types, notably the Spitfire, were proving formidable opponents. Experience gave German pilots the tactical flying edge but the British were aggressive, and learning.[24]

The French were fighting back here in the north, just as *Oberst* Liss at OKH intelligence had predicted they would; their finest units were in north-west France. These were the elite units pre-planned to attack forward into the Low Countries, and in so doing had ended up in the gigantic trap that had emerged against the Channel coast. Coming up the coast road via Étaples on 22 May was the *Kampfgruppe* von Prittwitz, the westward of two armoured columns converging on Boulogne. *Oberleutnant* Rudolf Behr's Mark III platoon was leading. 'A glance at the map tells me that we are approaching a small town, Nestes-Neufchâtel,' he recalled, about 5½ miles south of Boulogne. 'Soon we arrive at the first houses' and on entering a long high street '300 metres away we spot muzzle flash'. Neufchâtel was held by a rearguard from the French 48th Infantry Regiment. Four 25mm anti-tank guns covered the main through roads in the village, linked with a battery of 75mm guns supporting elements from the French 65th Regiment near Desvres. A brief firefight erupted in the village street and Behr's panzer lurched to a halt:

> Our shot is fired, and the shell hits home, tearing a hole in the protective shield of a French 75mm howitzer. Movement is still visible around the gun. A second shot falls among the crew. The third is a magnificent hit on the gun muzzle. The barrel is split and the howitzer is out of action.

Up ahead his leading panzer *Jochen II* duelled with an anti-tank gun. They were just off the town centre, a square where five streets converged. 'Barricades can be seen,' he remembered, with 'Frenchmen running up and down'. The panzer ahead fired from the edge of the main square, while 'my panzer is 10 metres behind, ranged a little to one side to keep its own field of fire clear'. His gunner shot two small Renault tankettes on fire 'when suddenly all hell breaks out at the crossing': 'There is shooting from the left, puffs of smoke on the right and gun muzzle flashes straight ahead. Where to fire first?'[25]

Low silhouette well-camouflaged anti-tank guns were difficult to spot. Sharp cracks from tank and anti-tank gunfire reverberated along the streets, producing disorientating echoes. Muzzle flash was the only telltale indicator of hidden positions. 'There's no time for long consideration,' Behr recalled, and as he 'feverishly' glanced in all directions, 'I see a small cloud of dust and smoke rise up from the panzer ahead'. 'That's a strike!' he realized. Hatches were flung open and the tank commander struggled out, collapsed onto the hull and rolled onto the street below, where he lay. Two other crewmembers baled out in rapid succession and took cover behind Behr's panzer. He watched the tank commander, seemingly wounded, drag himself off to a house to seek cover. His vehicle was hit next: 'A hard metallic blow strikes my tank, creating a display of sparks like a firework display inside the crew compartment.'

Down below, his driver slumped forward across the controls, blood cascading down his face. 'There is nothing for it but to get out,' was the immediate reaction. The gunner had the presence of mind to traverse the turret to one side, so escape hatches faced away from the enemy.

Behr shouted to his driver, 'but he does not move; he's probably dead'. They sprinted unarmed to the rear, under rifle and machine-gun fire, away from the stricken panzer, narrowly escaping French infantry, who attempted to apprehend them. A few hundred metres back they gained their own line, reporting the loss of two panzers and the situation to the detachment commander.

Fighting at Neufchâtel lasted over an hour 'to beat down the stubborn resistance', which accompanying rear companies bypassed, and attacked from the flanks and rear. It was a typical short sharp panzer meeting engagement, with casualties. Once the follow-up panzers passed through, Behr returned to the square to retrieve his fallen. His corporal driver was still sitting where they had left him, dead with a head wound. The lead panzer *Jochen II* still burned, the gunner (an *Unteroffizier*) was dead and the radio operator was still inside 'with his foot shot off, as well as other serious leg injuries'. The volatile blazing panzer with its fuel load and ammunition 'could go sky high' at any moment. A corporal 'achieves what is practically impossible,' Behr recalled: he donned a gas mask and crawled inside, managing to extricate the radio operator. 'With a tremendous crackling from the exploding ammunition, the tank is burnt out. And with it burns the dead gunner, whom we were not able to retrieve. His tank became for him truly an iron grave.'[26]

The dead were interred in a garden nearby, a few yards from where they fell. Von Prittwitz was pushing hard. Having lost two vehicles from the platoon, the third moved up and took over the point position and the panzers clattered on, just 5 miles from Manihen, the southern suburb of Boulogne.

During these fierce clashes the 10th Panzer Division was once again released from reserve to Guderian, during the afternoon of the 22nd. 'I decided to move the 1st Panzer Division, which was already close to Calais, on to Dunkirk at once,' Guderian remembered, 'while the 10th Panzer Division, advancing from Doullens through Samer, replaced it in front of Calais.' H-Hour for the new revised objectives required further planning and the revision of march routes, so was set for 10am the following day. 'There was no particular urgency about capturing this port [Calais],' Guderian later insisted. The new priority was the port at Dunkirk. With this further delay, the chaotic off-loading of Brigadier Nicholson's British 30th Infantry Brigade was enabled during the early morning hours of 23 May, unimpeded apart from intermittent

Luftwaffe air raids. A further 1,500 light infantry minus their vehicles and much equipment came ashore at the badly battered port, to join over 1,000 already landed. By the afternoon they were fanning out to the lightly manned outer perimeter, which had already been set up. Barricades were hastily erected to block through routes leading to the port facilities. Two battalions from the 20th Guards Brigade had likewise landed at Boulogne on 22 May, where another 1,500 men were moving out to over-extended defensive perimeters south and east of the port. German groups were spotted closing in during the afternoon.[27]

At first the 1st Panzer Division leading Guderian's XIX Corps advance drove through a seeming vacuum of enemy resistance. There was skirmishing, but prisoners taken the previous day, a mix of Belgians, British and French, suggested little uniformity or coordination for defence measures. When the 2nd Panzer encountered resistance at Neufchâtel outside Boulogne, the 1st detected opposition on its own axis, part of a thin defence screen between Questrecques and Desvres further to the north-east.

The *Kampfgruppe* Krüger in the vanguard, with a combined mix of motorized infantry, panzer, artillery and *Panzerjäger* anti-tank units, clashed with elements from the British 1st Searchlight Regiment at Les Attaques, securing a bridge across the Canal de Calais. German probing and fighting lasted three hours, confirming there could be no *coup de main* entry into the port of Calais. 'A raid is no longer achievable,' *Major* Graf von Kielmansegg accepted. Elements from the British 3 RTR, landed the day before, painfully clashed with Krüger's column in a sharp meeting engagement at Hames Boucres. After hitting a German convoy and setting trucks on fire, a confused, chaotic and rambling battle took place across open fields and on the by-roads and tracks around the village and beyond. 'It was very impressive to see the reaction of the German column on being attacked,' Major Bill Reeves with 3 RTR recalled. 'They very rapidly dismounted from their vehicles and got their anti-tank guns into action and soon shots were whizzing past our ears.' Four light and three Cruiser tanks were knocked out in the unequal fight against the superior firepower of panzer, anti-tank and artillery that was rapidly directed against them. Badly battered British tanks were withdrawn back to Calais. Guderian's change of orders, sent by radio, caused Krüger to change direction beyond Les Attaques from Marck and the outskirts of Calais towards Samer and Desvres, north-east towards Dunkirk.[28]

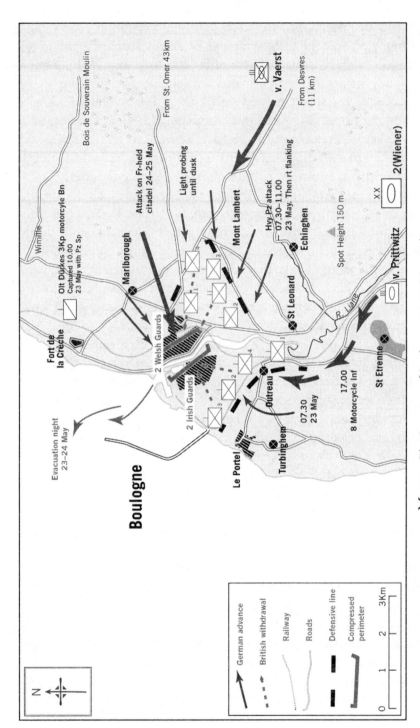

MAP 1: The Storming of Boulogne, 22–25 May 1940

Boulogne

v. Vaerst

From St. Omer 43km

From Desvres
(11 km)

Bois de Souverain Moulin

Wimille

Attack on Fr-held
citadel 24–25 May

Light probing
until dusk

Mont Lambert

Hvy. Pz attack
07.30–11.00
23 May. Then rt flanking

Echinghem

Spot Height 150 m

Olt Dükes 3Kp motorcyle Bn
Captured 10.00
23 May with Pz Sp

Marlborough

2 Welsh Guards

Fort de
la Crèche

St Leonard

R. Liane

2(Wiener)

XX

v. Prittwitz

2 Irish Guards

Outreau

07.30
23 May

17.00

8 Motorcycle Inf

St Etrenne

Le Portel

Turbinghem

Evacuation night
23–24 May

N

German advance
British withdrawal
Railway
Roads
Defensive line
Compressed
perimeter

0   1   2   3Km

The 2nd Panzer Division attacked Boulogne from the southern suburbs with the *Kampfgruppe* von Prittwitz and the *Gruppe* von Vaerst across Mont Lambert from the east. These attacks pushed the 2nd Irish Guards west of the River Liane, bisecting the town, and the 2nd Welsh Guards to the east, into the harbour area where they were evacuated in an epic fighting naval withdrawal. The French fought on around the citadel and cathedral Haute Ville area on high ground to the north for a further day.

The 1st Panzer Division main body fought engagements at Maninghem and Zoteux until encountering a seeming brick wall of French resistance at Desvres. This was a fight to clear the final intersection leading on to Gravelines outside the port of Dunkirk. Desvres and its environs were defended by two battalions from the French 65th Infantry Regiment with a battery of 75mm guns at nearby Questrecques. Graf von Kielmansegg recalled, 'the enemy was tough and gave no ground against assaults from different sides'. Four days before, *Oberstleutnant* Hermann Balck had taken over command of the 1st Panzer Brigade. In a statement highlighting the remorseless nature of the *Blitzkrieg* advance, he recalled 'my predecessor had suffered a total breakdown, caused by the horrific physical exhaustion and the constant tense situations'. His superior had balked at an attack just once too often and was replaced. Balck attacked with his panzers directly off the line of march. His 7th Company attacked into the rays of the setting sun, against well-camouflaged French low-profile anti-tank guns, and came to grief. The company commander was killed by a direct impact from a 25mm round, and three other medium Panzer IIIs were knocked out, one after the other, around him. Blinded by the low sun, the tanks suffered heavy losses. These were no longer the 'champagne campaign' skirmishes they had become accustomed to. Bitter fighting continued long into the night. The shattered 7th Company was withdrawn, and there were heavy losses among the motorized infantry companies. The rail station at Desvres was captured by the 5th Panzer Company, which captured a fully laden military transport waiting at the platform.

Krüger's *Kampfgruppe* advanced further west and captured Samer during the afternoon and reached Wirwignes, from where he detached an infantry battalion mounted on armoured half-tracks to assault Desvres. They crashed into the hotly contested town from the northwest and broke the impasse, overrunning a French engineer battalion, Balck recalled, 'but unfortunately my best battalion commander Major von Jagow was killed in the process'. The action, however, had opened up a clear route to Dunkirk. Guderian radioed they should proceed the following day. The 10th Panzer Division would follow and the 2nd Panzer was already penetrating Boulogne. H-hour was set for 10am on 23 May on receipt of the code word 'March eastward'.

As fighting intensified at Desvres, at 5pm the 2nd Panzer Division was approaching Boulogne. Von Prittwitz's battle group came from the south along the coast road, and *Gruppe* von Vaerst closed in from the east. *Oberleutnant* Rudolf Behr's reduced tank platoon still led the southern column. Speed was paramount; experienced crews were pushed forward as vanguards despite the losses. They were nearing the suburb of Manihen on the southern outskirts, just short of Outreau, where the main route into town forked. The road to the right led directly to the harbour. Hemmed in by a steep ridge on their left and a railway to the right, there was no room for approaching tanks to manoeuvre. Covering the key intersection with a 37mm Peugeot gun was Sergeant Arthur Evans, the Guards' anti-tank platoon second in command. Just 36 hours before they had been taken off gunnery ranges in southern England, trialling the new Peugeots, which they had just learned to fire. A private car with Frenchmen sped by their location, momentarily distracting them, Evans recalled, when they 'heard the distinct rumbling of tanks approaching our position':

> Sure enough, one appeared unconcernedly round the bend and then stopped. I could clearly see the tank commander's head above the open turret with field glasses to his eyes. We opened fire and the tank rocked as we scored two direct hits. The crew baled out and abandoned it. Soon a second appeared and that too was effectively disposed of.[29]

Panzer platoon commander Rudolf Behr was watching behind as his lead tank came out of the bend onto the straight stretch of road. 'There is a flash of fire,' he recalled, 'and a blow! An anti-tank strike.' The *Unteroffizier* commanding the tank had spotted the gun and ordered his driver to halt, so as to fire from a stabilized platform. 'But the tank drives on, without a human hand on the controls. For the driver is dead from a head wound from the first shell.' With his foot inert on the accelerator the panzer drove into a wall at the side of the street, which collapsed on impact. More strikes clanged into the hull 'and some penetrate the crew compartment'. The crew scrambled out under machine-gun fire, the radio operator shot in the head as he ducked down. Behr's platoon was virtually wiped out in a single afternoon, 'four dead, three seriously and one lightly wounded'.[30]

German motorcycle platoon commander *Oberleutnant* Künzel's men were riding just behind Behr's tank platoon, when 'suddenly the advance stops,' he remembered: 'From ahead a vicious sound of fighting can be heard; the sharp bark of our 20mm guns and furious machine-gun fire from the tanks. In between there are dull heavy thuds. An anti-tank gun?' A dispatch rider came down the road; 'motor cyclists forward' he ordered. They dismounted and wormed their way forward, where they could see 'the road bends sharply to the left' a few yards forward. 'Two of our own tanks were standing there, struck by the enemy anti-tank gun.' Künzel's company commander closed up and pushed a platoon left of the road and another to the right, while the third 'vanishes into houses on our right' to provide covering fire. Künzel led his platoon through a thick hedge, creeping unseen to the forward edge of the ridge overlooking the road 'just in time to see the flash of a shot from the direction of the enemy's position'. When his own machine guns opened up, 'the fat was in the fire' because the enemy occupied the houses ahead and a little wood. 'Burst after burst of machine-gun fire comes whipping into the long green grass.' They were pinned down and over-exposed. 'Where are the bastards?' he wondered, 'we can't find where the shots are coming from.'

They were still pinned when it grew dark. One of his corporals was killed trying to locate the enemy machine gun. 'Every attempt to get within grenade throwing distance,' he remembered, 'fails because of his defensive fire.' There was confused fighting 'when suddenly we hear several sharp explosions and shouting,' after which 'all is quiet at the gun position'. The third platoon, initially left behind, had located the enemy position and grenaded the two anti-tank guns; the platoon commander was, however, severely wounded. Sergeant Arthur Evans with the Irish Guards remembered the cascade of 'potato masher' grenades, and assumed one of their guns had blown up. 'We were in imminent danger of being surrounded,' he recalled, 'so I gave the order to disable the guns and withdraw.' They moved across the fields and garden allotments and made their way towards the port area.[31]

Further right *Oberleutnant* Dietz, with the motorized infantry southern column, recalled 'the blown-up bridge at Pont de Priques makes further progress impossible'. They were unable to cross the Liane River bisecting the town and casualties mounted from increasing machine-gun fire. Panzer support clattered up and raked the facades of enemy-occupied houses with intense automatic fire, while shells 'swept away whole rows of houses'. Gradually and systematically the streets in the southern suburbs of Boulogne were steadily cleared.

On the other side of the Liane River von Vaerst's battle group closed in from the east and north-east, gradually encircling the town. There was busy probing of the Mont Lambert ridgeline overlooking the town from the east. The 2nd Welsh Guards had four companies here, occupying an over-extended 'V'-shape configuration of hastily prepared shallow defence positions covering the high ground. Panzer *Pionier Abteilung* 38 moved into the village of Bainethun, bulldozing and dismantling barricades and erecting some of their own to hinder any future British attempts to escape. Throughout the night German probes around the northern suburbs towards Wimereux encountered strong French resistance at Fort de la Crèche. This citadel-like fortress overlooked the harbour from its lofty northern perch and most of the lower town of Boulogne.

Oberleutnant Dürkes commanding the 3rd Company of the 2nd Motorcycle Battalion had driven through the Forêt de Boulogne from the east on the St Omer road. As it grew dark they saw a car emerge from the town into the village of La Cappelle, where Dürkes and a group of Germans were standing in the twilight. When they waved it to a halt they were surprised to be cordially greeted by an English Major: 'At first we were startled, but after a few words the reason for his friendliness became apparent, he thinks we are Dutchmen who had managed to break through to Boulogne'. After a while the Major picked out the swastika emblems on their uniforms 'and realized his mistake, which he found intensely irritating'. By nightfall Boulogne was completely surrounded on three sides.[32]

Early on 23 May the 10th Panzer Division command staff steeled themselves for yet another day of frustrating stop-start indecision. Held back as the *Gruppe* Kleist reserve, they had to watch, with some exasperation, as their two sister divisions sped off towards Boulogne and Calais. 'We had just sat down to lunch in our small château near Boulogne,' war correspondent Edwin Dwinger recalled, 'when a staff officer from corps brought us our marching orders.' This had happened before, with monotonous regularity. 'Everyone looked tensely at the General – was there a possibility of action after all?' something denied for days. *General* Schaal passively examined the document until breaking into a satisfied smile. 'Gentlemen,' he announced, letting the order drop on the table, 'All of our wishes have been fulfilled. We are to move out to the north at once, the division is being deployed towards Calais, and our division will take it.'

Guderian had in fact confided the likelihood of this mission to Schaal the previous day. 'For the panzer divisions,' he allegedly remarked, 'the Knight's Cross hangs on the gates of the city of Calais!'[33] The 10th Panzer Division set off in two parallel columns, with the *Kampfgruppe* 86th Regiment, a powerful mix of motorized infantry, artillery and *Panzerjäger* units under *Oberst* Fischer, to the west, and on the east side, 69th Regiment under *Oberst* Menny. The 7th Motorcycle Company, part of Fischer's group, paused for supper at a height overlooking Calais, where 'we got a view of the open sea'. The second platoon remembered their commander's no-holds-barred brief:

> The final word was that the British should get the right impression about us, right from the start. We want to see him running before us. We'll hunt them through the streets of Calais with hand grenades. Everyone knows casualties only occur when you crack, so keep together and get stuck in like before – then they won't get on the ships.

We understood.[34]

More British infantry were disembarking in the port, even as he spoke.

Dwinger recalled a swift uneventful approach march: 'It seemed as if there were no enemy left throughout Artois,' he remembered. 'Had the English already withdrawn to the coast?' The *Hauptmann* leading their convoy laughed and claimed 'if it continues like this, we'll end up driving the column into Calais itself'. The other parallel armoured column could be seen intermittently in the distance 'moving through fresh greenery like a grey centipede' radiating 'an atmosphere of evil intent'. As it grew dark 'the northern sky over the Flanders meadows was flashing yellow from heavy artillery'. March planning had been complex; they needed to avoid resupply columns belonging to the 1st and 2nd Panzer Divisions crossing their north-south route, moving east. Enemy air attacks were becoming troublesome. 'We always sought good tree cover at our halts,' Dwinger remembered, because 'they were rapidly narrowing the distance to English based airstrips'. Lights from moving rail traffic could be seen in the distance, as if it was peacetime. Both columns approached Calais in the receding light of dusk. Fischer's column came in from the left, south-west along the Marquise road; Menny striking north from Guines was on the right.[35]

Guderian was taking a considerable risk. Despite advancing through the enemy rear combat zone, he felt confident enough to divide his corps into three separate formations with independent missions. Each, geographically remote from each other, was going for one of the three main Channel ports. The enemy situation, apart from being chaotic, was unclear. Contrary to accepted Prussian General Staff practice, Guderian had not designated a *Schwerpunkt* or main point of effort. This meant that his corps' artillery, *Luftwaffe*, and fighting support assets were not prioritized against any of the three ports. The 2nd Division was already bogged down street fighting in the southern suburbs of Boulogne – hardly panzer terrain. Calais was in the process of being enclosed on all sides by the 10th Panzer Division. The 1st Division had been launched against Dunkirk, where even a conservative estimate of the odds would suggest it was likely outnumbered. Guderian was driving through an audacious and unconventional strategy; tactical opportunity was driving operational considerations. Small wonder therefore that *Gruppe* Kleist's Headquarters was nervous at developments and the *Führer* especially so. *Blitzkrieg* gave every indication of outrunning political direction, and, since the scare of the surprise counter-attack at Arras, operational control. The nearest panzer division to Guderian's XIX Corps was the 8th at Montreuil, part of the *Gruppe* Reinhardt. Guderian had launched the 1st Panzer Division into the first direct attack on the port of Dunkirk with no reserve, banking resistance would collapse like a deck of cards as it had done during his epic dash from the River Meuse to the Atlantic.

PANZERS AGAINST SHIPS: BOULOGNE, 23 MAY

The two armoured battle groups from the 2nd Panzer Division converged on Boulogne, from either side of the River Liane. The panzer heavy *Kampfgruppe* von Prittwitz penetrated the southern suburb of Outreau, while the motorized infantry heavy *Kampfgruppe* von Vaerst closed in from the east, working its way around the eastern and northern suburbs of Boulogne to the sea. By dawn on 23 May, the day von Rundstedt announced a panzer pause, Boulogne was surrounded, the British with their backs to the Channel. Despite the pause order, von Rundstedt had agreed that Guderian could proceed with the capture of the Channel ports. The ports might be used to land reinforcements in his flank or rear, or conversely for an evacuation.

The German philosophy for city fighting was to drive unexpectedly into the heart of the administrative centre and paralyse the defence with a *coup d'état*. Von Prittwitz's battle group tried this, but had been thwarted by the 2nd Irish Guards' anti-tank guns blocking the main thoroughfare leading to the harbour area at Outreau. Should such a surprise raid not achieve entry, the next stage was a succession of probing attacks supported by infantry to identify the weakest point. This would then be subjected to a heavy deliberate attack. German probing had gone on all night.

Two British Guards battalions had set up a hasty defence. The 2nd Irish Guards were west of the Liane River, blocking von Prittwitz's southern approach. On the opposite side the 2nd Welsh Guards held a 'V'-shaped perimeter on the high ground at Mont Lambert, overlooking the town and port. Both battalions had been spirited across the Channel by destroyers the previous day from England, with virtually no warning. Arrival had been piecemeal and chaotic. When maps were unrolled, they were found to be of Kent, with Calais just on the bottom right-hand corner. Much of their equipment and only eight of 12 anti-tank guns had arrived. They had to march on foot against the refugee flow coming into the harbour and docks to hastily prepared defence positions. All this happened in an atmosphere of crisis. German tanks were reported to be nearby but nobody knew where. There was little time to assimilate their surroundings before it got dark. By the time the Welsh Guards companies reached the high ground at Mont Lambert, all they could do was barricade the road coming from St Omer to the east with abandoned carts. There was only time to dig shell scrapes, shallow pits sufficient for a man to lie prone just beneath the surface, with a Bren light machine gun or Boys anti-tank rifle. I Company, the last to arrive at the end of the 'V'-shaped line, arrived just as the first German patrols were spotted.

Oberleutnant Dürkes commanding the 3rd Company of the 2nd Motorcycle Battalion with von Vaerst was probing along the St Omer road, around the northern outskirts of Boulogne in darkness. When his point platoon reached a castle park, bordered by a massive stone wall, they were fired upon by a machine gun to the right. Unable to see anything, he recalled they 'returned fire relying on luck' and threw some hand grenades over the wall for good measure.

> There was an ear-splitting crack and a column of flame that reached the tree-tops. The British sitting in the castle had exploded a part of the stone wall alongside the road. The air pressure was stupendous; the jeep with the lead platoon next to the blast went up in the air and skidded along its side for a few yards. There was a moment of confusion, wounded called out to medics. One of our men had his eardrums burst by the air pressure and another was flung so violently along the ground that he broke his arm. Most of the forward platoon could not see anything, the air was so full of dust and dirt.

Dürkes' platoon reorganized and fought its way through a road block to reach the northern suburb of Boulogne.[36]

Dawn rose on 23 May, another hot day with thick ground mist hugging the ground around the heights at Mont Lambert. At 7.30am both German battle groups launched heavy deliberate attacks, supported by infantry, south and east of the town. Von Vaerst launched heavy panzer attacks mixed with infantry at an over-extended 2nd Welsh Guard's infantry company manning the apex of the 'V'-shaped defence position. 'I saw German tanks come bursting out of the village [of Mont Lambert],' recalled Lieutenant Colonel Stanier, commanding the Welsh Guards:

> and start firing at the little anti-tank guns which were just in the hollow below me. They were in threes; one would be in front and the other two would be looking out either side to protect it. They moved quite fast ... they were light tanks.[37]

The rudimentary road block obstructing the road to the village was soon blazing after being lashed by tracer fire. One of the light tanks was shot to a standstill by a trio of Boys anti-tank rifles. 'We thought they were British tanks!' Stanier recalled, surprised at the aggressive mobility of the assault. He had been driving back in a car.

> They'd come round from Number 3 Company and were already down as fast as me motoring down the road. They were belting out as fast as they could and it was all smooth fields. There was nothing to stop them... They were very bold. They were fairly charging about.[38]

The tanks started to rattle around the right flank of the Welsh Guards' 'V'-shaped position, heading towards St Martin Boulogne and the northern suburbs. The panzers systematically worked their way through the positions as platoons, forcing the Welshmen to break cover as they moved in; a support tank stood off and cut down any men that emerged to fall back. Stanier had to concede the German troops were 'very, very well trained'. It was an unequal battle. 'A German officer or whatever he was laughed his head off when we fired at his tank and it bounced off,' Guardsman Doug Davis with the 3rd Company recalled. They had been assured the 'Boys anti-tank rifle with its .5 bullets was invincible,' he claimed, 'and they weren't.' There was no option except to fall back down the slopes of Mont Lambert and make their way through the back gardens of houses to the centre of town. 'We just kept dodging and dodging and diving into shell holes or whatever.' There was no chance to consolidate. 'The Germans came down [the slope] and away we went again – only singly.' Some platoons managed to fight brief strongpoints as they fell back, but were overwhelmed by superior firepower. Doug Davis remembered, 'we dribbled our way back.' There was little they could do; 'I eventually found my way dodging the Germans to the fish market.' By late morning and into the early afternoon the Welsh Guards were driven back to the streets bordering the east side of the Liane River and the harbour area. Davis recalled:

We hadn't a dog's chance. Just the tanks came on, with a few infantry behind. They didn't have hordes of people. They didn't need them. When they got us in Boulogne we were near enough surrounded. We could see the tanks on the hills and the infantry sitting around.[39]

By 2pm they had been compressed to a north-south line running 500 yards from the quays, with their backs to the Liane River facing east. C.C. Christophé with the 2nd Panzer Division looked across the town from his vantage point on Mont Lambert:

The harbour and sea were only hazily distinguishable. Numerous English destroyers were sailing to and fro like grey silhouettes, their muzzle flashes were the only thing that could clearly be seen.

Down below he observed:

> The tanks still working together with the infantry make several probes against the edge of the town. Here, Englishmen and French were retreating by platoons, leaving their guns behind in position, and by about midday were falling back.[40]

At 7.30am von Prittwitz's *Kampfgruppe* opened its attack against the 4th Irish Guards Company area at Outreau on the other side of the Liane River. *Oberleutnant* Künzel's motorcycle platoon had formed part of the force that had knocked out the Irish Guards' anti-tank guns covering the main road to the harbour area. They watched this morning in reserve as the panzers, working in concert with infantry, switched the focus of the attack onto the 4th Company, to the right of the 1st Company, hit the night before. It took an hour of street fighting before it dawned on the German attackers that they were up against just light infantry with no anti-tank guns. The panzers seized the opportunity and drove straight over and through the Irish Guards' positions. The prisoners shortly came down the road past Künzel's platoon, 'at the double', he recalled, 'all races: Frenchmen, Belgians, Dutch, Negroes from the Belgian Congo, Algerians, Moroccans – and the Englishmen'. The British stood out, 'showing proud dogged faces'. Presently they picked out the crews 'who had manned the anti-tank position' that had blocked their advance. 'All tall fellows, Irish Guards we learn.' They regarded them with interest; 'they had behaved tough'.[41]

One of the Irish 4th Company platoons was cut off and overrun during the withdrawal. 'German tanks came up from a direction we weren't expecting,' remembered 2nd Lieutenant Jack Leslie, 'they came from the direction of the railway' and outflanked them. Supporting gunfire from the Royal Navy straddled the road, 'to break up the German advance', but to no avail:

> There were bullets flashing all around us in our trenches and a lot of noise – people were shouting at the tops of their voices and the next thing we knew a German Sergeant appeared some yards off wielding a stick grenade shouting *Raus, Raus, Raus* [out, out, out].[42]

Street fighting raged the rest of the morning until, at 1pm, Lieutenant Colonel Haydon commanding the Irish Guards ordered a withdrawal to the docks. Soon they were fighting from the quaysides. Some Bren guns were left behind, with barrels warped by the heat from the intensity of firing. Chaplain Julian Stoner was assisting at the Regimental Aid Post, by the rail line leading into the port. He recalled the assault against the senses by the incessant din from hundreds of men, Guardsmen and Germans, firing rifles and machine guns and throwing grenades at each other. Yet on poking his head outside the garage sheltering the wounded he was surprised to see just one man, a platoon commander, pistol in hand, taking cover behind a wall. This was one of the incongruous images of urban fighting: overwhelming noise, but not a living soul to see. Everyone was hidden.[43]

Just to the north of Boulogne was the French Fort de la Crèche, close by the village of Terlincthun. It sited four heavy 20cm coastal guns, facing seaward, an anti-aircraft battery and another of four 75mm field guns. The strongpoint, commanded by a naval artillery colonel with 15 officers and 300 men, blocked any approaches from the north. *Oberleutnant* Dürkes, trying to locate it in the dark, had clashed with the garrison, with his motorcycle vanguard, and was beaten back. His panzers awaiting the call forward advanced prematurely, resulting in a chaotic night action. Dürkes had to personally explain the failure to his *Gruppe* commander von Vaerst, who sent him back with reinforcements.

A deliberate attack with synchronized artillery support followed at 10am with two companies of infantry, each directly supported by a company of panzers. Under cover from a deluge of shellfire Dürkes' motorcyclists rode on the back of the bucking panzers, careering down a steep slope for 1,000 yards, before gaining cover beneath the fort's stone walls. Assault pioneers cut paths through the wire followed by infantry, who forced an entry, scrambling over obstacles into the interior of the fort. French gunners penned inside bunkers below ground by howling artillery strikes had to endure the humiliation of having to queue on the steps to the exits to be taken prisoner. The fall of the fort closed the final ring around Boulogne.[44]

By late afternoon both Guards battalions had been compressed inside dockside and quayside houses and streets around the harbour, on either side of the River Liane. Both sides were completely exhausted. *Oberleutnant* Dietz with the 2nd Panzer Division staff observed the port area from the high ground overlooking the harbour. Using scissor scopes and binoculars, he recalled seeing 'eight warships in all, laying down constant accurate fire on the attackers'. It was clear their attacks were running out of steam and there was insufficient infantry. Despite the overwhelming preponderance of German firepower, street fighting was an experience and quality leveller. Combat is essentially man-on-man, close in, virtually hand to hand, conducted in confined spaces from hidden and sheltered positions. Once men closed, it tended to favour defence. Men from the Auxiliary Military Pioneer Corps (AMPC) under Colonel Deane, labourers and craftsmen, whose fighting ability was disdained by the Guards, could offer resistance from behind barricades in street fighting. 'We miss the 3rd Battalion of our rifle regiment more all the time,' Dietz complained, 'it is still waiting on the Somme to be relieved.' Fighting in built-up areas is manpower intensive. A single house could swallow a platoon in defence or attack.

Another leveller was gunfire support from British Royal Navy destroyers and the French Destroyer Flotilla. They were able to observe groups of German soldiers and panzers moving down from the high ground and laid down effective supporting fire. Guderian's Corps Headquarters was impatient for increased *Luftwaffe* air activity over Boulogne, where it reported:

> The enemy is fighting tenaciously for every inch of ground in order to prevent the harbour from falling into German hands. *Luftwaffe* attacks on warships and transports lying off Boulogne are inadequate: it is not clear whether the latter are engaged in embarkation or disembarkation.

Dietz remembered that 'at about 1600 hours the attack peters out under the well-directed fire of the destroyers'.[45]

Formal cooperation between the Guards Brigade and French troops in the town was virtually non-existent. Brigadier William Fox Pitt commanding the 20th Guards Brigade force was dismissive: 'We were supposed to have a French division in front of us, but it never materialized.' French General Pierre Lanquetot had elements of the 21st Division holed up behind the thick medieval ramparts of the Haute Ville, a citadel in the old town. These were mainly French recruits, some 2,000, as well as about 4,000 raw Belgian recruits, youngsters aged between 16 and 24, largely ineffective, who had been evacuated from Étaples. Many British Guardsmen were also newly recruited.

Contact with the French was largely ad hoc, mainly at junior officer and NCO level, where jointly located. British soldiers shocked by the mayhem they had witnessed in the port area on arrival were disdainful of French efforts, as they generally were of most 'foreign' troops. Mistrust and language difficulties stymied the liaison needed to cope with a crisis already well beyond control. Welsh Guardsman Cyril Sutton's only glimpse of the French was the one he saw 'lying in the gutter with his intestines in his hands' as he stepped off the boat. By late afternoon the British government decided unilaterally that Boulogne was no longer defensible, and at 6.30pm the order to evacuate was passed to Brigadier Fox Pitt. Neither General Lanquetot in the citadel nor the French government was consulted, and neither was notice of British intentions given. Prime Minister Winston Churchill was uncomfortable with this decision; it was hardly likely to promote Allied solidarity.[46]

Eight British destroyers, supported by the French flotilla bombarding offshore, had now to move in and disembark troops, fighting to contain the German advance just streets away from the quayside area. The warships had by now come under fire from German artillery, newly established on the commanding heights around the town. On the ramparts of Fort de la Crèche a German artillery crew were trying to get one of the four heavy coastal guns to work against the destroyers. *Oberleutnant* Dürkes' motorcyclists looked on as, eventually, the experts especially commandeered to get them working gave up, claiming as he recalled 'the mechanism of these special [naval] guns was too complicated'. *Hauptfeldwebel* (Master-Sergeant) John, who commanded his motorcycle engineer platoon, stepped up to assist. He was a trained ex-infantry *Geschütz* – light gun man. They watched as 'again and again he tries, adjusting levers and turning wheels and cogs – until suddenly, it was working!' The skilled artillery experts were eclipsed by a veteran infantry gunner, covered in filth and dirt, who contemplatively smoked a pipe as he worked. The German press made much of the few shots fired, allegedly setting a destroyer on fire before it capsized, a veritable propaganda scoop. It is more likely that fire coming from the fort may have achieved some hits, and encouraged the ships below to keep a wary distance.[47]

Disembarking soldiers under fire and the seamanship needed to manoeuvre ships inside the close confines of Boulogne harbour was a challenge for the Royal Navy. French captains saw it as suicide, and remained outside, firing in support. Lieutenant G.J.A. Lumsden, the navigator aboard the destroyer *Keith*, explained:

> Boulogne harbour is approached by a narrow channel between long stone piers with a kink to the right in the channel just before it enters the harbour proper: there is a small spinney to the left there and the close packed town rises up the hillside to about 150 feet behind it and along the road lining the quay.

Manoeuvre had to be done against variable wind and tide states. Destroyers could only enter two by two to lift off troops. The *Whitshed* came in under fire with the crew watching in awe 'open-mouthed' at the discipline of the Guards, coolly and methodically engaging a German machine-gun post set up in a warehouse on the waterfront. Her two forward mounted 4.7-inch guns fired virtually at point-blank range, from a few hundred yards, collapsing the entire edifice. Lumsden remembered that a midshipman, sent ashore to find the naval officer in charge, walked across the quay and around a building to find himself confronting a German tank.[48]

Dietz and the 2nd Panzer staff viewing proceedings through scissor scopes on the high ground anxiously scanned the skies while watching the warships manoeuvring below, looking for any signs of the long-awaited *Luftwaffe* support. The final signal confirming the evacuation reached Brigadier Fox Pitt at the same time as a massive *Luftwaffe* air raid appeared. 'Now is the time to come in, comrades of the *Luftwaffe*,' Dietz recalled with relish. Lumsden, on the bridge of the *Keith* monitoring troops coming aboard, saw them: 'We heard and sighted a large force of aircraft approaching from the northeast, there were two forces of 30 Stuka dive-bombers each and a third force of 30 twin-engine planes.'[49]

The latter were Messerschmitt (Me) 110s, which 'moved in to attack the area of the town which our soldiers held on the north side of the harbour opposite us'. Dietz and the elated staff also picked up 'a faint howling of sirens' at 6.30pm, 'swelling within minutes into a deafening roar.'

> The first, second, third – the eye can no longer follow them as they sweep down through flak bursts toward their victims. Explosions, jets

of flame, enormous plumes of water, the howl of engines, and then they are off.[50]

Destroyers berthed inside the harbour basin were in no position to take evasive action. At this point 12 Spitfires from 92 Squadron RAF tore into the *Luftwaffe* formation, with British Hurricanes also joining in. Most of the Spitfires were holed several times during the massive swirling dogfight that ensued. The 92 Squadron intelligence report claimed seven Me 110s shot down and five more including possibly Junkers 88s 'probably' destroyed. Most of the fight was visible only by following crisscross vapour trails and the odd low-level pursuit. Stuka dive-bombers reduced the French destroyer *L'Orage* to a flaming wreck and her sister ship the *Frondeur* was also put out of action. They were easier to pick out from the air in the open water, away from the combat haze obscuring the harbour basin.

Throughout the late afternoon and into the early evening eight British destroyers took it in turn, two by two, all guns firing, to enter the embattled harbour to embark troops. German fire intensified as the evening wore on, coincidental with a lowering tide, which had the effect of keeping hulls well down by the quayside, offering protection to superstructures from direct fire, while dock installations provided cover from line of sight. When German machine guns opened up from waterside hotels against evacuating troops, whole buildings were simply swept away by 4.7-inch turret fire.

The captain of the *Keith*, 47-year-old David 'Ginger' Simpson, was cut down on his own bridge, mortally wounded by a sniper bullet to the chest. He had married just six months before. The destroyer *Vimy*'s bridge was also raked by fire as she was backing out of the harbour, coming from one of the waterside hotels. Signaller Don Harris saw the captain, Lieutenant Commander Colin Donald, hit when 'a bullet inflicted a frightful wound to his forehead, nose and eyes. He was choking in his own blood.' Their situation was perilous; a sub-lieutenant 'directly in front of me' was propelled backwards by a burst of fire, instantly killed by 'four bullet holes in line across his chest'. The first lieutenant scrambled up onto the bridge and the destroyer began to reverse astern at full speed. He ordered the 'A' gun crew to traverse onto the hotel and fire 'at point-blank range, no more than one hundred yards'. The deck reverberated with the ear-piercing crack and 'the result was devastating indeed'. They had then to contend with air attack, passing the French destroyer *L'Orage* bombarding the shore. She 'suffered a direct hit' Harris recalled, 'and disappeared in a gigantic mushroom of flame and smoke'.[51]

Suburban houses bordering the quayside area offered numerous approaches for German snipers and machine-gun groups to harass the harbour area. Set back in the streets was *Oberfeldwebel* (Senior Sergeant) Langhammer's Mark IV heavy panzer, with 3rd Panzer Regiment. It had been a hot day of intense fighting in the town, and he recalled the 'haze and smoke' hanging 'heavily, streaking the blood-red sky above the channel coast'. The crew was eating a snatched meal around the open turret. 'Oskar the driver had just uncorked a bottle of champagne' while his crewmates looked on expectantly. Suddenly the company commander *Oberleutnant* von Jaworski ran up, urgently gesticulating at the harbour, having picked out a destroyer approaching through his binoculars. 'He is going to land troops,' he shouted 'Alarm! Two heavy panzers prepare for action!' Whereupon he leapt aboard the leading Mark IV and they both sped off. Metal tracks squealed and sparked off paving stone corners as the two tanks skidded across the loose rubble littering the streets. Von Jaworski, perched behind the turret, radioed 'take the tank immediately to the port, we are going to spoil a destroyer's entry into harbour'.

The crew did not say a word; 'no one dares say anything', Langhammer remembered, an ambitious task. The two panzers clattered along the most direct routes available. Langhammer watched the lead tank 'driving through a lovely vegetable garden', seeking a fire position from a vantage point overlooking the port. 'I see our company commander jumping down from the leading tank and waving both arms energetically towards the harbour.' As they drove by they felt the concussive impact of the first round being fired. It was difficult to pick out the ship amid all the houses and dock installations, and it was low in the water. 'We can already see his smoke-stack', he recalled, as the ship hove into view, 'and the tip of his mast.' The tank had to be driven onto an open slope in order to achieve a clear shot.

This had to be one of the more bizarre episodes in the fighting for Boulogne, much hyped subsequently for propaganda consumption back in the *Reich*. At 490 yards Langhammer's first 75mm shot from the turret's stubby main armament followed a languid curved trajectory until 'there – a flash, a blue grey jet of flame shoots up the mast'.

They were certain they had hit the bridge. Swarms of British soldiers, likely already embarked, sought cover on the forecastle. In all the crew fired 10 to 12 rounds in a hasty action against the sleek ship, whose superstructure was soon wreathed in smoke, as it responded with its main armament. Thick smoke made accurate fire control difficult.

There were numerous instances of tanks, but more particularly German field artillery, firing on ships in the harbour basin. Half-track tractors towing field guns appeared at the north end of the harbour and allegedly engaged three destroyers. Langhammer's tank, out in the open, 'shivers and quakes from end to end and shrapnel clatters against its right-hand wall,' he recalled. Naval return fire straddled both tanks and the company commander jumped down and sought cover. German propaganda accounts claim, as did Langhammer, that the crippled and blazing destroyer backed out of the basin. 'Two hours later,' he recalled, 'our destroyer, completely burnt out, is consigned to the bottom of the sea for ever.' Although there are British accounts of tank-on-naval gunfire duels, the ship in question has never been positively identified. Subsequent popular German publications showed photographs of Langhammer's proud panzer crew, gathered triumphantly around their open command turret, with the painted victory symbol of a ship 'kill' beneath, with the date 23.5.40 inscribed. They probably caused fires onboard ship with 75mm strikes, but were unlikely to have sunk it.[52]

The destroyer *Venetia* was badly damaged by German tanks firing at her from the Quay Gambetta on the east side of the Liane River, as observed by Lieutenant Colonel Stanier commanding the Welsh Guards. He noticed 'a terrific explosion' which set her on fire, and displaying magnificent seamanship her captain got her out of the harbour. 'She went out stern first – blazing at the stern and with all guns firing – a magnificent sight!' This was an epic action.[53]

By 10.30pm that evening the Royal Navy had lifted 3,000 men from the hotly contested quaysides, in the midst of a graduated street-fighting withdrawal. *Oberleutnant* Dietz recalled the infantry battalion commander fighting for the quayside requested a momentary respite to the 2nd Panzer staff to rest his exhausted men; it was refused. Street fighting was exacting a considerable toll. The staff argued 'various reports indicate that the British have stopped landing troops, and are planning to pull out'. Shiploads of infantry sighted on board had suggested reinforcement rather than evacuation up to this point. As midnight approached the Germans according to Dietz were content that 'an iron ring has been formed around the town'. Von Vaerst on the east side of the Liane had blocked off the north, while the *Gruppe* von Prittwitz 'has a tight grip on the south of Boulogne, the port area and station'. Convinced they had the situation in the bag, Dietz remembered, 'to avoid further casualties, the troops were withdrawn from the [built-up area of] Boulogne for the night'.

Ninety minutes before, the destroyer *Wild Swan* had radioed that further evacuation was impractical, despite there being considerable numbers of troops still on shore. Another destroyer, the *Windsor*, which had departed Dover at 8.30pm, arrived in darkness after all the other ships had left and took on another 600 men. With evacuation apparently still achievable Vice Admiral Dover dispatched the *Vimiera* as a last resort. She tied up at 1.30 in the morning but found the quayside silent. Hailing shadows ashore, the captain discovered there were still over 1,000 troops waiting patiently in the darkness. When she slipped out 75 minutes later troops were packed tightly across all the decks to the tiller, with space only for gun turrets to revolve. She had to leave 200 men behind. Shore batteries opened fire on the jetty five minutes after departure and there was a 20-yard near miss from a German bomber when she reached open water. The *Vimiera* was so overloaded that just 5 degrees on the helm made her list unpleasantly. She reached Dover just before dawn, landing 1,400 men.

The Royal Navy managed to lift off some 4,368 men from Boulogne during the battle. One in three of the Welsh and Irish Guardsmen failed to get back. Lieutenant Colonel Stanier estimated he brought back 623 of 944 men with the Welsh Guards, of which 62 were immediately admitted to hospital. Lieutenant Colonel Hayden's Irish Guards contingent fared similarly, losing 196 from the 699 who had set off, again about one-third of the force. 'I got the whole of the Irish Guards off, and I got the Welsh Guards bar two companies off,' Brigadier Fox Pitt recalled, 'two companies were put in the bag.'[54]

Neither the Germans nor French were aware that the evacuation had finished.

Chapter 4

24 May, The Day of the Halt Order

COMMAND POLITICS

On 23 May, Hitler still basked in '*Führer* weather,' that happy combination of good weather that coincided with German fortune. Many of the meetings at the *Felsennest* headquarters were held in the open, taking advantage of spring-like balmy conditions. Eva Braun, Hitler's mistress, took photographs of the wicker-cane chairs and tables where they were conducted. Hitler was, however, by no means complacent. The British counter-attack at Arras had created a momentary stir. *Generaloberst* von Kluge, the commander of the Fourth Army, in whose sector the setback had occurred, admitted 'today was the first day in which the enemy scored a result'. It emphasized the urgent need for the marching infantry to close the gap with the panzers. Although Halder, the OKH Chief of Staff, was reassured the crisis was quickly settled, it did promote uneasiness. The enemy could still bite, and he acknowledged it would take 'some days' before strong infantry forces some 50 miles to the rear could catch up. On 22 May, the day after Arras, a French surprise attack crossed the Canal de la Sensée with light tanks and headed south towards Cambrai. It was blocked by a hasty infantry defence and repeated *Luftwaffe* attacks before the end of the day.

The broadening of the panzer corridor to the south, as mobile units swung north to the canal lines south-west of Dunkirk, was aided by the westward progress of von Bock's Army Group B. This was compressing the Allied encirclement area into a tall boot shape against the coast. The sole from Gravelines to Douhai was formed by the panzers, which had

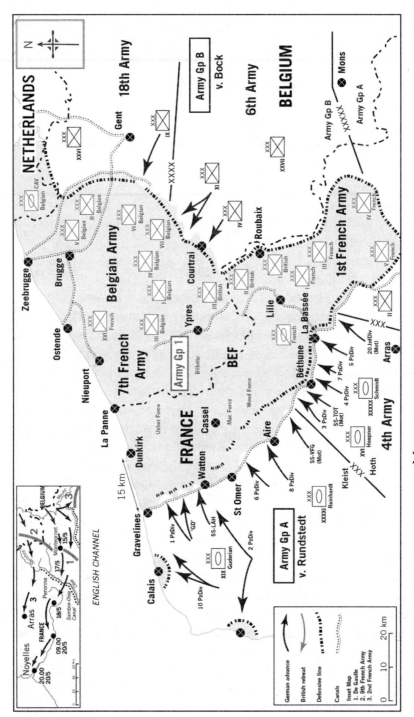

MAP 2: The Halt Order, 24 May 1940

Following an epic ten-day dash to the coast (inset), von Rundstedt's Army Group A panzers paused, stuck on the sole of a boot-shaped Allied pocket to its south west. Army Group B infantry divisions under von Bock continued their remorseless advance from the east. Severe coordination issues resulted for the converging German formations, bedeviling operations around the 1st French Army toe.

advanced to the Aa River and canal. On the coast, British TA divisions, 2nd Division and a number of ad hoc British units, such as Usher Force, Mac and Wood Force* tried, with the French 68th Division, to plug leaks in the heel around the Gravelines-Bergues area. The rest of the BEF held the toe and forefoot, separated 12 to 24 miles from the TA units holding along the sole. The long shin of the boot, from Courtrai north-east beyond Ostend on the coast and to Brugge inland, contained the hard-pressed Belgian Army. Elements of the First French Army occupied the toe area between Douhai and Valenciennes and Lille further up the foot. The ankle area, up against the Yser River inland from Dunkirk, contained French Seventh Army units. The boot outline created coordination problems between the advancing right wing of the German Fourth Army, with Army Group A and the left wing of von Bock's Group B Sixth Army.

At midnight on 23 May *General* von Brauchitsch, the Army Commander in Chief, uncharacteristically directly intervened in operations. He sent a telephone order to Army Group A detaching the Fourth Army and the mobile panzer forces from his command to von Bock's Army Group B. He aimed to rationalize command and control between the advances of two armies coming from different directions. This would simplify the reduction of the Allied pocket up against the Channel coast. Von Rundstedt's Army Group A, being the campaign *Schwerpunkt*, had priority for mobile units to execute the *Sichelschnitt* manoeuvre. Army Group B, which had crossed the start line on 10 May with 29 divisions, had meanwhile shrunk to 21. Von Brauchitsch decided Army Group A was too 'unwieldy', and was 'experiencing considerable difficulties' having expanded under pressure of events to 71 divisions. 'I have a good idea,' he suspected, that 'its staff have not been energetic and active enough'. Von Rundstedt's command

---

*These units had been hastily assembled from logistic and administrative units and remnants of larger dismembered formations.

was essentially 'disempowered' to simplify the command-and-control arrangements needed by von Bock's staff to destroy the pocket. Halder was not entirely in agreement with the timing of such a move, which was due to come into effect at 8pm on 24 May.[1]

Von Rundstedt had issued a 'close-up order' the very day von Brauchitsch decided to intervene. Von Kleist had been complaining his *Panzergruppe* had lost 50% of its armoured strength after 14 days' continuous fighting. He felt overtaxed by a succession of tasks requiring him to face units in different directions. Von Kluge commanding Fourth Army likewise complained about overstretch, because the ten panzer and six motorized divisions of the *Schnelltruppen* (mobile forces) were on the left wing of his army between the Channel coast and Arras, whereas his infantry divisions were only coming up slowly on the right wing between Arras and Valenciennes. Von Rundstedt fully agreed with von Kluge's need for a check by his *Schnelltruppen* to enable the infantry divisions to close up. In the midst of this, von Brauchitsch introduced his major changes of command and staff. Moreover, von Bock's Army Group B headquarters did not have the well-established radio means to talk with the panzer troops now placed under command. When the close-up order reached the mobile troops during the night of 23/24 May it was greeted with incomprehension and protests. They had their boot on the neck of the enemy running to their front.

Hitler had sent his senior adjutant *Oberst* Schmundt forward to find out what had happened at Arras on 21 May. The following day *Generaloberst* Keitel, the *Wehrmacht* chief, flew to Army Group A to personally relay Hitler's concerns about the slow approach of the infantry and the vulnerability of the southern flank. He was eminently satisfied when he heard von Rundstedt shared this disquiet. On 24 May Hitler personally went to von Rundstedt's headquarters, in a creeper-covered Ardennes town house at Charleville, to reassure himself about the further employment of the panzer forces.

Stepping directly from his black Mercedes staff car, he was surrounded by jubilant and adoring soldiers. Dressed as ever in an understated snuff-brown jacket and breeches, with single World War I Iron Cross pinned to the chest, he listened to the *General*'s report in respectful silence. Hitler was slightly in awe of von Rundstedt, valued his mature judgement, and could be almost docile in his presence. The calm and impassive *General*, who did not have a high opinion of his political superior, knew it. Asked what he intended to do with his armour, the puzzled von Rundstedt responded that surely the *Führer* appreciated the panzers were no longer his to command, having been transferred to Army Group B the previous day. The chilled silence that ensued signalled to all in the room that something was dreadfully wrong. 'That order will be cancelled,' Hitler quietly responded. He had not known of von Brauchitsch's intervention to hand over Fourth Army and the mobile forces to von Bock, to eradicate the Allied encirclement on the coast. Army Group A, he was told, was now no longer responsible for Dunkirk, just the Somme sector. The fundamental change had not only been ordered without Hitler's approval, it was even without his knowledge.

Hitler abruptly declared the OKH instruction null and void. He confirmed von Rundstedt's Halt Order, given the day before, and issued his own at 12.45 from Army Group A Headquarters. Only two infantry corps were allowed to advance east of Arras, the VIII and II Corps, engaged in compressing the Allied toe. The panzer and mobile forces were to halt on the general line Lens-Béthune-Aire and St Omer to Gravelines, following the line of the Aa River and canal. The panzers were to close up on this favourable defence line and be ready to compress and destroy the enemy driven westward by Army Group B. Moreover, as a personal slap in the face of von Brauchitsch's authority as Supreme Army Commander, his subordinate von Rundstedt was expressly given the freedom of action to decide when operations could be resumed westward.

Halder, the OKH Chief of Staff, had already drafted a battle plan. Army Group B was to hold the enemy in place, while the panzers of Army Group A 'dealing with an enemy already whipped, cuts into his rear and delivers the decisive blow'. Hitler reversed the scheme. 'I wanted to make Army Group A the hammer and Army Group B the anvil,' Halder wrote with frustration in his diary. 'Now B will be the hammer and A the anvil. As Army Group B is confronted with a consolidated front, progress will be slow and casualties high.'

Because of the drama and impact of its delivery, Hitler's Halt Order was assumed to be his personal decision, rather than forcefully confirming von Rundstedt's stop order issued the previous day. The infantry had now to close up to release the panzers.

The passions aroused by the 'Halt Order' were akin to live ammunition being fired off in the quietly efficient confines of army staff headquarters. This was high command politics, not necessarily replicated at the front.

Hitler's chief military aide, Schmundt, commented on the reactions of some corps commanders: 'They resembled a pack of hunting dogs that are halted at a dead stop, directly in front of the game, and that see their quarry escape.'[2]

Even von Kleist, who had argued he was overstretched, took the view 'to keep going' to achieve the high ground between Cassel and Dunkirk. The chance to pinch off the sack of the withdrawing French and British forces south of the Lys River and prevent them reaching the Channel ports was lost. *General* Reinhardt commanding XXXXI Panzer Corps argued: 'By remaining at the Canal d'Aire with weak forces at bridgeheads on the western bank did not do justice to either the special nature of the panzer as a weapon nor to the current conduct of the enemy.'

Reinhardt was convinced the enemy facing him had 'no offensive intentions' and the purpose of enemy actions was only 'to keep open the way to the coast'. The 3rd Panzer Division with *Gruppe* Hoth on the canal line both sides of Béthune concurred, observing: 'British columns flowing back deep inland to the north and north-west. The present enemy situation promises that the best chance of success is the immediate pursuit of the retreating enemy.'[3]

Von Brauchitsch was summoned to the *Felsennest* headquarters late in the afternoon, on Hitler's return. Before he could even broach the irrational halt to the panzer advance, Hitler vehemently upbraided him for his unauthorized chain of command action imposed on von Rundstedt. The Army chief was a sensible dignified aristocrat of the old school, and could not bring himself to answer back. What followed according to Halder was a 'very unpleasant interview', in which he was accused of creating a 'crisis of confidence'. The effect of a brawl with Hitler often made him feel physically sick. Von Brauchitsch was selected for his appointment because Hitler considered him the most obedient candidate. He was cultivated and sensitive and no match for Hitler's 'brutal personality', which made him feel in his dependency that Hitler 'had him by the throat', which was indeed the case. Irresolute briefings at the *Führer*'s headquarters and weak arguments against the order did not impress Hitler. He was tartly informed there would be no fresh restructuring of the armies – clearly within his remit as Army Commander – without Hitler's approval. Von Brauchitsch had lost his personal authority.

Senior officers at OKH were 'flabbergasted' by Hitler's seemingly incomprehensible order. *Oberst* Warlimont set off on the path 'up there' to the *Felsennest* accompanied by *Oberstleutnant* Lossberg, one of Jodl's senior aides, 'in order as a first step,' he recalled, 'to get some idea of the situation'. On gaining entry to the wire compound they found 'Jodl obviously did not want to see us and did not appear entirely convinced himself'. He rationalized, explaining Keitel and Hitler had both served on the Flanders marshy plain in World War I and would know armour could not be deployed there. Warlimont had vacationed there between the wars and appreciated drainage had considerably changed the terrain since 1918. What had still to be done in Flanders could be left to the *Luftwaffe*. 'Göring had given Hitler an assurance that his air forces were perfectly capable of completing the encirclement of the enemy on the seaward side,' Warlimont was told.

Göring's finely tuned political antennae had homed in on the potential kudos the high command spat offered the *Luftwaffe*. Sitting by his lavishly fitted special train *Asien*, outside a nearby tunnel at Polch in the Eifel, with his Chief of Staff *General* Jeshonnek, Göring seized the moment. 'This was a wonderful opportunity for the *Luftwaffe*,' he told him. It reminded him of a situation during the Polish campaign, when the *Luftwaffe* had smashed enemy resistance at Ilza and the River Bzura. The army had been left with a mopping up role. The developing situation had parallels, which would enhance his prestige. He picked up the phone to Hitler and made his case using 'every sort of language': 'If the *Führer* would give the order that this was an operation to be left to the *Luftwaffe* alone, he would give unconditional assurance that he would annihilate the remnants of the enemy.'

All he needed was a clear run. The panzers need only withdraw sufficiently from the western pocket to avoid danger from bombing. Strong protests came from the *Luftwaffe*'s senior commanders at what they viewed as an irrational mission. Göring was not general staff trained and had only ever commanded at air force squadron level. His morphine addiction, the legacy of a stomach wound from the abortive *Feldherrenhalle* coup in 1923, could well have influenced his optimistic assessment. Von Richthofen, commanding the VIII close air support corps, pointed out 'this was a typical army mission, which could best be accomplished by a sudden surprise attack on Dunkirk'. Jodl simply commented the notoriously vain Göring 'is shooting off his big mouth again'. Even so, Göring had a sure grasp of Hitler's personality, he was his trusted second in command, and had stirred him up even before his arrival at von Rundstedt's HQ at Charleville. The triumph of finishing off the Allied armies, he suggested, ought not be vested in the conservative army, rather the National Socialist *Luftwaffe*, created under Hitler's regime. Halder had also seen the link, presciently observing that, 'Göring warned Hitler against leaving such a success to the Generals, suggesting that if he did, they might win a prestige with the German people which would threaten his own position.'⁴

Hitler was acutely aware of the political risks he was running in this campaign. '*Führer* leads – we follow' was the party slogan. He had often successfully gambled on political instinct in the past. He was elected in 1933 on a minority vote and many of his questionable foreign policy initiatives had been taken in the teeth of military advice. The Nazi Party was all about control, the endless social pressure to participate. Hitler Youth member Alfons Heck recalled the Nuremburg Rallies were a 'gigantic revival meeting, but without repentance for one's sins'. The *Wehrmacht* was not quite in step with this control narrative, but uniforms were regarded with reverence; party officials even designed their own. The emotion engendered by the Army Staff stepping over his head was thereby acute. Halder correctly identified the issue; it was about the *Führer*'s personal prestige.

Hitler was in regular contact with *Reichsminister* Goebbels, who administered and monitored the *Reich* Home Front. Goebbels kept him informed with regular telephone updates. On 15 May, five days into the campaign, Hitler had asked about the mood back home. 'Wonderful naturally,' Goebbels responded, 'with Sedan and Rotterdam in our hands.' Hitler congratulated him on the propaganda measures he had led, in particular 'film, radio and the press, the *Wochenschau* [weekly newsreel] had pleased him greatly'. Courier aircraft flew out the latest newsreels every Tuesday to the *Felsennest*. Hitler watched them in the village pub and dictated changes, after which they were returned to Berlin to be screened on Thursdays. Goebbels wrote on 18 May that 'the radio is more important than ever before to the nation… Every German sits the whole evening up against the radio, picking up instructions and encouragement. We must beware that no psychological mistakes are broadcast.'⁵

'We're swimming in good fortune', Goebbels wrote in his diary after the fall of Brussels. Propaganda efforts bore fruit, the nation paid close attention to developments. Schoolchildren monitored the advance of the German armies across the Low Countries, sticking marker pins in maps.

Karl Kunze remembered his art teacher producing a 'roll of honour', painted on an old drawing board at high school. There were already six names from the Polish campaign 'and another six names after the French campaign'. As the war progressed 'the board was full, another was hung beneath, then one to the left, and then one to the right'.[6]

SS and SD secret security reports followed the home situation. Reports of success in the west were initially received with some reserve, swift advances like in Poland and Norway were unexpected. By 20 May talk of victories and a 'lightning campaign' were widespread. World War I veterans commented if they had enjoyed the same kind of leadership in 1914 then events might have turned out differently. Scepticism was transcended by the amazing accomplishment of German soldiers reaching the Channel coast. So acute was interest that a five-minute light break between newsreels and the main cinema feature film was inserted. This progressed to audiences thinning out without even waiting for the main film.[7]

Ironically the democracies were starved of the same quality information. British Home Intelligence Reports recorded complaints about an overemphasis of reporting on the RAF by an over-optimistic press, with little information on the land battle, where most relatives were serving. Reports before 20 May suggested that despite rumours of disaster, the front was holding the Germans. By the time of the Halt Order people in Britain thought they knew the worst and that the French were letting them down; even the German news appeared superior. 'We got a picture of how the battle was going by listening to the BBC on the wireless,' recalled Sergeant William Knight, with a Royal Engineer base depot: 'The impression they gave was that the British were advancing backwards and the Germans were retreating forwards'[8]

It was not the BBC's 'finest hour', which gave a positive spin on disasters unfolding in France. 'We were not really taken in by this,' Knight admitted, 'because it was obvious what was happening.' Recent research has identified that positive reports sent back by BBC reporter Edward Gardiner were completely at variance to the bleak comments he was writing in his personal diary. British troops on the ground appreciated the British public were being fed 'spin'. Most British reporters were evacuated before withdrawing troops even reached the coast. 'We were being pushed tighter and tighter all the time,' Knight recalled, 'and no amount of explanations could alter that.'[9]

Hitler checked with Goebbels on the home situation the day before the Halt Order. 'I briefed him on the *Reich* situation and he was very satisfied,' Goebbels remembered. Both were alert to negative reporting. Goebbels pointed out a degree of 'press stink' at the hands of the Americans. Fleeing enemy troops were mixing in with civilian refugees, 'and our attacking *Luftwaffe* can only exercise a degree of care,' he complained. 'The English were for the most part still fighting well,' he confided in his diary, but the news was all good. Hitler was clearly politically well in the ascendant: 'We have heard the French have their best troops, the elite, in the surrounded area at the front. Among them, probably the majority of their motorized units. What a haul!'[10]

PANZER ATTACK DUNKIRK...

On 23 May, *Generalleutnant* Friedrich Krichner's 1st Panzer Division approached Gravelines and Dunkirk from the south-west. To the left was the *Kampfgruppe* Balck, Krüger's battle group was in the centre and the attached motorized *Grossdeutschland* Infantry Regiment on the right. Balck's column captured the important bridge at Pont-sans-Pareil in a daring raid with a mixed mobile force of infantry armoured half-tracks and panzers. *Major* Graf von Kielmansegg remembered refugees caught up in the fighting, claiming 'the English drove French women and children toward our lines'. German soldiers momentarily ceased firing 'while the English behind this live cover intensified their fire'. The inevitable happened: 'our officers, with dread hearts ordered fire to be opened up, women and children were killed and wounded'.[11] Whatever the truth in this, there were numerous occasions when civilians were caught up in the chaos of these sudden meeting engagements.

'Motorcycles proved to be very useful,' Hermann Balck explained, employed 'to move out very quickly in advance of the main forces in order to grab a bridge'. They provided the means 'to get very quickly to the decisive point'. The imperative for a rapid advance was speed and surprise; the enemy should be immediately fought off the line of march. Armoured half-tracks, he explained, 'used to drive forward as far as possible, using our weapons from the vehicles if necessary, until we ran into anti-tank weapons strong enough to stop the vehicles. At that point we unloaded and proceeded forward on foot.'

Motorcycle units were often far out in front of the tanks. 'On the other hand,' Balck recalled, 'they had some drawbacks... They were very much restricted to paved roads and they were noisy, which made it difficult to do reconnaissance while on the motorbike.'[12]

By midday on the 23rd, 1st Panzer had reached the edge of the northern French hilly zone near the coast. Average heights of over 500 feet presented vistas of the sea and Channel coast. Von Kielmansegg recalled:

Before our eyes lay the flat expanse of Flanders, permeated by its network of canals running through. To our left you could almost reach out and touch the rising towers of Calais, and behind them, stretching out endlessly was the wide sea.[13]

The sea represented victory.

At dawn the next day the division commenced its attack on Dunkirk. The port was barely 10 miles away. Two columns advanced on a dual attack axis moving west to east, following two broadly parallel coastal approach roads against Gravelines. One was over Oye Plage near the sea, the second inland to the south through Vieille-Église and St Omer Capelle. Balck's panzer battle group attacked along the south route to St Folquin, to force a passage across the Aa Canal. The *Grossdeutchland* infantry advanced further right towards Audruicq, which was encircled. Two of its battalions then moved forward against St Nicolas and St Pierre Brouck, also on the Aa Canal.

Post-war historians have traditionally labelled this key attack on Dunkirk a 'missed opportunity', jeopardized by Hitler's Halt Order, which came into force later that night. Many of the German military histories during the 1960s and '70s were written by wartime veterans. These accounts laud the innate superiority of the German soldier against overwhelming odds. There never seemed to be quite enough manpower or tanks to achieve the decisive success sought. *General* Guderian's XIX Corps advance had probably ran out of steam *even before* the advent of the Halt Order, in the face of perceptibly increasing French resistance.

Casualties and strain had an insidious mental and physical effect on the advance. The nature of the terrain they were traversing was also changing. *Major* von Kielmansegg explained: 'The employment of our tanks in combined attacks is not possible over this landscape, which is crisscrossed by ditches, canals, water courses and across wet fields. Only single panzers can support the infantry.'[14]

The change in terrain 'made abundantly clear,' he recalled, 'the complete exhaustion and over-taxing that the men after two weeks of unbroken forward advances and heavy fighting had endured'. Troops were being steadily ground down. Fewer 'men with a calling', the experienced or daring tank and bunker-busters, who had habitually stepped forward, were left. *Hals-schmerz* or so-called 'sore throat' Knight's Cross hopefuls similarly advanced with less zeal. Death or the mutilation of close comrades became increasingly a stark restraint. *Oberstleutnant* Balck had replaced a combat-stressed failed commander, and he himself admitted 'while the losses of the preceding days had been minimal, they were now starting to add up'.

The 1st Panzer Division had lost 267 men killed up to this point, representing just 2.2% of the division total. When these ostensible figures are analysed a different perspective can emerge. Losses in wounded and missing would be two and a half to three times this figure, which means a figure of between 650 to 800 men taken out of action, mutilated rather than dead. The personnel divide between fighting 'teeth' troops versus logistics 'tail' soldiers in a typical panzer division is about 40% combat troops to 60% required to support. The revised casualty estimate seen in these terms is 12% of division strength and more likely 12% of the 40% of the fighting troops. The fall-out rate is something less than one-third. The infantry and panzer companies were actually suffering heavy losses, two or three men out of every ten. The casualties probably came from the quality element, exposing themselves to risks forward, a preponderance of junior leaders, officers and NCOs. Balck, the *Gruppe* commander, recalled 'every success we achieved had been paid for with the lives of some of our best troops, mostly officers'. Balck was one of those with a special calling. His philosophy after a costly set back on the Meuse crossing had been, 'gentlemen, we will attack, or we will lose the victory'.[15]

Other Clausewitzian 'frictions' similarly stymied momentum. Foremost among these were the huge crowds of refugees that got in the way of the columns. 'On the roads were scenes of the bitterest misery', recalled a soldier with the 15th (heavy infantry gun) Company from the *Grossdeutschland* Regiment. 'Endless columns of refugees passed by, we had no choice but to force them from the roads'.[16] They tragically got in the way of the fighting as well as marching. At the swing bridge on the

Calais road at Gravelines, several thousand Belgian refugees had crossed over seeking protection from the French-occupied Grand Fort Phillipe nearby. As the Germans approached the bridge swung closed, isolating many civilians and soldiers on a patch of ground called Cochon Noir on the west bank. Belgian refugee Clement Morel recalled:

> They are told the bridge will not be used again and ordered to clear out without delay in view of the impending battle... On the road from Calais many German tanks, armoured cars and guns [from the *Kampfgruppe* Krüger] have advanced through files of motor cars held up on the other side of the river and reached the left bank.[17]

Scores of civilians were shot down in the middle of the firefight that broke out between Krüger's speeding vanguard and the defending French and British. The French called in three RAF Blenheim bombers, which were observed by ten-year-old Eduard Timerman sheltering nearby; it was his birthday:

> The English or French air force bombed the area. I took refuge in a ditch near the port with a young man, shortly due to be 18. He was killed at the next bombing and I found myself alone again. I saw this road strewn with corpses.[18]

'The refugee muddle was indescribable,' *Major* von Kielmansegg recalled: '... on all the roads and byways, diving in the middle of fighting, they went in long columns, crossing and re-crossing, out of their heads with worry, and irrational from hunger and over-exhaustion.'

Four-seater cars drove by, with up to six or eight people squeezed inside, mattresses strapped to the roofs. 'These streams of refugees are a serious obstacle for military operations, and often so bad that only selfish resolve could free up the routes.'[19]

With the 2nd Panzer Division heavily committed to street fighting inside Boulogne and with 10th Panzer likely to be soon doing the same at Calais, Guderian likely suspected he had already overreached XIX Corps. Walther Nehring his Chief of Staff shared misgivings at the extent of resistance in the suburbs of Boulogne 'where unexpectedly hard fighting broke out'. Enemy fronts were hardening; 'it seemed that at last the influence of British leadership was beginning to make itself felt'. Infantry losses with the 2nd Panzer Division were well over 100 and the panzer regiment losses four times greater than those experienced by 10th Panzer en route to Calais.[20]

The main impediment to breaching the Aa Canal line at Gravelines and south of it was not British but French resistance. A few tanks from 3RTR (three light and one cruiser) that had escaped Calais did reinforce French firepower. There was a British Green Howard battalion partly securing Grand Fort Philippe with elements from 'Usher Force' and 23rd Division units in depth, but it was the French who were defending forward. First French Army, mauled during its fighting withdrawal north, and General Fagalde's 16th Corps had begun to coalesce inside the area of the future Dunkirk perimeter. About half of the French 21st Division, five battalions with training and labourr battalions, had also made it back. Crucially there were two intact French divisions *in situ* or nearby. Even as *Generalleutnant* Krichner attacked, the French 68th Infantry Division regrouped behind Gravelines and St Omer. The other division, the 60th Infantry, was with the Belgians on the east side of the perimeter, near Bruges.

Holding the line against Krüger, Balck and the *Grossdeutschland* were three reserve battalions from the 272nd Demi-brigade Infantry, assigned to the 11,000-strong *Secteur Fortifié de Flandres* or SFF under Brigadier General Eugène Barthélémy. The permanent SFF HQ was located inside the ancient walled and moat-bounded city of Bergues, 5 miles south of Dunkirk. The French defenders were rested in prepared entrenched positions, even if morale was not high. 'What was a little shocking was the sudden departure of the English,' Gustave Vancoille with the retreating First French Army remembered, 'because they had been in a way role models for us, models of discipline, preparation and command'. Events around them demonstrated things were going palpably wrong. The only British troops the SFF men had seen were rather disorganized and demoralized retreating line-of-communication troops. Vancoille likely echoed the view of many of his contemporaries: 'The departure of the British Army, that had been stationed with us during the whole nine months prior to the German attack, when we saw that they were pulling out, that was shocking. It was a sign.'[21]

With three rested and intact French battalions forward, on the home side of the canal line and occupying the few sectors of raised ground poking out of flat fenland, quality differences between attackers and defenders were levelled. Boots on the ground in difficult swampy terrain meant quantity became a quality of its own. The Germans attacked with superior firepower and armoured vehicles, but they were outnumbered. The 68th Division began to push forward units that gradually thickened up the defence line during the day. The French had a defence capability of 16,000 to 17,000 men, with 40 25mm or 47mm anti-tank guns and six battalions of 75mm howitzers and five heavier 155mm artillery battalions against a German division, whose combat strength was reduced by between a half and two-thirds. This suggested a breakthrough in such unforgiving terrain was unlikely. An after-action report by the *Grossdeutschland* observed for example:

> The terrain was completely flat, with fields and many canals. The only raised features were man-made: roads, railway embankments and villages. Visibility was excellent; the burning port of Dunkirk was the aiming point. Large palls of black smoke hung over the city.[22]

Despite this thickening opposition, the 1st Panzer Division attacks on 24 May made impressive headway. Before midday, Krüger's parallel advancing columns captured Oye on the coast and were hard up against the bridges at Gravelines. An attempt to bypass St Folquin inland to the south was beaten back at Hartevent. The 3rd Battalion of 1st *Schützen* Brigade reached the canal south of Gravelines, where the 1st Battalion temporarily got across. Balck's panzer *Kampfgruppe* attacked the canal bridge at Bourbourg Saint-Folquin after a systematic bombardment with six artillery batteries during the late afternoon and early evening. Exploiting the shock effect, an armoured half-track battalion under Eckinger forced a passage, supported by tanks, and established a bridgehead short of Bourbourg. 'Observing the attack from the roof of a house,' Balck remembered, 'I had the distinct impression nothing was going right.' It was a tense moment, but he left it to his commander's discretion and Eckinger forced his way over the canal.

Throughout these intensely fought actions, 'English fighter aircraft attacked us without interruption,' Balck complained, 'as my command post building shook constantly'. German veteran accounts around Dunkirk frequently comment on the unsettling effect of these RAF attacks. Ironically the retreating BEF complained loudly, both during and after the war, that they never saw them. Balck's son Friedrich-Wilhelm, a *Fahnenjunker* (Officer Cadet) with 1st Motorcycle Battalion, paid him a fleeting visit, and remarked 'we have it much better up at the front – you guys are getting bombed too much'.[23]

The situation was critical, but the French were holding the west side of the emerging Dunkirk perimeter. At dusk, the panzer division had closed up virtually to the line of the Aa Canal. 'The French had, in the course of the night heavily reinforced,' *Major* von Kielmansegg remembered, 'and fought with the courage of despair.' The *Grossdeutschland*, advancing up the lanes and byways from Hennuin after bypassing Audruicq, clashed with the 1st and 3rd Battalions of the French 137th Regiment in the wetlands bordering the canal. Opening the sluice gates and flooding the low ground paid dividends. It would take a week, but water levels were rising. 'The flat terrain offered little protection against enemy fire,' the *Grossdeutschland* after-action report noted: 'After two or three spadefuls of earth, the soldiers struck ground water. The many drainage ditches were filled to the brim with water.'[24]

The 2nd and 1st Battalions of the *Grossdeutschland* resumed the advance on St Nicolas and St Pierre Brouck at the canal line. Dinghies were brought forward to attempt an assault crossing. It was difficult to reconnoitre routes for singly deployed self-propelled *Sturmgeschütz III* assault guns through the low-lying fenland to offer support. 'We heard the sound of a motor growing louder,' *Gefreiter* Johann Neumann with 6th Company *Grossdeutschland* during the attack on St Nicolas remembered: 'the wide heavy tank moved slowly towards the canal on our left'. There was little room to manoeuvre, 'and it stopped several metres from the bank'.

> We described the target to our comrades. It was a single tree, at the foot of which was the enemy outpost. Turning its steel body slightly to align its gun on the target, the assault gun seemed to crouch like a beast of prey. Then there was a flash and a roar like thunder and a fountain of earth erupted at the tree. The assault gun fired shot after shot. The ground over there was torn up and clods of earth whirled through the air. It seemed impossible that anyone could be left alive. Then suddenly all was quiet; the target had been eliminated.[25]

The gun's motor was re-started and it ponderously moved further along the edge of the canal, shooting off sections from the facades of the nearest village houses on the opposite bank. Infantry sections scrambled across the canal road and launched their dinghies, pushing hard from the bank, rapidly paddling the 20 or so metres to the other side. Systematic house clearing began in the village, 'where the enemy was well entrenched'. They fought throughout the day against elements from the 1st Battalion with 137th Regiment, managing to establish a bridgehead up to 1,000 yards beyond the canal. The French line, however, held in depth, which meant the main bulk of the *Grossdeutschland* battalions stayed on the home bank.

'Then we were ordered to halt our advance,' recalled Balck. The reason was not clear. 'Before the attack could be renewed,' Major von Kielmansegg remembered, 'an order came from the *Gruppe* [von Kleist] that we're not allowed to continue and we were to hold the few bridgeheads we had taken.' *Oberst* Nehring, Guderian's Chief of Staff, recalled they were 'not to cross the River Aa, but to hold the line already occupied'. The attack on Gravelines and the coastal Grand Fort St Philippe had failed. 'For once the French defended bravely,' he acknowledged. Despite the pause, they were not overly troubled. 'Guderian and I assumed that the capitulation of the Allies was imminent,' Nehring suspected. Despite the apparent setback 'it was obvious to everyone present that the final phase of an overwhelming victory was at hand'. There was a degree of 'natural trepidation' but they looked ahead with confidence. Nehring was more relieved 'our temperamental general did not explode at this third order to halt'.[26]

The first attempt to carry Dunkirk had failed. The reasons why have since become steeped in myth. Dunkirk was after all barely ten to 18 miles distant, a half hour drive by car. Despite élan, determination and momentum, the 1st Panzer Division was not strong enough to break through. They were subjected to British naval gunfire and ever-increasing RAF air attacks. Furthermore, they were up against an established and rested French 137th Regiment, given time to entrench. This regiment was in turn reinforced inside 24 hours by the relatively intact 68th Infantry Division, which moved westward from along the Belgian coastline. The unit was familiar with the Gravelines area, because its three regiments had been based there since January 1940. Defences around Dunkirk had been set up and reinforced by the 53rd French Infantry Division during the Phoney War period, during which time 400 concrete and field fortifications were constructed, housing

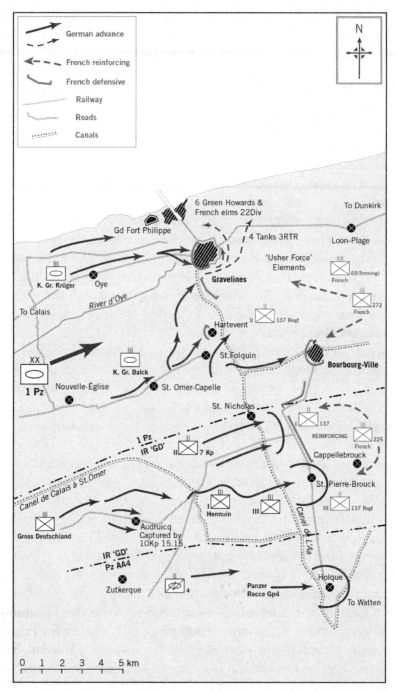

MAP 3: The Stalled 1st Panzer Division Attack Against Dunkirk, 24 May 1940

Two battle groups from the 1st Panzer Division advanced in parallel along the two west-east coast roads towards Gravelines and Bourbourg. The Infantry Regiment *Grossdeutschland*, supported to its right by 4th Panzer Reconnaissance Battalion, attacked into the marshy wooded area to the south. It was fought to a standstill against the canals on the west side of the Dunkirk perimeter by the French SFF Fortress Division, aided by the 68th French Infantry Division, even before the Panzer Halt Order was implemented. It was the only panzer division attack directed against Dunkirk.

---

artillery, anti-tank gun positions and machine-gun posts. It was to be the first of many failed attempts to capture the port.

Heinz-Günter Guderian, the XIX Corps Commander's son, with 1st Panzer Regiment, remembered:

When my Commanding Officer and I arrived at the division battle headquarters we were told the attack was cancelled, that the canal should not be crossed and lastly, which puzzled us very much – it was forbidden to ask the reason for this order.

They felt that Dunkirk was attainable. But after the Aa River there were three more canal lines to traverse: the Bourbourg, which canalized the advance, and the Mardyck and Bergues canals, both at right angles to the approach. The panzers were road bound, hemmed by canal lines and a myriad of herringbone diagonal ditches and waterways. It was virtually impossible for a panzer to be turned about on such narrow road tracks when it came under fire. 'Such a marsh is an obstacle for tanks,' Guderian's son conceded, 'but only a drawback when it is being defended', insisting: 'As far as I know the defences on the 23rd and 24th May were very weak. Therefore it was easy to see a way to punch through to Dunkirk.'[27]

This was the optimism that came with frequent success. They had no knowledge of the gradual French build-up. '*Führer* weather' was also about to give way to rain, which happened four days later.

'My father General Guderian told Kleist a panzer attack through the fen country, because of rain – being completely sodden – is useless,' the young Guderian remembered. By then a different situation, planning for *Fall Röt* – 'Phase Red' – the second phase of the battle for France had begun. Many of the signs suggest that *General* Guderian had already likely appreciated he had insufficient strength to punch through to Dunkirk on 24 May. He would have to cross four canal lines with depleted and dispersed assault pioneer and bridging assets. Armoured movement was only possible on predictable approach roads, hemmed in by floodwater and covered by French and British artillery and anti-tank fire. *Panzergruppe* Kleist Headquarters had likely arrived at a similar conclusion. Guderian was instructed to pass over all his attached heavy artillery to the 2nd and 10th Panzer Divisions, to bring the battles at Boulogne and Calais to a decisive conclusion. Dunkirk was clearly not going to be taken just yet.

...AND THE FRONT LINE

Historians are generally agreed that the Halt Order on 24 May was the primary event that prevented the panzers from capturing Dunkirk before the arrival of the withdrawing BEF. Many British units were about 80 miles from the port at the time. Two days later on the 26th, Operation *Dynamo*, the large-scale evacuation of the BEF from France and Belgium, was set in motion. Coincidentally it was the same day the panzers were let off the leash, but they could not get going until dawn on the 27th. A review of the front-line situation on the 24th, from the German soldier's perspective, is useful to ascertain whether the event was a command 'storm in a teacup' or was a missed operational opportunity.

One problem in resolving the conundrum is that the primary sources of contemporary comment are primarily officer driven. There are few down-to-earth gritty soldier accounts about this aspect of the 1940 *Blitzkrieg* campaign. Conclusions are generally derived from assumptions by senior commanders at the time. Soldier accounts tend to follow officer narratives because the average *Landser* did not necessarily know where he was geographically or where he sat in the overall campaign narrative, until his superiors published their biographies. Survival prospects of front-line officers, who rotated between staff and training appointments and regimental duty, were superior to soldiers and NCOs who remained at the fronts with their units. Many of these men would fall in Russia and other theatres of operations, leaving perhaps a more nuanced version of events. After the war *Alte Kameraden* veteran association meetings discussed events at division gatherings and came up with agreed formulated viewpoints. Few individuals, a characteristic old soldier culture, would stick their heads above a socially correct parapet to offer a contrary view to that of their comrades. After all, they stemmed from the society of the *Volk*, which was all about mass participation. These tribal division military associations, bonded in war, were solid in projecting an agreed viewpoint.

There was a totemic belief in the innate superiority of the German soldier over his enemies. Time and again the German leadership drew on these qualities and overtaxed the troops. Moreover, a plethora of contemporary 'derring-do' published personal accounts and propaganda cinema presentations like the grittily presented *Sieg im Westen*, 'Victory in the West', further propagated the myth of invincibility. German soldiers were understandably cock-a-hoop at their accomplishments. Hermann Balck with the 1st Panzer Division remembered, 'we encountered quite a bit of animosity from the old soldiers of World War I, officers as well as enlisted': 'There was quite a bit of tension. They were resentful that these young snots of the *Wehrmacht* had accomplished in six weeks what they had not been able to do in years.'

Post-war German accounts tend to ascribe lack of success in later years to Hitler's irrational decisions, insuperable odds and insufficient back-up resources. There were always *not quite* enough men, companies, battalions or divisions to achieve the objective. This tendency by officers to overplay the alleged superiority of the simple German soldier may well be a factor in subsequent Halt Order narrative myths.

The panzer attack mounted against Dunkirk on 24 May, often regarded as a foregone success, was beaten back on the canal line at Gravelines, apart from a few isolated bridgeheads. Halt Order or not, there was never a successful thrust west to east against the Dunkirk perimeter, until it finally succumbed to advances coming from the south and east ten days later. Rarely, moreover, did British Dunkirk veterans talk about the imminence of being suddenly over-rolled by panzer attacks. The three-day pause is often described as an interlude prior to the likely collapse of the perimeter defence, which never happened. Perhaps enemy resistance was as effective as the pause invoked by senior German commanders at Army Group A Headquarters and OKW. It was not aided by differing opinion on how next to proceed. Panzer generals at division and corps level wanted to attack and exploit as quickly as possible. Commanders at Army and Army Group level were pleading for a brief pause to enable the infantry to catch up. OKH was inclined to continue with a rapid advance, whereas Hitler and OKW wanted to apply the brakes to the panzer formations. There was scant unity of intent.

The spat at high command level assumed more significance in post-war biographical memoires because Hitler was by then blamed for numerous military debacles, notably at Stalingrad. That von Rundstedt was in agreement with Hitler's orders, having paused the advance the day before, was not generally realized at subordinate level. *Oberst* Warlimont pointed out that 'in view of the enormous respect in which von Rundstedt was held by all staff officers at the time' the decision would have been received with more equanimity. Controversy has raged ever since.[28]

The historical assurance that the Halt Order saved the BEF is based on later German officer assertions that success on 24 May was a virtual given. Similar assurances were given to Hitler about the airborne invasion of Crete in May 1941, which resulted in a crippling mauling of the German *Luftlande* (Airborne) arm. Likewise Moscow was to have fallen in the winter of 1941–2 to a *Wehrmacht* taken aback by a surprise Soviet counter-offensive. Stalingrad was on the cusp of falling in the late summer of 1942 yet transitioned to catastrophe after a series of over-optimistic assessments of success. The point to be derived is that the certainty of victory in May 1940 was based on assumptions that cannot be definitively proven one way or other, except through persuasion by the 'might have been' school of history.

Another way of assessing the significance of the Halt Order within the Dunkirk narrative is to drill down into the perspective of German soldiers manning the Allied pocket fronts on 24 May. The day dawned misty, which cleared and became warmer with a cloudy afternoon. The panzer and motorized units were manning the sole of the boot-shaped pocket from the heel at Gravelines to the toe south-east at Douai. From left to right they were the *Panzergruppen*: Guderian, Reinhardt, Hoepner and Schmidt. Numerous officer accounts voice frustration at the pause, yet few soldier accounts and diaries appear to identify 24 May as being particularly significant.

Panzer crewman Gerd Ahlswede recalled advancing with the 1st Panzer Division to within 10 miles of Dunkirk at Gravelines and Bourbourg: 'We positioned ourselves in this area but we didn't get an order to attack. Our forward artillery observers were not deployed, but we could see the coastline from where we were.'[29]

Grenadier Wolfgang Müller, to the right with the 7th Company *Grossdeutschland*, remembered the night hours preceding their attacks on the 24th: 'What would be awaiting us now? All around everything was dark. A fine Flemish drizzle sprinkled our helmets, dripping onto the tent squares we had draped about us, leaking into our tunics.'

They did not appear to be on the cusp of victory. Their platoon commander told them to dig in, 'we'll likely be getting artillery fire,' he advised: 'And so we spent half the night digging our foxholes, hoping that the rain would cease ... one spade cut, two, three, then four spade cuts down we could go no farther as we had reached ground water'.

Only a few isolated bridgeheads were created during a day of attacks. The main body of the regiment remained behind on the home bank, and waited two days in the same positions, 'with no significant combat,' the regiment's official account read, 'only positional warfare with the usual artillery fire'. No explanation was given for the pause in operations, which was not after all unusual. Troops rested gratefully where they were, with time to forage among the British supply dump they had located behind them, which uncovered 'many delicacies, which improved the food rations noticeably'.[30]

Von Kleist, commanding Guderian and Reinhardt's corps, set the drama of the Halt Order rolling when, feeling overtaxed by a multiplicity of tasks, he declared: 'Following the losses suffered during the past 14 days of fighting, particularly in terms of tanks, which amount to more than 50%, the *Gruppe* is no longer strong enough to mount an attack to the east against strong enemy forces.'[31]

Advising that his force was running out of steam prompted his superior von Rundstedt to institute the 'close up order' of 23 May, the day before Hitler confirmed it. Von Kleist's figures do not coincide with the detail reported by the 1st Panzer Division, rebuffed at Gravelines, indicating it had lost 10% to 12% of its fighting strength. Further to the right was Hoepner's XVI Panzer Corps and Schmidt's XXXIX Motorized Corps, under the *Gruppe* Hoth. They had closed up to the La Bassée Canal, which they reported clear. Each of Hoth's four panzer divisions declared losses of up to 30% of their tanks and armoured vehicles. The divisions were averaging 50 dead and 1,500 wounded each.

The seeming discrepancy between the losses officially declared by panzer corps commanders and the detail shown at division staff returns raises the question, was there indeed a need for a panzer halt on 24 May, or was it the victim of higher headquarters politics? One recent assessment has calculated that of 2,428 tanks that had crossed the frontier on 10 May with von Kleist and Hoth, 30% had been lost in combat or were irreparably damaged. Another 20% had been left behind because of mechanical breakdown or were in need of repair in order to cross the Aa and strike at Dunkirk. This left about 1,220 operational tanks ready for battle. A three-day delay could mean 730 incapacitated vehicles could be returned to running order and back with their units. This represented a shortfall variable of some 20% of 50%. On this basis a pause would appear advisable.[32]

Numbers of casualties and destroyed tanks are meat and wine to historians, investigating surviving documents to interpret past command decisions. Staff officers manning wartime headquarters in reality have more to do than assemble such lists, so in effect they come with a health warning. Under pressure to provide daily statistics, officers invariably made informed guesses, secure in the knowledge they could be amended if necessary later. Casualties are an emotional tally and are often reported as greater than they are at first, because of the psychological unease of coming to terms with the credibility of the evidence. The figures often reduce on close scrutiny. The most serious losses leading up to 24 May were among infantry and assault pioneer units. These were the men required to carry the assault across many canal systems and waterways and build bridges. There is also a tendency among some staff subordinates to defer in reports to what they feel their superiors would wish to hear. Another inaccuracy was the 'black market' practice of counterfeiting casualty and fuel returns by staffs attempting to circumvent overambitious demands on their troops. The true situation on the canal line on 24 May was therefore more complex than it might appear to be. Subjective facts produce subjective decisions made by commanders who are, after all, human beings, and will attempt where possible to lighten the burden on their men.

Von Rundstedt decided to halt before Hitler intervened. The situation was not regarded as optimistically as hindsight suggests. There was a fear the Allies might attempt a major break-out to the south. Von Rundstedt later admitted to his counterpart von Bock that 'I was worried that Kleist's weak forces would be overrun by the fleeing English!' Von Bock was disparaging about such a likelihood, 'having no worries of this sort whatsoever'. His Eighteenth and Sixth Armies had 'got the English by the throat, making them happy just to escape with their lives'. Having reached the coast and bottled up the Allied armies, von Rundstedt believed his army group mission had virtually been achieved. 'The battle in northern France is nearing its conclusion,' his war diary announced; there were unlikely to be crises except from 'a purely local nature'. He needed to husband his panzer forces for the next phase of the campaign, *Fall Röt*, 'Case Red', the advance south to Paris and the destruction of the rest of the French Army. As one Fourth Army staff officer put it: 'the Flanders pocket can be finished off co-laterally'.[33]

The *SS-Leibstandarte Adolf Hitler* (LAH) Regiment further along the sole of the boot-shaped pocket was in the process of attacking the 230-foot-high Watten Hill feature. The summit was crowned with ruined castle walls, totally commanding the surrounding marshy area. *Sturmbahnführer* (Major) Kurt Meyer was left 'speechless' by the sudden announcement of the Halt Order, just as the 3rd Battalion was about to assault the hill, which left them 'now out in the open, on the west bank of the canal'. His flamboyant commander *SS-Obergruppenführer* (Lieutenant General) Sepp Dietrich decided, unusually, to ignore Hitler's order and signalled the attack should go ahead. He was not prepared to have his regiment 'served on a plate' on this exposed sector dominated by the only high ground. Dietrich had no formal high-level staff or other training and had only reached *Feldwebel* during World War I. Wolfgang Filor served with him and recalled his unconventional leadership style:

> His briefings were strange to say the least. He just said 'attack this, attack that'. You all then had to come to some kind of arrangement. It was like no briefing we were used to, with clear boundaries and goals. Rather 'we will do it like that, then you go to the right and you to the left and I'll watch out' – and so on.[34]

The LAH had been formed from the 'asphalt' or parade ground soldiers of Hitler's personal guard. Well equipped and motorized, they had nothing like the depth of practical experience as the equally well-provided, but tried, *Grossdeutschland*. The SS were not yet the seasoned elite they would become in Russia, and were regarded in fact with disdain by the more conservative and traditionally trained *Wehrmacht*. Dietrich's regiment had, in fact, been cut off at Pabianice during the Polish campaign and was rescued by an army regiment.

Meyer recalled 'we sighed with relief' at the decision to go, because open ground and 'stubborn resistance by the English and French hindered the progress of the units that made the crossing'. *General*

Guderian came up shortly after to question this creative interpretation of the Halt Order. Dietrich explained: 'those bastards were able to look right down our throats', Meyer recalled hearing, 'that is why I decided to take the hill'. Guderian wryly accepted a *fait accompli*. Casualties among the LAH had risen exponentially since leaving Holland, from five or six a day to triple and quadruple this amount of dead and wounded in France. Eighteen men were lost on 23 and 24 May, and a further 20 over the next two-day pause as they prepared to cross the canal as soon as the release order was issued.[35]

Right of the LAH was Reinhardt's XXXXI Panzer Corps, with the 6th Panzer Division south of St Omer and the 8th north of Aire, facing Merville. The day before the Halt Order *Leutnant* Helmut Ritgen managed to capture the railway bridge across the Neuffosé just in front of Lord Gort's BEF HQ at Cassel. He had been fighting a mobile reconnaissance in force, managing to shoot up a French logistics column just short of the bridge. His panzer Mark IV threw a track on the bridge itself, while suppressing French and British opposition. His unit had insufficient strength to do little more than shoot up retreating enemy columns, so that 'many Englishmen were able to escape'. After establishing a precarious bridgehead 'a civilian told us the English were in position on both sides of the road leading to Cassel'. Rowland Young, one of the British defenders, recalled, 'it was about the 22nd May that some 2,000 men were drafted to Cassel to protect the way to Dunkirk'. They were to subsequently prove a tough nut to crack. Then 'at midday' on 24 May, Ritgen recalled the deliberate attack set up to take Cassel 'was suddenly and incomprehensibly cancelled on the orders of the *Führer*'.[36] They would not be released for two days.

Fritz Kanzler, a panzer crewman with the 3rd Division on their right, appreciated, 'its through the speed of the panzers that we've managed to come round to the back of the English'. Progress had been good; 'we can still feel a pleasant warmth from the burning town we've just come through,' he recalled. They had driven up to the canal line but remained wary:

> So far, everything is going as if on the practice ground, but still everyone had the feeling that the enemy, who are holed up in the positions in the hillocks over there, are only letting us advance so as to be able to wipe us out at the closest possible proximity.

These pauses were a characteristic of attacks from the line of march, following stiff resistance. H-Hour to cross the canal was announced for 3pm; motorcycle troops, reconnaissance and infantry were already formed up in the assembly area when the attack was called off.[37]

A general advance on the port of Dunkirk after 24 May, from whichever of three landward directions – west, south or east – would have to cross either four, six or seven canal lines. The land area between these waterways was fast filling with water, now that the defence flood sluice gates had been opened. Armoured vehicles would have to negotiate a latticework of drainage ditches and minor watercourses. One 3rd Panzer Division artillery officer could see the village of Robecque, 'already alight in several places' on the far side of the La Bassée Canal. Burning 'barges in the canal,' he recalled, 'also illuminate the night with an eerie red glow'. Their transport was starting to flounder in the 'marshy and black' soil. Vehicles leaving the roads 'sink up to the axles in the morass, settling deeper and deeper until at last the tractors pull them out again'. Resistance was stiffening. 'Tommy is tough and does not put up his hands so fast as the Frenchmen.' He was observing for the artillery, but 'everywhere damp ground mists destroy all visibility'. Only as the morning light came up 'does our opportunity come'.[38]

The soldiers with the panzer and motorized forces stalled on the canal line were not especially disconsolate. They faced scenes of the most amazing destruction, the abandoned detritus of a defeated army, whose eventual destruction could only be a factor of time. For this land-centric army, the sheer scale of an evacuation by the enemy across the sea was simply unimaginable. The *Luftwaffe* could comfortably seal off this exit, they imagined. Like all combat pauses, relative ceasefires gave soldiers time to ponder their survival prospects. Sacrifice at this high point of certainty in the campaign would be meaningless. The situation was analogous to that faced by coalition forces that had trapped Saddam Hussein's Iraqi Army in a huge pocket outside Kuwait city in February 1991. Nobody questioned the ceasefire; officers and soldiers alike believed it was all over. Within ten years there was a repeat invasion to destroy a resurrected Iraqi army. In similar circumstances in late May 1940, it was not nonsensical to sit back and let the *Luftwaffe* finish off the opposition. Ostensibly, the situation suggested there was not much more to do. *General* Guderian issued a congratulatory order to his troops two days later, confident in the belief they had already achieved their mission: 'I asked you to go without sleep for 48 hours. You have gone for 17 days. I compelled you to accept risks to your flanks and rear. You never faltered.'³⁹ Victory for the panzer and motorized forces appeared to be in the bag already. It would be the infantry who would have to finish the job.

The infantry were battling around the 'toe' of the boot, an Army Group A and B fault line, where there were difficulties coordinating the joint efforts of the Fourth and Sixth Armies. First French Army was falling back on Lille, where they would be besieged by up to seven German divisions. Following up along the line of the Somme, the 24 May was not a particularly significant day for the Army Group A German infantry division. Signaller Erich Kuby recalled 'the landscape was already empty' of French troops and civilians, with scenes of 'senseless destruction meeting us at every third house'. The campaign was going well as he washed down his 'dry blackbread' with 1910 brandy; 'that's how the Germans celebrate victory'. He still felt somewhat uneasy, 'and feared they might yet suffer a setback against their expedition, but they were steadily moving westward'.⁴⁰

Infantryman Karl Schönfeld had reached the World War I cemeteries on the famed Loretto Heights near Arras, 'where the swastika flags were already flying'. Hardly any trees remained on these 1914–18 battlefields, 'as if the blood-soaked earth had kept its cold and shivering nakedness, to show later generations what had happened here'.⁴¹ They spent the day preparing defensive positions as flank protection. Ernst Kleist was also fighting in a cemetery just under 10 miles beyond Courtrai. He wrote home describing he was amid some 6,700 graves of German soldiers, lying beneath an artillery duel. As the shells whistled overhead, 'one of the soldiers said "the dead are waking up"'. He too would be dead within three weeks.⁴²

Hans P. with 6th Mortar Battalion spent the 24 May at rest. 'At first we were really pleased,' he remembered, 'but what a disappointment for us.' Before they were hardly awake they had to 'clean weapons and equipment and parade in our field uniform and boots for lessons'. Ninety minutes of physical exercise followed. 'It couldn't have been worse as if in barracks – and we're off on a new operation next morning.' Company commanders felt they ought to be kept busy, with no time for negative thoughts. He did not even have time to read all his *Feldpost* letters, which had arrived for the first time in two weeks.⁴³

Fifteen infantry divisions from five corps with Army Group B were attempting to crush the toe of the First French Army in the boot-shaped pocket, and the BEF on the forefoot, and kick in the shin area of the Belgian Army, extending north-east. They were attempting to force the line of the River Lys. In the 18th Infantry Division area near Courtrai, rubber dinghies had been shot to pieces. *Feldwebel* Thiel and *Unteroffizier* Bednärek with the 51st Regiment recalled 'wooden planks and barn doors were thrown into the river, but to no avail'. Many attempts were swept away by the strength of the current. *Feldwebel* Brachmann took the initiative; 'he undressed and swam across the Lys armed with a pistol and hand grenade'. An NCO and soldier went with him in support, floating across with a machine gun and ammunition on a farm animal stall door. A small company bridgehead was cleared, but Brachmann was mortally wounded shortly after reaching the far bank. Thiel and Bednärek were twice attacked that day by highflying British bombers, which caused limited damage, 'but made a big impact' on soldiers unused to air attack. They were about 70 miles from Dunkirk.

The *Niedersächsiche* 216th Infantry Division attacked across the Lys River with two regiments forward near Macheln and between Olsene and Zutte, in concert with the 56th Division on their right. It was the 216th Division's baptism of fire, having remained behind defending in the west during the Polish campaign and *Sitzkrieg*. Two-thirds of the division were either World War I reservists or so-called poorly trained 'eight-week soldiers'. Despite being in the *Schwerpunkt* or main point of effort attack sector, they received no reinforcements and only light artillery support. Thus far in the campaign they had crossed over 20 river obstacles with little appreciable resistance, losing only 80 men.

The Lys gave every appearance of being a similarly easy obstacle to surmount. Not a shot was fired during the initial approach, and there was no sign of any Belgian defences. As soon as the attack was under way, however, artillery barrages ranging from light to heavy effectively straddled the advancing infantry battalions. When the dinghies hit the water they were riddled by heavy and sustained Belgian machine-gun fire and shot at by tree snipers. Within minutes most of the officers were either dead or wounded. The unexpectedly intense fire hit the inexperienced troops particularly hard. 'It cost nerves', the post-action report read. The soldiers felt they had been left unsupported in the open with insufficient artillery support. Many of the division's music corps bandsmen perished, acting as stretcher-bearers. Even the insufficient German artillery suffered notable casualties when an entire gun crew with the 4th Regiment was wiped out, 26 men and 21 horses lost, during a position change. The attack ground to a standstill on the home bank, beaten and pinned down by intense fire, as the villages of Macheln, Olsene and the Château at Karteelhoek burned around them. It was a debacle; two battalion commanders and 280 men were killed and 600 wounded. Even at night incoming Belgian fire did not slacken off. Two more days of painful casualties passed before the 56th Division crossed the Lys followed by the 216th. The 24 May was therefore a bleakly memorable event for many, who had no inkling whatsoever that operations had paused on the other side of the boot-shaped pocket.[44]

Infantryman Helmut Neelsen fought his way across the Lys near Armentières some 47 miles from Dunkirk. His task was to provide fire support for the assault pioneer river crossing. He remembered moving forward under harassing artillery fire 'through gardens, over squares and through houses' to reach their fire positions on the riverbank.

> Shell after shell howled overhead as they sprang, one after the other, rushing to the other side of the street. A Belgian family sat in the cellar. In the halflight we identified a young mother with a newborn child. Outside shells whined and whistled, mixed with the barking sound of heavy Belgian machine guns. We went out into the street, where we found a white horse streaming with blood. One of us dispatched the animal with a pistol shot.

They watched as, ten minutes into the attack, severely wounded medics and soldiers came doubling back, with civilians mixed in between, indicating a failed assault.

> We got the order to assemble near the church. This was totally destroyed but the enemy artillery still shot inside. Beneath the vaulted cellars we found long dead or likely wounded comrades. Distressed nuns from the Kloster sat in the middle under the soldiers, helping wounded civilians, left to their fate by God, to whom they earnestly prayed.

Neelsen and his men suffered the same fate as the assault pioneers, as the next attack was broken by two Belgian machine guns:

> At first the second attempt appeared to be succeeding. Our Company commander *Leutnant* S. was severely wounded. He lay on his stretcher with a pale face, with a bunch of flowers overhead on the roof. He was wounded in the same place where, over 20 years ago his father – who also gave his life for Germany – lies. Shortly after he died himself, in the Field Hospital.

They reached the other side of the Lys by dinghy, where the Belgians resisted bitterly, fighting from an excellently laid-out trench system.[45]

The vanguards of von Bock's Army Group B were more fought out than the masses of infantry marching behind Army Group A. The 216th Division had covered 190–220 miles on foot in 14 days and 56th Division had marched about 160 miles having lost 1,300 men fighting across the Maas, the Dyle line, Antwerp, Ghent and the River Scheldt. The division's experience was not untypical. It had not yet had a single day without combat or losing casualties. Despite their losses after the difficult Lys crossing, *Hauptmann* Schimpf who commanded the 1st Battalion of the 192nd Regiment felt able to report the next day: 'The battalion was in excellent spirits. Every battle group wanted to be the one most forward and every group competed to take the most prisoners. It was a storming victory.'

Belgians 'were absolutely terrified at the appearance of German aircraft,' he recalled; 'they would break in all directions' even when only a reconnaissance plane flew over. They lost their regiment commander *Oberst* Wolff, hit in the head by a machine-gun burst, but took 5,000 prisoners the same day. The Belgian Army was clearly falling back. *General* Hermann Geyer commanding the IX Infantry Corps watched swarms of prisoners mingling with the flow of refugees from Ghent heading south: 'There were thousands of soldiers there, either in half or full civilian garb. It was always simpler to just let them go.'[46]

They were 68 miles from Dunkirk.

Chapter 5

Panzers Against Ports

BOULOGNE *COUP DE GRÂCE*

At dawn on 24 May, smoke and haze hanging over the high ground of the Haute Ville and Citadel to the north of Boulogne echoed with the pick-pock sound of rifle fire and ripping bursts of machine guns. The occasional crack from a heavy gun reverberated among the densely packed streets. *Oberleutnant* Dietz with the 2nd Panzer Division staff remembered the morning was taken up with reconnaissance of enemy positions and a general reorganization when it was found the British had slipped away during the night. French General Lanquetot's headquarters were in the Rue d'Hautmont inside the protective ramparts of the old town. He had not been informed the Guards Brigade would land two days earlier, and he did not see them go. Coordination between the two had been minimal. Under command was a mixed force of French infantry from the 13th *Regionale* Regiment and sailors, marines, some engineers and raw recruits. They defended the narrow streets around the thick medieval ramparts enclosing the cathedral area and citadel inside the old town. High thick-walled terrace houses fronted both sides of the narrow streets. Singly deployed 75mm howitzers at corners provided the only effective opposition to panzers at street level. French troops manned windows and balconies, concentrated around the narrow approaches to the gates leading into the old town.

The *Kampfgruppe* von Vaerst with its infantry heavy 2nd *Schützen* Regiment and motorcycle infantry battalion was tasked to winkle them out. *Generalleutnant* Veiel co-located division headquarters nearby, to personally supervise his new *Schwerpunkt*. Von Prittwitz's panzer heavy battle group was to offer support from the south-east, after clearing the eastern suburbs. Battle groups were already short of infantry and had no reserves. H-Hour for the concerted deliberate attack was set for 1pm.

'Together with panzers – behind each of them a machine gun group – we advanced through the town,' *Leutnant* Künzel with 2nd Motorcycle Battalion remembered. 'Cautiously we secure all sides, the advance is slow because all the cellars have to be searched.' Künzel was mopping up near the Maritime station, where there was an intense firefight with Welsh Guards stragglers left behind the previous night. They cleared out a block of houses 'and have about eighty Englishmen come out of the cellars'.[1]

C.C. Christophé, a reporter embedded with the 2nd Division staff, watched as the infantry, closely supported by panzers, systematically cleared the narrow streets rising up towards the cathedral and citadel area. The French fought around four gateway entrances through the walls. Light tanks led, neutralizing and suppressing defensive fire, while medium and heavy tanks clambered over barricades hastily put together with paving stones. They crushed down lorries and cars sited to block the streets. 'Rattling machine guns and anti-tank guns can be heard,' Christophé recalled, trying to monitor progress through clouds of dust and billowing smoke ahead. By 6.45pm they were at the foot of the ramparts, 'but after a few hours one saw the vehicles rumbling back to occupy cover'. 'The fire was too murderous, the citadel was not yet ripe for assault.'

Another attack went in at 8pm, this time heavily supported with artillery fire, directed by a forward observer from one of the house balconies. 'Salvo after salvo came down at steep trajectories to erupt behind the barricades and walls in the middle of the enemy position.' Lanquetot's defenders were running short of ammunition and the water supply leading to the high ground had been cut. Progress was slow; 'the infantry worked their way forward from house to house', Christophé observed:

Again and again single heavy-calibre rounds sped along the length of the street, or bursts of enemy machine-gun fire. Every cellar hole, every roof window was occupied by the French. Time and again heavy tanks traversed their barrels onto another house and with a loud bark, shells struck the target, propelling debris across the street.[2]

This attack was also beaten off by tenacious French resistance from the 13th Regiment in the old town and 21st Division elements still battling around the four key gates.

Oberleutnant Dietz recalled the atmosphere in von Prittwitz's *Gruppe* headquarters where 'an oppressive silence reigns'. *General* Guderian had arrived. *Schnelle* or 'speedy' Heinz, as he was nicknamed, was as usual in a hurry. *Generalleutnant* Veiel had captured the port and most of the town, but the citadel and old town area were holding out. All three of Guderian's panzer divisions were fully committed fighting assaults against the built-up areas of the three Channel ports. Word was received that morning that the 10th Panzer's attempted *coup de main* had been checked by clashes on the outskirts of Calais and that they would have to resort to a deliberate attack, with all the combined planning and resources that would entail. The 1st Panzer Division was meanwhile fighting hard along the two parallel coast roads leading to Gravelines on the western outskirts of Dunkirk. There was no immediate corps reserve.

Guderian was well aware of the panzer and infantry attrition being imposed on the 2nd Panzer by its street-fighting operations in Boulogne. The *Führer* was in the midst of the Halt Order altercations and taking an unhealthy interest in panzer numbers, particularly as von Kleist had claimed he was overstretched. A repeat of the panzer debacle when the 4th Panzer Division was launched against the southern suburbs of Warsaw in September the year before was to be avoided. Only 57 tanks had returned from the 120 that had started the advance. Panzers operating in Boulogne had been reduced to the role of slow-moving mobile pillboxes, trying to negotiate narrow streets and the dock installations around the port. They were vulnerable to concealed French 25mm anti-tank guns and satchel charges and grenades tossed down from upper-storey houses. An explosive charge hurled from a cellar entrance could snap a track or tear off a wheel. Gun turrets snagging on crumbling walls could not traverse. Crew casualties were mounting; some 80 technically trained panzer crew from 3rd and 4th Regiments were down. Infantry losses were already approaching 100, with overall losses about 200. Guderian was fighting three battles in different dispersed locations. Those for Calais and Dunkirk had just begun. He needed a reserve and the Boulogne fight was the most advanced; he had little sympathy therefore for *Generalleutnant* Veiel's protestations about exhaustion and heavy losses. A siege was not wanted; it needed to be finished.

Dietz recalled how his division commander was summoned to the telephone 'person to person' by his corps commander. The corps commander could be starkly direct when results were not forthcoming. The staff looked on amid 'an anxious silence'. Guderian was succinct: 'We must take Boulogne today gentlemen – the men are to be informed.' The assembled officers were instructed to copy down his attack orders. 'The general takes up his map,' Dietz recalled, 'and the way he does so tells the officers to keep their distance.'[3]

The increasing significance of maintaining panzer strengths for the next phase of the French campaign, *Fall Röt*, projected Guderian into an unwelcome limelight. Not only had the issue attracted the *Führer's* full attention, the rancour over the impending Halt Order was starting to concentrate minds. Halder was already beginning the operational planning for the next phase during the enforced pause. Guderian's drive against the Channel ports was sucking up his panzers, so much so that the following day OKH forbade their employment specifically in Boulogne and Calais.

That night the area around the old town 'was lit up like a gigantic torch,' Christophé remembered. *Schwerpunkt* lay with the *Gruppe* von Vaerst, whose two infantry battalions closed in on the medieval ramparts. Two 88mm Flak guns were set up in the ground role, and, personally directed by Vaerst, hammered away at point-blank range to create two break-in points, opposite the rue Flahaut and just north at the Porte de Calais. They pounded all night. Christophé watched as 'armoured self-propelled guns and heavy tanks combined fire, systematically firing shot after shot from 150 metres against the rectangular-shaped walls. The first cracks started to appear.'[4]

A breach was achieved and at about 5.30am on the morning of the 25th the infantry stormed the walls, with a parody of medieval siege tactics. Guderian described 'a curious form' of attack whereby 'a ladder from the kitchen of a nearby house' was erected against the collapsed masonry of the breach point. Dietz saw infantry dash to the wall: 'Ladders are rushed up, and in an instant the first shock troops, with flame throwers and hand grenades are pouring over the wall – one battle group has already penetrated the north-east side of the citadel.'[5]

French General Lanquetot received a stark ultimatum at 8am: surrender or Boulogne would burn. He telephoned Admiral Abrial at Dunkirk and received permission to capitulate, but asked for time to convey the message to the rest of his beleaguered outposts resisting in the town. This was not easy, and even as Lanquetot was taken to see Guderian and Veiel, Commandant Berriat's mixed force of infantry was fighting off a German assault pioneer attack on the Château. The building was of some poignant historical significance as the overnight resting place for Britain's Unknown Warrior, en route to Westminster on 9 November 1920. The coffin was embarked on ship at the Quai Gambetta, where the Guards had conducted a fighting withdrawal 36 hours before. The last 300 exhausted defenders of the Château marched out at 10.30am and through the Porte de Calais under the admiring gaze of *Oberstleutnant* Decker, whose infantry from the 2nd *Schützen* had stormed the citadel. Isolated pockets of French resistance, ignorant about surrender, continued to skirmish with German infantry into the afternoon. Welsh Guards stragglers picked up at the Maritime Station were among the final prisoners. 'You can't describe how you felt', recalled Guardsman Doug Davis, about the humiliation of defeat; 'terrible, terrible'.

They took your watches off, your rings off. There was no problem with their attitude at all. No brutality or anything like that, they just came as normal blokes. I had shrapnel wounds – lot of blood but no damage and they, the front-line troops, made you take your jacket off and they bandaged it up. They did it with all of us.[6]

THE CRUCIBLE OF CALAIS

Calais was two to three times larger than Boulogne, which, being bisected by the River Liane, made its two halves more easily digestible to an attacker. The 2nd Panzer tanks were able to swiftly overrun the over-extended Welsh Guards' defence on the open slopes of Mont Lambert. Calais, with many ancient ramparts still standing, was more defensible in haste. When *General* Ferdinand Schaal set up his headquarters in sight of the town, the prestige of a Knight's Cross beckoned, but he knew it would probably be a tough nut to crack. Unlike Boulogne, where the harbour was overlooked by heights, Calais was flat. Only in the Courgain, the narrow-lane fisherman's quarter next to the harbour, did ground rise to a modest height. The countryside surrounding the town was also flat, sprinkled with villages, crossed by embankments and cut by numerous canals and ditches.

The Germans viewed this objective with relish. 'We were all joyfully excited and moved, from the commander of the rifle brigade to the private soldier,' front-line photographer Hubert Borchert remembered. He was observing from 'the last hill' where 'we stop and wait for the dawn' to rise on 24 May.[7] Edwin Dwinger with the 10th Panzer Division staff 'could taste the salt of the sea on the breeze' and was equally moved; '26 years ago this was regarded as the gateway to victory', but despite millions of German lives lost during the Great War, 'it was never reached'. The 1914–18 heroes of Langemarck, buried nearby, had claimed 'when we reach Calais, we also have England!'[8] Now it lay invitingly prostrate before them. Borchert recalled the panoramic view:

> ...this moment at Calais, as if emerging from the sea. The sun rises, red like blood. The many roofs, gables and towers, the old lighthouse and the rows of cranes are in silhouette. The town hall's tower tops them all.[9]

Schaal considered his options as he observed from the high ground at Coquelles, south-west of the town. From above, the town was in the shape of a plum. The outer fringe enclosed the flesh of the plum, coinciding with a rail line for much of its length to the south and west. The tracks followed the course of the old ramparts that had protected Calais when it was a fortified city. Its defences had been built in stages since the mid-16th century, 12 bastions linked by ramparts and earthworks, erected between 1880 and 1900. In 1940 the ramparts and bastions on the east side were still standing, as was much of the west side. The southern approaches, however, were weakened by the egress of railway lines and bastions 7 and 8 had been partially demolished to get the track into the town. This was the identified Achilles heel of the defence. Whereas the outer line enclosed the new town, the core of the old town formed the inner perimeter or stone of the plum, inside the canals that surrounded Calais Nord. These canals also encompassed the Petit Courgan harbour area, Fort Risban, which guarded the harbour entrance and the citadel. The latter, a massive rectangular-shaped fortress begun by Cardinal Richelieu in 1636, provided a fortified inner keep. Its large vaulted cellars provided a ready-made air raid shelter, housing the French and in time Brigadier Nicholson's 30th Brigade British Headquarters.

Claude Nicholson at age 42 was highly promoted in the rather traditional British peacetime army. Having taught at the Staff College and commanded his 16th/5th Lancer Regiment well in India the year before the war, his future was assured. Command at Calais, however, was a poisoned chalice in such confusing circumstances. He gave the defence its psychological and tactical backbone, but was stymied from the start by conflicting orders from three directions. Prime Minister Churchill had placed the Channel ports under the direct responsibility of the CIGS, Lord Gort commanding the BEF had given the same task to his adjutant general, while more orders came from HQ BEF direct.

Nicholson came ashore at Calais, like the Guards at Boulogne, amid chaotic conditions. He was immediately subjected to a rash of ill-considered missions, assisting Boulogne and sending logistic material to Dunkirk when his own resources were distinctly lacking. He had four highly trained battalions, maybe 3,000 men, two regular battalions of Rifles and the Queen Victoria's Rifles – a Territorial battalion – and 3rd RTR, whose 50 or so tanks were frittered away on contradictory missions. The force arrived piecemeal, packed in four ships, over two days between 22 and 23 May, just as the Germans were arriving. Half the brigade's vehicles, ammunition and stores were mistakenly left on the transports in all the confusion, and returned to the UK with refugees, wounded soldiers and 'useless mouths', training and administrative units. Only eight of the twelve 2-pounder anti-tank guns were landed and the troops were pushed out at once to occupy hasty defence positions, with little or no reconnaissance. During the first half of the battle Nicholson was assured his force would be evacuated, so five 3rd RTR tanks were destroyed to prevent their falling into enemy hands, leaving just nine. Then the following day Nicholson was told to resist to the end for the sake of Anglo-French solidarity.

There were probably about 800 French soldiers in Calais, dispersed manning heavy weapons inside the bastions that guarded the main approaches to the city. Overall French command was with *Chef de Bataillon* Le Tellier in the citadel, while the French Naval Reserve Officer's HQ was at Fort Risban. With him were a company and a half of reservist infantry, a machine gun company and two 75mm field guns in the citadel. Captain de Lambertye commanded naval guns at Bastion 2, 11 and 12, Bastion d'Estron and Fort Lapin mainly facing out to sea. Franco-British military cooperation was only between the junior commanders fighting adjoining defensive positions. Panzer crewman Otto W. had already identified bad blood between the two; 'the English were hated all over,' he recalled. When the prisoners started to come in, he saw 'the English were getting a lot of digs in the ribs from the French'. The Calais defensive force was outnumbered by two or three to one in infantry and faced about 120 tanks, two-thirds of them light, the rest medium and heavy. Tank odds were ten to one. Division commander Schaal was unaware of his complete superiority, but based on previous experience anticipated a swift victory after a brief fight.[10]

Panzer Aufklärungs Abteilung 90, a reconnaissance unit, was dispatched from the south-west to probe the defences and rush the town centre to achieve a *coup de main*. It had a motorcycle squadron to recce information and a heavier armoured car squadron to fight for it. By 5am on 24 May, Schaal appreciated this was not going to work, as each probe was pinned down by intense fire. He would have to resort to a deliberate attack with tanks and artillery. The reconnaissance unit was therefore sent around to the east of Calais to block any possible reinforcement from Dunkirk. Storming the town would be the task of his four motorized infantry battalions, supported by the division's heavy artillery. Three of the panzer brigade's four battalions leaguered in the Bois de Guines and Bois de Fiennes north of Desvres to start servicing and refitting for the next phase of the campaign. The remaining brigade would directly support the infantry attacks.

Two *Kampfgruppen* or battle groups approached the town from two directions. The 86th Regiment *Gruppe* under *Oberst* Wolfgang Fischer, the stronger of the two, came along the Boulogne road from the south-west, to clear Coquelles village, take Fort Nieulay west of Calais, and penetrate the inner town from the west. *Oberst* Menny came up from the south with the 69th Regiment through Guines to break in at the weak point south of the town, where the rail lines pierced the ancient embankment and ruined bastions. The attacks started before the panzer companies allocated to each attack group from 2nd Panzer Division's 7th Regiment, two with Fischer and one with Menny, had a chance to join. At first it was thought the Panzer *Aufklärungs* raid was succeeding, so the deliberate attack was mounted virtually off the line of advance.

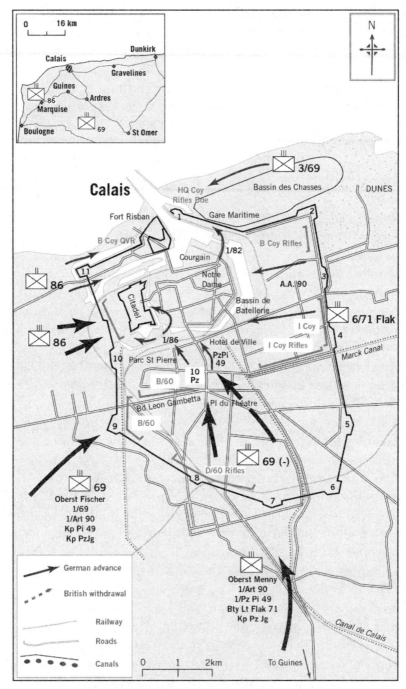

MAP 4: Calais Enfiladed, 24–26 May 1940.

The 10th Panzer Division advanced on Calais with the 86th Regiment *Kampfgruppe* Fischer from the southwest, and the *Gruppe* Menny 69th Regiment from the south (inset). The Rifle Brigade was gradually pushed into the citadel and old city harbour area, where it was surrounded and fought to the finish.

Lieutenant Airey Neave, a troop commander with a searchlight unit, recalled 24 May as 'a clear day and I could see the cliffs of Dover'. The situation with home in sight was parlous, the Germans were closing:

> The sad corpses covered in grey blankets had begun to stink. Shells burst among the cranes or landed in the sea. A mile out, the destroyer *Wessex* struck by *Luftwaffe* bombs, was sinking. Black smoke from the blazing oil refinery billowed across the harbour and, to the west and south of the town, there came the growing noise of rifle and anti-tank fire.[11]

The real battle was about to begin.

General Schaal urgently requested heavy flak and fighter support. The division was repeatedly harassed by high-level RAF bombing and low-level strafing attacks. Henschel spotter planes could not be employed because they were such easy prey for the British fighters. Edwin Dwinger remembered a squadron of RAF Blenheims flying over followed by a series of dull crumps in the distance. 'One could clearly hear each bomb, sometimes singly, sometimes even two even three times in succession.' The direction was division headquarters, where on arrival they found a line of craters just over 50 yards next to the small wood that concealed it. Schaal moved his headquarters 300 yards further towards Calais. He was promised *Luftwaffe* sweeps against shipping and fighter protection at 3pm, shortly after the raid that narrowly missed his command post.[12]

Menny's 69th Regiment battle group had begun to penetrate the southern outskirts of Calais two and a half hours before. Pushing through the gaps created in the embankment by the railway line, three combat teams of mainly infantry attacked along three main streets heading north towards the Parc St Pierre and town hall. At first they made good progress. There was little to see in an advance monitored by sound. Exchanges of machine gun fire rose to a crescendo, punctuated by shouts and screams amid the thump of hand grenades as infantry attacks went in, supported by ripping bursts of Spandau machine gun fire and the pock-pock of rifle reports as positions were cleared and consolidated. British soldiers soon realized it was not just a question of numerical inferiority. 'What amazed us,' recalled Lance Corporal Edward Doe with the 2nd King's Royal Rifles, 'was that when you looked at the German soldier, he had his jackboots on, a belt around his uniform, a canister at the side, but he wasn't lumbered down.' They were better equipped for the agile nature of fighting for buildings, scrambling, climbing and jumping from cover to cover. 'He wasn't tied down with packs and equipment like we were':

> Furthermore, he was armed with an automatic. He could just point it and let go! We had to fire a shot and eject the cartridge and reload again. We were not only outnumbered in Calais, but out-armed in every way.[13]

By 4pm Menny's force, held short of the town walls, paused to reorganize with the newly joined 5th Panzer Company from the 7th Regiment. They had also to produce an artillery fire plan for the next phase of the advance. Flat ground impeded effective artillery spotting because there were no vantage points. 'Everything was burning, the whole town was alight,' recalled Lance Corporal Doe, who remembered local British counter-attacks back down the main road came to naught:

> All of a sudden, and where it came from I didn't know, a machine gun opened up. I was fortunate, along with a few others, that I was in the middle of the formation, because the left and right simply disappeared! They just went down. By God I was scared.[14]

Solidly built houses in Calais were virtual fortresses. This was not like the shallow shell scrapes at Mont Lambert Boulogne; Nicholson's infantry fortified buildings as much as digging in nearby. 'Every house in Calais had a cellar', Doe recalled, and terraced in straight lines with shuttered windows. Streets at right angles to the German advance offered a ready-made rampart with window openings as defensive portholes. Street fighting was a series of isolated actions, unseen but noisy skirmishes. Second Lieutenant Davies-Scourfield with the Queen's Victoria Rifles pulled his friend Lieutenant Dick Scott into a cellar entrance under sniper fire:

> I grabbed him to pull him in. The bullet went right through his head as I held him. He did not die at once, but he never recovered consciousness, lying still and peaceful till he had gone. For a moment I was overcome with anguish, but the battle had to go on.[15]

The difficulty for British defenders with houses built back-to-back with no rear entrances was that they had to expose themselves on moving. Back doors tended to open into small enclosed courtyards. Communication between defending platoons was as difficult as it was for the attacking Germans, having to hug walls to approach. The only way to get from one house to another was to run down the open street, a perilous enterprise. Cooperation between sections and platoons was further impeded by the mind-boggling noise. Lieutenant Airey Neave recalled:

> This was my first experience of street fighting and I was acutely frightened. It was difficult to understand how others could remain so collected under fire. Throughout the battle, the noise was so great that if you were more than ten yards away it was impossible to understand what was said to you. Fatigue, thirst and the need to do the right thing, made it difficult to think clearly.[16]

Oberleutnant Botho König with the 7th Panzer Regiment was monitoring the progress of cellar clearing. 'House after house had to be taken,' he recalled, 'stormed by infantrymen'. He too recalled the cacophony of noise as 'machine guns cover the break-in, doors splinter, windows rattled and hand grenades exploded with sharp cracks'. Men would spring forward a few steps to post grenades while being covered by fire, each action intermittently costing a casualty. 'It soon became apparent, as the veterans knew, that the approaching noise of a shell told when it was getting dangerous, and one had to flop down.' Naval gunfire was not the same. 'You hardly heard them coming before the explosion,' König admitted. The infantry he was with were pinned down ahead awaiting tank support. The platoon commander's helmet had already been gouged by a near miss. Amid the noise of battle, 'There, you could hear a light drone and the earth starts to shake a bit, that must be tanks. Already the first was in sight – *finally* – exactly at the right time.'[17]

Three rumbled up, 'and then a hellish fire broke out, you could hardly differentiate different shots'. An anti-tank round 'hit the wall of a house, and tore out a substantial hole'. One of the tanks suddenly reversed, hit on the front, after directly engaging machine gun slits shrouded by smoke. König saw his platoon commander caught by a burst of machine gun fire, disappearing in the cloud of brick dust up against a house wall. As he hit the ground his helmet bounced away. One of his men scooped him up and brought him back:

> It was too late. His eyes were closed with a thin stream of blood running from his mouth. The back of his uniform collar was stained red. The shot had gone through between the shoulder and throat striking either his heart or vertebrae.

He was dead.[18]

On the west side of town the vanguard of *Oberst* Fischer's 86th Regiment *Gruppe* was fired upon by a French machine gun from Fort Nieulay, as it emerged from Coquelles village. They battled for the fort throughout the afternoon. The 7th Motorcycle Company recalled, 'there was not a favourable position either wide or deep' at the fort approaches. Its walls were battered by heavy artillery and direct tank fire. Shells were lobbed perpendicularly into the fort and started to crack the vaulted ceilings of the cellars beneath. By 4pm the 48 French defenders and a contingent of the British Queen's Victoria Rifles were eventually overcome at great cost. Two popular *Leutnante* with 7th Company, Pohl and Stoss, were lost, killed by a direct shell strike. *Leutnant* von Seggen assumed command; according to the company post-action report:

> He assembled the fought-out platoons that evening in one of the fort casemates. The tired men squatted on ammunition boxes or leaned up against the dusty walls in the half-light. Sweaty faces provided the only glimmer of light in the evening twilight. Tension and a questioning uncertainty could be seen in their eyes.[19]

The newly appointed *Leutnant* 'only spoke a few words, because he knew how they felt'. Words of encouragement were offered to prepare for what was still to come. The fall of Fort Nieulay enabled Fischer's *Kampfgruppe* to close up on the western perimeter of the town. Artillery and tank fire had blasted some local penetrations. Naval shipping could now be observed in and around the harbour for the first time. The Stuka attacks requested to suppress them two hours before had still not appeared.[20]

At 5pm *General* Guderian turned up at the division commander's command post. After his experience at Boulogne he accepted that 'an attack at Calais is likely to be accompanied by serious losses'. He called for a more systematic and deliberate approach. Stukas and heavy artillery would be released from Boulogne and could appear within 48 hours. Meanwhile 'the enemy is to be ground down,' he instructed, 'no unnecessary casualties'. Calais and Boulogne were offering a microcosm of what to expect if they broke into Dunkirk, which was more strongly occupied and five to six times bigger. Surrounding the town before dissecting it was sound policy. They were approaching from west, south and east, but the fourth side, at the defender's backs, was the sea. Only the *Luftwaffe* could secure this because the German destroyer fleet had been badly mauled by the Royal Navy at Norway the previous month. An option might be to isolate rather than besiege the Channel ports, because laying siege was not a suitable deployment for panzer troops. Marching foot-borne infantry with their horse-drawn heavy artillery was needed for this, but they had yet to close. Twice more during this war, at Leningrad and Stalingrad, the water flank was to be left open in a German siege, with fatal consequences. The attrition of effort and resources at Boulogne and Calais did not bode well for what could happen at Dunkirk.[21]

Anticipated Stuka support materialized at 5.30pm, but dive-bombed British positions in the dunes west of the town, instead of bombarding the destroyers. Fischer's *Kampfgruppe* derived little benefit. By last light Fischer's force had captured the embankment on the western outskirts of Calais beyond Fort Nieulay and linked up with Menny's 69th Regiment *Gruppe* at the railway intersection. They were now moving beyond the outer perimeter and into the flesh of the plum-shaped British defence.

Oberleutnant König's unit with them tried to penetrate the inner town near the station. He was suddenly accosted by a panzer crewman, having baled out of the tank ahead, who appealed for assistance to help his radio operator, still pinned inside the vehicle. 'His hair was congealed together with blood, his face and hands burned black and blood ran down his forehead.' He was in a bad state, with a charred back, and 'his whole body shook, he was wheezing and his hands were trembling'. An anti-tank round had punched through the driver's hatch, spraying his face in blood. His *Leutnant* had ordered: 'faster, drive on,' when the second high-velocity round bored in and the panzer burst into flames. The crewman managed to raise the hatch and scramble out but the officer 'climbed up and then sank back down inside'. The oxygen had been sucked from his lungs by the intensity of the conflagration below. Severe burns to his back came from being pinned against a house wall by the burning tank. He managed to escape through a window but the back of his shirt was on fire. Despite overwhelming fire superiority, the battle was proving costly. Panzers were vulnerable in street fighting and had to be closely protected by accompanying infantry.[22]

Nicholson managed to thin out the British defence to the inner perimeter when light faded, without his attackers realizing. He withdrew inside the canal line enclosing the dock area, the old town and Petite Courgain fishery district. The Germans, equally exhausted, went over to the defensive in the sectors they had penetrated deep in the town. Guderian's corps HQ, caught up in urgent returns feeding the panzer halt debate, requested a strength return from 10th Panzer. *General* Schaal responded with: 'Troops tired, need several days rest. Losses in personnel, material and vehicles amount to one-third, tanks are at half strength.'[23]

Schaal's problems multiplied when OKH directed that 'the use of tanks fighting in built-up areas, especially in Calais and Boulogne is forbidden'. Tank support had got the advance to where it was, but with losses. A number had already been knocked out and the panzer battalion commander *Major* von Grundheer was severely wounded. The tanks were pulled back. Attacks were to be conducted solely by infantry, supported by all heavy weapons at the division's disposal. Stuka coverage and the heavy artillery deployed at Boulogne would be switched to Calais as soon as it became available. The citadel at Boulogne was still holding out.

Attacks resumed at dawn on 25 May, the second day, and by 8.15am Menny's southern *Kampfgruppe* reported its swastika flag was flying from the roof of the town hall and that Calais was occupied. This proved premature. *Oberst* Menny plucked the mayor of Calais, André Gershell, from his desk, and sent him to the heavily sandbagged north-east bastion to negotiate a surrender with Brigadier Nicholson. He did not return and nothing happened. Schaal concentrated his artillery to lay down a massive barrage to grind the defenders into submission.

Meanwhile Fischer's 86th Regiment *Gruppe* fought its way along the streets to the citadel. The commander of its 1st Battalion, Major Graf Strachwitz, was severely wounded overrunning the northern railway station. The 86th Regiment's 2nd Battalion meanwhile fought its way along the beach road through the Les Baraques village towards Fort Lapin near the harbour entrance. 'The British defended bitterly,' the 7th Motorcycle Battalion recalled, 'through sand dunes, soon through gardens and streets, we advanced under the protection of our machine guns and mortars'. That night most of them slept in beds, unlike their companion companies freezing outside in the sand dunes. The objective was marked by huge flames and bulbous smoke boiling out of the huge oil storage tanks, set on fire by artillery the day before.[24]

By midday the scene was set for a major deliberate attack, supported by massed division artillery fire and Stuka attacks. Forward artillery observers were on the balconies and rooftop of the Opera House and Town Hall, which gave unimpeded visibility across the old town laid out invitingly before them. At 1pm a second invitation to surrender was sent to Nicholson. Problems piled up for Schaal when it was realized Menny's previous optimistic report of gains was inaccurate. The old town was not occupied; indeed the bridges crossing the Canal de Calais to gain access were still hotly contested. This meant a further revision of the artillery fire plan. Guderian's HQ next advised Stuka support would not be forthcoming, maybe the next day. At 4.30pm Schaal learned the second surrender ultimatum was rejected; the emissary *Leutnant* Hoffmann had returned slightly wounded. Nicholson had been emphatic: 'No – as it is the British Army's duty to fight as well as it is the German's.' Tension rose when the reconnaissance unit *Aufklärungs Abteilung* 90 at the east side of town reported two warships and 31 freighters sailing by. They might be reinforcements; but they passed by the harbour and continued on their way towards Dunkirk.[25]

Meanwhile *Stukageschwader* 2 led by *Major* Oskar Dinort was flying along the Calais coastline, homing in on the brown-black smoke mushrooming up from fires that now engulfed the town. They were flying Guderian's original mission to silence the troublesome British destroyers bombarding off the shoreline. This was actually a challenge, because attacking weaving dodging warships that fired back was a 'knack' few of his pilots had yet acquired. Dinort was blinded by the glare radiating back from the sea, which in the fine weather below was like an endless pane of frosted glass. 'Attack by *Gruppen*,' Dinort ordered his two *Gruppen* commanders *Hauptmann* Hitschold and *Hauptmann* Brückers, 'choose your own targets'. This was a tricky manoeuvre for the approaching waves of 40 or so Stuka aircraft, subdivided into *Staffeln* (squadrons) of nine to 12 aircraft each. These had first to reduce height, because dives on such small targets had to begin from as low a height as possible, certainly below the standard 12,000 feet.

Each aircraft rolled over and peeled off in succession, aiming for one of the larger ships. In so doing they found their prey tended to wander out of the bombsight and disappear beneath the engine cowling. The solution was to 'staircase' the approach by diving until the target was lost, then pulling out, re-sighting and diving again, perhaps several times. The initial 'specks' in the water transitioned to sleek destroyer hulls, which swerved from the dive turning sharply to port or starboard in a foaming propeller-fuelled froth, marking their escape. At the same time a wall of light flak and tracer spat up. A full half-circle turn could not be matched by the aircraft, meaning the whole staircase graduated process had to begin again. Many of the Stuka bombs cascaded into the sea, sending up impressive but useless fountains of water designating near misses. A few hits were achieved on a guard boat and transport, but most were unobserved results.

Once the *Staffeln* had delivered their attacks, the *Gruppen* had to re-form at sea level and head back south, towards their bases. The machines seem to hang in the air during this manoeuvre, the moment of greatest vulnerability. Speed was reduced as pilots became preoccupied with reseating diving brakes, dealing with radiator shutters, bomb release switches and adjusting airscrew and elevator trim. Pilots had also to watch for the leader so they all emerged from the flak zone heading in the same direction so as to tighten formation and augment their rear machine gun defence. 'No easy job when you've got three English fighters sitting on your tail,' recalled one pilot. This was the optimum moment for British fighters to attack, and they knew it. 'English fighters behind us!' was sufficient call for pilots to pull their machines into a tight turn:

They had appeared out of nowhere from a cloud and had already turned my starboard wing into a sieve. '*Ei, Donnerwetter*, [literally thunder and lightning]' I thought, 'three fighters, that makes 24 machine guns – and all shooting at me.'[26]

With his rear gunner wounded the pilot had to crash-land inland, after spotting marker panels that German infantry had laid out in a large field. The aircraft landed heavily, with its tyres shot to pieces, and flipped over on its back.

Dinort had seen the flashing circling dots of their escort fighters dogfighting the enemy, but a number of Spitfires had broken through in search of more vulnerable quarry. Ironically, he was obliged to replicate the destroyer's antics they had all missed below; 'evade, counter-turn, give no time to aim!'[27] An intelligence report from 17 Squadron RAF claimed its 12 Hurricanes clashed with a Stuka formation over Calais, shooting down four, including a Dornier 17 bomber and an HS 126 reconnaissance aircraft, for nil casualties.[28]

General Schaal reset his attack with an H-Hour of 18.30pm, this time reinforced by massive corps artillery assets. Nicholson's shrunken perimeter was to be ground down as Guderian had advised with an artillery concentration of 22 x 105mm and 18 x 150mm guns, with a battalion of six 210mm heavy howitzers. The latter aimed to lob its 260lb HE shells onto the citadel. *Artilleriekommandeur 101, Generalmajor* Berlin prepared the detailed firing plan. After a 70-minute artillery barrage the infantry would attack. *Oberst* Fischer's 86th Regiment, reinforced by a company of assault pioneers from the 43rd Battalion, would assault from the west against the citadel and Fort Risban. Menny's 69th Regiment would storm the canal bridges, coming in from the south, and force an entry into the old town and harbour area, while the motorcycle infantry and armoured cars of *Aufklärungs Abteilung* 90 would shoot them in from the east.

'Shell after shell roars out of the German barrels towards the bunkers and heavy fortifications,' observed Herbert Borchert overlooking the canal bridges. It started at 6.30pm: 'A surprising hurricane of fire, hit after hit crashes high over the citadel and Fort Risban at the mouth of the harbour.'[29]

Fountains of earth and flying masonry shot up amid huge smoke puffs that lazily rose with the dust into the air. 'My God this is it,' recalled Second Lieutenant Philip Pardoe with the King's Royal Rifles as a shell screeched in and landed barely feet away. 'I was completely covered in sand, absolutely winded, thinking my last hour had come.'

One of his soldiers started to crack up under the shelling, shouting out 'we can't hold out under this much longer'. 'I remember the sergeant dealing with him very peremptorily,' Pardoe remembered.[30]

On the town hall and opera house, 'the officers look to their watches,' Borchert recalled, 'ten minutes, five, now the firing stops! The sudden silence is very impressive.' Then disturbing news: the heavy corps artillery had dropped short, on top of Menny's men poised to assault from the south. His second battalion of the 69th had suffered casualties and the attack had descended into confusion. Units dodging unexpected incoming friendly rounds had split in all directions to seek cover, and became mixed up with those coming forward. They needed to regroup. The ensuing silence was soon punctuated by a steady rise in the volume of stuttering Bren gun and British rifle fire. 'There is only a slow advance,' Borchert observed. 'The adversary defends himself with the courage of despair. From all sides German storm troops were fiercely fired upon. But they advance.'[31]

There was bitter fighting for the three bridges spanning the canal, barricaded by the British to block entry into the old town and harbour area. The 3rd Company of 49th Panzer Pioneer Battalion brought up three Mark I Panzer 'destroyer' tanks to plant heavy demolition charges at the bridge barricades. Rifleman Lance Corporal Doe saw:

> The infantry was bunched up behind the tanks. Following behind in bunches using the shelter of the tank. And once these tanks started blasting [with 20mm cannon], there was little you could do. You couldn't stop a tank with a rifle bullet.[32]

A Boys anti-tank rifle [14.5mm] was brought forward and Doe fired it for the first time. 'It was a terrifying weapon,' he explained. 'To even fire it, you had to hang on to it like grim death, because it would dislocate your shoulder if you didn't.' He fired at one of the tanks coming over the bridge: 'I couldn't miss – it hit the tank – and knocked the paintwork off', totally ineffective. The strike 'just bounced off, making a noise like a ping-pong ball'. Major Puffin Owen and several men were killed in the attack on the barricades. One of the panzers struck a mine and the assault faltered until, under cover of a mortar barrage, another of the engineer panzers levered aside the vehicles making up the roadblock. In the ensuing British counter-attack, the panzer trundled back, but some of the 69th's infantry managed to occupy some houses on the British side of the canal near the citadel. By 8.40pm Menny reported his 1st Battalion had created a small inroad into the east side of Nicholson's inner perimeter, and the 2nd Battalion was still attempting to re-assemble after the disastrous friendly fire incident. All three of his engineer tanks had been knocked out.

Fischer's battle group coming from Menny's left was still immobile, having hardly advanced beyond their jump-off positions, pinned down by heavy machine-gun fire coming from the apertures in the citadel walls. These could only be subdued by manhandling the 37mm anti-tank guns forward to blast them into submission. Bugler Edward Watson with the Queen Victoria's Rifles was a crack shot, but not a sniper. He observed a party of Germans behind one of these guns at an angle, about 100 yards away. 'This is your job,' his officer had directed, well aware of his marksmanship skills. 'There mustn't be any missing, because if you miss, they'll know where the shots are coming from.' Watson accepted there was little choice; 'you must kill!' his commander insisted:

> It was a bit frightening at first, but after a while, it felt quite fun, just to kill them. I vividly remember the look on the faces of the people you hadn't killed, who couldn't work out where the firing was coming from. After four or five of them were dead, they pulled the anti-tank gun away and went back round the corner.[33]

By dusk the attack was losing momentum; the artillery was short of ammunition so Schaal called a pause at 9.45pm. 'There was deep disappointment at the failure of the evening attack,' according to the division log. Complications piled up. The Stuka attack planned against the citadel for the next day could not be switched to the old town for the 69th Regiment to get across the canal. *Luftwaffe* planning staffs required 24 hours' lead time to change a mission objective. Schaal, in discussion with Guderian's Chief of Staff Nehring, was given the option of delaying by one day. This prompted debate among his subordinate commanders, who felt the men 'were spent and finished', not what the division commander wanted to hear. He was determined the enemy 'should not be given a moment's rest,' and pressure must be maintained. The attack would go in the following day with an H-Hour at 10am, as the last Stuka bomb hit the citadel.[34]

On the morning of 26 May key commanders assembled at the fourth floor of the Calais Opera House, on the Boulevard Leon Gambetta. It provided excellent observation, completely overlooking Nicholson's perimeter. They gathered amid an air of tense expectancy. At Saint-Pol airfield Messerschmitt fighter pilot *Leutnant* von Kageneck with *Jägergeschwader* 1 recalled, 'we were waiting ready strapped into our cockpits as the bomb-laden Stukas crossed over'. Three fighter *Gruppen* were to escort the Stuka fly-in, because 'after yesterday's unpleasant experience with the Spitfires, Corps HQ was determined to run no risks'. After forming up they flew on to the target, which 'even without a compass one could not have missed, owing to the column of thick black smoke that showed the way'.[35]

Edwin Dwinger with the 10th Panzer staff watched the approach. He heard the excited warnings, 'The Stukas are coming!' and they all looked up. 'Three *Staffeln* [over 30 aircraft] according to hearsay, like a flight school.' 'It was a most dramatic thing to watch,' Second Lieutenant Philip Pardoe agreed:

I remember a drone in the distance, getting louder, and out of the sky in perfect 'V' formation, came these planes towards us. One by one, these Stukas peeled off, and dived vertically towards their targets. It was an absolutely breath-taking sight.[36]

Oberst Fischer, looking on from the Opera House balcony, remembered:

with deafening crashes, bomb after bomb does destructive work... Red flames flicker in various places, thick smoke and sand clouds rise skywards, and large chunks of masonry spin through the air. The effect is overwhelming.[37]

Dwinger watched as 'huge clouds of smoke rise skyward, and then the muffled clap of thunder passed over us'. Some Stukas dived so steeply they appeared to disappear into the smoke spurting up from the bombs of their predecessors.

British fighters appeared on the scene again and dogfights developed at high altitude, unseen from the ground apart from wispy trails of vapour. Dwinger saw at least one Spitfire shot down when some of the weaving dodging aircraft came down to low level. When

Stukageschwader 2 appeared to conduct the second wave of the attack, the dust and smoke pall hanging over the citadel and harbour was such they could hardly distinguish the target area. Nevertheless, they tipped over and dived, adding their bombs to the seething cauldron viewed from the air.[38]

The artillery barrage was under way at 8.30am, followed by 69th Regiment attacking from the south and 86th Regiment to its left out of the west. Phase two of the artillery preparation began working the citadel over from 9.30 to 10.15am. The last Stuka bomb landed 15 minutes later. Direct fire was opened up at the barricades on the canal bridges at point-blank range by 100mm guns firing directly over open sights from the edges of buildings. *Aufklärungs Abteilung* 90 provided intimate fire support from 20mm cannon mounted on armoured cars, shooting in three companies of infantry from the 69th Regiment advancing from the east, to complete the concentric nature of the attack.

Optimism reigned on the Opera House balconies at what looked like a series of successful assaults. But as *Oberst* Fischer recalled, 'we hear increasing machine gun and rifle fire, the enemy had come back to life, and is fighting for his very existence'. They watched as the preliminary penetration of the citadel by 86th Regiment was 'pushed back by a British counter-attack almost to their starting point'.[39] The street network of the old town channelled German probes into British killing areas, wrecking the symmetry of the advance. The built-up area of the old town was shaped like a five-cornered island, separated from the mainland by canals to the south and west, with harbour basins to the south and south-east, and by the large Basin de Chasses outer harbour to the north. The Germans attacked from the modern outer periphery estates into a confusing network of enclosed streets and waterways. These watercourses, bordered by buildings, were bitterly defended.

'I saw a fellow from the King's Royal Rifles [near the Clock Tower] who had a bloody great hole in his back,' recalled Edward Watson with the Queen Victoria's Rifles, 'probably from a lump of shrapnel'. He received scant sympathy:

This fellow was crying and laying on the floor. There was a Sergeant Major standing over him, shouting at him to get up. I was standing there aghast. I'd never seen anything like this before, and much to my amazement, the fellow did get up, and was able to walk.

I thought this Sergeant Major was a rotten sod – but he really made the fellow move![40]

Fischer was monitoring the attempts to breach the barricades blocking the three canal bridges into the old town. 'Almost all the enemy's machine guns are back in operation' like phoenixes rising from the ashes. 'Courageous and determined officers, NCOs and men trying to cross are shot up,' he recalled. Slow-firing stuttering Bren guns were clearly distinguishable. Eventually they were drowned out by the ripping-canvas sounding bursts of rapid firing Spandaus and the steady *thump-thump-thump* of 20mm cannon, engaging muzzle flash at aperture slits on the citadel walls and ramparts. Nicholson's men were running desperately short of ammunition.[41]

German infantry began to clamber across the barricades. Rifleman Eric Chambers with D Company of the 2nd Rifles saw the spot where his captain, Bower, had been killed at the Pont Freycinet. Suddenly his Bren opened up again beneath the wrecked barricade truck where he lay. It swept away several Germans. It seems Bower's finger had tightened on the trigger with the onset of rigor mortis.[42]

Brigadier Claude Nicholson demonstrated remarkable psychological and physical resilience during this fight. He had fought a good battle despite competing distractions of 'mission creep' imposed on him by the War Office and Lord Gort's BEF Headquarters that had stretched and reduced his force. Despite being outgunned, he had succeeded in keeping the port open, reassured that an 'evacuation' for his men 'had been decided in principle'. This changed on the second day of the fight when French General Fagalde at Dunkirk insisted the Calais garrison should hold fast. There would be no dashing rearguard extraction by the Royal Navy, which had so upset the French at Boulogne. Nicholson's dispositions for a fighting evacuation had then to transition to a Last Stand. The War Office insensitively directed 'you must comply for the sake of Allied solidarity' despite the 'harbour being at present of no importance to the BEF'. Churchill, incensed by the tone of 'this very lukewarm telegram', wrote to General Ironside, the CIGS. 'This is no way to encourage men to fight to the end,' he admonished, suggesting, 'Are you sure there is no streak of defeatism on the General Staff?'[43]

Fischer was correct to assume he was up against the courage of despair. Nicholson's promising career would now be at an end, with only the prospect of death or humiliation as a senior prisoner. He would now have to watch the rapid promotion of his contemporaries that would come with an expanded wartime army. At 2pm the day before, Secretary of State Eden wrote a more inspiring telegram at Churchill's urging: 'The eyes of the empire are upon the defence of Calais and His Majesty's government are confident you and your gallant regiment will perform an exploit worthy of the British name.'

Churchill was nauseated by the imperative to sacrifice Calais. Anglo-French solidarity was going to be vital for the forthcoming evacuation from Dunkirk. Nicholson remained in ignorance, because the signal explaining the link, 'that every hour you continue to exist is of the greatest help to the BEF', was dispatched only that evening and never received.[44]

By midday, *Oberst* Fischer on the fourth floor of the Opera House remembered, 'the mood in our command post is really depressed'. The final assault was not going to plan, there were even British counter-attacks and the division log reported 'lots of shooting from the roof tops into the rear of our advancing troops'. The situation, looking at the seething cauldron of burning buildings before them, tracers ricocheting skyward and smoke obscuring everything, was unclear. 'It soon transpires that casualties are low,' Fischer recalled, 'but that the failure of the attack has had an unnerving effect.' Then in the midst of this crisis of a faltering attack *General* Guderian, the corps commander, chose to make an unexpected appearance at the division command post. *General* Schaal found himself in the crosshair of his often pleasant but uncompromising senior commander.[45]

Guderian's XIX Panzer Corps had effectively run out of infantry. His 2nd Panzer Division was regrouping and licking its wounds after an unexpectedly hard fight at Boulogne, while the 1st Panzer Division was stalled in front of Dunkirk for lack of infantry. Guderian's infantry reserve, the *Grossdeutschland* Regiment, like 1st Panzer, was fully committed across an over-extended front, unable to penetrate the canal girdle to the west and south-west of Dunkirk. There was no infantry reserve available for Schaal. Guderian was concerned about his casualties. Schaal's two regiments were essentially fought out, and the extent of their losses not yet known. Casualties at the sharp end of conflict, at the emotive point of loss, are often over-reported by harassed staffs. Many were in fact missing, caught up somewhere amid the constant rolling skirmishes around buildings and docks that characterized this street fighting. Even Nicholson's situation report dispatched home at 8am that morning had commented that the 'enemy are definitely weary'.

Because of the 24-hour lead time required for *Luftwaffe* support, Guderian, well aware the 10th Division's attack was stalling, asked Schaal if he would still need air support the next day. Schaal had already been asked by Corps HQ if he was able to take Calais that day, otherwise he was told the attack would be postponed and final British resistance subdued by the *Luftwaffe*. Schaal responded he could do it, but, just as Guderian appeared, this appeared not to be the case. Guderian wanted the Calais operation settled; it was taking too long. His instinctive opinion was it ought to be settled by artillery and dive-bomber attacks. Cut-off time for additional *Luftwaffe* support was 3pm that afternoon. Schaal had either to complete the operation or hand it over to the air force. Two hours remained to force a decision. Schaal was not about to hand over Calais victory laurels to the *Luftwaffe* after all the blood he had expended, with a Knight's Cross still hanging tantalizingly from the city gate. The British were most certainly running out of ammunition and space.

After a brief pause, the attacks were renewed at 2.15pm. White flares shot up among the buildings to mark the progress of the advance to artillery observers. Men from the 7th Company, 86th Regiment loaded dinghies aboard an armoured half-track to rush the bridge leading to the south gate of the citadel. Four men were picked off in the open fighting compartments during the desperate drive. There was another check when the assault pioneer *Leutnant* claimed he had only eight men left, and needed an armoured vehicle to gain access to the gate to blow it. *Oberleutnant* Botho König remembered his men were pinned down by 'a hurricane of fire' that spewed out from the citadel. 'It was impossible to go one step forward or go back,' he recalled. 'With wheezing lungs' after short sharp dashes between cover, 'we lay in a small ditch' in the afternoon summer heat, 'pressed up against the hot sand like glue, with our faces running with sweat'.[46]

The 7th Company motorcycle troops stormed Bastion 11 nearby, 'destroying' the four machine guns blocking the entrance to the citadel southern gate, 'thereby creating a little air for our attacking comrades':

> The intensity of the bitter fighting was such, that no prisoners were taken. The French shot back at point-blank range – luckily very badly in their fear. It was a fierce long fight, until mortars, Schmeisser

machine pistols and hand grenades finally broke resistance. The first prisoners cried out in fright and could not be coaxed from their trenches. Those trying to escape – so they said – were shot at from behind, so despite doubts, they fought on.[47]

Fischer remembered the attack on the bastion was a turning point. Three hundred men were captured, weakening resistance at the citadel. 'Englishmen escaping to the harbour area,' he recalled, 'were shot to pieces.'[48] The 7th Company after-action report noted the reduction in enemy fire, as 'we penetrated the citadel from two sides and split up inside'. British Lieutenant Austin Evitts's signallers with brigade HQ were pulled out and made their way out of the Boulogne gate in single file, hands on heads. He was accosted by a *Feldwebel* leading a group of German soldiers:

The *Feldwebel* carried a revolver in his hands and a few grenades in his jack boots ... and he looked at me with a face full of scorn and hatred as if he would rather put a bullet through me than look at me.[49]

Casualties had been heavy.

At the 10th Panzer Division command post the atmosphere changed from high tension mixed with hope, to doubts, then confidence, and then again extreme concern. Good news finally emerged. Three companies from Menny's 69th Regiment advancing from the east had linked up at the lock in the north of the old town, moving beyond the cellulose factory to the *Gare maritime*. With penetrations in and around the citadel, the two *Kampfgruppen* were closing the pincer about the old city. *General* Schaal felt able to report to Guderian at 2.30pm that fragmentary reports suggested the attack was making good progress. He requested his division be allowed to remain in place and finish the job, which might take two hours. A large-scale Stuka raid would not be required. Guderian agreed and returned to corps headquarters. By 5.30pm Fischer observed they had the old town, the citadel and the entrances to the port, recalling, 'a jubilant mood prevails in the command posts at the Opera house'.[50]

Defeat for Nicholson's men was bitter. 'We felt that this was defeat with a capital 'D' to no purpose,' Philip Pardoe with the 2nd Rifles recalled. Edward Doe was taken in a shed nearby. 'Somebody called out "Come out! You haven't got a chance! If you're not out in within five minutes, we'll blow you to pieces!"' Edward Watson heard: 'Yelling outside the house, and they threw some hand grenades in. They were shouting, "Tommy for you the war is over!" They must have been taught to say this.'[51]

Sam Kydd's group of men with the 1st Queen Victoria's Rifles was surrounded by 30 to 40 Germans: 'They were bellowing and motioning with their machine guns and the awful thing was you didn't understand a word they were saying and they in turn took it for dumb insolence.'[52]

The Germans took 20,000 prisoners, 3,500 of them British. Four quality British infantry battalions had been overrun. The true extent of British casualties was never recorded; possibly 400 dead while 200 wounded were evacuated before the fall alone. The Germans recovered about 500 wounded, so about 2,400 able-bodied or slightly wounded men were taken prisoner.[53]

Edward Dwinger walked the ruined barricades and streets near the harbour soon after the surrender: 'Some houses fiercely burned radiating an unbearable heat, streets were covered in a grey smoke haze, and every face abruptly turned as a burning building collapsed in on itself.'[54]

The Mole was covered with British bodies, cut down as they had attempted to flee. *Oberleutnant* König with 7th Panzer Regiment checked over booty, vehicles and bodies at the Mole. 'Black clouds of smoke from the burning oil tanks hung over Calais,' he recalled. His men tried to 'get a lovely two-seater Austin into gear'. Dead were sprawled among discarded weapons and vehicles; 'one of them was only a head connected to a chest'. He was fascinated by the head, which appeared unmarked with 'wide open eyes looking questionably into the distance'.

German casualties were also high. König remembered the welcome arrival of the *Spiess* (the colloquial term for the rank of sergeant major), shortly after the citadel was taken, with extra meat rations. They licked their wounds and contemplated the campaign odyssey thus far:

> About the Stonne [river], the endless drive through the flat approaches to the Pas-de-Calais, and then three days street fighting. Three long days that had torn several holes through the ranks of their platoons. Squad leader Milddieb was not there, and Holsteiner, slow talking, but always there – and others.

Sleep with food and a break came easily. That night 12 British Lysander light aircraft flew over dropping bombs attached to parachutes, which caused some alarm and a fusillade of light flak and tracer. One of them crashed, leaving star-shaped wreckage on the low embankment leading to Fort Risban at the harbour mouth. Three were shot down in all. The soldiers were intrigued to discover the 'bombs' were food and ammunition containers.[55]

Brigadier Claude Nicholson, captured in the citadel, was taken before *Oberst* Fischer, now appointed *Stadtkommandant* (Town Commander) of Calais, who remembered: 'Blackened by smoke and dust, we could still see the exertions and trials of the past days and nights in his face.'

He would only give his name, rank and number. A senior French officer captured with him, according to the division log, had only fought-out units under command, and preferred not to fight. He claimed the British had confined them to houses and cellars. Fischer further recalled:

> Despite his exhaustion, [Nicholson] asked if he had caused me any sleepless nights in Calais. I merely replied that his appearance suggested his time in Calais had been something less than comfortable and that the days and nights to come would surely be more comfortable for me than those which lay ahead for him. I then wished him a pleasant trip to Germany.[56]

Fischer was correct. Nicholson was wracked with guilt for an operation he considered a failure. In June 1943, suffering from depression, he threw himself from an upper floor window in the German city of Rothenburg an der Fulda.

He was never made aware of the impact his last stand at Calais had had on the subsequent fighting around Dunkirk. This has been debated ever since. Guderian's XIX Panzer Corps raids and attempted *coup d'états* against all the Channel ports had failed, including the 1st Panzer Division's attack off the line of march against Dunkirk on 24 May. The panzers got into trouble at both Boulogne and Calais and were withdrawn at the insistence of OKH on 25 May. The difference in panzer crew casualties between 2nd Panzer's three-day battle for Boulogne and the 10th's against Calais were stark. Schaal's tanks were committed for one day only, and only one regiment, the 7th, which lost 18 men. Both the 2nd's regiments were committed and lost a total of 79 panzer crewmen. On average one or two crewmen were killed or wounded for every tank knocked out in combat. This meant theoretically the 2nd

Division could have lost 30 armoured vehicles in Boulogne, whereas 10th Panzer lost perhaps nine or so. Many of the damaged tanks would have been repairable if they were not burned out, a possible restoration of as many as 50% to 60% of the number.[57]

Heavy infantry casualties incurred by Guderian's mobile formations was probably the main lesson derived from fighting in the built-up areas in Boulogne and Calais. The two motorized infantry regiments belonging to 10th Panzer took no further part in the fighting in northern France. The delaying actions at Boulogne and Calais removed two panzer divisions from the German order of battle that might otherwise have been available for operations against the port of Dunkirk. The checks imposed by the enemy in the streets and docklands of the Channel ports suggested tanks were not the best means to occupy them, as recognized by the OKH decision to pull them back. More infantry would be needed for Dunkirk, and these divisions were still attempting to close up, with the panzers halted along the canal lines around Dunkirk.

Oberst Fischer met with the restored mayor of Calais and his 25 senators that night, in the badly damaged city. He called upon the population to remain calm, not to seek to harass German troops, and to go about their normal business. Shop owners who had not fled were allowed to reopen for business at 12 o'clock the next day. There was relief on all sides that the fighting was over. Even as these discussions drew to a close, the last 47 British soldiers who had hidden beneath the slimy green piers of the outermost northern breakwater were taken off by a small Royal Navy yacht. They had kept above water at high tide. Another landing party went back to seek more, but was challenged by a German sentry and met with machine gun fire.

Victory for the Germans was complete. 'Calais had once been a lovely city,' recalled panzer soldier Otto W., 'but our Stukas have been hard at work.' It still burned:

The Tommies have fled Calais, seeking safety in England, but their fate was settled en route. Not many got back because our flyers had a conversation with them on the high seas. I saw how our bombers bombarded three English ships, marvellous to see.

He was writing home on captured British stationery, part of his loot. The panzers were being refitted, 'likely the calm before the storm', he wrote, but 'which direction we will then strike, is not yet known'. They were buoyant about the outcome; 'the war will be over soon,' he insisted, 'no way it was going to last four years'.[58]

Botho König remembered one of the infantry platoons swimming in the Channel after the operation:

In an instant the war was forgotten. Thoughts dwelt on home; everything was still and wonderfully calm, sun, warm sand and the endless expanse of the sea. Only when they put uniforms back on was the dreamlike world of peace pushed aside; reality again intruded on the mind. In the haze across the Channel England's steep coastline was just visible.

At dusk on the day after the capture of Calais, the 105th Artillery Regiment with the 10th Panzer Division, newly deployed for coastal defence, reported a large number of enemy ships offshore. The guns opened fire at 8.10pm on warships and transports out to 15,000 metres at sea, claiming some hits. The convoys, however, continued on, heading for Dunkirk.[59]

'PAUSE'

There was no pause for the BEF when the German panzers halted along the canal line. The attacks by Army Group B in Belgium snapped aggressively at the heels of the retreating British. 'My overriding impression at this time was one of great tiredness,' remembered infantry captain Gilbert White with the British 4th Division. His battalion with the East Surrey Regiment 'would fight all day and then perhaps for two days on end, patrol at night and then withdraw by motor transport at night. It was an exceedingly exhausting business'.[60]

The BEF had started the campaign moving 65 miles forward to the Dyle river line east of Brussels. Its 3rd Division fought three days in this position, then fell back to the River Dendre. After 24 hours it withdrew to the River Escaut, where it was attacked again, holding for three days. Bill Stanton, a machine gunner with the 5th Gloucesters defending the line of the Escaut, recalled the perfect view of the enemy approach:

And I could see them dragging things down to the river edge, and I could see it was rubber boats. If you're fighting a war you wait for the best chance, which I did. I waited until they were in the centre of the river, and that was it. I can see them now jumping out of the boats, the bullets splashing in the water. Then you could see people jumping up in the boats their arms in the air and the equipment going over board, and men jumping or falling into the water. At the time I was really in the glory of doing it, because that was my job. Dicky Bird was shouting *Keep it going!* He was bloody patting me on the back all the time, and he was really feeling good, I was too.[61]

These instances of euphoria were fleeting. The retreat continued to the Gort Line and held for five days. Bill Weeks, a Coldstream Guardsman with the 1st Division, described the typical experience of fight and fall back:

And the stuff started flying about, you sort of laid down – move out, dig in – move out – until you get up into the action yourself. Get close to them and try to take the high ground. Take the high ground? You couldn't even get up! Not only were you crying, you were probably sick as well, and you had probably messed yourself as well with the sheer fright! You can't explain it really – you're petrified. Bang! Crash! This stuff whistling about all around you, and you're thinking 'What's going on here?' Someone shouts *lay down! dig in!*[62]

By the time the 3rd Division reached the coast, it had held six defensive positions, was attacked on nine days and spent seven days on the move. Outflanked by the panzers to the south, the BEF had little choice but to continue the retreat. 'It was terrible really', Joe Trinder with the Gloucestershire Regiment recalled, falling back through Belgium with the 48th Division. 'So many times you got ready and keyed up to have a go, and then you would have to retreat, and you hadn't fired a shot.'[63]

By the evening of 25 May, the first day of the Panzer Halt Order, Lord Gort had appreciated the gravity of the threat facing the BEF. On his own responsibility he called off a projected Allied attack to the south, supposed to combine with a projected but over-optimistic French thrust north, as part of the Weygand Plan. Two British divisions, the 5th and 50th, held in reserve for the attack were instead sent north to restore the widening gap opening up between the British and Belgian armies. On 26 May British and French forces east of Lille started to withdraw to the coast. *General* Hermann Geyer commanding the German IX Army Corps caustically wrote in his log 'that the English, despite the energetic holding of the Dyle, Schelde, Lys and Yser by the Belgians were thinking only of disembarking', he recalled, 'we only later were astonished to find out'.[64]

As the Allies retired the boot-shape outline of the pocket changed to that of a deflating sack, as the race to the coast began. The momentary respite granted by the panzer halt enabled the 2nd Division and widely dispersed 44th and 48th Divisions with ad hoc units like Woodforce, Macforce and Usherforce to shore up the shrinking west side of the pocket. The other east side was covered by the British regular divisions. Inside the sack, the mass of the BEF ran the gauntlet between advancing Germans to the coast. The 48th Division set up a series of village strongpoints screened by canals at Socx, Wormhoudt, Cassel and Hazebrouck. Only slowly did the realization dawn that the panzers had paused in the south. The 48th was a TA division, occupying six defensive positions in all, being attacked on four days. It spent nine days marching and counter-marching to hold the line before disembarkation. Royal Artillery gunner James Bradley recalled:

> There is a time that you do begin to worry a little bit and get a little concerned, because they are saying 'you're in a position here or dug in there, and this is *really* the place to be'. Then the next thing is we're all hooking up the guns and we are pulling back again. We're pulling back again and you were really getting a bit of a downhill feeling, weren't you.[65]

French Captain Marc Bloch retreating to Dunkirk with part of the First French Army's logistics staff felt the planners had 'displayed blindness to the Germans' capacity for speed'. The problem was that 20- to 30-kilometre withdrawals were not far enough, because 'the Germans advanced a great deal faster than they should have done according to the old rules of the game'. The British 42nd TA experience was typical. Badly rattled by its piecemeal deployment on the Escaut, it occupied five defensive positions and was seven days on the move, eventually losing communications. 'And so it went on,' Captain Bloch explained. 'The only hope of re-establishing the general situation lay in our "disengaging", and establishing a new defensive line sufficiently far back to ensure that it would not be overrun before it had been properly organized.'

The BEF was as yet undefeated, but lost cohesion as it was outmanoeuvred from both ends of the line. As Bloch observed, 'small groups of reinforcements were continually dribbled into every breach as it occurred, with the inevitable result they were cut to pieces'. Advanced defensive positions often could not be withdrawn in time; now a general retreat to the coast begun.[66]

This retreat was a nightmare for British soldiers and peppered with indelible images that would remain with them for the rest of their lives. Bill Weeks' friend Ernie Costa 'came from Government's Lane' and was a local, who died in his arms: 'He was smoking when he got hit, and the cigarette was dangling from his lip, and it was burning all his flesh down here [indicating the lower jaw]. It didn't seem to worry him all that much you know.'

Weeks' abiding fear was an anonymous death. 'The only thing that bothered me,' he admitted, 'were bits of flesh, arms and legs that had been hit by shell fire and sort of disintegrated.' 'That's why you wear your dog-tags,' he pointed out. 'Even if you were decapitated, it's still around his neck.' James Bradley suffered similar anguish, holding his friend's face 'thinking he can't be dead', but the blood and gore suggested otherwise:

He's a chappie with whom I laughed and played football with, and now he's lying in a bit of boggy ground. His mother would die of shame if she saw her lovely baby being dropped in like this... If their parents could see them, like that, in a corner of a foreign field. They must never know![67]

Lord Gort had already sent Lieutenant General Sir Ronald Adam, the commander of III Corps, with his staff back to Dunkirk to organize the defence of the perimeter and the evacuation of the BEF. He met with French General Fagalde commanding the town and agreed a plan for the defence of a bridgehead. There were already strong French defences in place. What was left of the 21st French Infantry Division was already deployed behind the line between Gravelines, Watten and Cassel. General Beaufrère's 68th Division was reinforcing and entrenching along a secondary line of canals connecting Mardyck, Spycker and Bergues, with strong artillery support. With Fagalde already holding the west side of the perimeter it made sense to deploy arriving French troops into that area.

Adam established a British perimeter to the east, with II Corps covering two canals forming the corner at Nieuport extending almost to Furnes. I Corps would hold the centre around Furnes with III Corps filling in between there and Bergues. The planned area was 30 miles wide and up to 7 deep. The Belgian Army position was considered too 'obscure' to be included. The line maximized the terrain features governing the layout, a succession of concentric canal lines, virtual moats, around Dunkirk. The surrounding countryside was flat and low lying, crisscrossed by a herringbone pattern of ditches and waterways. The sea dykes were opened and the land behind the canal line began to flood. It was not good going for tanks.

Sid Crockitt, a Royal Engineer sapper, remembered receiving the word they were to head for the coast and home:

> The OC [Officer Commanding] now came and told us that we were going to retreat, and we are going to retreat to Dunkirk. You will live off the land, you won't get any food from the army now, you have to live on what you can find. It's every man for himself.

The BEF had to run a closing gauntlet, between the threat of collapse by the teetering Belgian Army to the north, fierce attacks by the pursuing German infantry divisions of Army Group B at its eastern rear, and a possible panzer advance by Army Group A coming up from the south. 'You couldn't put a pin-prick between the soldiers on the road,' remembered Sid Crockitt, withdrawing in the middle of this mass exodus. 'There were thousands – and all making for one place – Dunkirk.'[68]

On 25 May, *Luftwaffe* reconnaissance aircraft flying the Channel ports line between Zeebrugge in Belgium and Calais reported minimal ship traffic. No ships were spotted at Le Treport and Dieppe with maybe two dozen cargo ships loading and off-loading at Le Havre. The 'exception' was Dunkirk, with 14 ships in the harbour and six more standing offshore. Earlier *Luftwaffe* intelligence reports on 21 May had given fragmentary indications of many ships leaving and entering Boulogne and Dunkirk. *Oberst* Liss, assessing enemy intentions at OKH, claimed in hindsight that the intelligence officer Intelligence Section had been giving indications since this date that a sea evacuation was a possibility. Halting the panzers was ignoring the huge opportunity the 'critical situation of the enemy' invited. Prisoner of war reports suggested the process had already started on 23 May. 'It was not their [the intelligence staff's] responsibility,' Liss insisted, absolving himself of any responsibility, 'to direct troops on the basis of their conclusions.'

All this changed, Liss suggested, on 26 May – the second day of the Halt Order – 'in particular in terms of the enemy picture, one of the most dramatic days of the campaign'. *Luftwaffe* over-flights reported 'forty to sixty ships gathering off Dover and Ramsgate, of which one-third are warships (cruisers and destroyers)'. The shipping picture had drastically changed: 'twelve ships heading for Dunkirk and eighteen transports sighted going for Calais'. Air reports also picked up 'a succession of enemy march columns throughout the entire day, troops and all types of weapons, were sighted heading in a northerly direction'. 'So that strong enemy withdrawals from the surrounded pocket towards the coast can be confirmed.' Liss saw the evening *Luftwaffe* report which advised, 'it appears that at Dunkirk only troops without weapons and equipment are being shipped out'.[69]

Since 16 May Dunkirk had experienced three *Gruppen*-size air attacks. On 25 May, following Göring's assurance to Hitler that the *Luftwaffe* would settle the British in the pocket, raids perceptibly increased. Two days later, the first day of Operation *Dynamo*, it looked as though British hopes might well be dashed. Raids on 27 May exceeded the worst expectations. Ulrich Steinhilper, a fighter pilot with *Jagdgeschwader* 52, remembered 'the Dunkirk-Calais area was easy to spot as we flew in from our forward base, because the whole area is shrouded in smoke and fog'. At first light Heinkel III twin-engine bombers from *Kampfgeschwader* (KG) 1 and 4 unloaded over the port and town. Streams of bombers never let up; KG 54 hit docks and ships alongside the East Mole, breaking apart the 8,000-ton French freighter *Aden*. Raids were conducted by *Luftflotte* 2 based in Western Germany and Holland as well as *Dorniers* from KG 2 and 3, flown from the Rhine-Main region. They homed in on black smoke mushrooming up from burning oil tanks at Saint-Pol-sur-Mer in raids that lasted from dawn to dusk. Steinhilper had sufficient fuel for only 15 minutes over target, because flight times from their distant bases were between 65 and 75 minutes each way. 'We had been briefed about the quality of the British pilots and their aircraft, and expected a hard fight':

Indeed, when we first saw the Hurricanes and Spitfires attacking our Stukas it was immediately clear that we were up against very tenacious opposition. Equally clear now was the vulnerability of the Stuka when met by experienced and determined pilots. Inland from Dunkirk and offshore the RAF was exacting a very high price from our dive-bombers.[70]

The lightly armed Dornier 17 bombers with KG 2 suffered heavily. Major Werner Kreipe with *Staffel* 3 remembered how 'enemy fighters pounced on our tightly knit formations with the fury of maniacs'. Flying wing tip to wing tip to maximize the screen of defensive fire from their radio operator's MG 15s, they were outgunned by the eight.303 Brownings of the swooping Spitfires. Radios crackled with anguished calls from rear stragglers: 'badly shot up … must break formation … am trying forced landing'. The II *Fliegerkorps'* war diary described 27 May as 'a bad day', 'with 64 aircrew missing, seven wounded, and 23 aircraft gone, today's losses exceed the combined total of the last 10 days'.[71]

Damage below was fearful. Bombing went on from 8.30am to 7.30pm with as many as 300 aircraft counted above the skies at the height of the storm. Some 15,000 high explosive bombs and 30,000 incendiaries rained down. The fire bombs were light, about a kilogram in weight, but sufficient to penetrate house rooftops. People sheltering in cellars below did not often hear their impacts amid the din of the bombing and discovered the house was ablaze before they knew it. It is likely more than 1,000 of the eventual 3,000 civilians were killed that day; coffins ran out and mass graves were employed. Fire brigades short of equipment could not tackle the blazes, water mains had burst and water had to be pumped from the harbour basins and canals. Scores of public buildings were hit by bombs and entire streets in the centre and close to the port were completely collapsed. The Hotel de Ville town hall burned from 11.00 in the morning until 8pm that night. On the Place du Minck near the port, a number of injured left behind in abandoned ambulances burned alive. Around 1,500 civilians sheltering beneath the burning town hall survived the day but 27 sheltering beneath the Lefort Company building perished. The railway station was soon ablaze and 1,600 of a total 5,200 goods wagons in the marshalling yards burnt out.[72]

'By midday the cellar was becoming rather smelly,' recalled artillery Second Lieutenant Anthony Rhodes, 'it held 60 men only with difficulty.' He was part of the rear echelon troops due to be evacuated first. 'Nerves were becoming a little frayed' by 4pm: 'One of the NCOs wearing last-war ribbons was crying quietly in the corner and several men began to make queer little animal noises – rather like homesick dogs.' The incessant raids 'seemed to have a cumulative effect on one's system,' he noticed. Combat stress disorder was starting to manifest itself. 'After a while,' he admitted, 'the mere thought of a raid was worse than its reality.'[73]

Dunkirk harbour consisted of a chain of basins maintained at a navigable level by locks. The main lock gate had been knocked out of action by bombs the previous day, exposing the docks to the rise and fall of a 16-foot tide. The outer harbour appeared blocked with wrecks when Captain William Tennant RN, the senior Naval Officer Dunkirk, arrived to manage this first day of the evacuation. 'The town was heavily on fire,' he recalled, 'the streets being littered with wreckage of all kinds, and every window was smashed.' Dive-bombers pounced upon any ship trying to enter the harbour. Even the route to the port through town appeared unusable. Streets were blocked with rubble, framed with licking fires, and crammed with leaderless men, the stragglers and headquarters personnel not belonging to fighting units. 'Great palls of smoke from the oil depots and refineries enveloped the docks and town itself.'[74]

This was day one of Operation *Dynamo* and the evacuation seemed not to be working well. Up to 28,000 troops were lifted before *Dynamo* started, so-called rear echelon 'useless mouths', no longer with a role. Tennant believed only 6,000 were embarked and cleared that night in the dark. In fact the total was 7,669, with most from the beaches. The rate of disembarkation was less than before the formal evacuation process started. Tennant sent a signal to Vice Admiral Dover at 8.05pm: 'Port continually bombed all day and on fire. Embarkation possible only from beaches east of harbour. Send all ships there.'

Feldmarshal Hermann Göring felt his *Luftwaffe* was in the ascendant. He was relatively unconcerned about the observed rise in boat activity, humorously assuring Hitler: 'Only fishing boats can get over now. Let's hope the Tommies are good swimmers.'[75]

Chapter 6

Running the Gauntlet

THE PANZERS ROLL AGAIN — SOUTH SIDE

Von Rundstedt was aggrieved that OKH had sought to remove his panzers. Despite the operational imperative to release them and the mobile troops, he stuck to the Halt Order far too long. It was a matter of principle. As a consequence German attacks made little material progress. The north wing of Army Group A was attempting to overcome an organized and intact enemy, while the right wing of Fourth Army was still east of Arras. Army Group A was marking time in an area from which the rear of the enemy could be attacked with considerable effect. Von Brauchitsch, whose authority had been emasculated by the *Führer*, was on edge at the lack of progress. Von Rundstedt, similarly, began to have misgivings and went forward to consult with Hoth and von Kleist's *Panzergruppen* to see the situation for himself and perhaps reconsider. He 'apparently could not stand it any longer', Halder, the OKH Chief of Staff commented, clearly getting nervous. Both von Kleist and Hoth vociferously argued to be let off the leash. Six transports loaded with evacuated troops had been spotted leaving Dunkirk. *General* Anton Brennecke, the Fourth Army Chief of Staff, described what could be seen in the port: 'Large ships are being made fast to the quayside, planks are laid across and men swarm aboard. All material and equipment is being abandoned.'

He dryly suggested to *General* Blumentritt, von Rundstedt's senior operations officer, that he did not wish to meet these men again in the future, rested and re-equipped. At least, he advocated, everything possible should be done to prevent or at least hamper the evacuation;

even flat trajectory fire. Army Group A recommended the re-engagement of the panzer and mobile forces along the line from Béthune, St Omer to Gravelines. Hitler was unofficially informed and gave the go-ahead.

Von Brauchitsch received the assent around noon on the 26th and was summoned up the footpath to the *Felsennest* to meet with Hitler at 1.30pm. He 'returns beaming at 14.30', Halder observed in his diary. 'The left wing is authorized to move to within artillery firing range of Dunkirk in order to cut off, from the land side, the continual flow of transport (evacuations and arrivals).'[1]

Another 16 hours would pass before the mobile units would be in a position to move forward to attack Dunkirk and the Cassel heights. Panzer and motorized units had been resting, reorganizing, and fully engaged with vehicle servicing and repair. The new orders had to be drafted and fresh objectives drawn up before they could move off. Army Group A would push the panzers close enough to Dunkirk to bombard the road and railway points, and prevent shipping taking off troops even under cover of darkness. They were then to drive east and complete the encirclement of the port. Infantry forces would be moved up south of the town to block the Bailleul-Cassel-Bergues road with artillery, one of the main withdrawal routes.

Several enemy divisions had by this time gone into position in front of Dunkirk, fleshing out what had previously been a thin screen of companies. The sides of the withdrawing Allied sack had been strengthened, utilizing village strongpoints and concentric canal lines, as the mass of the BEF withdrew. Four British and several French divisions had already escaped a pocket forming around Lille. No effective German attacks were made during the afternoon of the 26th, and a general offensive could not be resumed until 8am on 27 May. Most of the panzer divisions were stationary at the canal line for a total of three days and eight hours. They suspected an immense opportunity had passed them by.

Leutnant Helmut Ritgen with the 6th Panzer Division had spent two days in the beautiful but rather neglected Château Campagne before the attack order for Cassel arrived on 27 May. This was three days after stopping short of the town as a result of the *Führer's* order to pause. He had plenty of time to observe this 'fortress-like terraced hill' which, at 577 feet high, completely dominated the flat surrounding countryside. War correspondent Christoph von Imhoff agreed: 'Cassel was created by nature as a natural fortress. The hill towered above the smooth flat Flanders countryside like a huge volcano, with the town laid on top.'²

Defending it were two infantry battalions from 145 Brigade, belonging to the TA 48th Division. Sitting on top, the men from the 2nd Gloucesters and 4th Battalion Oxfordshire and Buckinghamshire Light Infantry could easily see the Dunkirk coastline on a clear day. 'A blazing Dunkirk was just 10 miles away down a very straight road,' remembered Rowland Young. 'For a week we saw the bombers on their way to the beaches to drop their bombs and witnessed the Stukas dive-bombing our convoys passing northward up that straight road.'³

Clouds of billowing black smoke marked the burning refinery; aircraft, insect-like specks, buzzed over the port and coastline. They had barricaded the narrow streets of Cassel and loopholed its outer walls for artillery and anti-tank guns. Von Imhoff watched as 'our artillery salvoes detonated in the middle of these ramparts'. Fifteen British two-pounders, nine 25mm Hotchkiss anti-tank guns and four artillery 18-pounders were ranged in on five approach routes that met inside the town. Attacking it could replicate the 'Grand Old Duke of York's' folly of the 1790s when his 10,000 men were marched up before 'he marched them down again'. 'We were told that we were going to hold up the German Army as best we could, to the last man and last round,' remembered 2nd Lieutenant Julian Fane with the 2nd Gloucesters. 'I thought "oh dear" I didn't think I was going to be losing so soon in my military career.'⁴

Generalmajor Werner Kempf's 6th Panzer Division advanced on Cassel with about 60% of his original armoured strength. The majority of his tanks were 75 Pz35(t)s, a Czech-made Skoda variant, one ton heavier than the light Panzer II, but with a superior 37mm gun. They were part of the confiscated Czech booty from the 1938 Munich Appeasement Agreement. Kempf attacked at 10am with two panzer heavy *Kampfgruppen*: Koll, coming from Staple on the intervening canal line to the south, and von Esebeck, wheeling in from the west. 'They coated us attackers with a wicked fire,' Ritgen recalled: 'The terraced steep slopes were only negotiable by tanks on the roads, which the British 17-pounders dominated, from hidden positions in the old town wall above.'⁵

Fighting developed into a rolling duel between British anti-tank guns and the 37mm main armament of the Czech 38(t)s. Weaker British

25mm and 2-pounder rounds ricocheted off the 25mm frontal armour of the advancing German tanks until fire was redirected at tank tracks, or once they had passed, to hit less protected flanks and rear. 'We fired, they moved, halted and fired,' Bombardier Harry Munn recalled. After shooting 15 times the exasperated gun loader asked: 'When are you going to hit the bloody thing?' Munn shouted to the gun layer, 'Hit [it] in the tracks Frank!'

> Just as the tank moved we fired, hitting the track propulsion wheels… The tank halted abruptly, swinging to one side. Our next shell must have disabled the turret, as they opened the escape hatch and ran for their lives towards their lines.[6]

Tank after tank slewed off the roads, mortally stricken. 11th Panzer Regiment lost scores of tanks, the British claiming to have disabled 40 vehicles in all. 'Previous experience of the French led the tanks to be committed without adequate infantry support,' Ritgen admitted, 'but this was a different kind of enemy, and heavy losses were suffered.' Kempf paused the division to take stock; Cassel had at least been completely surrounded.[7]

Further south-east in Hoepner's XVI Panzer Corps sector the approaches to the La Bassée Canal were flat and marshy. *SS-Schütze* Herbert Brunnegger with the *Tötenkopf* Division recalled 'we had been told to expect heavy resistance from British elite forces and this proved to be the case'. *SS-Gruppenführer* (Major General) Theodore Eicke had already been thwarted at the canal line by unexpectedly fierce British resistance on the eve of the Halt Order. He had no formal military training, having been a political street activist, and lacked any understanding of complex military manoeuvres. He assumed energy alone was sufficient to meet the challenges posed. A mismanaged former attempted crossing had already cost the *Tötenkopf* 42 killed, 121 wounded and five missing.

The SS in the French campaign were not the vaunted elite they became later in Russia. Eicke's corps commander, *General* Erich Hoepner, harboured serious doubts about the regiment's reliability and competence. Eicke's stated indifference to manpower losses and his insistence that SS men do not retreat, whatever the enemy situation, led Hoepner to publicly reprimand him in front of his staff as 'a butcher'.

Training the fledgling division had posed problems because many of the soldiers had been elderly police reservists with scarcely any military training. This was especially true of the 6,500 concentration camp guards, incorporated when the division assembled at Dachau. These men were ominously menacing, with an indifferent moral compass. Rudolf Höss, commandant at Auschwitz, claimed Eicke instilled into his camp guards 'a hate, an antipathy against the prisoners which was inconceivable to those outside'. The Army and its customs were regarded with contempt. 'The combat training of the NCOs and men is inadequate,' *Generaloberst* von Bock had written following an inspection in April 1940. 'This will cost a lot of blood. It's a great shame, for they are a magnificent body of men!'[8]

Before dawn on 27 May the bulk of the division started to cross the La Bassée Canal. Dug in opposite was the 4th Brigade of the British 2nd Infantry Division. Private Ernie Farrow with the 2nd Norfolk Regiment was told to 'make sure that every round that we fired got a German'. He and his men scrambled up and down the canal bank 'just to try and bluff the Germans that there was a great company of us there'. 'We were being very hard pressed,' he recalled, but the German advance seemed unstoppable. 'They were even driving lorries into the canal and trying to drive their tanks across on these lorries.'[9] Artillery fire kept them momentarily at bay.

By 10am the village of Le Cornet Malo was fought through after heavy fighting. 'The village was burning in several places', *Untersturmführer* (2nd Lieutenant) Emile Stürzbecher, the adjutant of the 1st Battalion 2nd Regiment, recalled, 'and the noise of battle was deafening.'[10] *Scharführer* (Sergeant) August Leitl remembered the defence of various houses held them up for long periods in open countryside. 'We were very exposed, if somebody just lifted his head he was killed,' he recalled. 'The British used snipers very skilfully.'[11] The ferocious British defence brought the inexperienced *Tötenkopf* regiments to a virtual standstill.

Stürzbecher was assisting the medical officer attend a group of 25 British wounded prisoners sitting and lying on the road when he noticed a clearly stressed Fritz Knöchlein, commanding the 3rd Company with 1st Battalion 'came running from the road shouting very loud and very excited'. He roared at the adjutant and MO that 'these prisoners are nothing to do with you – they belong to me!' 'My impression of Knöchlein was that he had gone mad,' remembered Stürzbecher. Knöchlein's parent battalion had been virtually wiped out and the attack was degenerating into a series of vicious small actions. 'Only after some argument, during which he insisted the prisoners were his, did he quieten down.'[12] Signaller Robert Brown with the defending 2nd Norfolks recalled 'we were causing more casualties than they were causing to us, but they must have outnumbered us by about six to one'.[13] Eicke was struggling to gain control of his troops against stiffening and unexpectedly bitter resistance.

'The terrain immediately before Le Paradis,' the next objective, 1½ miles further on, 'was broad and flat,' Herbert Brunnegger recalled, 'which gave the British defenders an excellent field of fire'. Casualties were already high. 'Had our *Kradschützen* [motorcycle troops] not launched such a bold assault, our losses would have been considerably higher.'[14] Experienced leaders were falling right and left and the tactical recklessness that resulted was remorselessly punished by British fire. Unlike the helpless enemy behind the wire, to which the concentration camp guards were accustomed, these shot back with an accurate ferocity that belied their diminishing numbers.

Hearing that the 1st Battalion of his 2nd Regiment had been virtually wiped out, Eicke ordered the 3rd Battalion to come up and complete the assault on Le Paradis. Its commander, *Obersturmbannführer* (Lieutenant Colonel) Hans Götz, came forward to recce the task but was felled by a sniper at the crossroads near the village. In the middle of this crisis, Eicke's division operations officer then collapsed at HQ with a haemorrhaging stomach ulcer. By 4pm, however, the 2nd Norfolks' defence had been beaten down, reduced to about 100 all ranks. Fighting was savage and bitter at the end. Private Ernie Farrow, pinned down unarmed in a water-filled ditch, was traumatized when the man alongside him was 'shot right through the head', sinking back in the water with 'the back of his head missing'. Another of his remaining companions, 'an old soldier' who had served in India and had two gold teeth, was next. 'I felt something hit my face', he recalled, suspecting he had been hit and saw 'they'd shot his [friend's] jaw – and his jaw had smacked me in the face'. He too sank beneath the brackish water and 'the last thing I saw of him was these two gold teeth shining'. Farrow would see them for the rest of his life. An SS soldier jumped into the ditch to finish them off. As the German put his rifle to the shoulder,

'I said my last prayer because I knew I was going to die'. The loud click of a misfire, or no ammunition, suggested there might be a reprieve. But after all the heavy casualties his assailant's blood was up:

He turned his rifle round, got hold of the barrel and as he got close to us he took a swipe at my head. I put my arm up to stop him hitting me and the first blow smashed all my hand up. The next blow came down – I still had the strength to hold my arm up to stop him and he smashed my elbow and put my shoulder out of joint. One more blow and I'd be dead.

More Germans appeared amid much shouting. It was an officer ordering the soldier to desist. 'He ordered them to pull us out.'[15]

SS-Gruppenführer Eicke was not happy; by nightfall he had lost 155 men killed, 483 wounded and 53 missing. Results gained were considered mediocre, set objectives were not reached and his lines of communication remained fragile. It was a setback. Herbert Brunnegger remembered that as they were being regrouped, a large group of prisoners were rounded up and put against a wall at Le Paradis.

Those who were not wounded stood – the wounded men lay on the ground in front of them. As our platoon marched past, they imploringly held out pictures of their womenfolk – wives and girlfriends. I thought to myself, 'what a sad bunch'.

Two heavy machine guns were being set up in front of them, and he thought it 'an odd thing to take two precious machine guns out of combat to guard these prisoners'. They could just as easily been confined to a house or cellar 'where we'd only need one guard for the whole lot'. Suspicion made him to go back and ask one of the MG gunners 'what was going on here?' 'They are going to be shot,' was the response. Mistaking this for black humour he asked: 'Who ordered that?' When he heard it was *Hauptsturmführer* Knöchlein, 'I knew that he was being totally serious.' He broke away to rejoin his platoon; 'I had to get away from this place. I didn't want to see the execution'. The ripping canvas sound of sustained bursts of Spandau machine-gun fire sounded behind, followed by distinctive pistol and rifle shots as the wounded were finished off. More than 90 serge khaki figures from the

Norfolk Regiment were left sprawled at the base of the long wall of the Louis Creton Farm.[16]

The following day staff officer *Major* Hans Riederer von Paar drove forward to Eicke's headquarters to coordinate road column movement. He knew the *Tötenkopf* had lost about 450 men the day before and its units were scattered. 'Nobody knew where the vehicles were, and the regimental commander reckoned it would take at least four to five hours to collect the troops together.' On the way back von Paar came across 89 dead British men piled together along a wall, 'shot by the SS, an awful scene'. He wrote later in his diary:

> I reported it to high command. The case will be sharply followed up. Beyond that, the battlefield appeared grisly; a large number of dead German and English soldiers are lying around all about. Dead horses, cows, broken cars and fighting vehicles, destroyed and burned out houses, large and small shell holes show the bitter fighting that occurred over the past few days.[17]

Hoepner's XVI Corps immediately asked for a report from the *SS-Tötenkopf* and received an unsatisfactory, indeed insolent, response. The British were accused of using dum-dum [soft nose] bullets; swastika flags had been waved to entice German soldiers into ambushes. Most of the German wounds were described as being 'in the back'. Eicke's unit portrayed itself as the victims. A series of searching questions were sent back but ignored when the *Tötenkopf* were detached from Hoepner's command for the next phase of the operation.

Brunnegger, who had hastened away from the execution, argued: 'Any soldier who uses dum-dum bullets steps out of the ranks of decent soldiery and should expect nothing but the harshest condemnation.'[18]

Dum-dum bullets 'splash' on impact with the human body and cause catastrophic tissue damage. 'But did the men use the terrible ammunition?' he questioned; 'probably not'. Wounds inflicted by high-velocity rounds cause visceral injuries in any case. A small hole at the point of entry is the precursor to a kinetically propelled shock wave that follows the passage of the bullet punching out a fist-sized hole as the projectile exits the body. Wounds were worse if the bullet was 'tumbling', ricocheting off the ground or graze deflected by tree branches or undergrowth. Inexperienced SS soldiers stressed by unprecedentedly shocking casualties in their units were easily convinced such injuries had to have been applied with malicious and 'unfair' intent. *General* Erich von Manstein commented that the *Tötenkopf* could not be faulted for discipline or soldierly attitude: 'They always attacked with tremendous guts... But the force had above average casualties, because they and their officers had to learn for the first time in battle what the regiments of the regular army had long since mastered.'[19]

The SS in France had much to learn. The following morning the *Tötenkopf* attacked two regiments forward to form its bridgehead on the far side of the canal. Real progress was not, however, achieved until the morning of the 29th, when the British began to pull back what was left of the battered 2nd Division to Dunkirk.

Third Panzer Division to the left of *Tötenkopf* made better progress, pushing on to Merville on the River Lys, 2 miles further north of Le Paradis. Eicke felt the *Wehrmacht* was showing him up. The 2nd British Division was under enormous pressure along its whole front, as the panzers attempted to pinch off the general withdrawal of the BEF to the north-west behind them. River and canal lines were fought over as defence line obstacles, held together by village strongpoints like a string of defensive pearls. *Hauptmann* Schneider-Kostalski's 2nd Battalion of 6th Panzer Regiment with 3rd Panzer attempted to storm the bridge over the Lys Canal at Merville. Again, as at Cassel, the infantry-panzer coordination took time to coordinate. Rapid relatively unopposed advances across French countryside had encouraged a tendency for panzers to outdistance their motorized infantry, who had to dismount from their trucks on meeting opposition, and then keep up. The division also lacked motorcycle infantry. They were up against an enemy who was less off balance and fighting for its very survival within the restricted confines of the pocket.

The Lys Canal was surrounded by drainage ditches, which meant the only practical going for panzers was on the roads. Their approach was therefore predictable. The lead panzer belonging to *Leutnant* von Winterfeld was hit at the railway level crossing 165 yards along the main street from the bridge. He was victim to a British 18/25-pounder artillery piece firing over open sights. The turret was blasted skyward, knocking the tank violently about, blocking the road. British infantry from the 6th King's Own Battalion pinned down the accompanying German infantry and another panzer was destroyed and several damaged. Infantry attacks developed both sides of the road until by midday there was fighting in Merville town centre. By mid-afternoon the attacks tailed off and the Germans drew back. Panzer crewman Fritz Kanzler recalled:

> The Tommies would not let themselves be taken and are still shooting at us from a distance. An abandoned English anti-tank gun stands at the fork in the road – an evil looking thing with considerable gauge and power.[20]

An officer with 75th Panzer Artillery Regiment followed the engagement through his scissors telescope from a forward observation post at Calonne-sur-la-Lys nearby. 'The batteries fire on enemy movements and concentrations', he remembered, and 'the fire is only feebly returned'. By nightfall there is 'pitch darkness, rain and in between the firing a deathly stillness'. The town looked 'lonely and abandoned', no movement except for the odd motorcyclist or vehicle 'clattering over the cobblestones'. There was little to report: 'With an ear-splitting crash a shell bursts in the lonely village, followed by the splintering of glass and the rattle of slates falling on the road, till an oppressive silence again hands over to the village.' At daybreak they found the British had gone.[21]

Dawn at Cassel after the bloody rebuff of the two 6th Panzer Division *Kampfgruppen* remained a stand-off. *Leutnant* Ritgen, observing the hilltop through binoculars, saw the British were shaving. His 11th Panzer Regiment commander, *Oberstleutnant* Richard Koll, 'also called a truce for the morning ablutions, which both sides punctiliously observed for 45 minutes'.[22] Assaults were now more deliberately mounted. 'We were attacked repeatedly by infantry, tanks, artillery and aircraft,' 2nd Lieutenant Julian Fane with the 2nd Gloucesters remembered, 'so we had a very busy time and suffered quite a few casualties'. 'Of course,' he added, 'the chances of getting killed were quite great.' The 'hold until the last man' instruction transitioned to an order to break out on 29 May:

> We realized our chances were negligible; obviously the Germans had completely outflanked us. But one still had it in mind not to give in and to escape. Something had to be done to avoid dying. You don't just give in.[23]

During the early afternoon 6th Panzer reported that it had broken the bunker line around Cassel.

The British attempted to break out during the night. Early in the morning two villages further north-east towards Dunkirk – Steenvorde and Watou – were attacked by Stukas and overrun by the 6th Division's panzers. 'We destroyed the English brigade in the early morning fog at Droogland northeast of Cassel,' Ritgen recalled. Caught on the move the withdrawal transitioned to a debacle, and the 145th Brigade commander with 40 officers and nearly 2,000 men were captured. 'We were going in single file along a large field, when at a sudden signal, the whole hedgerow opened fire,' Fane remembered:

> We were easy targets. A hand grenade must have bounced just in front of my head. Suddenly there was an enormous bang on my head and my tin helmet took a glancing blow and did no more; another piece of shrapnel went into my shoulder and arm. Then I thought 'Oh dear, what was happening now?' Then I looked to my right, and another platoon commander, the second, Olive I think, was his name, was hit in the chest and died not long afterwards. The next thing the Quartermaster Sergeant was hit and killed. So I moved my way along, really crawling over these people who had been killed.

Collecting about '14 people' Fane moved south, keeping to ditches, trying to keep out of sight. It was a harrowing experience, but he was determined to make it to the coast and home. 'If you are a hunted animal,' he remembered, 'and put yourself in the same position, you escape as best you can, you're driven by the fear of not being captured.'[24]

German soldiers standing on the northern slopes of the Cassel hill feature could now direct observed artillery fire upon Esquelbecq and Wormhoudt, being attacked by the LAH under Guderian's command, moving before them from half left to right. They sought to cut the Wormhoudt-Bergues road, one of the main entry points to the Dunkirk perimeter 12 miles away. Formed from the original Berlin SS Headquarters Guard, the LAH formed the centre of an attack with the *Grossdeutschland* Regiment to its left and 76th Infantry Regiment right. The advance was hotly contested. They had lost 12 dead and twice that wounded the day before taking Bollzelle, and its 1st Battalion, 2nd Regiment, supported by tanks from the 2nd Panzer Division, was bearing down on Wormhoudt, tenaciously defended by the British 2nd Royal Warwicks infantry battalion.

A company of the Warwicks, the centre of two companies defending forward, had been hit by artillery and 15 Stuka dive-bombers early that morning, suffering heavy casualties. The SS advanced on a three-company front, 6th Company north of the Esquelbecq road behind panzer support, while the 5th and 7th Companies were attacking across very open ground southwest of the village. On the right Baum's 7th Company was overlapping towards Arneke, with 76th Regiment. Bill Stanton, a machine gunner with the 5th Gloucesters here, remembered holding fire from his railway embankment position as he watched up to 100 SS troopers advancing towards them across open ground:

> So I waited and waited, and when they got into the middle of the field I started firing, and they were dropping all around the field. Then in a second they started to run and they were coming to the embankment, and I knew we'd had it.

The second German wave watched what was happening forward, a dance of life and death viewed through the comfortable prism of distance. Figures darted urgently left and right at grass top level. Violent activity became sky lined when the forward assaulting platoons passed over the top of the British positions, pausing momentarily to mop up amid the crump of grenade detonations and pop-pop of rifle fire. Evidence of combat was more pronounced as the second wave drew near: empty brass cases, discarded equipment and the first bodies. Wounded were gathered in groups, retching, shaking and crying; others wide-eyed and staring.

'The ones coming around the house I got,' Bill Stanton recalled, 'they went down':

> I said to Dickie *another magazine!* He put a magazine in and I heard the click. Dickie then jumped up, ran about ten to 15 yards and then dropped. He'd been hit. I don't know what it was, something made him get up, I think it was the shock of being hit. He got up and ran, and then dropped, he must have died while he was moving.

Stanton saw he was dead and thought, 'well that's me'. Seconds later he was shot in the jaw. With blood streaming down his face he made it to a road, where a passing British truck heading for Dunkirk picked him up.[25]

SS-Sturmbannführer (Major) Schützek, the commander of the 2nd Battalion, entered Wormhoudt during the morning to coordinate the attacks by his three forward companies. He was next found lying inside his *Kubelwagen* (car), with severe head injuries. The men were enraged; Schützek was a respected and popular leader, and now the momentum of his attack faltered. Kurt Meyer, the 15th Company commander with the 3rd Battalion, had also penetrated the south-east part of Wormhoudt at about 3pm. 'They were defending tenaciously,' he recalled; 'our grenadiers dashed from house to house'. *Hauptsturmführer* Möhnke was called back from the advancing centre company and told to replace the critically wounded Schützek.[26]

Sepp Dietrich, the ever-flamboyant regimental commander, was impatient at delays from opposition he had confidently predicted would be swiftly overcome. He drove forward to investigate. 'The fighting started early in the morning,' Eric Maas, one of his adjutants, remembered, 'and was extremely severe'.[27] Dietrich drove along the Esquelbecq road past four burning 2nd Panzer Division tanks, knocked out by British anti-tank guns on the open ground to his left. His car was then shot up and set on fire by men from the 5th Gloucesters dug in nearby. For much of the rest of the day he was pinned down in a water-filled ditch alongside his wounded adjutant, seeking to avoid the flames marked by black smoke, which clearly delineated the beleaguered position to would-be rescuers. Repeated attempts to reach him were beaten back by intense British fire. Burning fuel, which set the grass on fire around the blazing vehicle, leaked into the ditch, and Dietrich and his injured adjutant had to plaster themselves with mud in order to dampen burns. Finally at about 4pm he was relieved by *SS Oberscharführer* (Senior Sergeant) Oberschelp's rescue group, who was killed in the attempt. Another popular figure, he had been the first regiment NCO to be awarded the Iron Cross First Class, during the Polish campaign. Emotions ran high.

The pressure on Dietrich had been alleviated by Möhnke's renewed 2nd Battalion attack on Wormhoudt, which got into the market square at 5pm. Fierce house-to-house combat developed, with repeated British counter-attacks at the point of the bayonet. Prisoners were taken, and SS blood lust rose accompanied by the first excesses, beatings and shootings of wounded and captured stragglers. Twelve guards from Möhnke's battalion marched about 90 prisoners across the fields to a barn at La Plaine au Bois, south of the Esquelbecq road west of Wormhoudt, where a clumsy massacre occurred. Grenades were posted in among prisoners herded together in the small barn. Not all were killed, so groups of five were taken out and shot and prisoners not emerging were sprayed inside with automatic weapons fire. Survivors were bayonetted or dispatched by a shot to the head. The final brutalities were cloaked by a violent thunderstorm, pouring rain sanitizing much of the bloody evidence. Kurt Sametreiter with the LAH later recalled the successful end of the French campaign. 'We were so happy,' he remembered, 'that for a few days we basically got drunk', tinged by an element of uneasy regret. 'Really you see,' he admitted, 'we just wanted to forget.'[28]

Dietrich was not best pleased. The official regimental history called the 28 May fighting 'the hardest yet in the West'. Twenty-four of his men were killed, many of these well-liked high-profile characters, with perhaps three times that number wounded. Guderian claims it was the 3rd Panzer Regiment with the 2nd Panzer Division that saved Dietrich from 'his unpleasant predicament', extracting him from his burning vehicle: 'He soon appeared at my headquarters covered from head to foot in mud and had to accept some very ribald comments on our part.'[29]

The *Wehrmacht* continued to have reservations about the military capability of the *Waffen SS*. Nevertheless, the Oost Cappel-Rexpoede road, one of the main British withdrawal routes into the Dunkirk perimeter, was reached at dawn the next day. Former determined resistance transitioned to rearguard skirmishing; the main British body had already passed by.

On the coast, Guderian's XIX Corps leading the drive against Dunkirk made surprisingly little progress. His panzers gained scarcely half a dozen miles in two days. No attack was even mounted against Gravelines on 27 May, the nearest point the panzers had reached on the day of the Halt Order. 'We were a little sad,' admitted *Major* Graf von Kielmansegg, hearing of the fall of Boulogne and Calais on 25 and 26 May, 'that these two names were not directly linked to our battle' for Dunkirk. Apparently ripe to fall, 1st Panzer Division was still licking wounds and refitting on the first day of the resumption of the panzer offensive. On the 28th, the previously contested villages at Bourbourg and Spycker – just over 4 miles from Dunkirk – were captured. Then during the night Guderian's corps was forewarned it would shortly be relieved by the 9th Panzer Division. Having visited his forward commanders that day, Guderian concluded 'the enemy was fighting very bitterly on the Cassel to Bergues road'. This experience was replicated by Reinhardt's intense fight for Cassel and Hazebrouck and Hoepner's faltering progress across the canal near Béthune. The British flank screens were holding firm, enabling the main force behind them to run the gauntlet to Dunkirk under protection.

Guderian probably appreciated his main chance had been the failed 1st Panzer Division attack of 24 May, beaten back through lack of capacity and the timely arrival of the lead elements of the French 68th Division. During the three-day pause, the flooding of the low-lying areas with the opening of the sluice gates had transformed previously seen grass meadows to shimmering expanses of water. He expressed his general appreciation of the situation in the Corps log on 28 May:

> Attacking across polder land with tanks would be wrong, a pointless sacrifice of our best soldiers. A rapid reconstitution of regimental offensive strengths would be ever more difficult. It makes more sense to hold the present positions and allow the attack by Eighteenth Army from the east to take effect.

He was more focused on the forthcoming demands of Operation *Röt* (Red), the conquest of the rest of France, which was why his corps was relieved the next day. Nevertheless, the 37th Panzer Pioneer Battalion did cross the Aa River canal and take Fort Philippe the next day and 1st *Schützen* Regiment occupied Gravelines. 'With that,' von Kielmansegg summed up, 'the last obstacle on the coast road along to Dunkirk had fallen.'[30] Guderian felt his mission was achieved; Dunkirk harbour was clearly within artillery range. War correspondent Christoph von Imhoff shared the elation of this progress:

> Gravelines was ours. German dive-bombers were already there, as days before at Boulogne and Calais, with their unmistakable intent. Day by day the German positions creep nearer to the town, smoke and dust lay before our eyes. The German Stukas hurl themselves against the enemy and transport ships in steep dives. Just a few days more will decide Britain's fate here![31]

Even on the night before the attack on Fort Philippe Guderian dispatched a general warning order to his *Panzergruppe*: 'All three panzer divisions are to be relieved, accommodation in Ardres. Get on with servicing of equipment. Personnel numbers will be brought up to strength by [transport] aircraft in three to four days.'

The capture of Fort Philippe merited only a single line entry to the log the following day; the rest of the content dealt with the proposed relief by the 9th Panzer Division. Guderian's final instruction to his commanders was 'to make map study appreciations to prepare for operations against the Lower Seine'. Dunkirk clearly was not going to be captured by any further progress coming in from the west side.[32]

The right wing of Hoth's panzer group further east, did, however, make commendable progress. Rommel's 7th Panzer Division made a determined crossing of the canal line between Béthune and La Bassée during the night of 26/27th May and managed to erect a bridge across the next day. Radio operator Hans P. with the 6th Machine Gun Battalion had reached the canal by morning. During house clearing they came across a young woman whose house had been badly damaged by shellfire. 'Her fear at us "barbarians" was greater than the shellfire,' he recalled. Rushing up to him, she said, 'for God's sake, spare her children and she would give us anything we wanted'. 'We're not murderers,' they assured her in French, they 'were only looking for weapons and Englishmen'. She did not believe them, and offered herself again 'with tears in her eyes'. It was a totally bleak scenario: 'I could only offer her a few supplies. The worse was likely still to come, a life of cold and hunger in the ruined house.'

Rommel was able to utilize better tank country on the far side, and by 28 May the 7th Panzer Division was sitting astride the road running west from Lille to Armentières, trapping a large part of the First French Army near Lille. Hoth's armour and Waeger's XXVII Infantry Corps from Army Group B's Sixth Army met and closed the trap on some five French divisions, almost half of First Army. They were hemmed in by between seven and eight German divisions. All the British forces in the city and two French corps did manage to escape. The receding Allied sack, deflating as it neared the coast, had just lost a substantial globule. As one *Landser* pithily put it: 'from the big sausage in the cauldron [pocket], we got a few smaller'.[33]

Determined resistance on the southern line of the pocket was enabling much of the BEF to exit, inside the gauntlet corridor. The

German Fourth Army with Army Group A had now managed to join Sixth Army coming in from the east with Army Group B. The pursuit continued, following the British retiring to the north-west. An officer with the 75th Panzer Artillery Regiment with an artilleryman's eye for ground described the horizon ahead as 'bounded by wooded ridges'. He atmospherically described the view:

> Columns of smoke half encircle us. The dust clouds of withdrawing English columns rise near the hills. Our infantry advance in open order, rifle on shoulder. The clouds of smoke emanate from St Venant, Hazebrouck and Ypres.

Advancing German soldiers were convinced they were witnessing the collapse of the Allied armies in Flanders:

> In front of the canal, which we can clearly observe, stand countless English vehicles, completely undamaged, with engines still running, abandoned perhaps two or three hours ago. They are in front of a bridge, prepared by Tommy for demolition. But there was no time for that... The booty is immense. Jams, delicacies, bottles of champagne and liqueurs, coffee, chocolate, cigarettes etc are found in the vehicles. Arms ammunition and equipment, too, fall into our hands and are at once utilized.[34]

The end must come soon, and then electrifying news: the Belgians had capitulated.

BELGIAN CAPITULATION — EAST SIDE

During the night of 27 May 'at about 4am came the totally surprising news about the capitulation of the Belgian Army', *General* Hermann Geyer commanding IX Infantry Corps remembered. Both OKW and OKH had been totally engrossed in the drama of the Halt Order. The panzers had just been released, but there is no indication in the diaries of Halder, the OKH Chief of Staff, or von Bock, commanding the main point of effort against the Belgians, that this was coming. Nobody, moreover, appears to have considered a plan of action against such an increasingly likely eventuality. Geyer's 216th Division had taken several thousand prisoners the day before, clearing a 3½-mile stretch of unopposed road towards Thielt. But when they got there urban street fighting cost them 140 men.

XI Corps to their left was also fighting hard. Artillery and Stukas were directed against Theilt, 'but nothing was showing us that the enemy was giving up,' Geyer recalled, 'and we had already lost over 2,000 men in our three divisions over the last four days'. *Leutnant* Otte and *Gefreiter* Lormes recalled waiting by the roadside with the 5th Battery of the 18th Artillery Regiment: 'As we waited for the order to continue the advance a Belgian officer came past on a bicycle. The Belgian Army had – *Ja* – capitulated, and he was heading home with a smiley face.'[35]

If the Germans were surprised, with no operational plan to call on, the British were not. They had seen it coming for days. A dangerous gap had opened between the Belgian right wing, when it was forced back to Menin by the IV German Corps, and the British left. General Sir Alan Brooke (later created Viscount Alanbrooke) commanding the British II Corps had been tasked by Lord Gort to salvage and screen this flank, over which he had been consistently nervous. 'I do not think much of the Belgian Army', he wrote with some exasperation in his diary. He was also damning about the French Army's performance, frustrated by the need for frequent withdrawals after the collapse of the French to the south. By 25 May he declared 'personally I am convinced that the Belgian Army is closing down and will have stopped fighting by this time tomorrow! This of course entirely exposes our left flank.' Gort gave him his reserve, Divisions 5 and 50, to shore up the flank and cover the withdrawal to the Dunkirk perimeter. On the day Geyer received the electrifying news, Alanbrooke had accepted the 'Belgians have practically given up fighting, so that security of eastern flank of retirement rests with II Corps'.[36]

Alanbrooke's view was uncharitable. During successive retreats forced upon the Belgians by the French catastrophe, they had held their own. Forts and defensive positions along canal and river lines had been tenaciously defended. Despite being battered by von Bock's infantry and Kesselring's Stukas, the Belgians never broke. Pressure to retreat on the left was occasioned by the same French failures that had compelled the British to fall back. For 18 days the Belgians held on beyond the point when the larger operational picture clearly spelt doom for Belgium's future as an independent country. The Allied left flank was still firmly anchored, with the Belgians lengthening and thinning their own front in response to pleas from the British and French. Von Bock's infantry divisions had suffered heavy losses at the hands of the Belgians, particularly on the River Lys. Now their retiring troops were running out of space. 'It was astonishing to see that the Belgians fought with increasing tenacity, the nearer the end approached,' recalled *Oberst* Siegfried Westphal, on the Eighteenth Army Staff. At the front German soldiers regarded the Belgians with wary respect.[37]

During the crisis leading to the collapse of the Belgian front between 25 and 30 May, British II Corps fought an adept 40-mile action, screening the vital flank. It withdrew in contact with the enemy, side-stepping three lines facing south, defending against successive pushes mounted by nine German divisions coming from the east, as they retreated north. It was a continuous mobile operation with successive fronts fighting off superior forces, responding to every enemy evolution without being seriously dislocated. German failure to break through and prevent it reflected the lack of coordination along this sector of front between corps seeking their own grandiose objectives at the seeming point of victory.

This developing scenario evolved into the biggest threat facing the forming Dunkirk perimeter since the failure of Guderian's thrust from the west on 24 May by 1st Panzer Division. The collapse of the Belgian Army now exposed the vulnerable east side of the perimeter to the likelihood of a crushingly swift German advance exploiting the emerging vacuum. Dunkirk port could conceivably be captured before the BEF could get away. *General* Hermann Geyer recalled the unexpected implications, pregnant with teasing but favourable possibilities:

> Did this mean the end of the Flanders campaign? It was only 50km to Ostende and 80 to Dunkirk. Was it only Belgians between these two objectives or also French and English? What about the lower Somme, are the French and English attacking there, or on the Aisne at last in full strength?

There was certainly no plan. Eighteenth Army HQ, to which he belonged, telephoned swiftly and told him to get the corps moving, at least to prevent the British and French setting up a new defensive line behind the Yser. It was obvious to Geyer 'that high command did not have a clear view about the big operational perspective'.[38]

Nor did British soldiers on the line of retreat. Durham Light Infantryman Fred Clapham recalled 'three weeks we were marching, digging in, battling, marching, digging in until we reached the coast'. The II Corps withdrawal involved defence by day followed by a succession of extensive night withdrawals, keeping one pace ahead of von Bock's pursuing infantry. 'Quite frankly I don't think by then anyone knew where we were.' They were harassed by dive-bombers which 'would attack us umpteen times a day,' Clapham remembered. 'We would have to dive off the road and spread ourselves in the fields until they cleared off.' They also suffered from the hot weather 'as we were all wearing army issue woollen "long johns" our crotches were all sore with constant rubbing of the garments and perspiration'. 'After about 10 days of this caper', he recalled, 'it began to dawn on us raw lads that something was sadly amiss.'

Despite severe pressure from the 61st, 31st and 18th German divisions Alanbrooke's II Corps extricated itself from south of Ypres, moving north towards the coast. Montgomery's 3rd Division managed to come into line to the left of 151 Brigade after an epic night march that gave Alanbrooke a sleepless night. 'The whole movement seemed unbearably slow', he wrote in his diary:

> The hours of darkness were slipping by, should daylight arrive with the road crammed with vehicles the casualties from bombing might well have been disastrous. Our own guns were firing from the vicinity of Mount Kemmel, the German artillery were answering back, and the division was literally trundling slowly along in the darkness down a pergola of artillery fire, and within 4,000 yards of a battle front which had been fluctuating all day, somewhat to our disadvantage.[39]

It was a very close shave, 'an eerie sight which I shall never forget'. Just before dawn 'the last vehicles had disappeared northwards into the darkness'. The line was closed against the German advance, just hours before the Belgian Army finally capitulated.

Infantryman Ernst Kleist with the 61st Division was part of the pursuit, in the Ypres area north of Comines, when the Belgians surrendered. 'The fighting is unbelievably heavy,' he wrote home. There had been many casualties; one of their regiments had lost over 60% of its men, 'with many of my old friends among them'. 'Even so, it's going forward even if a little slow':

> Yesterday evening saw an ugly reverse. The enemy sent heavy tanks, fired gas, and laid down the heaviest artillery fire on us, but this morning we made amends. We had our own dead, one of the youngest, barely 19 years old, we buried him early this morning.[40]

18th Division further north was pressing forward towards Ypres. *Unteroffizier* Sandau with the 5th Company of the 54th Regiment was part of a group ambushing retreating British lorries trying to break out. The British vehicles were running a gauntlet through the streets of St Eloi, south of Ypres:

> There – suddenly engine noises, single shots, then an English lorry raced down the street towards Ypres. The lorry is packed full with Englishmen. We shoot at the back of the vehicle, the English return fire and speed on. About 200 metres further down was our second platoon, and they prepared a warm reception for Tommy! One heard shots from a machine pistol (SMG) and the wagon stopped. Damage to the vehicle or was the driver hit? In no time the English were out of the vehicle taking cover in a street ditch.[41]

An intense firefight involving light mortars and rifle fire broke out. 'It was too late for them,' Sandau recalled. '*Gefreiter* Wygasch's machine gun had the lorry pinned.' Another German section joined in 'and Tommy was now sitting in a crossfire'. They surrendered, 19 prisoners, some of whom were wounded, from an original contingent of 45.

Another lorry drove up and was again shot to a standstill, the driver and co-driver pitching over as they jumped out of the cab. An anti-tank projectile struck the body of the truck and it burst into flames. After an hour a car came down the same street, with two men and an officer, who quickly accelerated. 'They shot back out of the car windows,' Sandau recalled, 'and at full speed they raced passed the first houses – he was plucky the Tommy!' But they found themselves blocked in by the two burning lorries up ahead and were taken prisoner.[42]

Advancing German soldiers were surrounded by the detritus of Allied defeat. Alfred-Ingemar Berndt with the self-propelled guns of *Panzerjäger Abteilung* 605 on the Tournai road heading for Ypres recalled, 'we saw something awful we couldn't forget'. The road ahead was obstructed by the remains of a British fuel and ammunition resupply column, hit by a shell. The fiery conflagration had immolated nine vehicles; 'the heat of the flames melted and made bizarre sculptures from some of the tin and iron'. It was thought upwards of 40 British troops had perished:

> They were burned so severely that it was hardly possible to remove their disintegrated remains from the wrecked autos. The corpses were ripped to pieces, rotten, broken, bent into half circles, arms and legs sticking out as though they didn't belong. Shredded uniforms are present on only a few, on the others burnt away with the rest of the body, without a trace.[43]

Only blackened soup-plate-shaped helmets and dog tags indicated they were British. German engineers were pulling out wreckage and human remains with long boat hooks to clear the debris. 'Our pioneers are not happy but are doing what they must,' Ingemar Berndt remembered. They watched them 'work robustly with equanimity to suppress their emotions'. Black *Landser* humour surfaced 'when one calls out: '*Roasted Tommies, anyone?*'[44]

Infantry officer Werner L. remembered retreating French and Belgian troops causing havoc on the line of march 'according to the locals, who had already enough misfortunes to complain about'. They were senselessly 'plundering the land they were supposed to defend'. His unit was now nearing the front, 'huge smoke clouds hang on the horizon with dull reverberations and thunder' showing the way.[45] There was no indication the fighting was slackening. German soldiers were phlegmatic, they lived for each day and survival brought another. Indescribably tired, they plodded steadily onward.

Ernst Kleist near Comines south of Ypres wrote home it had started to rain, 'the famous Flanders mud'. His 61st Division was trying to break through the 5th British Infantry Division fighting along the Ypres-Comines line, covering II Corp's northward withdrawal. 'It is impossible to describe what is happening in such an attack or counter-attack,' he wrote, 'except that one is unspeakably tired.' Nicotine and alcohol was what held them together and the hope that the assault on their senses by the din of artillery might eventually end. Murderous artillery supporting fire preceded their attack on the morning of 28 May; 'Tommies were lying in their hundreds, like mown grass,' he recalled. 'The one benefit of battle now', he remembered, 'was that one had just to react, because you can't think any more.' Shortly before his death in action three weeks later he wrote to his wife: 'only you, and our life together has given me the strength to get through all this.'[46]

Two days before the Belgian capitulation *Hauptmann* Schimpf, commanding the 1st Battalion of the 192nd Regiment with the 56th Division, discovered his regimental commander *Oberst* Wolff had been seriously wounded in the head by a machine gun burst. The day after, his battalion took 5,000 Belgian prisoners and then he heard that *Major* Haus, who had replaced Wolff, had also fallen. *Hauptmann* Reichard, who commanded Schimpf's sister battalion the 3rd in the 192nd Regiment, took over. Fighting continued throughout the night and Schimpf was warned off for yet another attack on 28 May, the next day. They had no idea that a Belgian delegation had been received at the XI Corps HQ requesting surrender terms.

At dawn a regimental communiqué announced that the entire Belgian Army had surrendered. Ceasefire would be at 5am. Schimpf was ordered to drive over to the Belgian division across the line to negotiate its surrender. 'That was practically unbelievable to us,' he recalled. Recent experience had given no sign a collapse was in the offing. 'It was a lonely drive,' he remembered, across no-man's-land after a white flag was hastily attached to his *VW* jeep: 'Our forward elements for the most part had not heard the news. They wondered why it was a solitary German vehicle should drive off in the early morning twilight towards the enemy.'

Schimpf soon appreciated there was 'huge astonishment also on the Belgian side'. They had no idea the Belgian king had taken the step. Schimpf was arrested at first by a Belgian major, but then allowed to continue on to Bruges for surrender negotiations. Schimpf's battalion drew breath, anticipating a long-awaited break, but was immediately sent off via Thielt to the coast.[47]

The Belgian surrender opened a demilitarized vacuum in the area between Bruges and Thielt inland, and Zebrugge and Nieuport on the

Channel coast. Army Group B now had the opportunity to strike at the coast, turn west, and roll up Dunkirk. At a minimum, the perimeter might be pierced from the east before it had a chance to effectively form. It offered the best opportunity to block the British escape since the failed panzer attack on the port four days before. Unfortunately for von Bock, the distractions at this pregnant moment were as immense as the opportunities. He had to coordinate negotiations between Army High command (OKH) and the Belgian king. This would preoccupy his Sixth Army commander Reichenau at a critical stage in the battle. 'I am worried,' he wrote in his diary, '… that the unavoidable negotiations with the Belgians will result in a halt of our forward movement, which abetted by the resulting tangle of German and Belgian troops, the English will be able to exploit for themselves.' The Belgians were told to stay off the roads. 'Issued orders for the motorized battalions to be driven forward,' he wrote, 'toward the Yser Canal between Nieuport and Ypres as powerfully and quickly as possible.'[48]

The news electrified tired troops and morale soared. Soldiers had appreciated the Allies were visibly teetering. One *Gefreiter* with the 77th Artillery Regiment wrote home:

> The three enemy armies are coming apart, which can only be favourable for us. The Belgians are out of it, which you would certainly have heard, the English wherever you meet them. It can't last much longer before they realize that further resistance is pointless.

Alfred-Ingemar Berndt was jubilant, he remembered: 'no reporting service is better or faster than word that spreads over the front from mouth to mouth.' His 2nd company with *Panzerjäger Abteilung* 605 reported: 'Masses of troops have approached carrying white flags. They leave their vehicles, hundreds of them, standing in the fields.'

The whole corps knew within two hours; 'one talked to another', Berndt gleefully recalled. 'Messengers carry the news, call out to everyone they meet on their way.' 'Early this morning I saw the Belgian negotiator that had signed the capitulation,' another *Leutnant* in a signals regiment wrote home, from near Ypres; 'today I experienced a small piece of world history'.[49]

General Geyer, commanding IX Corps, provided a vivid snapshot of the command situation on the German side, with the tumultuous news fraught with potential opportunity. Time was of the essence. 'Time meant advantage for the enemy,' he appreciated. 'He who dares conjures success out of the hand.' The clock was already conspiring against him. 'We should form advance guards,' he appreciated, as the Army Commander had already ordered; but Geyer had been in the midst of a corps reorganization when the news broke. With some effort he managed to scrape together a *Vorausabteilung* or advance guard under *Oberstleutnant* Rodt. This was an ad hoc assembly of a vehicle-borne *Aufklärungs* unit, a machine gun battalion and *Panzerjäger Abteilung* 563, with some artillery. Rodt was given total freedom of action to use his initiative to reach the coast and, at the minimum, hinder any British or French attempts to set up new defensive positions behind the Yser River.

Rodt's task was unenviable, requiring him to drive through 400,000 disassembling Belgian soldiers nursing hostile intent. Geyer appreciated: 'At no time was anyone certain if the Belgians, who were not friendly forces, would shoot, or whether the English or French might suddenly emerge.'

Geyer's staff group drove forward, bypassing Rodt's force, on a different road. After a few miles they felt impelled to turn back, 'because we saw absolutely no German soldiers, except Belgians to our front, next to and behind us'. Common sense tempered valour; 'here and there during the drive we heard shooting,' he remembered. 'It was about 8am, and the ceasefire had probably not got through to everyone yet.' Rodt's more imposing force came up and accelerated ahead north of Dixmude, 9 miles short of the Yser. 'There I left him in the pouring rain, with the repeated instruction to get across the river today if possible.'[50]

On 28 May '*Führer* weather' transitioned to heavy and prolonged rain, 'the first and only time in this campaign', Geyer commented. Many of the advance guards were clogged at crossroads, delayed by driving rain and roads jammed with Belgian soldiers mixed with refugees, which stymied progress even further. Roads were also snagged by wrecked vehicles, dead horses and the sinister presence of mines. As Geyer's staff drove from Thielt a Belgian nursing sister flagged them down, pointing out mines. During their conversation a German vehicle overtook the group 'and went up in the air'. 'Many a courageous recce cost lives,' Geyer grimly recalled, including that of *Hauptmann* Rockstroh, one of his artillery battery commanders. The enemy situation was uncertain and rain slowed the march of the advance guards. Geyer explained: 'It was an unusual act to force their way through partly, still armed, Belgians. Men who yesterday, no this morning, were still fighting; some ten thousand standing on the roads or resting nearby,'

Despite poor communications between units, 'we didn't need to give orders or wait for reports'.[51] It was obvious they needed to get to the coast.

'We counted 10,000 prisoners that filed by us in an endless line,' remembered Alfred-Ingemar Berndt, 'a beaten army': 'They ambled, laughing, gossiping, a loaf of bread under arm, repeating again and again the word *fini* finished! The weight of the German blow demoralized and broke them. They wanted to go home, nowhere but home.'

When German aircraft swept over they flinched and ducked their heads. 'They can't stand to listen to the drone of aeroplane engines,' Berndt recalled. 'Stukas [had] hacked their companies of soldiers to bloody fragments.' They moved by with bicycles, wheelbarrows, and children's prams piled high with possessions.[52]

The day of the Belgian surrender, 28 May, was a critical day. *Generalmajor* Moritz Andreas's 208th Infantry Division, part of XXVI Corps north of Geyer, likewise formed three motorized advance guards, one from each of his three infantry regiments. 'Here,' he directed, 'quick action could bring a breakthrough success, and prevent the English Army disembarking through Nieuport.' Each was a battalion-strong mixed unit of infantry, engineers, anti-tank and artillery, mounted on captured vehicles. The X Infantry Corps also hastily assembled vanguards that were directed to immediately press on to the Channel coast towards Dunkirk, on news of the surrender. They were delayed less by the reorganization and change of thrust lines, more from 'extraordinarily dense traffic jams which assembling Belgian units created on the roads'.

256th Division approaching from the north-east did not manage to get its improvised transport columns moving until 11am on the day of the surrender. They were then blocked by French Brigadier General Deslauren's 60th Infantry Division, which, alerted to the impending Belgian collapse, withdrew from the Léopold Canal Line north of Bruges, driving west in commandeered Belgian lorries. The 241st Regiment made it to Nieuport and set up a new line to the south behind the Yser. Its sister regiment, the 270th, marching on foot, was, however, caught, surrounded, and taken prisoner. A motorcycle borne *Aufklärungs Abteilung* from 256th Division reached Nieuport and captured the canal bridge intact, but was checked by a vicious firefight with British armoured cars from the 17th Lancers.[53]

Eighteenth Army's 256th Division reached the Channel coast at Nieuport, just 17 miles north-east of Dunkirk. Ostend had fallen and isolated advance guards marched straight through West Flanders, to exploit the vacuum created by the surrender of the Belgian Army. At the same time Reichenau's Sixth Army lunged at the Yser River north-west of Ypres. The manoeuvres were not part of a pre-planned operational scheme, but were rather exploitative measures taken at the initiative of individual corps commanders. The overall situation remained unclear. *General* Hermann Geyer got a radio call from *Oberstleutnant* Rodt between 3pm and 4pm that he had captured Furnes, on the east side of the Dunkirk perimeter. 'That's what I at least read from the report,' but 'in reality he had only reported he was on the east edge or edge of town,' he later remembered. Geyer was becoming increasingly uneasy about the situation of his staff HQ, because still fully armed and organized French and Belgian units were moving by his location: 'The Belgians with no escorts at all, the French with just a few German guards. There were hardly any German units at all in the area.'

His 56th Division had everything up front; 'we didn't have a corps reserve, and nothing else was following the 56th'. Improvised task forces of British and French troops were hindering the progress of many of the weak German advance guards, seeking to fill the empty space left by the Belgian surrender. The BEF main body of retreating units had reached the Poperinghe-Noordschote line during the night of 29 May and by morning the bulk were inside the Dunkirk perimeter that had been set up to protect the evacuation. 'And now,' Geyer recalled, after the heartening news from the advance Guard Rodt, 'there was strong resistance from an English machine gun battalion in Furness' and 'also the northern edge of the Furnes-Nieuport canal was occupied by the English'. The main German infantry marching groups following up behind the improvised vehicle-mounted vanguards were way behind, and clearly losing the race. All three infantry regiments with 56th Division were on the roads:

Meeting endless numbers of Belgian soldiers, either in small groups or properly ordered formations under their officers. There were also abandoned vehicles and weapons and equipment of all types piled up on the roads. Well-dressed Belgian soldiers could be seen, approachable and mightily pleased the war was over for them. All this frequently led to long march hold-ups with crowds of refugees, with their huge two-wheeled carts blocking the way. It also rained during the afternoon, the first time in this campaign, a cloud burst, an hour-long storm, that soaked us all to the skin.[54]

The Belgian surrender enabled von Küchler's Eighteenth Army to close up on the Dunkirk pocket. Infantry divisions were now available for a final assault. This was just as well, because the panzers had not been able to break into the south side of the gauntlet the BEF had run to the port. 'Now that the Belgians have capitulated,' Guderian concluded in his report to von Kleist's Chief of Staff Zeitzler, 'continuation of operations here… is costing unnecessary sacrifices'. With armour reduced by 50%, 'equipment is in urgent need of repair, if the corps is soon to be ready for other operations' south of the Somme. Guderian pointed out: 'a tank attack in this marshy, rain-soaked country is pointless. The troops hold the high ground south of Dunkirk… and have good artillery positions from which they can fire on Dunkirk.'[55]

The rain also slowed the final infantry advances to the Channel coast at Ostend and Nieuport. The infantry were also frustrated; firmer enemy resistance around the perimeter had obliged them to dig in. The 61st Infantry division complained: 'The arrival of constant rain fully soaked through the dry soil. The men stood knee-deep in water. Flanders mud glued itself to the entire body, clogging weapons and equipment.'

Rain hindered vision and machine gun belts plastered with mud became inoperable, creating 'a stark reduction in fire support'. Heavy weapon sights misted up and the flat featureless nature of the terrain was hindering the accuracy of observed artillery fire.' Eighteenth Army is approaching,' Guderian concluded, 'from the east, with infantry forces more suitable than tanks for fighting in this kind of country, and the task of closing the gap on the coast can therefore be left to them.' That night, at the point of victory, orders were issued for the withdrawal of Guderian's XIX Panzer Corps, to be replaced by von Wietersheim's XIV Infantry Corps.[56]

The weakest point at the coalescing Dunkirk perimeter was its east side. The Belgian surrender opened up a huge expanse of Northern Flanders territory between Zeebrugge and Nieuport on the coast to

Ypres, and Thielt and Bruges inland. Four German corps tried to exploit the windfall by pushing motorized advance guards ahead of their main march bodies, but were thwarted at every critical juncture by retiring British rearguards. Alanbrooke's British II Corps had effectively screened off the approaching forays from the north and east by deftly side-stepping advances while presenting a solid retiring front. As Geyer with IX Corps maintained, all his assets were up front; there was no reserve. A multiple corps-size redirected German offensive might well have been able to reach the coast in this area and roll up the Dunkirk perimeter from the east before it had time to coalesce.

There were a number of emotional and practical reasons for the failure to exploit the opportunity. Although not directly or explicitly stated, German commanders were starting to assume the Flanders area of operations was downgraded to a subordinate front. German *Landser* were sapped of élan; uninterrupted heavy fighting between forced marches dulled commitment through exhaustion. Having clearly won the battle, there was reluctance to risk life and limb at the point of victory. The wholesale destruction of abandoned enemy equipment suggested that the enemy was at the point of giving up. Mass evacuation by sea seemed an unrealistic option to a land-centric army and most soldiers assumed the British would surrender anyway with impending French collapse, even if they did miraculously escape to their homeland. Attention was increasingly being drawn to the next mission awaiting them beyond the Somme. Operations against Dunkirk were being prosecuted almost half-heartedly, despite the awareness the British were beginning to slip through their fingers across the sea.

The confusion that ensued after the Belgian collapse negated any possibility of a vigorous well-coordinated assault against the Dunkirk perimeter. If all the forces operating against the pocket had been placed under von Bock's command, as von Brauchitsch had wanted – rejected by von Rundstedt and Hitler – the town and port of Dunkirk would likely have been captured sooner. Organizational problems emerged. Two army groups were competing for space, trying to eradicate a bridgehead that was only 30 miles long. A plethora of higher headquarters, Army Groups A and B, the Fourth Army with the *Panzergruppe* Kleist, Sixth and Eighteenth Armies, were all tumbling over each other in this confined operational area. Only ten of their divisions were actively engaged. Seven German divisions had sealed off the Lille pocket on

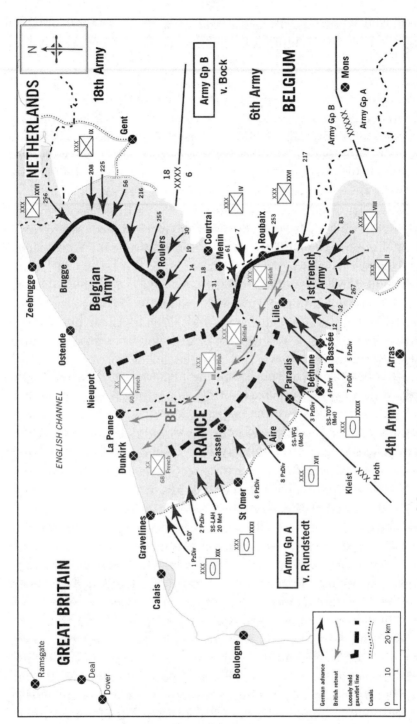

MAP 5: The Belgian Surrender Situation 28 May 1940.

The Belgian surrender nearly resulted in the Dunkirk perimeter being collapsed from the east by von Küchler's Eighteenth Army. Skillful intervention by Alanbrooke's II British Corps fenced off the Belgian collapse at Nieuport, forming the north-east side of a gauntlet, which, opposite a line held to the south west, enabled the BEF to escape to the coast.

28 May, reduced to four laying siege by the following day. Often cited as offering relief to Dunkirk, there would have been scant room for them to manoeuvre around the reduced perimeter even if they had been brought up.

The extraordinary complex command interface negated any focused attempt to exploit the vulnerabilities of the pocket as it was forming or a rapid *coup de grâce* thrust with the Belgian surrender. Halder glumly concluded on 30 May, 'we lost time, so the pocket with the French and British in it was sealed later than it could have been'. Eighteenth Army had not been able to exploit the Belgian opportunity because: 'Lacking unified leadership, our attack resolved itself into individual actions against an enemy stubbornly defending himself behind the canals, and so achieved only slight local successes.'[57]

These command and coordination issues delaying determined action against the perimeter occurred just as Operation *Dynamo* was achieving greater momentum with the evacuation process. Likewise, before the coming battle had even reached its height, mobile and panzer units were relieved in the line in preparation for Operation *Röt*, the offensive against the rest of France. Nobody was in clear overall command as these transfers took place. Relief in place is a complex and slow manoeuvre when in contact with the enemy, possibly the most difficult phase in war. Some units, such as the XVI and XIX Panzer Corps, had not at any stage committed their full resources to the battle. Fourth Army admitted to Army Group A HQ they had penetrated to within artillery range of Dunkirk as ordered, but that only four batteries of 150mm guns and part of von Kleist's light artillery were bombarding the town, 'so long as ammunition stocks allowed'.[58]

Success bred a form of inertia. The medieval town of Bergues, 5½ miles south of Dunkirk, was a future lynchpin of the Dunkirk perimeter defence. It was one of the primary entry points into the town for the retreating BEF; its ramparts, improved by Vauban, dominated the surrounding flat countryside right and left. Its importance was not identified by the advancing Germans and not targeted for days. The town lay within the attack perimeters of the *Grossdeutschland* Regiment attached to Guderian's panzer corps. Despite being one of the nearest units to Dunkirk, they were static as Eighteenth Army drove across the Northern Flanders Plain on the day of the Belgian surrender. 'The advance was greatly hindered by the need to cross many canals,' the regiment reported, 'and made only slow progress'. Much of the terrain to the left of their sector was already flooded, with the opening of the local sluice gates. 'Weather was rainy and dull,' and movement forward laborious and slow. 'As he had often done before,' the report reiterated, 'the enemy abandoned his field positions during the night and established himself further to the rear'. The French monopolized dominating dry ground, leaving the Germans a saturated lower water table. 'We were outside Bergues,' a soldier with the 8th Company recalled, 'we broke out the entrenching tools and began to dig into the clay'. This particularly vulnerable sector of the Dunkirk perimeter front had come to a complete standstill:

> On both sides clay. At the head and foot of the trench, clay. Beneath us clay. Over us a tent square [canvas protection] with the rain splattering against it. After the first hour the clay on the sides had become damned soft. Several litres of water had collected on the tent square. Bits of clay swam around in the water like goldfish. They came from fresh shell holes around us, and there were more and more of them by the minute. We lay stretched out in our holes and stared up into the clouds.[59]

It could have been a description of trench life in World War I. *Unteroffizier* Martin, a motorized infantryman with the 1st Panzer Division, was on sentry duty 'in this boggy trench, dreaming of home':

> With every step in the saturated earth you sink deeper. The water wells up all around your boots. They used to be black. But that was a long time ago. Your greatcoat is encrusted with mud, wet through and crumpled. Your hands are grey and cracked, your beard too long. Thick stubble on your cheeks and chin, coated with the dust and dirt of the last four days. Over your eyes there is a thin, dark veil of tiredness.[60]

German positions were completely overlooked by the town. A soldier with the heavy weapons support company of the *Grossdeutschland* remembered: 'Small hedgerows, bushes and gardens provided some cover, but we were unable to escape the sharp eyes of the enemy observers in the towers and churches opposite us.' Flooding restricted all digging options and very often 'a hail of shells, showered down on us'. Even the armoured self-propelled assault guns had to drive off to seek cover. Nevertheless, they frequently engaged Allied truck columns retreating through Bergues town. They also fired at French artillery observation positions looking down on them with heavy infantry guns. 'The 2nd Platoon aligned its gun on a very narrow church steeple, and the fifth and sixth shells scored direct hits.'[61]

The front on this west side of the Dunkirk perimeter had not moved. During the afternoon of 30 May, *Oberstleutnant* Rolf Wuthman, the Fourth Army Operations Officer, complained to Zeitzler, von Kleist's Chief of Staff, that his headquarters had the impression 'that nothing is going on today, that no one is now interested in Dunkirk'.[62] He urged that the town be bombarded to sow panic and stop the evacuations. Subsequent messages between Army Group A and von Kluge's HQ suggest that Fourth Army, Sixth Army and von Richthofen's VIII *Fliegerkorps* had no idea about each other's plans.

In summary, 30 May was not a good day for the Germans surrounding Dunkirk. The BEF was in the final throes of successfully running its gauntlet, gaining access to the perimeter before the sack was compressed from the south and north-east. With that the survival chances of the BEF had improved. During the previous evening 47,310 British and French troops were taken off by sea, virtually three times the number of the night before. The figure did triple the next night, 29/30th May, when 53,823 got away. This meant 126,000 troops evacuated in total, three times beyond the most optimistic figures naval planners had dared hope for. The men lifted were primarily logistics and line of communications troops, units that had sustained the BEF from the rear. Disembarkation figures were accelerating and now verged on the critical mass. The next troops to embark would be the actual fighting troops. These were the very men that *General* Brennecke, the Fourth Army Chief of Staff, hoped he would never have to meet again, rested and re-equipped.

The core of the British Army was its five regular divisions. Many of these men had seen active service fighting bush wars in the Middle or Far East. *Oberst* Liss at OKH had assessed these soldiers as 'very high quality,' emphasizing that 'the British Empire had occupied over a quarter of the globe'. Regular NCOs had 'long active service in the Colonies, which made them self-assured and totally reliable'. The TA divisions were also reasonable quality and were now veterans. Lord Gort had voiced concern to Rear Admiral Wake-Walker about the need to get the rearguards out. 'These troops are some of the best,' Wake-Walker recalled, 'and Lord Gort was very anxious that they should get away; there were about 5,000 of them.' They were the vital seed corn for any future British Army, the experienced trained cadre around which it could expand.[63]

If the daily evacuation rate was maintained, the fully trained veteran core, representing the British Army's future fighting capacity, could be taken off in four to five days. Such a contested evacuation process had to cope with three primary enemies: a *Luftwaffe* air blockade, German naval threats and the advancing German Army. The battle for Dunkirk had reached a decisive phase. If the *Wehrmacht* could capture these men, Britain might conceivably be knocked out of the war. Her army could be held hostage against surrender negotiations. The UK mainland would be vulnerable to German invasion, and at best, her capacity to influence events in Europe would be negated. The events of the next few days could determine the outcome of World War II.

Chapter 7

Sea, Air and Land

THE SEA

Kapitänleutnant (Lieutenant Commander) Siegfried Wuppermann cast off from the recently secured forward naval base at Flushing during the late afternoon of 28 May with three fast attack craft. His three *S-Boote*, or E-Boats, cruised stealthily through scattered rain squalls to lie in wait for Allied shipping near the well-lit Kwinte Buoy off Dunkirk. This was a turning point on Route Y, the easternmost of three sea evacuation routes across the English Channel, which ended at the North Godwin lightship off Ramsgate. Routes X and Z were shorter and more direct, which as a consequence attracted more enemy attention.* The sea state was smooth. The beaches of La Panne gradually came into view off the port bow after passing Nieuport. *Bootsman* (naval rating) Herbert Sprang, a war correspondent attached to the *Schnellbootsflotilla* (*S-Boot* flotilla), recalled how 'the fire from the huge battle in Flanders and Artois radiated across to them, flashes and thunder from heavy artillery fire'. It did not take long before 'the bright glow in the sky picked out Dunkirk, burning for days now'.[1]

E-Boats were powered by three 1,320bhp Daimler-Benz engines, a derivative of a civilian luxury cruiser, originally ordered by a wealthy American, that was powered by three Maybach engines. Its hard chine

*See map on p.228.

construction, producing a single angle between side and keel, had been much admired by *Kriegsmarine* (German Navy) officers in 1928. The profile cut water drag to a minimum, swiftly producing speeds of 30 to 35 knots (34–40mph) from a standing start. The rich man's toy transitioned to the 21-crew *S-Boot*, mounting a 20mm gun forward and a heavier 40mm aft. It carried six 21-inch torpedoes, with two firing tubes mounted at the bow. As a mine-layer or stealth-ambush weapon, it packed a devastating punch when employed as a low silhouette surface attack craft.

By late evening Wuppermann's 2nd *Schnellbootsflotilla* was off the Kwinte Buoy. The three boats dispersed into *Lauertaktik* formation, a lateral spacing of one nautical mile between each craft. They switched off engines and lay in wait. With the winking buoy flashing as a form of bait, the screen line presented a two-mile net opening, to scoop up any prey sailing by. The blacked-out boats bobbed gently on a flat calm sea state.

A protected sea evacuation from Dunkirk faced three enemies: hostile elements at sea, in the air, or land borne. All three mediums were influenced by the weather. The Dover Straits are an inhospitable environment if the wind blows hard, which it frequently does, even in spring or summer. A 30–40mph channel wind can produce waves of between seven and 11 feet high, seriously hindering light boat traffic between the beach and offshore ships. The weather in May and June 1940 was settled and warm, with abundant sunshine and light winds. One woman watching Dunkirk burn from the south-east coast of England remembered 'you could see it clearly'. The weather was clear and calm:

> It was marvellous! The sea was like a mill pond. It looked like God was there and he was watching over us, and there wasn't a wave, and I believe today that we were going to win the war because of that.[2]

When the battle of Dunkirk entered its climactic stage between 28 and 30 May a sluggish southerly airflow covered the British Isles and France. It produced a few fog banks in the Channel, but otherwise the weather was fine, with mirror-like seas. A weak frontal trough moved eastwards across south-east England during the night of 30/31 May preceded by isolated thundery showers. The wind veered north-easterly and freshened to force four, creating a slight chop on the sea surface and some surf on the evacuation beaches, the only time in nine days. Rear Admiral William Wake-Walker RN, in charge of offshore operations at Dunkirk, later admitted, 'an onshore wind of any force would have stopped embarkation completely'.[3] The momentary disturbance in the weather transitioned to sunny and benign conditions during the first four days of June as a large high-pressure system embraced England and Wales.

Veterans at Dunkirk recall a Mediterranean-like opaque hue to the sea, produced by the fine, calm and sunny weather. German bomber pilots found they could track British ships at night following the luminous wakes created by rising zooplankton and phosphorus in the water. *Bootsman* Herbert Sprang recalled 'sea lights' trailing in the water behind them; 'our boats were hunting in a silver bath'. Ship wakes produced an effect 'like a wheel skidding on the surface'. The phenomenon was two-edged, because with the appearance of British aircraft the hunters became the hunted. E-Boat captains would cut engines and wait for the aircraft noise to dissipate before continuing.[4]

After an hour of lurking expectantly around the Kwinte Buoy, the flotilla commander, *Kapitänleutnant* Wuppermann, moved west with S-25 and S-34 in search of prey. S-30 under *Oberleutnant zur See* (Naval Lieutenant) Wilhelm Zimmermann remained behind to monitor the buoy. Shortly after midnight the two E-Boats attacked the *Shearwater*, a British patrol sloop, near another buoy at Farey Bank. All torpedoes missed. At about the same time a small British convoy headed by the destroyer *Wakeful* approached the Kwinte turn, loaded with troops from Bray Dunes and Dunkirk. *Wakeful* had some 640 soldiers packed below decks. Following at intervals was the *Grafton*, another destroyer carrying 800 troops, and two minesweepers, *Gossamer* and *Lydd*, transporting another 720 troops between them.

Herbert Sprang's E-Boat crippled the French destroyer *Sirocco* two days later, and he described the typical sequence of actions that ensued. 'Black shadows off the port side,' shouted the lookout to the captain, 'and in an instant we were electrified'. Binoculars scanned the dark sea; 'there – a black shadow rose up. That must be a warship! Probably packed full with lots of soldiers'. The Captain ordered 'enemy crossing 15 miles, both tubes make ready!'

Oberleutnant Zimmermann's S-30 surged out of the darkness and closed to within 600 yards. E-Boats were aptly nicknamed the 'Stukas of the sea' because the entire craft, like the dive-bomber fuselage, was aimed at the target for bomb release. 'Starboard 15, fire torpedoes,' recalled Sprang in his atmospheric description of the attack. 'A splash, bang with a hiss [of compressed air] the torpedo shot out of the tube,' and soon 'we could see fine phosphorescent tracks running out to the destroyer'.[5]

Commander Fisher commanding the *Wakeful* recalled that, after clearing the buoy and beginning to zigzag at 20 knots, 'two parallel torpedo tracks about 30 yards apart, one slightly ahead of the other, were seen approaching 150 yards away on the starboard bow'. The light reflecting on the tracks made them look as if they were 'running practically on the surface,' being 'very bright with phosphorescence'. Sprang on the E-Boat watched while his Captain bit his lips with the tension: 'Still not yet? A Miss? *There!* It was as if hell had risen up. A flame shot up several metres from the after-deck.'[6]

Fisher steered hard to port, 'sufficiently to cause one to miss ahead', but the second impacted against the forward boiler room. The ship snapped spectacularly in half, both sections 'standing with its mid-ship end on the bottom,' leaving 'the bow and stern standing about 60 feet above the water'. Only one soldier standing on deck smoking, from 640 below, survived; 96 crew also went down inside the two halves. They were buoyant for no more than 15 seconds, before slipping beneath the surface. Zimmermann quietly withdrew his E-Boat into the darkness to reload.

Three hours later *Grafton* arrived at the scene, with two minesweepers and some converted drifters, including the *Comfort*, already alongside, picking up survivors. Numerous distress flares shooting up and winking signal lights attracted the attention of *U-62*, a German submarine commanded by *Oberleutnant zur See* Michalowski. She fired two torpedoes at *Grafton* with 800 troops on board, one of which blew off the stern, killing her captain, Robinson. In the darkness, the crippled and near sinking *Grafton* and rescue Minesweeper *Lydd* mistook the low-lying silhouette of the drifter *Comfort* off to starboard for an E-Boat. They unleashed a fierce barrage of heavy fire which straddled her and even machine-gunned survivors in the water after she was successfully rammed for good measure by the *Lydd*. This complete debacle resulted in the heaviest loss of life for the whole evacuation.[7]

Wuppermann tried unsuccessfully to launch further torpedo attacks that night with *S-25* and *S-34*, but achieved no hits. Two days later *S-23* and *S-26* crippled the French destroyer *Sirocco*, which capsized and sank with the loss of over 606 troops and 59 crew. Between the night of 23/24 May until the 31st, E-Boats sank or crippled four destroyers, which represented a carrying capacity of between 3,000 and 4,000 soldiers. With daily evacuation totals nearing 68,000, this was a sustainable loss. Reducing ship-carrying capacity was one way of negating the Operation *Dynamo* mission. Ship losses were making inroads into this capacity at this decisive stage of the evacuation, just as fighting troops were starting to embark. German artillery firing from Calais had nullified the usefulness of Route Z, 39 miles directly east–west from Dover. *Kriegsmarine* E-Boats and single U-Boats were impacting on Route Y, another mine-cleared path, an 87-nautical-mile trip passing the east side of the perimeter. This left Route X, a treacherous 55-mile sail through shoals and sandbanks, before going north-west to the North Godwin light and then along the south coast to Ramsgate and Dover. This cost the evacuation process time and concentrated ships, which made them even more vulnerable to *Luftwaffe* air attack.

The evacuation area stretched 30 miles from La Panne in Belgium to the port of Dunkirk in France. The coastline is a long stretch of sand dunes, rising steeply in places, bordering a gently shelving beach, exposed and dry for 200 yards or more at low tide. Water deepens only very gradually offshore, and a destroyer cannot get nearer than half a mile. Small boats were employed to ferry from the beaches to larger ships, if the port of Dunkirk was unusable. On 27 May, the first full day of the evacuation, one cruiser, eight destroyers and 26 other craft had gathered and were active. By 31 May, well into the evacuation process, an emergency call went out in England to produce 400 small craft, sailing boats and cabin cruisers, many crewed by enthusiastic volunteers. Along the evacuation coastline were small towns and seaside resorts, seemingly perched on top of the dunes when viewed from the sea, which sloped gently to the beach. These were the holiday resorts of La Panne, Bray Dunes and St Malo, with characteristic red-brick houses, pretentious villas and typical modern seaside architecture.

French troops from the 68th Infantry Division were already in place along the west side of the Dunkirk defence perimeter, facing the

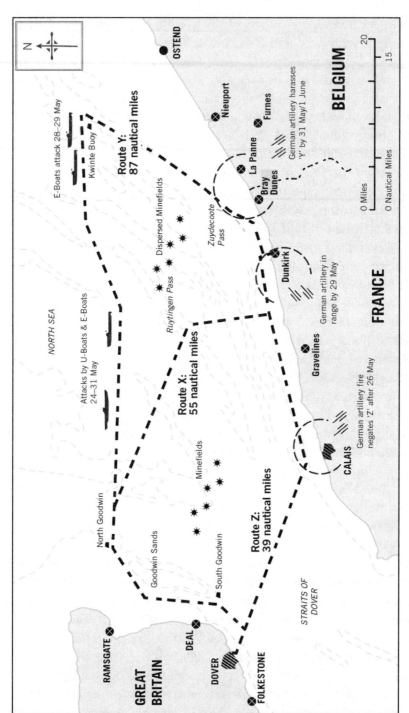

MAP 6: British Evacuation Routes by Sea.

By 26 May the shortest route 'Z' was invalidated by shellfire from Calais. The Zuydecoote route 'Y' was the longest and harassed by E-Boat and U-Boat attacks around the Kwinte and North Goodwin buoys. Bray Dunes and La Panne were under shellfire by 31 May. The *Luftwaffe* massively interdicted routes 'X' and 'Y.'

Germans from Gravelines to Bergues south of the port, on the canal of the same name. It was agreed from the outset, as the perimeter filled, that arriving French troops should be directed to the west side. The British II Corps had arrived barely in time to defend in the east, covering two canals that formed the perimeter corner near Nieuport to almost Furnes (present day Veurne). I Corps defended the centre around Furnes while III Corps held between them and the French at Bergues. The plan was to evacuate the BEF in reverse order, starting with III Corps from an assembly and control area at Malo-les-Bains, the eastern suburb of Dunkirk town. II Corps would leave from La Panne, 10 miles further east, and I Corps from Bray Dunes, 6 miles from Malo. Each day the 18-mile strip of coastline was crowded on average with 10,000 troops, assembling to board boats and completely vulnerable to air attack.

The *Kriegsmarine* had achieved a few notable successes and inflicted heavy casualties on single figures of ships sunk. The overall impact on an embarkation fleet in the process of expanding to over 800 vessels was negligible, however. For the 1944 D-Day landings it was assessed that 500 ships varying from 100 to 15,000 tons were needed to set a division ashore with its equipment and guns. Personnel alone would likely require 50% or less of this figure. Admiral Bertram Ramsay's evacuation fleet was ferrying at maximum over 60,000 per day at the evacuation peak at the end of May and first day of June. This was two or three divisions' worth at a time across a 24-hour period. The 800-ship assembly had to carry ten BEF division equivalents and a further three of line-of-communication troops as well as 27,000 French troops it also managed to take off.

Only the *Luftwaffe* could make any appreciable inroads on this carrying capacity. It had either to sink ships or so cripple the port and harbour installations that no ships could berth. Following the internecine political spat between OKH and OKW that had produced the Panzer Halt Order, Göring offered the *Führer* a grandiose and simplistic solution to administer the *coup de grâce* to the Dunkirk perimeter.

Hitler had been mightily impressed with the *Luftwaffe*'s performance in Poland, lingering over spectacular aerial newsreel footage of Warsaw's destruction. Dunkirk, he assumed, being much smaller, could well be bombed into a subservient capitulation.

Hitler, like the French, had a land-centric view of operations. General Sir Edward Spears described the difficulties he had conveying the 'Dunkirk idea' to the French Premier Reynaud and General Weygand, with whom he liaised. The French view was that: 'The sea was much the same thing as an abyss of boiling pitch and brimstone, an insurmountable obstacle no army could venture over.'

This view was shared by French engineer soldier Marceau Lantenois seeking to embark at St Malo with the BEF. He had never been on a boat before, and 'I was already afraid of the sea,' he admitted, 'and in addition to that there was the bombing'. Spears explained to his French seniors that 'beyond the harbours lay God's own highway, the greatest widest highway in the world, one that led everywhere'. The British had simply to cross the Dover Straits, some 20 miles as the crow flies, or 55 nautical miles on Route X avoiding minefields. The French had considerable doubts.[8]

Göring's view assumed the port of Dunkirk and the shipping assembling offshore would fall easy prey to the *Luftwaffe*. Hitler's attention was already elsewhere, dealing with the enemy south of the Somme and occupying Paris. Göring had not reckoned on the element determining success or failure for all three mediums effecting the evacuation, air, sea, or land; namely, the weather.

FROM THE AIR

Air attacks on 27 May had been a sobering experience for Dunkirk. 'It was the biggest bombing raid over Dunkirk,' Jean Coutanceau, with the Seventh French Army recalled. 'The planes came over in waves of 50 to 100 every 20 minutes, from nine in the morning until seven in the evening without stopping.' It seemed Göring would indeed honour his pledge to the *Führer*. Coutanceau remembered, 'all the docks, everything was burning'. The *Wehrmacht* high command bulletin broadcast across the *Reich* the same day reported that 'the port installation was in flames'.[9] Despite this, nearly 14,000 soldiers were evacuated, a poor performance, but this was the first day of the evacuation. The weather then worsened from hour to hour. By mid-afternoon the following day, the day of the Belgian surrender, it was raining heavily. Individual *Luftwaffe* bomber *Gruppen* found gaps in the cloud cover over Ostend and Nieuport but not at Dunkirk. Low cloud fused with the rising smoke and dust and blotted out the entire area.

Pouring rain heralded 29 May. Von Richthofen commanding VIII *Fliegerkorps* became increasingly exasperated:

> All levels of the higher command were clamouring today for VIII Air Corps to go again at the ships and boats, on which the English divisions were getting away with their bare skins. We only had a ceiling of 300 feet and as General commanding I expressed the view that the enemy's concentrated flak was causing greater loss to our side than we were to his.[10]

It was not just the weather creating difficulties. Göring's sudden and unexpected intervention to subdue the BEF *in situ* and prevent the evacuation was a major change for the air *Schwerpunkt*. Bomber units were configured and located to support ground, not anti-shipping, operations. Squadrons were frequently on call to protect the southern Somme flank and strike at the French traffic network. Building up *Luftwaffe* ground support had only just begun on airstrips in Belgium. Attacks were still primarily flown from available bases in Holland to the Swiss frontier. Long-range bombing attacks could generally only fly once per day and even then might be diverted elsewhere because of bad weather. *Kampgeschwader* 51, for example, was flying from its Bavarian bases at Memmingen and Landsberg and having to refuel in the Rhine Valley on the way back. Bomber units also flew at the limits of German fighter escort effectiveness, and their ground control agencies were too far away. The Ju 52 transport fleet had suffered disastrous losses in Holland, which impacted adversely on logistic resupply. Bomb ordinance for sea targets was different from that required on land. More fundamentally, Göring neglected to revise and define the nature of the new *Schwerpunkt*. Was the objective to neutralize all port and embarkation facilities at Dunkirk to prevent embarkation? Or was the imperative to sink ships with evacuated personnel on board to produce unacceptable casualties?

General Albert Kesselring, commanding *Luftflotte* 2 from Münster, had initially thought the Belgian surrender would bring some relief to his hard-pressed crews:

The C in C *Luftwaffe* [Göring] must have been sufficiently aware of the effort of almost three weeks of ceaseless operations on my airmen not to order an operation which could hardly be carried out successfully by [even] fresh forces.

'I expressed this view very clearly to Göring,' Kesselring recalled, 'and told him it could not be done even with the support of [von Richthofen's] VIII Air Group.' Kesselring complained about his 'groggy' and 'overtired' units which had to keep taking off'. Many of his squadrons were down to just half their authorized strengths.[11]

Fighter pilot Ulrich Steinhilper with JG 52 recalled the mistakes that could occur with such relentless cumulative combat flying. Standing on the grass at a forward airstrip at Charleville, 'my attention was attracted by the sound of an approaching *Dornier 17*' bomber. He was making his wheels down final landing approach:

Then I heard the approach of another engine but this time a 109 [fighter] at full power, for take off from the opposite direction. There was nothing we could do other than hope that by some miracle they would miss each other, but it was not to be. Just as the *Dornier's* engines were throttled back there came the sickening impact as the aircraft collided and wreckage scattered across the field. The 109 removed the whole cockpit of the *Dornier*, killing the crew instantly before breaking up and falling to earth. There were no survivors.[12]

During the early afternoon of 29 May, after 36 hours of marginal weather, the clouds parted and the sun shone through. By 3.40pm the first formations of *Luftflotte* 2 arrived over Dunkirk: *Kampfgeschwader* 30 from Holland and *Lehrgeschwader* 1 from Düsseldorf. Both flew the Junkers 88, the *Luftwaffe's* so-called 'wonder [dive] bomber'. Von Richthofen at his Saint-Pol headquarters had been assailed by a stream of telephone calls from Göring and his staff, complaining they were not attacking Dunkirk as they should. Low cloud cover had precluded this all morning. The disgruntled von Richthofen commented in his diary that 'the *Luftwaffe*'s supreme commander has the jitters over Dunkirk'. *Major* Oscar Dinort commanding *Stukageschwader* 2 at Beaulieu airfield was told by von Richthofen's Chief of Staff Seidemann: 'clear the decks for Dunkirk'. They began taking off in waves after 4pm; time over target was predicted for 5pm.[13]

Captain William Tennant's parties of Royal Navy personnel coordinating the evacuation from the shore had profited from the 36-hour respite. They had formulated a speedy evacuation process of forming groups of 50 men, led from the beaches to the East Mole pier. The embarkation rate steadily increased to 2,000 men an hour, screened by the murky weather and heavy smoke pall over the port and town. By 29 May they were achieving 3,000 to 4,000 per hour, and these were men from the fighting divisions, 2nd, 23rd and parts of 42nd and 44th Division. The non-combatant elements had largely been lifted. They had been relieved by the French and were moving through the town. 'Their conduct and bearing,' Tennant observed, 'was noticeably superior':

Previous detachments had reached the embarkation points in a straggling manner with scarcely any semblance of order. The corps troops marched in formation along the beaches, quickly scattering during an air raid and reforming and continuing afterwards. It was this order which enabled such a high rate of embarkation to be maintained.[14]

These were the very men the *Luftwaffe* aimed to stop.

Hauptmann Helmut Mahlke with *Staffel* 2 (9 to 12 aircraft) of *Stukageschwader 1* approached Dunkirk, flying between snowy white banks of cumulous cloud at 11,500 feet. He was sweating, 'in the thin air, with the summer's evening sun still beating hotly through the cockpit windows'. Looking about, he recalled: 'Today, it seemed as if everybody who *was* anybody in the *Luftwaffe* was heading for Dunkirk. The airspace around us was crowded with German aircraft.' 'The bad weather meant that we hadn't been able to lay our morning eggs'; normally the first sortie of the day, remembered another Stuka *Kettenführer* (three aircraft). 'Huge banks of clouds reaching down almost to ground level greatly hamper downward visibility.' It was difficult for his three aircraft to maintain visible contact 'through the scudding cloud and smoke from the burning town'. A curtain of flak rose up to greet them. *Oberleutnant* Dietrich Peltz, a *Staffelkapitän* (Squadron Commander) with *Stukageschwader* 3, recalled there were so many aircraft 'that a pilot had literally to watch out that he did not get a bomb in the neck from comrades flying above him'. Finding Dunkirk during the eight missions he flew against it was never a problem: 'Even hidden by banks of cloud, Dunkirk was not to be missed, because countless numbers of anti-aircraft shell bursts were to be seen, even above the clouds, at the point where the town ought to lie.'[15]

Robert Merle, a French liaison officer with the British at Bray Dunes, gazed skyward on hearing anti-aircraft guns opening up and saw 'the sky was again splattered with tiny black clouds'. He recalled: 'They were flying in close order, and all at once they began to peel off gracefully, as they had already done, separating, coming together again, then once more separating.'

Confronted abruptly with such a vast target array, 10,000 troops on the beach and scores of ships offshore and in port, pilots had to be directed to attack specific objectives. Hurried radio orders were transmitted. Merle, watching this from the ground, likened the process to 'the well-ordered figures of a ballet' as they organized themselves, 'a sort of ritual dance before the attack'.[16]

The *Kettenführer* spotted 'a nice fat freighter tied up alongside' a large loading ramp by a harbour wall. 'I run my hands over the controls almost by instinct,' as his three Stukas peeled out of formation to dive. 'Now it's stick forward, and the old crate stands on its head as down we go straight at the target.' Each time a Stuka pilot dived it was said he died a little, and the strain built up day by day. Mahlke accepted that individual dive-bomber pilots had 'different perceptions of the physical demands made upon them'. For some, 'those demands may even have been close to the limits of their endurance'. Mahlke personally experienced 'occasional and unpleasant build-up of pressure in my ears' which he alleviated by constantly swallowing until his ears popped.

The German propaganda magazine *Signal* published six sequential photographs of a Stuka pilot's face in the dive, as part of a psychological study. The first picture shows a clear-eyed pilot, who has identified his target. The next shows face muscles becoming 'painfully tense' as the momentum of the near vertical dive takes effect, reducing blood flow to the brain. Falling at 1,000 yards per second the face displays strain and intense concentration; the pilot is clenching his teeth. When the pilot pulls out of the dive, Mahlke explained 'crews [were] pressed down in their seats by some 3 to 5 G, but it is up to the pilot to judge his recovery'. The subsequent three portrait frames show the pilot looking drawn and relieved on straightening out; blood flow to the brain improves and he is looking alert again, seeking out the next target in the final picture.

'At first' during training, Mahlke admitted, 'an angle of 70° [to dive] seemed to me impossibly steep, but it soon became routine'. He found the altimeter always lagged a little behind the plane's actual height in a vertical dive, so a degree of judgement was required for this and a myriad of other lever alterations and instrument adjustments to control the dive brakes.[17] The tensions and exertions with each sortie led to the cumulative fatigue that afflicted most pilots, having seen uninterrupted combat flying since 10 May.

Robert Merle had no appreciation of this cockpit-eye perspective as he observed the Stuka attacks: 'They side-slipped, started a descent, pulled up again, banked, described circles, cut figures of eight; then suddenly forming a triangle forwards, they flew off like a flock of migrating birds.'[18]

The third wave of Stuka dive-bombers approaching Dunkirk harbour was attracted to a cluster of ten vessels berthed at the end of the east jetty: two destroyers, six armed trawlers and two paddle-wheel excursion steamers. The destroyer *Grenade* was hit twice, the bomb exploding in the forward fuel tank sluicing the innards of the ship with a slurry of oily flame. The doomed ship drifted stern first into the harbour channel. The Isle of Man paddle-wheel RMS *Fenella* had a bomb plunge through its promenade deck packed with 650 troops on board. Another bomb hit and exploded among the boulders upon which the wooden jetty of the Mole stood and wrecked the engine room and perforated the hull, so that she began to list and settle. Troops quickly clambered across to the other paddle steamer *Crested Eagle*, which later managed to clear the harbour. Three of the armed trawlers were crippled while the remaining destroyer, *Verity*, despite being straddled by water spouts for 35 minutes, managed to cast off, but empty.

Pilots looking down observed the harbour area erupt in a maelstrom of hits, evident from what Peltz described as 'an enormous black mushroom shooting up', amid water jets shooting up from near misses. Shrapnel lashed the harbour basin, multiple splashes and spray fanning out from hits on the harbour wall. Peltz observed 'flashes appear at a number of points on the ship' they were attacking. 'Several bombs also fall beside and behind it' as his *Staffel* dived down from all directions.[19] Robert Merle, possibly aboard the *Crested Eagle*, remembered the totally intimidating noise: 'so great that it was almost more than a human could stand': 'The enormous volume of sound vibrated through his body. He was no longer frightened, but he felt unstrung, shaken, exhausted by the noise. He wondered if death could be caused by noise, just as by concussion.'[20]

Crested Eagle managed to cast off from the harbour shambles at 6pm, according to seaman Frank Pattrick 'to the accompaniment of loud cheers from the troops and murmurs of relief from the crew'. Attacks had paused and 'being the only seaworthy vessel left we were inundated with survivors from the ships in the harbour'. Stukas approaching at high altitude immediately detected her wide wake, characteristic of paddle steamers, as she came abreast of Malo-les-Bains. Heavy wakes normally denoted a heavy cruiser. With no RAF opposition in sight, they came in 'unhindered', Pattrick recalled, diving to virtual mast height, 'where we could clearly see their crew through the transparent cockpit cover'. Four of five bombs hit the wooden steamer, three aft of the bridge, ripping into the oil fuel and diesel tanks, causing the entire rear section of the ship from bridge to stern to burst into an oily fire ball: 'As we rushed aft we saw men running with skin blasted from their faces and arms, some scalded and badly wounded and our First Lieutenant only recognizable by the emblem on his steel helmet'.

Horrified onlookers on the beaches at Bray Dunes saw men on fire 'shrieking and dancing like Dervishes'. Decks had been crammed with troops, and the wounded stowed on stretchers below. 'We made for the main stairway' to rescue them, Pattrick recalled, but 'we found everything a sea of flame and nothing could be done for them'. The Captain, Lieutenant Commander Booth, managed to skilfully run the stricken ship aground off Bray Dunes. Robert Merle remembered men were too scared to jump into the shallow water and seemed to succumb to 'an overpowering feeling of drowsiness'. They were likely incapacitated by shock and starved of oxygen, sucked in by the intensity of the fireball. Pattrick watched men jump overboard:

It was only when they reached the sea that they realized that the oil was lying some inches thick on the surface, it had not had time to disperse and they were unable to get their heads high enough to breathe.[21]

Two hundred survivors milling about in the water were heavily machine-gunned from the air and rescue boats were also bombed. The *Luftwaffe*, more National Socialist orientated than the other arms of the *Wehrmacht*, had no intention of allowing Tommy to get away to fight another day.

Seventeen naval vessels, varying in size from three destroyers down to drifters, were sunk on the afternoon and evening of 29 May. Seven more destroyers, a sloop and minesweeper were damaged and put out of action, as were a passenger ship and hospital carrier. Eight other merchant vessels went down, including the 6,900-ton *Clan Macalister*. It was a devastating blow, resulting in the eight modern destroyers left being withdrawn from the evacuation, leaving 15 older destroyers. The losses represented a 20,000-troop lift capacity, about a half day's evacuation rate up to now. That night over 47,000 troops got back to Britain, 2,000 of them casualties, about one-third lifted from the beaches and the rest from the devastated harbour. The fast and manoeuvrable destroyers were proving the most capable transports. Excluding further losses, the 15 remaining could maintain a flow of one per hour and lift 17,000 troops in 24 hours. If such an afternoon's *Luftwaffe* impact could be sustained, appreciable inroads might yet be made on the numbers of fighting men the Royal Navy could lift off.[22]

The weather the next day was disappointing. German observation planes reported damp grey fog rolling in across the Channel. After the promising results of the day before, von Richthofen was anxiously frustrated. He telephoned *Major* Dinort's *Kampfgeschwader* wing at Beaulieu and ordered his Stukas to strafe Dunkirk without delay. Inside an hour Dinort returned with bombs still on board. The fog was impenetrable, he reported; losses at low level would have been unsustainable. Von Richthofen insisted; looking out of his window, he could see Saint-Pol-sur-Mer basking in sunlight. Dinort took off again to mollify him; 'I expect no less of you,' was the icy rejoinder. When he returned a second time, von Richthofen, still experiencing fine weather, was uncompromising. 'May I suggest then,' Dinort proposed, 'that the General flies with us to check?' *Luftflotte* 2 and 3 also reported 'totally unfavourable weather'. Despite 'colossal achievements' on the 29th, von Richthofen knew Göring was becoming increasingly nervous at the situation over Dunkirk. 'Unfortunately attacks against Dunkirk were not possible today,' he wrote in his log, 'because of the bad weather'.

Results were also indifferent for *Luftflotte* 2 the following day and *Luftflotte* 3 was 'not operational on account of bad flying weather'.[23]

'It was funny weather over Dunkirk,' recalled Flight Lieutenant Brian Kingcome RAF:

A lot of the time there you saw nothing but aircraft because you were sandwiched between layers of cloud. An aircraft would suddenly appear and disappear... You fired at something which disappeared perhaps with some smoke coming out of it, into a layer of cloud below you.[24]

The morning of 31 May started with fog, which cleared by afternoon, enabling a few bomber formations to operate, but the Stukas were grounded all day. 'Still bad weather,' von Richthofen gloomily noted in the log: 'Yet heavy shipping traffic is reported around Dunkirk'. Recce flights despite all attempts are not able to get through. The Stukas are unable to attack.'

Von Richthofen was irritated at the operational impasse that had been imposed upon him and complained to his staff:

The whole situation is totally unsatisfactory. Because of the great flying distances, bound up with logistics difficulties, it is not possible for the VIII Fliegerkorps to establish a *Schwerpunkt* main point of effort. Moreover, my impression is that more energetic attacks by the army on Dunkirk would be the quickest way of clearing the situation and making the most British prisoners. It is not clear why orders are not following to execute this.

The issue was becoming a distraction for preparations for Operation *Röt*, the next phase of the campaign. Of six days since the beginning of Operation *Dynamo*, the *Luftwaffe* had only actively interfered for one and a half, 27 May and the afternoon of the 29th. 'So nothing is happening on the coast,' von Richthofen complained, 'and unfortunately we are losing time.' During this period the British evacuated its rear echelon troops and the I Corps, and was on the verge of starting to embark the II Corps. About one-third of the fighting troops were taken off during the poor weather: 54,000 on 30 May and nearly 68,000 on the 31st. Probably about 80,000 British troops remained to be evacuated.[25]

On 1 June the weather dawned sunny and clear. At forward airstrips, and inland on Dutch airfields and in the *Reich*, the start-up roar of aircraft engines and the reek of aviation fuel filled the air. The weather had at last opened a stable window of opportunity; this time, they should be able to finish Tommy off.

<h2 style="text-align:center">ON LAND</h2>

Von Richthofen was not the only one questioning inactivity by the German land forces. *Generalleutnant* Christian Hansen commanding the X Infantry Corps was also puzzled on 29 May and asking 'why high command was not concentrating the *Schwerpunkt* on the coastal area'. His corps 'was trying to gain territory to the west, to destroy enemy forces before they reached the coast'. But the British had successfully run their gauntlet. Hansen was distracted by command and coordination issues in the limited operational space. The 18th Infantry Division newly attached to his corps was snarled up on the roads with von Kleist's mobile 20th Division infantry. The motorized troops sought to disengage and move to new assembly areas for Operation *Röt*. He had to dispatch his operations officer to the 9th Panzer Division to regulate the move forward of the 18th and 61st Divisions, against the withdrawing flow. Army Groups A and B had come together on the south-east periphery of the newly formed Dunkirk perimeter and were competing for limited space for accommodation and assembly areas. There were also competing priorities for movement on the few arterial traffic routes. All this was further complicated, as Hansen observed, by 'unimaginable numbers of vehicles, guns, tanks and so forth' abandoned by the Allies, 'often in two rows lined up behind each other'. Traffic conditions were dire, 'roads and lanes were jammed up, mostly not even enabling a single traffic lane to flow'.[26]

The front against the west side of the perimeter was static. War correspondent Christoph von Imhoff described 'a pitch-black night, lit up by flames on the horizon to the northwest':

They silhouetted a few church towers here and there in the distance. A dazzling flare up and then a few dull thundery impacts! That was our artillery firing, then again, a muted flash in the far distance, a whistling, deep reverberations and blasts. These were the English naval guns, taking our positions under fire this night.

Von Imhoff thought the atmospheric scene 'conjured up images from the past war'. In the morning the sun's rays barely penetrated the silvery smoke from the fires; 'you would think night was not paying attention to day, night had descended again in the midst of the sunlight'.[27]

There was little activity in the *Grossdeutschland's* sector west of Bergues, where they were being relieved by Sixth Army infantry formations. Fighting appeared to be dying down; 'prisoners report that the defenders were being worn down by Stuka bombs and shells from German heavy artillery'. There were continuous RAF bombing attacks, hitting isolated vehicles and causing casualties among the regiment's 12th Company. The relief was slow and subject to niggling delays. Two infantry regiments, the 51st and 54th, arrived at the *Grossdeutschland's* 2nd Battalion area: 'The 51st Regiment was slated to attack the town, but the planned participation by 2nd Battalion in the operation was cancelled. Then the attack by the 51st was also put on hold.'

'The battle in Flanders was nearing its end', the regimental history recorded. The impression was that resistance is 'waning', and 'the lessening of enemy artillery fire was especially noticeable'. Soldiers knew they were about to be relieved and move to new assembly areas for *Röt*, the next mission. There was scant enthusiasm to take risks when the foe was clearly beaten. 'Enemy warships were anchored at sea', clearly outlined from the shore, 'and smaller craft could be seen shuttling back and forth to the beaches'. The BEF was busily embarking and evacuating its bridgehead, while a lack of urgency seemed to reign in the German lines around the perimeter.[28]

The French were holding the line with the 68th Division from the great naval fortress at Mardyck inland along the canal of the same name, and eastward following the Canal de la Haute Colme to the fortress town of Bergues. The medieval town was perched incongruously on an odd little hill overlooking the surrounding plain. The British held the line eastwards from here, along the Canal de la Baseé-Colme, running out eventually to the sea at Nieuport, 6 miles inside Belgium. Much of this line traversed the reclaimed sea marshland known as Les Moëres, the marshes. The long straight road leading to Ghyvelde village and Bray Dunes was now a causeway across a lake, which seemed to German observers to extend to the coast. On either side of the road was a double bank of vehicles, abandoned and driven cab-first into the water. Submerged side roads were only distinguishable by lines of trees poking out of the brackish water.

Opening the sea dykes had transformed the area into a shallow lake, which meant the British had only to defend two short sectors left above water. The first was the canal bank extending 2 to 2½ miles east of Bergues, tricky to defend because rows of houses on the southern bank allowed a covered German approach. The other weak spots in the British line were the dry sand dunes forming a 1,000-yard-wide strip behind the evacuation beaches at La Panne and Bray Dunes beyond. Fortunately, during the night of 27/28 May the 60th French Infantry division appeared in this sector. They arrived in Belgian trucks handed over as they had prepared to surrender to save their French comrades from encirclement.

On 30 May two regiments from the French 12th Division entered the perimeter, with artillery and elements of the 32nd Division, with two artillery regiments and two squadrons of tanks. These men were from the much-depleted French 3rd Corps commanded by General de la Laurencie. The general, whose troops had already been assessed as stout fighters by the British, was surprised to find the BEF had not troubled to man the existing strong defensive positions, bunkers and fieldworks, *in situ* along the French border with Belgium. This ran through the area just east of Bray Dunes. This he proceeded to do, offering a formidable depth position to the strung-out forces of II Corps, which had barely arrived in time to block German incursions coming from the Nieuport-Furnes area. The area was the most vulnerable sector of the Dunkirk perimeter. Harry Dennis, a driver with the 1st East Surreys, recalled the difficulty of establishing a line at Furnes after the Belgian surrender. '5,000 Belgian soldiers came through our line, all on bikes,' he remembered. His CO appealed for 'as many fighting men as possible', only to be told 'they had already been given orders to stand down'. British soldiers were not happy with their erstwhile allies. 'We couldn't understand their capitulation,' Dennis recalled, 'after all, there were 5,000 blokes sitting on their bums and our blokes out there were really struggling to hold the line.'[29]

Hauptmann Schimpf, commanding the 1st Battalion of the 192nd Regiment with 56th Division recalled by contrast that 'morale in the battalion was high due to the announcement': 'our final objective on the North Sea would soon be reached. We all felt good, beautiful and excellent weather on the beaches, which we could all well do with. However, it did not turn out that way.'

Schimpf learned 'that there should only be weak English resistance in Furnes'. The 1st and 2nd Battalions of the Grenadier Guards had arrived just in time to occupy the solid red-brick town with its old stone walls. They knew it was vital to block the German advance as the BEF embarked, which they were to hold until told otherwise. Signalman George Jones was with the 1st Guards marching towards the town when 'Harry came up alongside and with a backward jerk of his head drew my attention over to our right rear':

> About a mile away and out of range as far as we were concerned, a party of Germans could be seen marching, wheeling bicycles at about the same speed as our own column. Friend and foe arrived in Furnes at about the same time. We took up positions on one side of the canal and most of the Germans the other.[30]

The town was divided by a fly-infested scum-covered canal, full of sunken barges. The approaching 56th Division infantry had every reason to feel confident, as Schimpf explained:

> Veurne [Furnes] was empty this side of the canal. Abandoned French ammunition, baggage and horse-drawn wagons were lying all about. It was an awful picture, bloated cattle and dead and wounded cows and horses were strewn about in the no-man's-land between our furthest forward company and the canal.[31]

They assumed a walkover. He set up his command post in a loft, where he could observe the whole canal bank.

On 30 May *General* Georg von Küchler's Eighteenth Army was appointed the lead headquarters to reduce the Dunkirk perimeter. Battles until now, he recalled, 'were conducted with no overall coordination', commenting 'corps and divisions were apparently doing their own thing'. Attacking units had defined their own axis without reference to neighbours while infantry divisions had been unclear about their command relationships with panzer and motorized forces. Von Küchler's Corps was doubled overnight from 11pm. His first task that morning was to visit his four commanders to find out what was going on around the perimeter. Two of them were his own, the IX and XXVI Corps, and two newly attached: X Corps from Sixth Army, and XIV Corps from the *Panzergruppe* Kleist. It became clear the enemy was defending on a line from the French fortress at Mardyck, next to the port of Dunkirk, through Brouckerque and Bergues in the south, and east to Furnes and Nieuport.

Haphazard attacks were conducted that afternoon. On the west side of the perimeter, in the Kleist sector, light tanks with the 9th Panzer Division attacked towards Spycker supported by infantry from 11th *Schützen* Regiment. They were repulsed, as was another attack by 9th *Aufklärungs* (Recce) Battalion, again beaten back by the French 68th Division. In the south and west an LAH assault was stopped on the Canal Haute Colme line, while the 18th Infantry Division moved up in the X Corps area and mounted an evening attack from Warham. *Generalleutnant* Halder remarked that von Küchler 'apparently has not been able to reach all units now under its control'. As a consequence: 'Our attack resolved itself into individual actions against an enemy stubbornly defending himself behind the canals, and so only achieved slight local successes.'

Focus in any case at OKH was on forthcoming operations for *Röt*. 'Regrouping is making good strides,' Halder reported. 'Fourth, Sixth, Ninth and Second armies will take over their sectors by noon tomorrow, next to Twelfth and Sixteenth armies.'[32]

Von Küchler was left with ten infantry divisions and four corps' worth of heavy artillery to compress and subjugate the Dunkirk bridgehead. This meant about 92,000 British and 156,000 French troops were cornered by about 120,000 Germans, for the first time under single unified command. This needed another 24 hours to practically enact because the staffs and logistic systems from three different armies, Fourth, Sixth and Eighteenth, had to rejig and come together in order to work. These complicated command arrangements had to be rationalized just as the panzer and motorized units had to be relieved in place from the western and southern end of the perimeter and marched off to new assembly areas. Geyer with IX Corps remembered how boundaries between units had been repeatedly changed 'in the past few days and hours'. He had heard it 'from higher headquarters there had been some debate whether the final battle for Dunkirk should be directed by Eighteenth or Sixth Army independently, or both together'. He craved clear orders 'because the situation was developing very quickly, and direction forward was urgently required'.[33]

A point often overlooked by many historians at this stage of the campaign was this fundamental change in the ratio of attackers to defenders. On 28 May there were some 30 German divisions operating around the Allied pocket; of these 20 were being relocated for the next phase of the campaign, leaving ten *in situ* to reduce the perimeter. The accepted military convention for success in attack is a 3 to 1 superiority, yet with this revision of command responsibility, German attackers were outnumbered by British and French defenders. The ratio would diminish as more troops were lifted from the beaches, but it indicated the extent to which both OKH and OKW had accepted Dunkirk was a subsidiary front – a mop-up action. Urgency appeared lacking to finish off the BEF, the difference between victory and total annihilation. *General* Geyer remembered 'we had the order to attack energetically, Eighteenth Army should end the Dunkirk matter'. Von Bock commanding Army Group B commented a few days later that 'the business at Dunkirk is finally drawing to an end,' adding 'we could have achieved that eight days earlier if a unified command had been created there sooner'. Britain's fighting troops might well then have been netted if an aggressive attempt had been made to roll up the perimeter from the east after the Belgian surrender. Geyer commented, 'army high command not only failed to bring the appropriate force to bear to speedily clear up the pocket, they even took them away'. He understood why; 'they were already preparing for the new bigger objective, the concluding attack against the French Army'. Kesselring, commanding *Luftflotte 2*, like many others in high command underestimated the ingenuity, resourcefulness and determination displayed by British planning to set up Operation *Dynamo*. 'We had no idea in 1940,' he later admitted, 'that the number of British and French who escaped was anywhere near the figure of 300,000 given today. Even 100,000 we believed to be well above the mark.'[34]

The 56th Division bearing down on Furnes still had potential to cut off the British II Corps combat troops seeking to evacuate from La Panne and Bray Dunes. The British Guards battalions, occupying the town barely in time, complained 'British and French soldiers holding the town on the previous day' were 'drunk when we entered it'. With 256th Infantry Division pushing hard against Nieuport to their right and the 216th approaching the Bergues-Furness canal south of the town, 56th Division was in a prime position to threaten the II Corps' evacuation. This was just at the moment when the 4th and 3rd British Divisions were seeking to thin out the line, preparatory to moving down to the beaches. Unbeknown to von Küchler, there was an outside chance of penetrating into the sand dune zone, extending from La Panne to St Malo and the vital East Mole in the port of Dunkirk. It was a pivotal moment in the battle, recognized only on the British side, grimly set to hold their rearguard positions until the combat divisions had been safely embarked.

Hauptmann Schimpf with the 1st Battalion of the 192nd Regiment watching the fierce artillery bombardment of Furnes recalled, 'there was not much to see or hear from the enemy'. It appeared 56th Division was pushing on an open door. Houses were blazing around the outskirts of town and thick acrid smoke filled the air. 'It made us think that in fact we should only expect weak resistance.' Grenadier Guardsmen had meanwhile managed to occupy houses overlooking the canal in extremely testing conditions. Most took cover in cellars, sheltering from the intense artillery shelling. Schimpf watched his sister battalion, the 2nd of the 192nd, go into the attack and saw 'the complete point platoon pinned to the ground by rifle and machine-gun fire, they made no progress across the flat ground'. They paused and waited for their own artillery to have a greater effect.[35]

Schimpf attacked further south at the north-east entry point of town, profiting from the protection of houses that covered his approach. Even so his men were being picked off by British snipers from as far away as 500 yards. Once they got in among the houses, 'you had to take great care,' he recalled, 'and *marsch-marsch* [move-move], to quickly clear squares and streets', to maintain the tempo of the assault: 'This was often seriously impeded by destroyed houses, broken street lights, fallen telegraph poles and shell craters.'[36]

They were halted by heavy British artillery fire and machine-gun fire from the flanks and took cover in houses. They brought forward their own heavy machine guns and wheeled up anti-tank guns to shoot up the houses opposite as they prepared an inflatable dinghy assault across the canal. Schimpf decided to pause and take stock; their own artillery support was too weak and the smoke cover they were firing was insufficient. Darkness would soon cover the crossing. Forward artillery observers spotted from the railway station buildings directly behind them.

At about 6.30pm Schimpf's battalion line was rocked by an enormous explosion that suddenly erupted in the railway station. An ammunition train, unnoticed for what it was, had been struck by artillery fire. 'The effect was shocking,' division staff officer *Hauptmann* Sprenger recalled; 'heavy losses, especially among the 1st Company Pioneer Battalion 47,' earmarked to transport Schimpf's battalion across the canal. Three of the battery commanders from the 4th Artillery Battalion supporting them were also killed. 'The detonation was so strong,' Sprenger remembered, 'that back at the division command post in Avecappelle [a village 3½ miles to the east] they thought an aircraft bomb had exploded next to the headquarters.' All the houses around the station were completely flattened.[37]

Hoping to profit from the fall-out from the massive blast, Schimpf launched his 2nd Company across the canal. Frantic paddling propelling a variety of heavily laden four-man and 12-man pneumatic rubber dinghies, or *Flosssacks*, got them over. The company commander soon came back, 'and on my question what's wrong?' Schimpf recalled, he got a shaken response: '*Impossible!* My company is down to around 30 men and all the rest are dead or wounded.' The regimental commander *Hauptmann* Reich simply ordered a resumption of the attacks. The 4th Company, moving its dinghies from cover to cover, pushed off but got no nearer than 30 yards to the opposite bank. 'Our heavy machine guns and anti-tank shot blindly into the darkness,' Schimpf recalled, to no result. The British did not return fire, waiting for boats to enter the canal, then they 'shot from the overhanging bank, directly across the water, shooting up a number of dinghies'. These scythed through rubber dinghy sides and tossed men and equipment into the water. Despite casualties, much of the battalion got across and momentarily pushed the British back from the canal bank. 'All hell broke out here,' recalled one of Schimpf's company commanders: 'The English lay just over three yards away in their positions, and covered us with machine-gun fire, which went too high, and with hand grenades and mortars.' An oil-carrying barge moored nearby burst into flames and illuminated the entire surrounding area.

We still had not got into the British positions and every minute of additional delay cost us even more blood. After a quick reorganization and a salvo of hand grenades and a *hurrah*, we were in amongst a completely surprised enemy.[38]

Meanwhile elements from the 2nd and 3rd Battalions of the 192nd, the rest of the regiment, had got across the canal, trying to bolster Schimpf's precarious bridgehead. The left flank of the Furnes defences, manned by depleted Berkshires and Suffolks infantry, was crumbling. A distraught sapper rushed inside the British 2nd Grenadier Guards HQ and announced the Germans were getting over the canal unopposed. Acting CO Major Richard Colvin dispatched 2nd Lieutenant Jones to investigate, just as the Suffolks and Berkshires, with 246 Field Company Royal Engineers, were pulling out. 'Jones attempted to reorganize and rally them,' the 2nd Grenadiers' war diary records:

> But when some broke under further heavy shellfire he found it necessary to shoot some of the men, and his NCOs turned others back at the point of the bayonet. Jones then organized and led a counter-attack, which not only resulted in the re-establishment of positions along the bank, but which also seems to have restored the men's morale.[39]

'We had hardly seized the English position,' Schimpf's company commander recalled, '... when we were confronted by heavy machine gun fire. Right and left from me wounded were shrieking and groaning, with difficulty we placed them under much needed cover.'[40]

Forward artillery observers joined in to help carry them back to the rear, 'and fought with naked spades and bayonets at our side'. Attempts to cross the canal came to naught. The 192nd Regiment attack was bogged down, with Schimpf's battalion marooned on the enemy bank. The blazing oil barge 'lit up the entire area like daylight', and any movement caught by its reflected glare came under machine gun or mortar and artillery fire. 'The English constantly tried to reach the canal edge through counter-attacks,' the division reported. By nightfall 56th Division had lost 33 killed and 71 wounded trying to get over the canal.

Elements of the 1st Battalion of the 192nd remained cut off all day on 31 May, perched inside a few isolated houses at the canal edge. They could not even consider withdrawal because virtually every dinghy had been shot to pieces. Attempts to get the wounded back across were repeatedly fired upon. One British fighting patrol's attempt to cut off *Leutnant* Richter's beleaguered group of houses on the far bank from the flank came to grief when it was seen at the last moment and shot to pieces. The regiment was at an impasse.

Schimpf's battalion alone lost 39 killed in this action, the worst loss of the French campaign. Some 54 dead German soldiers were later laid out in multiple lines at the canal edge for identification and burial. Photographed by a 56th Division soldier, most are on their backs, plaintive hands raised skyward as if in supplication, stiffened by rigour mortis in the poses in which they died. The *Spiess*, or sergeant major, can be seen moving among the lanes of dead, retrieving identity discs. These thin metal ovals were snapped in two, one segment buried with the corpse, the other for unit records. Civilians are visible beyond, digging a mass grave, overseen by German soldiers, who are also wandering about checking for friends and unit members. Smoke from the burnt-out oil barge permeates the scene, rising from the skeletal outline in the canal. The 56th Division losses on 31 May were severe: 77 killed and 158 wounded, with two missing. The 192nd Regiment was withdrawn from the line that evening, to recoup and replenish. Men were exhausted and depressed; they had reached the limit of combat effectiveness.

There was, however, progress either side of Furnes. To the north-east the 256th Infantry Division, heavily supported by artillery, made inroads into the British 12th Brigade defence, establishing a bridgehead across the Nieuport-Furnes canal. South of Furnes, 56th Division's 171st Regiment broke into the periphery of the marshy Moëres area, crossing the Bergues-Furnes canal at Bulscamp, in the teeth of resistance from 151 Brigade. It was now floundering in the flooded area. The British II Corps line hastily established to the east had bought time for evacuations at La Panne and Bray Dunes. The British plan was for the 4th Division to begin thinning out from 2am during the night of 31 May/1 June and for 3rd Division to fall back an hour later to beaches at La Panne and Bray. The thinly held line proved both costly and exhausting for 256th and 56th Divisions to penetrate. It was only at early dawn on 1 June that German reconnaissance patrols, probing the canal bank in the British 7th Guards Brigade sector, discovered they had gone.

Ground bombing support by the RAF struck elements of the 256th Division on the Westende crossroads near Nieuport during the late afternoon, causing heavy casualties and spoiling their intended advance. RAF bombing attacks on the pontoon bridges across the Nieuport canal also checked progress and Blenheim bombers interdicted troop columns moving up to Furnes from Ypres. *Generalleutnant* Karl Kriebel commanding the 56th Division reflected 'a heavy day of battle has passed us by,' acknowledging 'the English had held their bridgehead both sides of Furnes with astonishing tenacity'. RAF raids continued to niggle at a sensitive German infantry nerve; they were unaccustomed to such unprecedented enemy air activity. The 3rd Battalion with 156th Artillery Regiment was hit by two bombs in the middle of a street near Bulscamp; its 8th horse-drawn battery had been static, waiting for the call forward. Seven artillerymen lost their lives and eight were seriously injured, losing 18 horses killed in their traces. 'The strong presence of the English air force, day and night,' Kriebel admitted, 'even achieved air superiority, and showed the enemy had to commit everything, so that his transports could still rescue what remained to be picked up.'[41]

Now, for the first time, von Küchler's Eighteenth Army was beginning to impinge on the evacuation space on the east side of the Dunkirk perimeter. A German artillery spotter plane radioed 56th Division's headquarters that there were about 15 British transports lying off Bray Dunes. They were obviously intending to pick up the British, who were starting to thin out before them that night. Von Küchler was an artillery general, and handled his guns effectively. He was pushing them forward as far as possible beyond Nieuport and Furnes to shell the disembarkation beaches.

The late evening of 31 May also proved a testing period for the newly appointed commander of the British II Corps, Major General Bernard Montgomery. He had imaginatively ordered lines of 3-ton lorries to be driven into the rising surf and connected together with wooden planks. These so-called lorry piers were to assist in the loading of small boats. His problem was that the tide receded and negated their effectiveness. An intercepted British radio report suggested the enemy was starting to assemble at La Panne and Bray Dunes, and that they would be taken off in three waves beginning at 2.30am. Orders were given by the IX German Corps to engage approach roads leading to likely British assembly areas as soon as darkness cloaked the operation. *Artillery Abteilung* 445, an artillery unit with 100mm guns, and heavy 210mm mortar unit 735 were instructed to lay down fire on the transports identified offshore by the spotter plane during the afternoon. Suppressive fire 'against this rare target of opportunity', the division log reported, was brought to bear, 'with the result that 13 transports fled seaward at full steam, one was beached on the sand and another left burning'.[42]

Montgomery's former 3rd Division and the badly battered 5th Division managed to embark from Bray Dunes, starting at 11pm that night. Major General Dudley Johnson's 4th Division, which had held the line to the east at Nieuport and Furnes, had problems. Very few ships appeared offshore at La Panne, driven off by the earlier shelling. By 1am only about 300 to 400 of Johnson's 8,000 survivors had been taken off, and the surf was up. Montgomery recalled the impact of the shelling, which 'smashed the piers and caused a great many casualties to the troops'. Low tide had also made the piers unusable. Naval onshore beach staff had also departed, assuming German shelling was the precursor to the arrival of German troops on the beach. 'It was clearly impossible,' Montgomery remembered, 'to continue embarkation at the beaches': 'I ordered the troops to move on to Dunkirk and embark there; this they were loath to do as they saw the ships lying off and hoped boats would come to the shore; but no boats came.'[43]

Oberleutnant Joachim von Oelhaven's Ju 88 had been shot down by Hurricanes over Dunkirk two days before; he was the squadron commander of 6 *Lehrgeschwader* 1. He belly-landed his badly holed aircraft in a cascade of spray in the shallow water overlooked by the holiday apartments at Nieuport beach. Two of his crew were killed and he and *Feldwebel* Notzke were hauled from the wreckage. As a prisoner of war he was led over the planks of one of the lorry piers to be taken aboard a British vessel. Seizing an opportunity during shelling, he leapt into the water and hid between the lorries under the planking. There was too much going on around for his captors to bother looking for a prisoner amid all the chaos, who had likely, in any case, been killed by his own countrymen. Von Oelhaven lay motionless in the darkness and watched the tide going out.[44]

Lance Sergeant Robert Green with the 2nd Bedfordshire and Hertfordshire Regiment recalled being held up outside La Panne 'because there was a whole column moving through it':

Away ahead of us a shell pitched right in the middle of the road, and you could see bodies staggering away. One-half of me, my hair was standing on edge with terror, and the other half was thinking in a very resigned sort of way, we've got to go through this, so we might as well make a start.

The troops set off on a ten-mile march through soft, leg-fatiguing sand to Dunkirk. 'Come on, follow me,' Green heard: 'Who the devil's that? Oh my God, it's me. I was so tired I didn't realize it.'[45]

The British II Corps was getting away. The tenacious defence of the east side of the perimeter meant 53,000 French and British troops sailed on the night of 29/30 May and a further 68,000 the following night. In six days, Operation *Dynamo* had lifted 259,049 troops, two corps' worth, including virtually three-quarters of the combat soldiers.

Poor weather was impeding the effectiveness of *Luftwaffe* attacks and the *Kriegsmarine* at sea were only having a negligible impact upon Allied ship-carrying capacity. But for the first time German land forces had seriously shrunk the beach area from which evacuees could leave. La Panne was out of commission and Bray Dunes seriously menaced by artillery fire; this left only the beaches at Malo-les-Bains and the vital East Mole jetty in an increasingly devastated Dunkirk harbour. There was still opportunity to reduce Britain's ability to withstand an invasion or hold hostages to fortune if the Wehrmacht could prevent the remaining 25% of the BEF's veteran combat elements from getting away. With increased flooding and concentric canal barriers obstructing most German avenues of approach from west and south, the narrow dune strip along the coast from La Panne through Bray Dunes and Malo was the most favourable German attack route. It could still conceivably be done.

Generalfeldmarschall von Küchler's Eighteenth Army had spent two days regrouping, setting up land communications and dealing with the distraction of reliefs in place for departing panzer and motorized forces. During this period the *Luftwaffe* had remained broadly ineffective, while repeated land attacks coming from west, south and east against the perimeter had lacked uniformity of effort. The withdrawal of the British II Corps had reduced the land area of the perimeter by about one-third. A new line had to be established to block off the approaches by the 256th, 56th and 216th German divisions coming from the east. Von Küchler planned a general offensive from all directions beginning on 1 June. This was to be in concert with an announced supreme effort by the *Luftwaffe*. Several *Luftflotten* were to attack the Allied bridgehead and transports offshore.

Generalleutnant Kriebel's 56th Division intended to mount a two-regiment attack westward along the coastal strip, alongside 216th Division to its left. Prisoner of war reports suggested that 'behind the Bergues canal English and French troops were deployed to hold to the last man'. The former French frontier line had been manned, with its mix of field and concrete bunker positions, whose substance had yet to be appreciated.[46]

Lieutenant Colonel Anzemberger's 8th French Zouave Regiment arrived at Ghyvelde and Bray Dunes on 30 May, after a weary and tumultuous retreat. The 900-strong battalion, part of General Janssen's 12th Division, had anticipated being evacuated by sea. They were instead ordered to dig in by the village of Bray Dunes and defend the beach strip at the eastern periphery of the perimeter. Departed French units had left a lot of weapons and equipment before embarking, so that the Zouaves were able to re-equip themselves and gain access to a generous stash of 81mm mortar rounds and 75mm shells. They were in fact almost better equipped than at the start of the war. Existing bunkers were occupied and the already prepared field positions dotted along the frontier line improved. Supported by the 15th Artillery Regiment, they had in addition two 75mm and four 95mm guns permanently mounted on fixed concrete mounts covering the direction of the likely German approach.

During the night of 31 May to 1 June they watched the last British 4th Division rearguards crossing their lines. Shortly after they detected German recce and scouting groups drawing near. After wending their way through the wreckage of abandoned British vehicles and bodies, the Germans at last sensed an opportunity to finish the job. The 56th Division was extremely fatigued. Its 192nd Regiment had already been withdrawn, fought out, from the line. The two remaining regiments had no reserve, and certainly did not anticipate meeting an entrenched bunker line after the British had thinned out ahead of them.

Chapter 8

The Great Escape, 1 June

AIR BLOCKADE

Dawn on 1 June emerged clear and bright as mounting *Luftwaffe* airfields buzzed with activity. *Hauptmann* Erich Groth commanding the *Haifisch* ('Shark') *Gruppe* of II/ZG 76[*] Messerschmitt *Zerstörer* aircraft, twin-engine fighters with sharks' teeth painted on the aircraft snout, briefed his men in the rustic setting of the *Geschwader* (squadron) operation room farmhouse. 'Very well gentlemen,' he began:

> For the next few days Dunkirk is the target for our attacks. The enemy is cornered there by our panzers and has fallen back in rapid retreat to the harbour. Almost the entire British Expeditionary Force is trapped. Obviously they will be trying to get as many of their troops back to England as possible, while the French fight a rearguard action.[1]

Generalmajor von Richthofen had received the order for VIII *Fliegerkorps* 'from above' during the night, instructing 'early attacks on Dunkirk'. 'Throughout the whole day,' it ordered, 'rolling attacks on Dunkirk'. 'It will be just like Calais all over again,' Groth summed up, eying his officers crowded around him, 'but this time we can reckon on even stronger British resistance'. These were prophetic words.

[*] II. *Gruppe, Zerstörergeschwader 76*

The Messerschmitt 110, flown by Göring's favoured elite pilots, was inferior to the newly introduced British Spitfire.

Richard Marchfelder flying an Me 110 with II/ZG 1 remembered the 'huge column of smoke ascending from ground level way up into the blue sky' always over Dunkirk, 'serving as landmark for the battle ground'. It was his first sortie over Dunkirk where he saw an Me 109 'engaged in a dogfight with an odd-looking aircraft'. 'Spitfires!' somebody shouted over the intercom. They tried to cut them off heading back to Britain, but were easily outpaced. 'We were too slow,' Marchfelder recalled; 'it was then that we found out how vulnerable our Me 110 was.' Me 109 fighter ace Victor Mölders agreed; 'the Spitfire was considerably superior to our clumsy and slower Bf 110.' He felt 'the steering was too heavy, in tight turns it slid about and fell out of the sky like a leaf from a tree'. Spitfires flying from the English south coast were appearing in larger numbers. Marchfelder appreciated 'after out first encounter with British fighters it became soberly clear to us that the holidays were over and we had to use all our wits to fight a desperate enemy'.[2]

The first German raiders showed at 4.15am, before the British had put in an appearance. *Luftflotte* 2 and 3 were still flying long sorties from the *Reich*. 'Quite a mission,' one He 111 bomber *Staffelkapitän* remembered. 'The various *Ketten* [wings] from the *Staffel* had first to form up and then head west.' Gaps in the cloud opened as they neared the objective, offering the first view of the ground. Nearing St Quentin, 'below us it is possible to pick out places where many towns are burning'. They passed over a smoking Amiens and were soon at the coast, where '*kette* after *kette* of German bombers were already in the attack'. They unloaded over ships in the harbour and others offshore. 'A 200-metre-high eruption of flame showed the impact of a hit.' As they turned away, 'the harbour was burning literally from all sides and huge smoke clouds indicate where the oil storage containers used to be'. Newcomers flying over Dunkirk from the *Reich* for the first time, like Heinkel 111 bomber pilot *Hauptmann* Alfons Vonier with 3/KG 4, were amazed as the spectacle off the beaches unfolded before them. 'This is fantastic,' he called to his radio operator Paul Strobel; 'just look at that shipping!' Vonier had always believed, like the majority of Germans, that once the British were surrounded, they would make peace with Hitler. The magnitude of the exodus below suggested otherwise. His instrument panel suddenly disintegrated before his eyes as a Spitfire made a pass.

They managed to cripple it with defensive fire, but had to pull out of formation to make an emergency landing at Ghent.[3]

The massive fly-in continued. *Hauptmann* Helmut Mahlke commanding 2nd *Staffel* of *Stukageschwader* I flew the first leg of his 117-mile sortie from their forward base at Guise, approaching the target zone, clearly outlined by a screen of flak above a level of thin cloud. He would fly back and forth three times this day. 'By this time,' he remembered, 'the British were sending every vessel – naval, merchant or civilian, which was capable of carrying troops across the Channel, in a desperate attempt to evacuate their expeditionary corps from Dunkirk.'[4] *Luftwaffe* reconnaissance reported, 'in the morning in the coastal region of Dunkirk were numerous commercial ships, about 60, and a few warships'. This was the finale for the II British Corps evacuation, which had been going on all night. 'During the afternoon, 15 to 26 small to medium freighters between Dunkirk and the English south coast, increasing during the day with warships escorting the ship traffic.' The *Luftwaffe* operations report also pointed to 'heavy flak and fighter opposition around Dunkirk'.[5]

There were still 10,000 civilians in the town. 'Many houses were demolished,' recalled French engineer soldier Marcel Lantenois; 'the dead litter the streets, and how many were there under the ruins?' At 8am, following the initial bombing attacks, an air raid shelter in the cellars of the Gondrand Company in the citadel of Dunkirk collapsed. Glass demijohns containing ether and alcohol immolated at least 50 people in the ensuing fireball. Lantenois recalled one soldier losing his mind when he found his house partially collapsed and his repair shop in flames. 'Our comrade couldn't find his wife in his house,' and, believing the family to have perished, 'went to commit suicide in the countryside'.[6] Another shelter imploded at Saint-Pol-sur-Mer at the Comtoir Linier building, entombing 67 civilians.

Paule Rogalin remembered, 'since I was just a little girl, I was hoping my father would be the hero and save us from these bad people'. He was missing and then abruptly turned up, having 'left the army, because they had no guns, nothing to fight with'. 'He was almost crying when he found us, saying "we can't fight. We don't have anything".'[7]

The family agreed he should try and evacuate with the French soldiers being taken off. Lantenois, waiting at Bray Dunes, had not yet succeeded; 'we were placed in a group of the "isolated",' he remembered, joined together to form a boat. 'But alas,' he appreciated, 'this cannot yet be today.'[8]

After Rogalin's father left for the beach, 'my mother wanted to see for herself whether he had made it'. The intensity of the bombing offshore and strafing on the beaches was evident to all and civilians had begun to appreciate the din from the front around the town was getting nearer. Paule and her mother moved down to the confusion on the beach:

> We took advantage of the breaks between the bombings to look for my father among the dead men on the beach. It was a horrible sight, all these men lying there, and when I would see a dead man with his eyes open, I'd say to my mother 'He's awake! He's not dead! Maybe we can help him'.

'Luckily', they did not come across her father. 'When is it going to end mother?' she plaintively asked, 'maybe tomorrow?' and she replied 'Yes, maybe tomorrow'.[9]

As *Hauptmann* Mahlke began his Stuka attack approach he saw 'the *Luftwaffe* was up in force, with formations of aircraft attacking in waves one after the other'. It was a confusing melee of aircraft with 'a tremendous amount of activity in the air, from both friend and foe alike'. Arriving at such a target-rich environment,'it was difficult' at the height 'to make out which of the vessels had already been hit and which were still seaworthy'. Their escorting fighters 'seemed to be keeping the other side in check' and 'we arrived over the target area unmolested and split up into smaller formations to carry out our attacks'.[10]

Göring, realizing the British were escaping despite effusive claims to the *Führer* to the contrary, was getting nervous. He interrupted a tour of Dutch cities confiscating loot for his art collections and rushed back to his headquarters in an attempt to re-energize the air blockade over the beaches. *Luftflotten* 2 and 3 were launching primarily from the *Reich* and VIII *Fliegerkorps* from forward airfields in the St Quentin, Guise and Cambrai areas. This shortened sortie runs for the Stukas and some fighters. Göring had not, however, nominated any of the *Luftflotten* for overall command. As a consequence, operations for four *Fliegerkorps* (flying corps) and two *Jagdfliegerführer* (fighter commands) were uncoordinated. The respective headquarters were, moreover, separated by geography: *Luftflotte* 2 in the Ruhr and *Luftflotte* 3 in southern

Hitler in conversation with his adjutants alongside his specially commissioned *Reichsbahn* train *Amerika*. The modern equivalent would be the US president's Air Force One. The *Führer*'s supreme commander, *General* Walther von Brauchitsch, is conversing with *Generaloberst* Keitel, his chief of staff, to the left. (Getty Images)

Hitler's *Luftwaffe* adjutant, Nicolaus von Below, at the *Führer*'s left shoulder as he converses with OKW Chief of Operations Jodl, checked the weather for the 10 May western offensive en route. (Getty Images)

Hitler took advantage of the fine weather at the *Felsennest* (Crag's Nest) bunker headquarters. He was much taken with the natural beauty of the site. (NARA)

Inside the Spartan briefing hut at the *Felsennest* HQ outside the village of Rodert, overlooking the Belgian frontier. The *Führer*'s intention was to make it a symbolic pilgrimage site after the war. (Getty Images)

War correspondent Leo Leixner filmed this bitter Belgian holding action at the Ghent-Terneuzen canal, typical of the German infantry *Blitzkrieg* progress through Belgium, published in the German propaganda magazine *Signal*. The Germans regarded the Belgian Army with wary respect. (*Signal*, July 1940)

The impetuous panzer corps commander *schnelle* or 'speedy' Heinz Guderian in his armoured command half-track directing operations from the front, constantly pushing for greater freedom of action. (Bundesarchiv, Bild 101I-769-0229-15A, Fotograf(in): Borchert, Erich [Eric])

General von Brauchitsch, commander in chief of the German Army (right), closely conferring with his chief of staff at OKH, Franz Halder (left). They repeatedly clashed with Hitler about the pace of the panzer advance. (Getty Images)

Generaloberst Fedor von Bock commanded Army Group B, which penetrated Holland and Belgium, taking on the main bulk of the Allied armies. (Getty Images)

Hitler (left) confers with *Generaloberst* Gerd von Rundstedt, the commander of Army Group A, at Charlerville on 24 May. He seconded his desire to pause the panzer advance and censored Brauchitsch for over reaching his decision remit. (Getty Images)

The 1st Panzer Division's attack on Dunkirk was road bound, threading its way through villages encumbered by canal lines. It was fought to a standstill by the French 68th Division before the Panzer Halt Order was applied. (Bundesarchiv, Bild 101I-126-0321-03, Fotograf(in): Boesig, Heinz)

Hermann Göring, the commander in chief of the Luftwaffe, conversing with his senior officers. He flamboyantly assured the *Führer* that the *Luftwaffe* was all that was required to finish off the BEF in the Dunkirk pocket. (Getty Images)

A German tank from the 2nd (Vienna) Panzer Division is knocked out at a village intersection as the von Prittwitz battle group battled its way into Boulogne from the south on 23 May.

Oberst Balck commanded one of the 1st Panzer Division's battle groups during the abortive advance on Dunkirk on 24 May, and was halted at the canal line on the western outskirts. (Getty Images)

Hauptmann Edwin Dwinger was with the 10 Panzer Division headquarters during the concentric attacks on Calais and observed the final attacks on the citadel.

Oberfeldwebel Langhammer and his Panzer Mark IV crew proudly display their turret victory tally for sinking a British destroyer in Boulogne harbour. (Getty Images)

The destroyer *Venetia* backs out of Boulogne harbour on fire with all guns blazing during the evening of 23 May – 'a magnificent sight', according to one eyewitness.

Generalleutnant Schaal's 10th Panzer Division commanders at Calais: *Oberst* Menny commanding the 69th Regiment battle group (second from left), *Oberst* Fischer with 86th Regiment (second from right) and artillery commander *Oberstleutnant* Gerloch listening far right. Schaal is centre, third from right.

A British Blenheim bomber photographed attacking an 18th Division infantry column. The RAF severely harassed German ground troops for the first time in the war outside the Dunkirk pocket. Veteran and unit accounts often complain about the loss of a previously overwhelming air superiority.

SS soldiers with the *Totenkopf* Division at rest outside the pocket. Far from being the vaunted elite as later in Russia, many were ill-trained ex-concentration camp guards who attracted *Wehrmacht* criticism following atrocities against British prisoners.

The *Kriegsmarine* and *Luftwaffe* were never able to seriously diminish the carrying capacity of the evacuation fleets, unlike the sinking of the *Lancastria*, shown here, following Dunkirk, which cost an estimated 4,000 lives.

German E-boats lurked around the Dunkirk navigation buoys, causing costly sinkings at night. (Getty Images)

The arrival of another mass Stuka assault viewed from the beaches. The vagaries of the weather meant that *Luftwaffe* attacks were effective for only two and a half days of nine.

The beaches were an inviting target, crowded with on average 10,000 troops each day, awaiting evacuation. Air attacks failed to prevent the embarkation of the key fighting troops of the BEF. (Getty Images)

Two consecutive views of a Stuka attack against ships off the open beaches. Troops are lying on their backs and firing back. (Getty Images)

The second picture shows ships straddled and hit by bombs offshore (visible at center). The bulbous smoke signature registers a major strike. (Getty Images)

De Oogen recht op het Doel Gericht,
in zijn hart stoutmoedige vastberaden-
heid. daarmede begint de Stuka-vlieger
zijn duikvlucht

De Duik in de Diepte is Begonnen,
de razende snelheid veroorzaakt een bloedeloosheid
in de hersenen: de gelaatsspieren zijn kramp-
achtig vertrokken . . .

Binnen Enkele Seconden
1000 Meter naar Omlaag . . .
gestort, is de vliegenier. De bom verlaat't vlieg-
tuig. De sterke inspanning doet hem de tanden
op elkander klemmen maar hij blijft volhouden

De Duik is Achter den Rug,
het toestel vliegt weer rechtuit.
Het gelaat vertoont duidelijk de
sterke lichamelijke inspann...

This interesting *Signal*
magazine photo essay clearly
shows the strain reflected on
a Stuka pilot's face during
the attacking 70° dive and
subsequent recovery.
(*Signal*, August 1940)

De Spanning Verslapt,

En wéér: De Oogen op het Doel Gericht

The flooded road leading from Ghyvelde village to Bray Dunes (distant skyline) with abandoned Allied vehicles driven off the dyke road either side. Flooded terrain effectively denied German attackers access to the Dunkirk pocket in strength, creating an impassable moat obstructing the advance of five of ten attacking divisions.

General Georg von Küchler commanding Eighteenth Army was appointed to coordinate and command the ten divisions tasked to reduce the Dunkirk pocket. The Germans failed to capitalize on the Belgian surrender by rolling up the beaches from the east. (Getty Images)

German infantry trying to assemble for the attack in flooded landscape; the defenders dominated the exposed dry ground. (© Pierre Metsu)

A photograph showing the main attack axis of the German 18th Infantry Division towards Bergues and Dunkirk. The 51st Regiment attacked left and the 54th Regiment right of this road.

Final Stuka attacks against Bergues, which breached the town wall, the lynchpin of the French defense of the Dunkirk pocket to the south.

The only infantry recourse to advance over a half-dozen concentric canal lines was to assault the crossings in vulnerable dinghies, which was immensely clumsy and costly. (Getty Images)

The German dead from 192th Regiment laid out after their costly advance from the east of the Dunkirk pocket at Nieuport. The *Spiess* or sergeant major has the grim task of harvesting identity discs while soldiers look for missing friends.

German soldiers advance across a totally flat and fire-swept landscape. The axis of attack was always billowing clouds of smoke bubbling up from the blazing refineries at Dunkirk.

Dune positions held by the 8th Zouaves to the east of the perimeter, blocking attacks by the German 56th Division, which had to be withdrawn totally exhausted and 'fought-out' from the line.

Just one part of the 51st Regiment's haul of French prisoners once the 18th Division penetrated the harbour area of Dunkirk on 4 June. (Getty Images)

Generalleutnant Friedrich-Carl Cranz, the commander of the 18th Division, takes the final surrender of Dunkirk alongside his staff. The perimeter was held for a further three days after the last British had departed.

Germany, while von Richthofen's close air support VIII *Fliegerkorps* was forward in the St Quentin area. British fighters swept the coast at 50-minute intervals, often appearing when there were no Germans and vice-versa. British coastal radar gave Air Vice Marshal Keith Park's 11 Group squadrons some visibility of what was going on. This enabled standing patrols to be increased at times to substantial fighter sweeps, able to intercept the larger German bomber formations.

Göring was out of touch with the air situation and had little experience of the interface between logistic resources and the need to build a coordinated *Schwerpunkt*, or focus for the main effort. He had finished the previous World War as a *Hauptmann*, then had a decade in civilian life before being abruptly elevated to *General*. Not only had he no formal staff training, he also missed out on-the-job education, climbing through the ranks. He was also addicted to morphine, which contributed to his shortcomings becoming increasingly apparent. Von Richthofen commanding VIII *Fliegerkorps* complained: 'The Stuka sorties were too far distant, with too few sorties possible. There were resupply problems at the forward airstrips, not enough bombs or fuel.'[11]

Admiral Wake-Walker, the senior Royal Navy officer coordinating the British evacuation offshore, remembered the inconsistent nature of German air attacks. At first 'they were chiefly occupied in wrecking Dunkirk and the port' before the focus changed:

> During the morning they made attempts to machine gun the beaches, but were held off by anti-aircraft fire. The beaches were also bombed but only for a brief period. Had they persisted, they would have inflicted terrible losses on us, for there were seldom less than 10,000 troops on the beaches. They later attacked the pier with dive-bombers, sunk three ships and damaged the pier. Had they persisted in these successful attacks on the pier and ships alongside, the evacuation could never have been achieved.[12]

Göring essentially left the operation to his air fleet and corps commanders to sort out, not far removed from the land situation before Eighteenth Army was nominated to reduce the perimeter. Subordinate commanders exercised commendable initiative, but were getting in each other's way. Clear leadership was required to direct focus on either wrecking port facilities to block disembarkation, or sink ships to reduce Allied carrying capacity preferably loaded to inflict unacceptable casualties. No attempt was made to seriously interdict the Channel crossing or disrupt disembarkation at reception ports, such as Dover and Ramsgate. The truth was the full extent of the evacuation was never appreciated by *Luftwaffe* high command and Göring never personally intervened in the battle in any meaningful way to impose an air blockade. Ironically, one of the specialized anti-shipping *Gruppen* was transferred to Norway ten days before.*

Admiral Wake-Walker then noticed 'they soon turned their attention to ships lying off the beaches'. This was the primary threat on 1 June, the first real break in the weather and visibility since 29 May. On the 31st, Wake-Walker claimed 'no less than 100 bombing attacks were made on ships within 2 miles of the pier'. Clearly 1 June was a supreme effort, but coordination over the target area was rare. 'Happily,' Wake-Walker observed, 'at least 24 bombs were dropped on one large wreck and many bombs on other wrecks.' Mahlke recalled 'on this particular day, 1st June, we had been ordered to attack shipping off Dunkirk's beaches'. The British II Corps was in the process of escaping and were largely clear by morning. British I Corps, the final rearguard, was still on shore, hoping to get away that night.

'I led my *Staffel* down against a fair-sized steamer that was getting under way just offshore,' Mahlke remembered. They scored several hits. *Wochenschau* newsreels recreated these dramatic moments in German cinemas, which gripped audiences. Filmed through the propeller ring during the dive, ground features gradually expand into clear focus. Attacks on the thin pencil-like protrusion of the East Mole show detonations rising from previous Stuka bomb releases. Cascading spray obscures the outline of vessels dodging and weaving between near misses, curving wakes sketching evasive actions on the sea's surface. Flashes can be seen from ships firing back amid wakes studded with circular patterns from waterspouts, which are run over by the fleeing ships. Mahlke remembered:

There were some heavy bursts of flak to port, but as we couldn't hear the crump of exploding shells, they were clearly too far off to be of

---

*This was *Kampfgeschwader* 30.

any danger. Then more flak to starboard. This time it was pearls of little red 'mice' chasing each other through the air, indicating tracer fire from light or medium weapons. We hurriedly jinked away – turning sometimes gently, sometimes sharply – until we were safely out of range.

French soldier Marcel Lantenois watching from the beach saw one plane 'hit by a shell literally flies into pieces.' After a pause, 'two occupants descend by parachute, one of the two is dead perhaps, he is cut in two'. As Mahlke's *Staffel* flew back to Guise, 'I couldn't get the horrific spectacle that was Dunkirk out of my mind,' he remembered, 'an absolute inferno!' On landing, they were told 'same situation, same orders'. The objective was to take out the big ships, preferably loaded, heading back to England. 'Those men down there,' Mahlke reflected, 'trying to escape, but packed together so tightly on board their ships that they could hardly move, didn't stand a chance if set upon by Stukas.' Lantenois, waiting to be picked up at Bray Dunes, did not relish the prospect. 'The ships, whether coming or going,' he observed, 'are sprayed with bombs.' 'We see jets of water rise up around them, as three-quarters of the bombs didn't hit their targets.' His day had begun 'with a sad spectacle' at dawn, observing 'sunken ships where only the masts could be seen'. At the water's edge 'corpses black with oil were brought back to the shore, with all kinds of objects, buoys etc'.[13]

The *Luftwaffe* aimed to kill these men before they could be brought back to Britain. On his third sortie Mahlke attacked one ship, 'by no means huge – perhaps 1,000 to 2,000 tons – but big enough':

There was an almighty explosion immediately under the middle of the ship. It seemed to lift right out of the water and bits of wreckage were hurled a good 50 metres into the air. A fascinating sight – but a horrible one.[14]

The toll on shipping began to mirror the effort the *Luftwaffe* combined air fleets applied. Four destroyers were lost and three damaged. Three minesweepers went down with three damaged; a personnel vessel was also sunk and five smaller boats and another passenger ship seriously damaged. Shipping losses at Dunkirk were to total 236 from 845 vessels participating in the action, of which 30 were substantial tonnages; 61

others were put out of action. Admitted casualties from the carnage were ostensibly 3,500 troops from the 68,111 lost during the three-week campaign in Flanders. In hindsight the figures appear a substantial underestimate, averaging about 25 men from each vessel that went down. The numbers may have been massaged to fit the 'Dunkirk Miracle' narrative, which the British government projected to calm a pensive population worrying about possible German invasion.

It is impossible with the passage of time to meaningfully interpret casualties lost at sea, because who amid the chaos and emotional loss is actually counting? At this juncture, with the BEF steadily slipping away, the best the *Luftwaffe* could hope for was to inflict heavy casualties, which they likely did. One estimate of about 6,000 deaths is probably nearer the mark. The sinking of two French destroyers, the *Bourrasque* and *Sirocco*, resulted in 300 and 750 deaths respectively. Some 640 soldiers and 96 crew went down with the British destroyer *Wakeful*. One French auxiliary vessel, the *Emile Deschamps*, lost 400, and the *Brighton Queen* and *Scotia* passenger ships lost 300 men apiece. These are just a few grim statistics in isolation, which suggest likely heavy losses overall.[15]

The *Luftwaffe* threw all its serviceable aircraft into the fight. Stuka pilot *Oberleutnant* Dietrich Peltz recalled his ground crew joking about the frequency of sorties. 'Third class ticket for Dunkirk,' they called out, 'without changing!' Entire groups of Heinkel 111 horizontal bombers were frequently seen passing through swarms of dive-bombing Stukas. Despite Admiral Wake-Walker's fearsome predictions, the soft sand dunes on the beaches absorbed the worst of bomb-blast effect. Strafing by low-level fighters brought better results as well as being profoundly scary. Me 109 fighter pilot Paul Temme, racing up and down the beach at 300 feet with all guns blazing, admitted, 'I hated Dunkirk, it was just unadulterated killing.' 'Now the small fry are for it,' recalled Dietrich Peltz, after the Stukas had unloaded against ships offshore:

Motor boats, yachts and fishing cutters. Craft of every description are swimming about… These provide targets for machine-gun fire, not very different from the way the squadron has had sufficient practice of in Poland and France in low-flying attacks on marching columns. These small craft also try to escape by zigzagging, but it doesn't help much.

'We put one chap on a Bren gun, anti-aircraft, you could mount them on a tripod,' recalled Lawrence Bennett, on the beach with the Lancashire Fusiliers. 'They split him down the middle more or less,' on a strafing run; 'killed him instantly, when they fired at him'. It was not difficult to miss, as Dennis Avon with a Field Park Company explained: 'On the beach, it was just black with troops, from the harbour as far as you could see, it was just troops.'[16]

Veterans soon appreciated the shortcomings of *Luftwaffe* strafing tactics. 'They didn't go down the queue direct from inland to sea,' driver Ray Corbishley with the RASC pointed out: 'They went across, parallel with the beach line, and of course passed through [at right angles] the queues of soldiers standing there.'[17]

Captain Humphrey Bredin with the Royal Ulster Rifles saw phlegmatic soldiers playing cards in the sand during attacks, remarking 'he can't shoot very straight' when the bullets missed them by a few yards.[18] Corbishley remembered those unaffected by the strafing carried on as if nothing had happened. 'Nobody else moved, the people behind them just walked over the top, around them, and kept moving towards the boat.'[19]

RAF Fighter Command put up eight patrols of three to four squadrons over Dunkirk throughout the day. Maximum effort was seen as early morning and late evening, when it was planned the bulk of the ships would be either leaving or approaching the port. Seventeen precious British aircraft went down with the loss of 12 pilots in an effort that clearly failed to prevent serious losses of men, ships and materiel. The destroyer *Ivanhoe* barely made it back to Sheerness without sinking. She limped in on a beautiful summer morning, with 'an unnatural quietness hanging all around'. Royal Navy medical orderly Silvester MacDonald watched, waiting to board with medical assistance when she came in. 'Even the view from the dockside brought a hushed feeling to all who looked,' he remembered:

It was a macabre scene that the devil himself could not have imagined to see bodies hanging over the bridge rails, lying around gun turrets, sprawled on the decks both fore and aft, and the bodies in navy blue and in khaki that were entangled in death in a grotesque heap on the after-deck.

It took little imagination to hear the ghostly echoes of far-off bugles calling for their spirits to assemble again and be counted.[20]

It was a rude awakening of the power of the *Luftwaffe* and what they were up against. 420 Me 109 and Me 110 fighter aircraft had successfully enabled their bombers to operate with relative impunity. Only two bombers and two Stukas were lost. The RAF lost 16 fighters to ten *Luftwaffe* 109s and 110s shot down.[21]

'Where were the "Brylcreem Boys"?' troops commented. They had been portrayed as *Boy's Own* (comic strip) heroes in showy publicity during the Phoney War period before the *Blitzkrieg*. Royal Engineer sapper Sid Crockitt, like many Dunkirk veterans, was puzzled by their absence, even well after the war:

> Where were they? Where the hell are they? Why aren't they helping us out? This was all wrong. They had left us on our own. They just didn't care! That kind of stuff. This was what the attitude to the RAF was.[22]

'I'm afraid that the fighter boys are in very bad odour at the moment,' Tony Bartley, a Spitfire pilot with 92 Squadron, admitted, writing to his father:

> The BEF have started stories that they never saw a single fighter the whole time that they were being bombed. The feeling ran very high at one time and some fighter pilots got roughed up by the army in pub brawls.

He argued the Germans 'had layers of bombers and fighters, with which 12 Spitfires had to cope'. Bartley recalled fighting off 30 He 111s 'which we drove back', to no avail, because 'below us the dive-bombers were operating the whole time'. He commented: 'No wonder the soldiers did not see us up at 10,000 feet, but little do they realize that we saved them from the "real bombs", 500 pounders carried by the Heinkels.'[23]

The *Luftwaffe* had mounted a ferocious strike, 160 bomber and Stuka sorties arriving in five major raids; the RAF flew 267 fighter sorties in response. Under clear blue skies, the heavy air assaults wreaked havoc on the evacuation fleet. At 6pm Captain Tennant, directing the evacuation from on shore and watching the disaster unfold from atop Bastion 32, the large French HQ bunker in the port, signalled Admiral Ramsay in Dover: 'Things are getting very hot for ships... Have directed that no ships sail during daylight. Evacuation by transports therefore ceases at 03.30.'[24]

The heavy *Luftwaffe* fighter presence was effectively shielding its bombers from the British fighters. Pilot Officer J.E. Storrar with 145 Squadron RAF remembered the remorseless pace of operations, which began with patrols from first light:

> Each day started the same with the batman bringing in a cup of tea while it was still dark and I would have five minutes to think about the day to come, and used to pray just that I could have a cup of tea again the next morning – I thought no further than that.[25]

German fighter pilot Ulrich Steinhilper with *Jagdgeschwader* 52 had his squadron withdrawn for rest just as the good weather emerged once again. 'We suffered only at the hands of bad weather and bad luck,' he maintained, 'we didn't feel much like heroes.' He managed to extract one of their injured pilots from hospital, *Feldwebel* Munz, a Spanish Civil War veteran from the Condor Legion, to take back to Germany. He was being treated among army casualties at a Trier monastery. For the first time in the war Steinhilper glimpsed a world apart from the sanitized cockpit view he normally experienced far above the battlefield. Munz was found in an 'aspect of pure misery and utter depression', shockingly lacking care and medical resources. Soldiers in beds around vented frustration and anger at the sight of his officer's uniform. '"To hell with the whole bloody lot of you!" they shouted: "Now we're wounded and not much use, we're on the scrap heap. Nobody cares!" It was a shock to me to see how men who had been wounded fighting for their country were being left to die.'

He was sickened at the shortage of medical staff. Men were 'badly wounded, obviously in need of attention, others were plainly too far gone for any help from this world'. These were not the triumphant scenes played out in the weekly *Wochenschau* newsreels. Victory here came at a cost: 'A little of the glory that I youthfully saw in this campaign was left among those stinking rows of blood-sodden mattresses.'[26]

Despite the awful air attacks and the cost to the evacuation fleet, 64,000 troops were lifted this day from the Mole and beaches, even more French than British. Some 22,000 to 23,000 British troops still remained on shore, the British I Corps and rearguards. German shore batteries had closed to the extent that all three sea approaches could now be interdicted by enemy shellfire. Göring's supreme *Luftwaffe* intervention had its limitations, but the *Wehrmacht* anaconda had closed on the perimeter and was now squeezing.

THE TIGHTENING VICE: EAST AND SOUTH

War correspondent Christoph von Imhoff could watch the sea approaches to Dunkirk harbour from the coastal sand dunes at Loon Plage. Stuka dive-bombers hurtled down from the clouds onto their targets. 'Every movement could be followed,' he observed, 'despite the great distance' using an artillery scissors scope. 'There, a flash of flame, a cloud of smoke and a number of explosions in the distance.' He felt with aircraft wheeling and diving and ships capsizing that he was viewing a 'death dance'. The thud of detonations 'was making the sand tremble slightly'. 'The other transports were fighting back with anti-air and machine guns – hopeless.' There was 'suddenly a deep rush of air over us' following a distant firing report; the noise made them jam their heads into the dunes, coming up with 'faces full of sand'. The artillery observer had not ducked down, looking out for muzzle flash, and soon an artillery duel was in progress. The evacuation beaches were not visible to von Imhoff from his standpoint, but he could see ships coming and going and black silhouettes of aircraft overhead in the distance, like insects, buzzing over wounded prey. The French 68th Division was still holding firmly here on the west side of the perimeter, with four infantry regiments, engineers, two field artillery regiments and naval artillery firing from Fort Mardyck. Von Imhoff was convinced he was reporting on 'the last days of the final battle'. Encircled French troops under General Molinié at Lille had surrendered that very morning with 35,000 troops.[27]

The most vulnerable point of the Dunkirk perimeter was its east side, known by the British and suspected by the Germans. *Generalfeldmarschall* von Küchler, now in command of the overall effort with the Eighteenth Army, had directed two divisions, the 56th and 216th, to force their way through the narrow 2-mile-wide dune strip between Bray Dunes next to the sea and Ghyvelde village at the edge of the inundated zone inland. Unlike the other approaches from west and south, they had only to cross one canal, des Chats, to get into the heart of the evacuation zone. By doing so, they would be in a position to cut off the remaining British I Corps, still holding a six-battalion front to the south of Dunkirk. The scheme was to capitalize on the supreme *Luftwaffe* effort and break in.

The problem with *Luftwaffe* support was that the tasking process, including any changes of plan, took four hours to enact, so it could be passed to widely separate mounting headquarters. These were geographically dispersed between the Ruhr, southern Germany and north-west France. The sudden change in the ground situation resulting from the rapid 4-mile thinning out and disembarkation of the II British Corps to La Panne and Bray Dunes and beyond, the night before, bedevilled the agreed *Luftwaffe* ground support plan. The perimeter had shrunk by about one-third to the Franco-Belgian border overnight. The 56th Division was able to rapidly advance beyond Furnes at dawn to fill this vacuum created by the departing British. Air attacks, therefore programmed to support an 11am move forward, had to be called off. It was not possible to coordinate air assistance until the FLOT (Forward Line of Own Troops) had been discerned and marked on staff situation maps. In essence, the opportune advance by 56th Division became a victim of its own success. Throughout the day they would witness swarms of *Luftwaffe* attacks passing overhead, none of them in support of them.

By 9.30am the unit's 234th Infantry Regiment had overrun Adinkerke village inland. Progress was not, however, without damage. Marching columns and artillery battery positions in the villages nearby had been strafed and bombed by the RAF, leaving 13 dead and 20 wounded. The artillery lost a further four men killed and many horses, which impeded the forward passage of the guns. They did manage to cross the Nieuport Canal despite its blown bridges by wending their way across a small coastal steamer, which was fastened to the canal sides. 'Finally the last!' triumphantly exclaimed the IX Corps Commander *General* Hermann Geyer, 'the last canal before the coast overcome'.

Two hours later 234th Regiment was on the beach at La Panne, which *Hauptmann* Sprenger described as 'a cruel picture'.

Houses demolished, and in the streets countless dead and wounded. The beach was completely covered in abandoned vehicles, guns and military equipment of every kind. There were many ships stranded on the beach, some still smoking.

Lorry piers were seen for the first time, doubtless saving many men, 'but many must also have been driven to Dunkirk by the division's advance'. Thick oil slicks covered the surface of the sea, much of it seeping from the lorry piers. The 234th Regiment soldiers were in high spirits; they had finally reached the sea and joked about the possibility of a quick bathe. Sprenger remembered in La Panne 'groups of civilians started to surface from the cellars, partly refugees from Brussels and Antwerp seeking to flee, but with the speed of our success, did not find a way'. Ominously, he observed 'most of them are Jews'. Their sister 171st Regiment reached the coast further along at 1.45pm, emerging between La Panne and Bray Dunes. Its 3rd Battalion attracted heavy fire to the flank, coming from the direction of the French fortified frontier zone. The battalion wheeled west to face this new threat, with the Channel to its right. By now the sun was high in the sky and the heat became oppressive.[28]

Well-spaced bunkers set amid sand dunes lined the old Franco-Belgian border, occupied by the depleted 12th French Infantry Division. The 8th Zouaves, recruited originally from North Africa, but now also metropolitan France, were defending this sector with two battalions forward and another in reserve just east of Bray Dunes. The 150th Regiment closed the gap to the inundated area to their right at Ghyvelde village. 92nd Regiment held the line of the Canal des Chats overlooking this inundated area, where the water level still rose. The French line was heavily supported with five regiments of artillery, naval artillery at Zuydcoote and Bray Dunes as well as a battalion of infantry from the 60th Division. The Germans had no idea this new line existed.

The advance continued with the 2nd Battalion of 171st Regiment leading, traversing flat open fields, crisscrossed with numerous water-filled ditches. As they approached the open meadowland west of Ghyvelde they came across thousands of grazing horses, left behind by retreating French and British artillery columns. The advance sector became increasingly constrained by the flooded area to their left and sand dunes rising to their front. The Furnes Canal was the axis and also the divide marking the two-division approach, 56th Division north of the canal to the sea, and 256th Division left to the south. 56th Division could only commit 171st Regiment inside this narrow boundary and that on a battalion frontage; the 3rd Battalion followed behind the 2nd. Spirits were high; *General* Geyer, taking in the catastrophic signs of destruction, was exuberant. 'This was no withdrawal,' he recalled, following the British trail, 'this was flight! Overpowering! Hardly imaginable annihilation!'

'On the horizon Dunkirk was clearly visible, beneath a huge black cloud,' remembered *Hauptmann* Sprenger, 'from which again and again, pillars of flame and smoke shot out.' The *Luftwaffe* were hard at work:

> Nobody, standing in wonder overlooking the remains of where the English Army had stood, could avoid a deep impression that here, the division's breakthrough to the Channel coast had been an amazing success, decisively contributing to the destruction of the BEF.[29]

As 171st Regiment attempted to negotiate the sand dunes in front, it came under increasingly heavy fire from the left flank. This was because the 216th Division advancing on Ghyvelde village had been pinned down by the French 150th Regiment, and fallen behind. Constrained by the flooded area and this heavy flanking fire, the 171st Regiment's follow-on battalions were unable to manoeuvre further right. Attacks on the 1st Zouave Battalion defending here, next to the sea, carried on all afternoon as the sun remorselessly bore down and slowed the pace of operations. Heavy support weapons could only be trundled along the wet beach when the tide was out. They were virtually immobile in the soft shifting sand inside the dune belt and could not be brought to bear on targets. Zouave Pierre Dehay recalled chimneys and the bell tower in Bray Dunes village 'jinking and houses collapsing' under the impacts of artillery. Massive abandoned horse herds panicked and stampeded while 'men were falling'. The Zouaves manned pre-war concrete-built bunkers supported by two 75mm and four 95mm artillery pieces, permanently mounted amid the dunes on fixed concrete plinths.[30]

The 171st Infantry Regiment suffered in 'stifling heat which hung over the hot sand,' Sprenger recalled. 'They desperately needed water, but there was none to be found.' They faced masterfully sited bunkers and field positions. Concrete shelters were only used for cover or assembly points, Sprenger recalled 'their machine guns were between the bunkers in excellently camouflaged, hardly visible positions'. All the time 'French artillery was active'. Some German infiltration caused the Zouaves to cede ground, but they counter-attacked with artillery support to regain it.

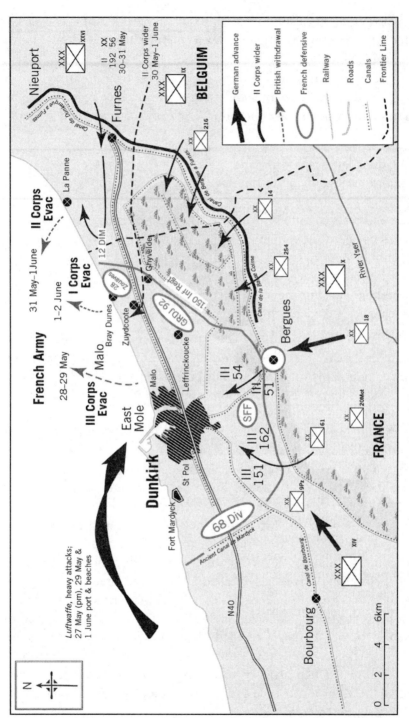

MAP 7: Concentric German Attacks Against the Dunkirk Pocket, 1–2 June 1940.

The crisis points were the 56th and 256th Division attacks directed at the east side of the perimeter from Nieuport and Furnes. The 18th and 254th Divisions attacked from the south against Bergues across flooded areas in concert with the 61st Division attacking from the south-west. Heavy effective Luftwaffe attacks were flown on 27 and 29 May and especially during clearer weather on 1 June, but insufficient to block the evacuation of the main fighting elements of the BEF, which got away. Overcoming flooded canal lines proved the main obstacle. Bergues, the lynchpin of the French defense, fell on 2 June.

'The dune landscape with sand hillocks up to 100 and 130 feet high is extraordinarily difficult to traverse,' Sprenger explained:

Cars and cross-country vehicles remain hopelessly stuck. Everything the troops needed, ammunition and rations etc, had to be brought forward by porters. In this amazing heat every step in the sand is an effort. Boots drowned in the soft sand. It was hardly possible to get a machine gun into position; they immediately sank in the sand, which quickly rendered them inoperable. Only the 98 rifle and hand grenades could hold their own. Endless patience was needed during ebb tide to get some heavy infantry guns and rations forward.[31]

Undulating sandy mounds and hills, covered with rough brown sea grass, made it difficult to see or engage targets. Sand whipped up by muzzle velocity pressure on firing made it easy to pick out opposing automatic weapons, and increased their vulnerability. They might just as well have been fighting in the Arabian desert, which some of them would be doing within a year in any case. *Führer* weather was a boon for the *Luftwaffe* this day, but less so for the infantry.

The battle in the dunes was difficult to control and transitioned to stalking raids by strongly formed fighting patrols against identified positions. The division operations officer came forward to investigate lack of progress for himself. He found the 171st Regiment 'in a difficult situation', observing 'the regiment was fragmented and the battalions not firmly gripped by the battalion commanders'. He remembered how 'you had to creep along to reach the regimental command post, as the route to it was dominated by French snipers, who brought you under fire'. These snipers also penetrated the rear through gaps in the line German soldiers were unable to close. Clearly, the attack was not going well. That evening at 7pm the ops officer quickly convened a planning conference at the Adinkerke railway station, bringing together the artillery regiment commanders and the 171st Regiment commander. As soon as it began, French artillery straddled the location and they had to reconvene elsewhere.

It was decided to resume attacks, reinforced with a battalion from 234th Regiment and supported by all of 56th Division's artillery and that of Geyer's IX Corps. They had lost 11 killed and 55 wounded, including three officers that day, to no appreciable end. The French were denying access to the remaining evacuation beaches by blocking this eastern dune thrust. They held the vital ground. The German troops were completely exhausted. *General* Geyer felt the attacking force was proving insufficient for the task and called upon the lead regiment of the 208th Infantry Division to be brought up. 337th Regiment was ordered forward by forced march with bicycles and lorries. It had to travel via Furnes to go into the line south of the pinned 171st Regiment, but got stuck in the darkness on the Furnes-La Panne road. Geyer was impatient to regain momentum; the eastern segment of the closing German vice was labouring to apply pressure. The British I Corps still remained potentially at their mercy.[32]

The shortest geographical thrust line into the depth of the Dunkirk perimeter and port lay due south. The southern jaw of the vice needed to compress just 6 miles, an 18-minute car drive. Here, the X German Corps was poised to advance with three infantry divisions: the 18th, 254th and 14th. Before them lay the final defending BEF elements, a six-battalion front formed by rearguards from General Alexander's I British Corps. French troops from the three infantry regiments of the Fortified Sector of Flanders (SFF) were holding either side of them and in depth, supported by two artillery regiments and naval artillery. The French now held the west and eastern sides of the perimeter, poised to relieve the British in place, so that they could thin out to the beaches. This could not happen during daylight hours on 1 June.

Generalleutnant Christian Hansen was in charge of this southern offensive sector. Captured documents recovered by XIV Corps on their left suggested four divisions were holding the line of the Dunkirk perimeter, with two each side of Bergues, the defence lynch pin. Extensive flooding on both sides of the town along the line of the Canal de la Baseé-Colme restricted attack options to a narrow dry land peninsula at the dividing line of Hansen's 18th and 254th

Divisions. This was where the blow was aimed, starting at 11am. *Luftwaffe* attacks were already well under way, attacking Bergues and the forts to its rear.[33]

Hansen pinned his hopes on an 18th Division *Schwerpunkt*, led by *Generalleutnant* Friedrich-Carl Cranz. The 18th was a crack unit and Cranz the consummate military professional, totally objective driven. His Polish campaign veterans experienced more casualties in 1939 than any other infantry division. They had performed well at the Lys crossings and mercilessly harried the British and French to this point in the battle. His current casualties were in the process of surpassing those lost in Poland. The 254th Division would attack to his right and the newly arrived 61st Division had already been dispatched west of Bergues, to attack towards the port of Dunkirk from the south-west.

Major Georg von Altenstadt, a newly promoted staff officer with the 18th remembered, 'we had no clear picture' of the enemy in front of the division, and 'an apprehended radio transmission had said the last Englishmen had disembarked during the night of the 31st May to 1st June'. They were confident of making rapid progress. 'The division had an unusually strong artillery support at its disposal on the first attack day, 31 batteries, of which 13 were heavy.' This was in addition to howling Stuka support 'which repeatedly bombed Dunkirk and the many forts of its old fortifications'.[34] The division would initially assault over the canal to the east of Bergues with the 54th Regiment before its 51st tackled the town's ancient Vauban ramparts.

Gefreiter Lachmann with the 51st Regiment remembered moving up to the assembly area prior to the attack the night before: 'We moved out. Again the fiery ball of the sun slipped beneath the smoke and cordite haze on the horizon. In the distance we heard a constant and loud rumbling of thunder, which became even louder as darkness descended.' As they marched, 'the nearer we came, the more violent the sounds at the front'. He thought of home, a reminder why he was doing this, 'and felt content to be among his circle of comrades'.[35]

H-Hour was 11am and *Oberst* Recknagel's 54th Regiment was soon mired in the flooded terrain and funnelled onto constricted dry land approaches, which slowed them down. Hit by artillery, they sought cover after being unexpectedly raked by tank fire across open ground 2,000 metres away, losing heavy casualties. The attack carried on despite losses and they took about 100 prisoners. 'Frenchmen!' Von

Altenstadt recalled; 'once again the British were making others bleed for them'.[36] The attack by 51st Regiment against Bergues to their left stalled beneath the 12-metre-high Vauban walls and a well-entrenched enemy. A 'forlorn hope' rush by 20 volunteers, led by the regimental adjutant *Oberleutnant* von Wensky-Petersheyde, came to naught when he was cut down beneath the rampart wall. When night descended Cranz ordered the troops to dig in along the line they had achieved and hoped for progress further to his right.

This was *Generalleutnant* Walter Behschnitt's 254th Division, which attacked out of the village of Wareham. War correspondent Dr Storz was with its 454th Regiment and approached the blown bridge at Pont à Moutons, where 'the flat open terrain very much favoured the defence'. He remembered the pre-attack briefing conducted in a barn 'only 500 metres from the Tommies and Poilus'. All around him, the attacking companies:

> were lying, one behind the other in mud-filled ditches alongside the narrow roads and tracks, rifle in hand and a bag filled grenades slung across the shoulder. They had that grim look on their faces, as always, at the decisive moment before life or death.

The barn briefing outlined infantry would be in the first wave to reach the canal, followed by engineers and an anti-tank company. Another company of guns was in reserve.[37]

The official 2nd Battalion of the 454th Grenadier Regiment after-action account is not the same as the idealized action Dr Storz describes in his propaganda reportage. It notes they were under fire even as they moved into their assembly area prior to the attack 'from houses, hedges and trees'. They were not aware the enemy was still on their side of the canal bank. When they burst from cover the 6th Company commander *Leutnant* Sievert was cut down and wounded alongside several other soldiers. A pause ensued to bring more artillery fire down on the objective, some of it 'direct fire onto the identified enemy nests, and soon several houses were in flames'. Storz remembered that, when the *Oberleutnant* issued his instructions inside the barn, he had to shout over the rushing howls of outgoing German artillery support. By 11am the 2nd Battalion attacked two companies forward, six left and five right. They gained the south canal bank ahead of the 3rd Battalion attacking on their left, at which point they were pinned down by intense machine-gun fire.

Directly opposite were elements from the British 1st Battalion the East Lancashire Regiment, where Private Frank Curry remembered 'we could see hundreds of Germans appearing in front of us'. Captain Ervine-Andrews, their commander, shouted, 'don't fire until they get right down to the canal'. Curry's friend Paddy reassured him by saying: 'don't worry, we'll be prisoners of war' and 'he convinced me that Captain Ervine-Andrews would have to surrender'. Fighting, however, went on throughout the day. 'We repulsed them, simple as that. We were behind the hedges with Bren guns and plenty of ammo and we just riddled them like stupid. They were like suicide squads.'

Ervine-Andrews, perched on a barn roof, dispatched runners to warn 'somebody coming on the left-hand hedges!' or 'enemy troops on the far right!' The 454th Regiment described 'painful losses'. A stalemate of sorts developed; 'well camouflaged, the enemy sat in houses, trees and above all in numerous hedges, and a tremendous fight developed'. Ervine-Andrews knew what he was doing, and later recalled:

If you fire accurately and you hit men they are discouraged. It's when you fire a lot of ammunition and you don't do any damage, the other chaps are very brave and push on. But when they are suffering severe casualties they are inclined to stop, or as in this case, they move round to the flanks, because there is no point in going up and getting a bloody nose.

He allegedly brought down 17 Germans with rifle fire and more with a Bren gun.[38]

Lieutenant James Langley with the Coldstream Guards defended further along the canal to the east. He also suspected the Germans did not realize they were holding both banks of the canal; they 'didn't really know what was happening', he recalled. Manning the perimeter defence, they watched as British troops retired through them, but 'we didn't even know where the sea was'. Looking behind, 'one could guess where it was, because we could see the aircraft being shot down'.

Then on the morning of 1st June, we saw the Germans on the other side here. I don't think they knew where we were. They were digging in quite comfortably. When the mist rolled back there were about 400 to 500 soldiers sitting, gossiping, packing up their tools and marching back. Then we let them have it, undoubtedly causing very heavy casualties.[39]

'At about midday,' the 454th Regiment account read, 'in stifling heat' the 6th Company had reached the canal edge, with the 5th hanging back, unable to attain the bank. Storz recalled enemy 'from left and right tapped his machine guns and the light *pff-ffs* zipped by, rifles firing over the ground'. The Tommies, he realized, 'must have thinned out and left their foxholes on the other bank'. Artillery descended and 'amid the shrieks and cracks and deep thunderous artillery reports, and the lighter singing of machine gun and rifle shots, came the bellowing from frightened cattle'.

Lorries loaded with dinghies and more on trailers behind were driven down dirt tracks to the canal edge. Storz observed the engineer major, 'an example to all his soldiers', standing 'in the middle of the street giving instructions'. His act of bravado resulted in severe wounds. An engineer platoon supported by another platoon of infantry, and even staff from battalion headquarters, began manhandling these dinghies through the streets. They got to within 200 yards of the canal bank before a flurry of intense fire pinned them all to the ground. The dinghies were left hastily abandoned in the road; there would be no crossing at this point. The battalion commander intervened, cajoling his men until they managed to throw two small four-man and one large 12-man dinghy onto the back of another lorry, which was driven off to 6th Company, who had reached the canal bank.

Frank Curry watched 'hundreds' of 'Germans stacking up on the hill – hundreds of them', and began to suspect: 'We can't keep this up. If a hundred come at us and we shoot half of them, some of them are still going to get across.'[40]

Ervine-Andrews, his commander, was still shooting from the barn roof when it caught fire, but continued to snipe and machine-gun Germans on the flat expanse of open ground before them. He eventually clambered down and ordered, 'tell them all, when I blow my whistle, to make a hasty retreat. It'll be every man for himself'. 'We got moving,' Curry recalled. After about 100 yards his friend Paddy was struck in the back by a bullet that exited through his chest. With blood streaming from his mouth, 'he looked at me, this poor old bugger, who'd been taking care of me and said: "Get going son!"' His companion Johnson also shouted 'get the fucking hell out of here. Go on lad – run!'[41]

The 454th Regiment observed: 'Although now, already the greater part of the battalion had managed to cross, the enemy still fired heavily from positions and cover south of the canal, partly in the rear and right flank of the battalion.'[42]

The 1st Battalion of the 454th was now brought forward and its 7th Company tasked to mop up the south bank of the canal as 'the enemy continued to fire out of burning village houses and barns'. Shortly after the company was so depleted by heavy casualties the entire battalion was ordered in to finish the job.

Lieutenant James Langley with the Guards thought the Germans 'were extremely brave, and very, very tired, like we were':

> They had been following up [the BEFs retreat] on foot, without any change of clothing or very much sleep. When they did advance, it was through their own shellfire barrage, but nothing stopped them. The first wave were killed but they managed to cross the canal.[43]

Fighting developed on both sides of the canal. Langley's men climbed inside the roof rafters of a house to dominate the ground to their front. 'We moved just three tiles and put the muzzle of the Bren gun through,' he remembered, and:

> All through the morning of 1st June we swept the country in front of us. I had about 20,000 rounds of ammo. In fact the Bren guns got so hot we had to dip them in white wine, we found, to cool the barrels off.[44]

At about midday the British unit to their right claimed they could not continue with their defence and were going to withdraw. 'My company commander was quite ruthless,' Langley remembered, and said, 'if you go back beyond that tree [which he pointed out] over there, I will shoot you'. Half an hour later they did start to withdraw. Thereupon Langley's company commander called him over and said they would both lower their rifles and 'both fire to kill'. 'I don't know whether we killed or not,' Langley admitted, 'but they did not go back to or beyond that point.'[45]

When French soldiers tried to retreat through their lines, the Guards turned them back too.

'Towards the evening, the Germans got into the cottage opposite,' Langley remembered:

There, they tried the same game as us. We saw them starting to move a tile or two and we let them have the blast of all our three Bren guns, and drove them out of the cottage, which enabled us to hold this vital point until six in the evening.

Langley stayed in the rooftop, vigorously sniping at anything that moved, until he was injured by a shell that exploded inside the rafters. His men carried him out of the building and trundled him away from the fighting in a wheelbarrow. Remarkably, he was to get back to Britain.

The 1st Battalion of the 454th was bogged down in bitter house-to-house fighting around the canal until late evening. The 2nd Battalion occupied the north bank by late afternoon, where it found itself opposite a flooded landscape it was unable to cross. They had lost 46 men during the crossing, of which eight were killed. 'Darkness descended,' the after-action report noted, which was 'a little restless'.[46]

After 10pm the Guards began to thin out and move down to the beaches; their line was never broken. The small German bridgehead established on the north bank of the canal was contained by elements from the French 137th Regiment with the SFF. There was friction between French and British retreating troops. The British assumed they had unstated priority and the French sensed it. 'There were moments when we were given orders to change position,' recalled Seventh Army soldier Jean Contanceau, 'and sometimes we would come across British officers who would threaten us with guns, not letting us get past. That was very hard.'[47]

That night, during the hours of darkness most of the 1st British Division and the 46th Division's 126 and 139 Brigades were taken off the Mole and beaches, including the I Corps' artillery and support units, some 15,000 or more men. During the afternoon, in the face of the massive air attacks, it was decided not to continue embarking stretcher cases. I British Corps had achieved the great escape beyond all expectations. Seventeen ships were lost, including four precious destroyers, with another two seriously damaged to be laid up for months.

Clearly, daylight evacuation was no longer tenable. Captain Tennant ordered 'evacuation by transports, therefore ceases by 0300 hours'. Royal Engineer sapper Sid Crockitt was caught up in the final rush:

> Captain Tennant said 'Now, you are going off the Mole. I want you to run as fast as you possibly can, because the more you run, the more we can get off.' I looked round, I was the last man, and I wasn't going to get left.

He ran as fast as he could, but the steps had been removed and he could not climb to reach the ship. At first dismayed, 'a big sailor simply leaned over, grabbed me rifle in one hand and me in the other, lifted me straight up and dumped us on the deck'.[48]

Admiral Ramsay ordered all ships to clear Dunkirk before sunrise. The destroyers *Whitshed* and *Winchelsea* pulled up their gangplanks and boarding ladders at the allotted time and cast off. Standing in grim lines on the East Mole jetty were shadowy silhouettes identifiable by distinctive soup-plate-shaped helmets. They were the Loyals, who had fought all day alongside the French at Bergues, holding off the German 18th Division attacks. They force-marched 5 miles through the gathering darkness to reach the port, having endured two days of non-stop artillery bombardment and close combat on the perimeter defence. They were the very rearguards that Lord Gort had instructed should be saved. After dejectedly watching the ships reverse out of harbour, they were 'about faced' and marched off to the sand dunes beyond Malo-les-Bains. They joined another 3,500 British troops positioned inside a final redoubt secured by a dozen two-pounder anti-tank guns and seven bofors. The isolated enclave would soak up further units and stragglers during the coming day. They dug in and waited for the daylight hours to pass and for the Royal Navy to return. Up to now 285,000 British and French troops had been evacuated from the perimeter, leaving behind about 95,000 soldiers. About 7,000 of these were British, the final rearguards and BEF stragglers.

The French now manned the entire outline of the Dunkirk perimeter.

Chapter 9

Elusive Victory

'On the horizon a black smoke cloud darkened the sky,' recalled an artillery observer with the 18th Artillery Regiment: '… the smoking silhouette of the town harbour can be clearly made out beneath. That signposts our objective, Dunkirk.'[1]

Infantry up front, could see it too, visible from miles away. The 18th Division pushing from the south had stalled, with 51st Regiment left, pinned down along the 4-mile length of the Bergues' Vauban ramparts and canal moats and 54th Regiment right. The main entry point, the Cassel Gate bridge, was blocked by a huge caterpillar bulldozer, filling the entire gate post. 54th Regiment was struggling across flooded terrain to the right of the medieval town and Hoymille. 'Deep water ran either side of the roads, where the water had risen over the meadows,' remembered *Major* von Altenstadt with the division staff. 'Flooding constantly necessitated changes of position, many experiencing an involuntary dip, which impeded forward movement.'[2]

Then at 6am came a remarkable sight; waves of French infantry were bobbing up and down in the flooded landscape coming towards them. Sloshing through thigh-deep water, they were supported by Somua S35 tanks and armoured cars, wading along tracks and byways visible above and just beneath the surface. This was the 550-strong French 21st Division Training Centre, flinging itself recklessly against the German advance. The French, now isolated, sought to regain some initiative. The ragged files floundered nearer and nearer, starkly silhouetted against the silvery sheen of the early morning sun rising above the water. Advancing waves were abruptly torn apart in a welter of bloody foam by crisscrossing Spandau machine-gun fire. Badly wounded men slipped beneath the surface of the water. Only 65 French soldiers survived to give up. So devastating was the German riposte that it is hardly mentioned in surviving German unit accounts.

Two hours later the *Luftwaffe* was back over Dunkirk. Heinkel III bombers from *Kampfgeschwader* 54 and Stukas from *Stukageschwader* 2 swept into view but found the shallow waters offshore empty of ships. Reconnaissance flights reported 'scant shipping movement in the area of sea between Great Britain and Dunkirk'. Fierce air battles developed when the bombers, escorted by four Me 109 squadrons and one of Me 110s, came up against five RAF fighter squadrons. Once again the formidable force of 120 German aircraft held its own, losing just one fighter to six British, but at the cost of seven to eight bombers.

Numerous 'false crests' had marred ascent towards German victory at Dunkirk. *Luftwaffe* high points on 29 May and 1 June had not materially diminished the carrying capacity of the British evacuation fleet. Despite vacant seas this morning offshore, the evacuation was not over yet. Belgian surrender had not precipitated an expected Anglo-French collapse. The vulnerable coastal dune strip from La Panne to Bray Dunes on the east side of the perimeter was still blocked by the French frontier bunker line. Bergues, the shortest direct line distance to Dunkirk harbour, was holding out to the south. German soldiers found themselves in the invidious position of fighting and dying for objectives already proclaimed a victory back home in the *Reich*. They were as exhausted as their opponents.

German schoolchildren had followed the advances across France by sticking pins on maps displayed in classrooms and newspapers. 'Even to a 12-year-old,' Hitler Youth member Alfons Heck recalled, 'the radio news of the enemy's attempts to escape was an admission of utter defeat.' German soldiers knew victory was in the bag. One *Gefreiter* with the 77th Artillery Regiment wrote home: 'The Belgians are out of it, as you have already heard. The English are trying to escape over sea to their island, and the French give up wherever you meet them.'

'Further resistance was pointless,' he suggested. An anti-tank gunner with the 44th Infantry Division was convinced the 'next phase of the war will in all probability be played out in England'. 'Strength of will,

will always triumph,' he wrote home, 'the impossible has certainly been achieved'. Schoolboy Heck remembered that 'after Dunkirk, no German doubted the outcome of the battle for France'.[3]

Secret German SS home front reports commented the week before that 'the entire German people are completely engrossed, tirelessly following the development of the huge encirclement battle in Flanders and Artois'. Their view was 'they firmly believed they stood on the threshold of a great German victory'. News of the Belgian capitulation 'had spread like wildfire among the population', the reports noted on 30 May, 'and had made a deep impression on the German population'. Moreover, the 'approaching annihilation of the French and English armies in Flanders and the successful attacks on 60 English war transports ... had strengthened the belief that the war would soon end'. Considering whether to risk life and limb for a pre-determined victory provided an element of drag in the minds of wily German *Landser*. Hans S., with the 12th Infantry Division, writing home to his parents from Béthune on 30 May, crowed 'we will be counting the Tommies at their home, if I can be there to take part?' Although this outpouring of emotional satisfaction at home was heartening, German soldiers around the perimeter knew further sacrifice would be required.[4]

General von Küchler's Eighteenth Army planned an H-Hour of 3pm on the afternoon of 2 June for the final attacks on the remaining perimeter, which would launch from the south-west, south and east. Seven German divisions would assault three French equivalents in defence. That night the Royal Navy still intended to get the last of the British off. A German thrust along the evacuation beach line by the 56th Division had the potential to completely negate this. Stuka attacks hit French General Janssen's 12th Division Headquarters at the Fort des Dunes, west of Malo-les-Bains, which was coordinating resistance along this line. Two bombs exploded in the officer's courtyard, mortally wounding Janssen and a number of accompanying officers and NCOs. More attacks the following day killed scores, so the headquarters was relocated to a school in Dunkirk, near Leffrinckouke railway station. Janssen's body had to be temporarily rolled into a ditch, alongside other victims of the raid.

56th Division had been pushing against the 8th Zouaves on the frontier line since 9.30 that morning. La Panne and Bray Dunes beaches had already been overrun; just Malo-les-Bains, east of the Mole jetty remained. Lieutenant Colonel Anzemberger's Zouaves observed German motorized columns crossing the Furnes Canal as the 337th Regiment from the reinforcing 208th Infantry Division was brought up. Heavy artillery fire descended on the French positions after a calm night. Zouave Pierre Dehay, manning the telephone at the 15th Artillery Regiment concrete observation post, remembered, 'a 105mm shell landed 10 metres away and killed a telegraphist and ripped off the hands of another'. His friend Maurice standing at the edge of the shelter grimly reminded them 'this was not a healthy place'. Paul Weber passing mortar shells to his sergeant, Ramos, frequently passed his friend Flory Gruile from his home village. He next saw him carried by on a stretcher five hours later with a serious head wound. The Zouaves beat back all attacks; they were firmly ensconced and well fed on horse steaks and potatoes. Their concrete-mounted 75mm artillery pieces and 81mm mortars could be directly resupplied from abandoned piles of shells left on the beach; German infantry attacks were decimated by a steadily maintained fire.[5]

Hauptmann Sprenger with the 56th Division remembered 'deep sand and enemy defensive fire meant the attack only went forward slowly'. Heavy direct fire support weapons could not be pushed or pulled through the deep fine sand. The 2nd Battalion 171st Regiment managed to close up on the left of its stalled sister battalion, the 3rd, but 216th Division to its left lost 120 men, failing to achieve its objectives. This resulted in 171st Regiment being lacerated by galling fire in the flank from the French 150th Regiment, which stopped progress.

The 56th Division's artillery regiment and battery commanders made their way forward by horse and motorcycle along the wet sand of the ebb tide to try and resolve the impasse with directly observed artillery fire onto the Zouave positions. Hardened concrete bunker shelters could be picked out but not the well-camouflaged mortars and machine guns sited in the dunes between. Sprenger recalled: 'Because of the exhausting efforts of the past few days, unbearable heat in the dunes and the scarcity of water, the 171st Regiment infantry were so fatigued, that one could not count on any vigorous forward movement.'[6]

They could only engage visible resistance points and 'the infantry could only manage to win a little ground'. Division commander *General* Kriebel sent his operations officer forward to assess progress. It took him some time to find even the forward elements of the reinforcing

337th Regiment. 'Even this regiment is not fresh,' the operations officer reported; 'worn out, the people were lying fast asleep by the roadside'. Kriebel was resigned to accepting 'it was becoming increasingly clear, that this first part of the western campaign had come to an end for the division'. Failure to achieve an objective was not something this army, underpinned by National Socialist ideals of innate superiority, could easily encompass. Combat stress was recognized in the ranks, but not as an officially accepted medical condition. The soldiers tended to look after their own, away from public gaze.[7]

Kriebel's 56th Division had formed up just ten months before, on the eve of war in August 1939. It had played an inactive support role during the Polish campaign and had only managed six months of solid training to prepare for the western invasion. It had performed well in the attack and forced marches over the previous 23 days, breaking through the Dyle position, then Antwerp and Ghent, and the Lys crossing, and reached the sea. Kriebel's post-operation report exposed the weaknesses through which it laboured. 171st Regiment had only one young *Oberleutnant* who was a regular officer when the war started; the rest were reserve officers. The battalion commanders were all reactivated reserve officers and none had commanded in peacetime. There were just two regular NCOs on average per company and the reserve NCOs drafted in were only short service or administrative personnel. These ad hoc assemblies of officers and NCOs had to learn the whole gambit of discipline and administrative practice that underpinned a typical division.

Although the reserve officers performed well in combat, they, like their men, lacked practical experience. The after-action report admitted big holes in discipline, particularly on the march. All three infantry regiments with the 56th Division had endured 'bloody losses'. One in two officers – 50% – had become casualties, as had two in ten NCOs, losing 75 officers and 250 NCOs. The infantry regiment losses were some 1,554 men, a staggering 21.7% fall-out rate. Kriebel also complained about the shortage of medics and stretcher-bearers throughout the campaign, ill prepared to pick up the heavy losses from the field. Overall, the division lost 105 officers and 2,146 NCOs and men. On 2 June 56th Division was fought out and its attacks were faltering; 75 men had been lost during the day. No further progress would be made until the next morning, when the 208th Division would replace it in the line. 'A period of recuperation and replenishment is necessary,' Kriebel accepted, 'Above all everyone needed a break. There is, however, great disappointment not to be involved in the final storming and annihilation of Dunkirk, as the crowning achievement of many hard days of battle against the enemy.'[8]

The most powerful German attacks against the perimeter on 2 June came from the south. Three French divisions, the 68th, the SFF and the 12th, faced seven German. Four of these were restricted by flooded terrain to floundering laboriously forward. Three, including 56th Division from the east, applied forceful pressure; two others – the 18th and 61st – were utilizing dry land causeways to further the advance. An area of flat flooded terrain, dominated by the French 92nd Infantry Division Recce Group (GRDI), checked the 14th and 254th Divisions.

The medieval town of Bergues with its Vauban-restored massively thick fortifications and ramparts was the key obstacle, and road junction, for any move on Dunkirk. A junction of three canals, its walls surmounted and dominated the totally flat landscape to the south and east, inundated by floodwater to its west and further inland. *Gefreiter* Vater, an anti-tank gunner with *Oberst* Bohnstedt's 51st Regiment, recalled 'our artillery had worked over Bergues with its remorselessly destructive and annihilating fire the whole night'. His platoon commander told them, 'Bergues must be taken today'. For Vater 'the 2nd June began with a gigantic sun ball rising up over the horizon,' another stiflingly hot day. Bohnstedt's 51st Regiment was held at the moats beneath the town walls, while Recknagel's 54th Regiment was channelled by inundated flooded terrain to the right, coming under fire as it tried to bypass Bergues to its left.[9]

Battery commander *Oberleutnant* Richtsteig with 156th Artillery Regiment remembered the gradual concentration of artillery units the preceding night, with 'still other artillery units gathering here'. There were 31 batteries, including his 5th, of which 13 were heavy, setting up across a 2½-mile front:

> What a gigantic artillery offering, we thought, we are going to let loose here! We had strong enemy resistance to crack, because over there in the heavily fortified town, the enemy had set himself up behind thick medieval walls. He held the key position for Dunkirk in his hands, he knew it, and so did we.[10]

The barrage opened up as 'battery after battery sent their whistling and howling salvoes over'. Nicknamed the 'bloody dog' division, Bohnstedt's point battalion, commanded by *Major* Mohr and supported by assault pioneers, was earmarked to storm the walls within minutes of the Stuka attack between 3pm and 3.20pm. Operational planning had been laborious because of the three- to four-hour reaction time lag needed for *Luftwaffe* mission targeting. Although it was difficult to precisely steer Stuka support onto identified enemy batteries, 'the Bergues fortress', the X Corps log noted, 'offered a clear target'. It clearly stood out from flooded terrain surrounding it on three sides.

Artillery *Oberleutnant* Otte recalled 'smoke still lay over the town, flames raged from the burning town tower and the tip of the church tower had been shot away'. Troops withdrawn to 1,000 metres for safety called out, 'our Stukas are coming!'

> We tensely observed the approaching formation, the so-called 'Sky Wolves'!
>
> Enemy flak started to shoot. Already they swarm and wheel coolly in circles like vultures, over their victim. We watch this beautiful destruction delivering performance. *Achtung!* [Watch out!]. The first tips over and dives down, sirens howling. The second, third, all go into a steep dive. The bomb release can be clearly seen and terrific detonations assault our ears.

Time and again the aircraft dive, 'smoke and dirt fountain high into the sky'. Watching troops were intimidated by the effect of the spectacle, 'would the enemy surrender? Must surrender!' At the final bomb release at 3.20pm massed artillery opened up again and fired in depth as the Mohr battalion stormed forward.[11]

The French 137th Regiment with the SFF had taken over from the British Loyals battalion and was caught up in this inferno. The noise and blast waves from the 500kg bombs battered them into a form of insensibility. Soldiers in unprotected overhead positions had simply been swept away. Those cowering and dazed in underground shelters awaited the alarm to man the ramparts at the first pause in bombing. An incandescent glow from flamethrower jets shone through billowing clouds of smoke and dust as German assault pioneers closed up on the walls. *Schütze* (Private) Linke with Mohr's battalion identified a narrow breach in the Vauban ramparts blasted open by a Stuka bomb that left 'a church-high smoke cloud from the explosion'. It was wide enough for two men to scramble through. The breach was pointed out to *Oberleutnant* Voigt, the 2nd Company engineer commander, who went in with men wielding pistols and hand grenades supported by a flamethrower. They came up against dazed Frenchmen 'who looked as though they had experienced an earthquake, written on pale faces'. Creeping over the rubble they clashed with Frenchmen scrambling from bunkers and casemate shelters to reoccupy the wall, cutting them down with rapid fire. Voigt called upon survivors queuing to get up the stairs outside, to surrender. Hands were raised and the wounded commander, a grizzled veteran, decided to capitulate. Many of the shocked garrison gave up without firing a shot; 16 officers, 44 NCOs and 809 men were taken, an exploit that earned Voigt the Knight's Cross. A short fight in the depth of the fortress yielded a further 200 prisoners.[12]

Another 24 Stukas meanwhile attacked Fort Vallières 4½ miles beyond, killing much of the garrison. Bohnstedt's 51st Regiment got across the now undefended Bergues canal and overwhelmed the surviving defenders, capturing a 150mm-long barrelled artillery piece in the process. The advances enabled *Oberst* Recknagel's 54th Regiment to close up on the right, gaining ground that now enabled the port of Dunkirk and beaches to come within range of all of the 18th Division's artillery. A potential stranglehold had been applied that could yet halt further evacuations.

Gefreiter Vater's 14th Company's anti-tank guns provided flank protection to Recknagel's attempt to bypass Bergues to the right. 'The merciless rays of the sun shone down on us on the only negotiable road,' he recalled, as they towed and manhandled 37mm guns forward. 'Right and left of us, the enemy had flooded everything.' As they moved nearer to Dunkirk the advance was halted amid 'the distinctive sound of tank shells'. Two of their forward guns were already in position on the macadam road ahead, barking out the sharp crack reports of return fire. Despite the road stretching straight for 200 to 300 yards, they could not see the enemy tank, 'although the enemy could obviously see us' because tank rounds were bursting ahead and behind. Eventually they picked out his superbly camouflaged position, 'but despite 60 well-placed rounds from the guns up front, he was still maintaining a lively engagement'.

When a French lorry moved forward to resupply the tank with ammunition, they managed to hit it after two to three rounds, rewarded by the sight of a huge jet of flame and smoke rising into the sky. 'Celebrations all round' from the gun crews, and 'the tank took flight inside the smoke clouds, and we could continue with the advance'. Seeing the collapse of French resistance with the raising of a swastika flag in Bergues to their left, they pressed on, hoping to get into Dunkirk by dusk. Dry ground came into sight at last protruding above the level of the flood plain as they reached the outlying houses of the next village. A flurry of detonations and shooting indicating a French counter-attack came in against the 5th Company on their left. When a convoy of French lorries tried to bypass their advance, it was halted by knocking out the first and last vehicles. Vater remembered:

> The Frenchmen jumped from their wagons and ran for their lives. Ten minutes later they came by with raised hands, the shock of the past few minutes still in their eyes. They warily eyed the Pak guns, these 'wonder weapons', from which there was no escape.

Having reached its intermediate objective, the battalion started to dig in. As night fell, 'rumbling and light flashes on the evening horizon showed smoke clouds rising up from Dunkirk's burning docks'.[13]

Even as the Stukas were diving on the ramparts of Bergues, *Generalleutnant* Siegfried Hänicke's newly arrived 61st Division attacked from the 9th Panzer sector of the perimeter, north-east towards Dunkirk. They were traversing a dry land bridge area both sides of the village of Brouckerque, with the 151st Regiment left and the 162nd right. The attack was hemmed in by the Bourbourg and Colme canal lines at each side. Both regiments had an engineer company in support to get across the myriad water obstacles they faced, as well as an artillery group and a company each from *Panzerjäger Abteilung* 560, with 88mm guns towed by 8-ton half-tracks. The 176th Infantry Regiment followed on behind in reserve, prepared to exploit any breakthroughs.

The infantry laboured forward with a miscellany of ladders and planks to traverse the ditches and watercourses they needed to cross. 'The flat wide and completely open ground', the 151st after-action report noted, 'impeded the approach against the enemy'. The 162nd Regiment commander repositioned his heavy guns to protect his right flank and as his vehicles drove through the village of Brouckerque, they were spotted by French artillery, who brought them under fire in the village streets. *Hauptmann* Hauboldt with the 151st Regiment, 'one of our best officers', who had taken the initial Belgian surrenders at Fort Eban-Emael, was cut down by a hail of shell splinters. *Oberfeldwebel* Borbe with the 1st Battalion, pinned down by the heavy fire, recalled 'we couldn't even get eye contact' with the attacking 3rd Battalion on his left. 'The attack was stuck fast' and 'despite energetic and intense observation, we couldn't pick out any enemy ahead, because he was very well camouflaged'. Borbe's battalion started to lose cohesion, fragmenting into individual battle groups, over-committed against ever newly surfacing French strongpoints.

Borbe's battalion was pinned down for at least an hour. 'Our artillery fire lay far to the right,' he complained, 'and did not help us at all'. Crawling through ditches was laborious progress, despite intensive mortar and machine-gun fire support. They were 'not dealing with foxholes', they gradually realized; 'the French had constructed well-built field fortifications'. On working their way forward to bunker apertures, his men found, with hindsight, that although the positions were well built, the firing ports were obscured by undergrowth. 'We threw several grenades at the firing apertures and shouted *Raus!* Out!'; Borbe shot up the slits with his machine pistol. White flags were gradually waved here and there, but the majority of positions had to be stormed. Borbe lost a number of his NCOs, 'so sad were these losses that the enemy were roughly treated', he recalled, exasperated by what was considered pointless resistance. Clearing the positions they found ten dead Frenchmen and took 60 prisoners. By nightfall the 61st Division had penetrated the strongpoint at Spycker village, which the French abandoned during the night, having resisted stubbornly all day.[14]

Oberst Ulrich Liss was correct with his original OKH enemy forces assessment that the French armies of the north-west would prove their most doughty opponents. The Ninth French Army had collapsed quickly in the south while the Seventh Army had been a different proposition. *General* von Küchler commanding the German Eighteenth Army had grudging admiration for the bitter resistance and counter-attacks encountered around the Dunkirk perimeter. 'I see in these soldiers the same ardour as those at Verdun in 1916. We are unable to break through anywhere and suffer terrifying losses.'[15]

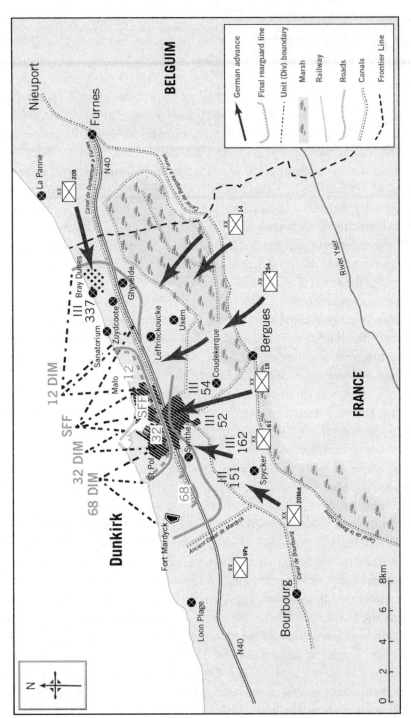

MAP 8:   The Collapse of the Dunkirk Pocket, 3–4 June 1940.

After the fall of the fortress town of Bergues to the 18th Division, four German divisions closed from the south and penetrated the suburbs within easy artillery range of the port area. The German 208th Division replaced the fought out 56th Division and penetrated Dunkirk from the east side. French resistance from remnants of four divisions was finally overcome during the morning of 4 June.

French soldier Jean Coutanceau with the Seventh Army on the perimeter remembered 'we had a lot of deaths, we lost comrades': 'We could see them all around us, dead, wounded, and our morale was dropping. We still had courage. We were afraid, but never "disarmed" if you see what I mean. We always had a desire to fight.'[16]

The French had been off balance ever since the collapse along the line of the River Somme. 'It was incredibly sad,' admitted Gustave Vancoille with the First Army:

It was above all surprising, because we hadn't been warned. Everything that happened was surprising, because it was unexpected and murderous. There were bodies everywhere because of the bombings. I had two friends who were killed right next to me, Arcole and Predel. What a disaster.[17]

Hoping to be evacuated from the beaches, they resisted fiercely. The perimeter was still holding on the evening of 2 June. One French soldier confided to his diary: 'Dunkirk is nothing but flames. The enemy planes attack us relentlessly. Perhaps our last hour is not far off. But we hold on to the end, knowing full well that we will be the last to be withdrawn.'[18]

After losing 17 substantial vessels the day before, it was a considerable risk for Admiral Ramsay to send back even more ships to ferry out the last contingent of 7,000 British troops. The beaches and Mole jetty were now under regular artillery bombardment with 75mm, 105mm and heavy 150mm German shells. French engineer Marceau Lantenois remembered, 'we spent the whole day [2 June] again waiting, in fear of being bombed, but throughout the day it's only the ships that attract attention.' Vancoille had all day to ponder his chances:

The worst sight was in the morning, when we would see all the dead bodies lying along the beach. The tide had brought them in. It was terribly sad, it was dangerous, but you had to take risks, and I didn't want to be a prisoner.

'Finally at dusk, our time has come to embark,' Lantenois recalled. 'We feel that we are going to be saved, we prefer to face the risks at sea than to stay in this sinister place.' After the final *Luftwaffe* raids, Ramsay's ships began to arrive after 9pm in gathering darkness. Emerging from the gloom into the reflected glow of the burning port came 11 destroyers, eight personnel ships, 14 minesweepers, nine drifters, six Dutch schuyts, two armed yachts, a gunboat and a tugboat towing small craft. Three passenger ships had refused to sail after the carnage of the day before.

Captain Tennant remembered this last night of shore organization. 'At dark vessels of all kinds arrived further up the harbour.' Movement was organized by a berthing officer, who stood at the head of the pier with a loudspeaker. The French also participated with a supreme effort: 43 ships, including the large destroyer *Leopard*, two torpedo boats, six smaller warships and an assortment of 34 French and Belgian fishing boats. Gustave Vancoille remembered 'there were some who stayed, who didn't dare go, because it was dark, there were mines and boats were sinking'.[19]

By 10.30pm the last elements of the BEF were embarking from the quayside. Less than 4 miles away to the south the French 407th Regiment was blocking the road just north of Coudekerque. The furthermost elements of *Oberst* Recknagel's 54th Regiment were still digging in, while its artillery commanders were looking around in the dark for dry spaces where the guns might deploy. To the south-west, 61st Infantry Division was reorganizing beyond Spycker, which put it 7 to 8 miles from the port. It was held in place by elements from the French 225th Regiment. Just 7 miles to the east of the docks the 8th Zouaves and 150th Regiment were holding back 56th and 216th Divisions in the area of Bray Dunes.

Major Donald Wilson-Haffenden with the headquarters of the 1st British Division appreciated their precarious predicament. 'We reckoned that this was to be our last night of the evacuation,' he remembered. He spoke to General Alexander, commanding this final rearguard contingent, feeling they should start carrying the wounded to the end of the Mole before the last of the British troops put in an appearance. He was totally taken aback at Alexander's uncompromising response: 'Haffie, no casualty is to be moved on to the Mole until the last of the fighting troops are away, because the country needs fighting troops now, and the casualties will be protected by the Geneva Convention.'

Wilson-Haffenden had hardly slept for eight days and this was too much; he promptly 'burst into tears'. 'Don't be a fool, Haffie,' Alexander gently reminded him: 'You've got to realize that we're custodians for the whole of Britain and we've got to get the fighting troops back!' 'I saluted smartly,' his distressed staff officer remembered, 'and said "Yes Sir".'[20]

Captain Tennant watched the last of them, the 1st Battalion the Kings Shropshire Light Infantry, board the 1,952-ton ship *St Helier* and cast off at 11.30pm. He signalled Vice Admiral Ramsay at Dover 'Operation complete. Returning to Dover', which was reworded for posterity as 'BEF evacuated'. By midnight 7,208 British troops had been taken off from under the noses of the German Army. On average, they were merely a ten-minute drive from the port. Only 19,800 French troops got away that night. German shellfire stopped the evacuation from the Malo-les-Bains beaches next to the Mole. When Captain Tennant's control team departed, embarkation ceased. A series of mistaken communications resulted in most French troops not arriving at their eastern jetty until 2.30am. Up to 10,000 were left at the quayside and around the dock area. Gustave Vancoille at least got away. 'I was young, I knew how to swim, I could risk it,' he remembered, picked up naked beneath his greatcoat. 'I'm glad I did, because it turned out well.'[21]

Offshore, Admiral Wake-Walker had done his best to salvage what he could from French confusion on shore. 'One ship lay three and a half hours at the end berth waiting for men,' he recalled, and he had to send back many empty ships. The East Pier situation went from bad to worse as it grew light. 'As the time of leaving got closer,' he recalled, 'I was hailing them to make them run down the pier.' Lack of organization and language was all against him: 'I can remember seeing men, who were on their way to a ship that was alongside the end of the pier, turn and run back down the pier because they saw another ship coming alongside further in.' They had to cast off to avoid inevitable *Luftwaffe* retribution. 'This had been a very disappointing night,' he concluded. Nevertheless, the last of the BEF was on its way home.[22]

THE RACE TO THE SEA, 3–4 JUNE

Haze and a heavy ground mist hampered air operations over Dunkirk in any case during the early morning hours of 3 June. On landing the previous evening most *Luftwaffe* units were warned off for Operation *Paula*, a mass attack on airfields in and around Paris, the precursor to Operation *Röt*. Von Richthofen, commanding VIII *Fliegerkorps*, had already accepted the *Luftwaffe* limitations at tackling a task 'so to say at the last moment, that could not further hinder English embarkations from Dunkirk' despite what they had achieved on 1 June. This was particularly as 'the army had not gripped it before'. He wrote resignedly in his diary, 'a victory over England has shrunk!' Diary entries for the next few days are headlined 'preparations for new operations in the south'; he had already moved on.[23]

That afternoon 640 bombers escorted by 460 Messerschmitt fighters hit French air bases and aviation industry targets around Paris. *General* Kesselring commanding *Luftflotte* 2) remembered 'more than a hundred French aircraft were shot down and three or four times that number destroyed on the ground'. Likewise, as von Küchler's Eighteenth Army geared up for the final assault on the shrunken Dunkirk perimeter, *General* Geyer commanding IX Corps complained they 'received a surprising order during the night that all the heavy artillery apart from a heavy mortar unit and their own heavy division artillery, was to be taken out of the line'. Yet more assets were being stripped out to support the coming new offensive below the River Somme.[24]

The debacle in communications on the French western jetty the previous night meant five destroyers and a personnel ship cast off at 3am virtually empty. Some 10,000 disappointed French troops were left behind. This left General Alfred Fagalde, Admiral Abrial's subordinate land force commander, about 25,000 troops to man the much-reduced Dunkirk perimeter. With the Germans between 4 and 8 miles away from the port, 22,000 Frenchmen were ready to embark. Another likely 20,000 were unaccounted for, disparate elements spread about in hundreds of tiny groups, hidden in cellars and cowering amid dugouts in the dunes. An appeal was made for yet another naval lift, a final effort, despite the chronic fatigue of ship crews, for the sake of Allied unity. The Germans had to be denied entry for this to happen.

General Friedrich-Carl Cranz's 18th Infantry Division was poised to administer a *coup de grâce* from the south. Two regiments were forward, the 51st left and 54th right, with just 4 miles to go. Theirs was the nearest and most dangerous approach to the port. 'For seven days now,' recalled *Unteroffizier* Järisch, an assault pioneer attached to Bohnstedt's 51st Regiment, he had been staring 'at the dark shadow of an unbelievably huge smoke pall, which glowed during the night hours'. It clearly marked the final objective for every German soldier, from whichever direction he advanced. 'Inside it, you could hear the drones from Stukas and bomber squadrons,' Järisch recalled, 'the whole horizon, as far as you could see was flashing'. *Major* von Altenstadt with the division staff remembered H-Hour had been set for 11am. 'But before it begins, the division has to give up 19 batteries' for redeployment further south. Not a propitious start. However, 'this painful shortfall in artillery was remedied by increasing the ammunition state for each gun by three times,' he explained, 'to even out the loss'. One of Järisch's companions pointed out the objective, 'the glow over there,' he gesticulated, 'should be Dunkirk – that's where we have to go to clear them out'. They trudged forward, exhausted, looking for their company assembly area, an estate farmhouse, 'just for something to eat and drink, not to sleep,' he remembered. RAF aircraft swept overhead eliciting nil response; 'we were too tired to pay them any attention', Järisch explained.[25]

The French did not wait for the inevitable onslaught; they put in an early morning spoiling attack of their own, against the forward jump-off positions of the 18th and 254th Divisions. General Lucas's 32nd French Division attacked the 18th with the 122nd and 143rd Regiments, while another two battalions from the SFF's 137th Regiment attacked the 254th. It was a powerful push supported by six S 35 medium and four light H 35 tanks with 47mm and 37mm guns. They advanced from Teteghem village south towards the Canal de Moëres, a surprise attack with no artillery preparation, astride the dividing line between the two German divisions. *Oberst* Recknagel's exhausted 54th Regiment soldiers were dozing at the bottom of their foxholes when it came in, waves of infantry and tanks streaming past their flank unobserved. Eventually one of the 14th Company anti-tank guns opened up against the French tanks. Two rounds cracked out, narrowly missing the target but waking up the entire German front. At the third round the tank ground to a halt and the crew baled out, cut to pieces by machine-gun fire as they scrambled from the turret and hull. By now eight to ten tanks were grinding down the Teteghem to Boomkens road north of Coudekerque village, and the 18th Division had a crisis on its hands.

The violence of the French assault bore testimony to their desire to safeguard their planned evacuation, and was pressed home with fanatical bravery, even though there was little hope. *Oberleutnant* Pickart commanding the division's 7th horse-drawn artillery battery came galloping up and went into a heroic action that elicited cheers from the hard-pressed 2nd Battalion infantry. It was ironic that after the mechanized *Blitzkrieg* dash to the sea, a Napoleonic horse artillery action was needed to block modern French tanks. This imbalance of horse to engine power was not portrayed in victorious German newsreels. The vast majority of the German Army's support weapons and logistics assets were still, as in 1914, horse drawn.

Taken in the flank by direct fire 75mm artillery pieces, five tanks were shot to a standstill. Further to their right *Oberleutnant* Manitius's 9th Battery located behind the 3rd Battalion also engaged the tanks with direct fire. The battery commander, crewing one of his own guns in the emergency, was riddled across his chest by French flanking machine gun fire. By 6.30am four French companies of infantry closing in on the 2nd Battalion had not recognized their own flank was exposed to a completely alerted 3rd Battalion. The Germans opened up with every weapon at their disposal. Even the administrative staff had been packed into the line to contain the French attack, which collapsed in a welter of withering fire. 'In one place alone,' recalled one 54th Regiment soldier, 'over 50 French bodies were counted.'[26] The tank attacks reached the forward 54th Regiment command post before being shot to a standstill by the 8th battery and 88mm guns from *Schwere Panzerjäger Abteilung* 2. During the distraction the 2nd Company from the 1st Battalion captured a lock gate, which crossed the north-south Dunkirk-Bergues Canal, and established a small bridgehead. The rest of the battalion followed, advancing on Fort Louis, where they linked with Bohnstedt's 51st Regiment, held at this point. By midday the 18th Division had penetrated the south-eastern outskirts of Dunkirk and Fort Louis, but was checked by unremitting concentric French artillery fire.

The area around the captured canal bridge was a picture of devastation. An 18th Artillery Regiment forward observer remembered how the hot sun accelerated the decomposition of unburied horse carcasses, 'so that the whole surrounding area was polluted'. Amid the stench at the canal bridge he saw:

> three civilians, a man, woman and child, who clearly had left it too late to leave the town. They were lying dead in the road, a shell crater right next to them. One of our safe pass leaflets was in the man's outstretched left hand, a shocking picture.[27]

Bitter house-to-house fighting continued on the outskirts with no appreciable result until darkness. The division had fought to within 3 miles of the port. Artillery gunners were confident they would be able reach the embarkation areas. 'With the highest elevation and number six charge, we sent our greetings directly into Dunkirk,' one of them recalled. The infantry geared themselves up for the final push, confident 'we would serve Dunkirk up for breakfast in the morning', recalled *Unteroffizier* Järisch with the Pioneer Battalion.[28]

To the left, 61st Division attempting to force the dry land bridge from the south-west made steady progress in dry sunny weather. The 151st Regiment took increasing numbers of prisoners as it pushed against a French line identified between Fort Mardyck, the Dunkirk-Furnes canal and Synthe to Fort Louis and Coudekerque village, where the 18th Division was attacking. At midday *Generalleutnant* Hänicke committed his reserve 176th Regiment, enabling him to penetrate the perimeter as far as the high ground at Cappelle, bringing him into line with 18th Division. As it grew dark his forward outposts were stuck fast 300 yards short of the canal, mercilessly pounded by French artillery. Suspecting this was the final night's resistance, the French fired from every barrel, unsparing with artillery ammunition readily retrieved from abandoned beach ammunition dumps. The German 88mm flak guns were brought up to directly engage house walls at the canal crossing, but 61st Division could not get across. The sharp cracks of the flak guns were easily audible in the dock area only 4 miles away.[29]

In the east, the fought-out 56th Division was in the process of being relieved in the line by the newly inserted 208th Division. The 337th Regiment leading the advance was tasked to attack directly down the dune road with its 3rd Battalion under command of *Hauptmann* Pöthko, reinforced with heavy weapons, to break through the 8th Zouave line. Its 2nd Battalion followed behind, tasked to mop up the dune positions, while the 1st Battalion waited in echelon as reserve. Pöthko created strong reconnaissance groups, able to fight for information and identify French heavy weapon and bunker positions.

Delays occurred relieving 56th Division's forward 171st Regiment, but by late morning the 208th Division advance was well under way. It was soon subjected to the same devastating concentration of machine gun, mortar and artillery fire that had stymied 56th Division. It quickly became apparent it faced a well-established and formidable bunker line. 2nd Battalion was pushed out to the right to fight along the hardened wet beach sand, finding it impossible to progress along soft sandy beach trails. The first houses in Bray Dunes were stormed and occupied by the 11th Company, but two anti-tank guns in direct support were knocked out by the French, causing heavy casualties among the crews. Further south, on the enemy right flank, German 14th Division elements managed to get across the causeway through the flooded Les Moëres village, attacking the 3rd and 92nd GRDI French Division recce groups. Fighting was fierce around the village of Uxem, where a platoon of light French H-35 tanks repulsed repeated German assaults until it was knocked out and the village captured at 6pm.

By nightfall the 2nd Battalion 337th Regiment was still trying to bypass the dunes by working its way steadily along the firmer damp beach sand. It aimed to get into the rear of Bray village which Pöthko's 3rd Battalion, aided by its concentration of heavy weapons, had already reached. To support assault pioneers 37mm Pak guns were laboriously wheeled through deep sand, attacking identified French bunker locations. Lieutenant Colonel Anzemberger's 8th Zouaves and the French 150th Regiment were still holding firm. The 337th Regiment after-action report observed 'the enemy had not left his positions':

> Prisoners were saying there were strong enemy forces standing prepared in positions to resist. As before he was shooting along well-selected arcs of fire with machine guns, anti-tank guns, trench mortars and above all artillery, including heavy calibres.[30]

Pressure was increased on the French. Zouave Willy Hertzog fighting with the 1st Battalion along the beach water line recalled 'our Adjutant Chief was shot through the head' the day before, and his diary entry for 3 June simply reads 'bombarded all day. In the evening we left to embark'. They were warned off during the afternoon that they would embark that night. This meant holding their positions until 9.30pm, at which point they would begin to thin out. The line had held firmly all day, 8½ miles from the port.[31]

Knowing this would be the final night's effort overruled the chronic fatigue felt by all evacuation ship crews. Admiral Ramsay sent everything he had available: all nine surviving destroyers, nine passenger ships – a tenth refused to go – 11 minesweepers, sloops, a gunboat and numerous small craft. The French came with 63 vessels, four destroyers, eight smaller warships, 18 trawlers and a host of small boats. At 7pm French Admiral Abrial, in overall command at Dunkirk, closed down his headquarters at Bastion 32. He calculated 25,000 men were left to embark; Ramsay had organized sufficient lift for 30,000. Fleets aimed to converge on the harbour at 10.30pm and needed to be away by 2.30 in the morning. Admiral Wake-Walker commanding offshore recalled, 'the small craft were to go right up to the quays and docks on the inner harbour, the transports, destroyers and four paddle steamers were to use the East Pier and the remainder the West Quay'.

General Barthélémy's SFF troops had begun exiting the line two hours before, a calculated risk with the forward elements of the German 18th and 61st Divisions only 4 miles from the port. A number of depleted battalions held the final bridges at Chapeau Rouge, unable to disengage. It was his men that had defended against the first and only panzer attack against the port on 24 May and they would now be the last defenders of Dunkirk to leave. The *Luftwaffe* was less in evidence and German artillery had broadly checked fire to avoid hitting their own troops. Even so, the evacuation did not get off to an auspicious start. 'I got over at 10pm,' Admiral Wake-Walker recalled, '… to find the harbour swarming with French fishing craft and vessels of all sorts. They were yelling and crowding alongside the East Pier, which was already thick with French troops.'[32]

A fresh easterly wind pushed against the west-going tide, which 'could hardly have been more difficult', he remembered. Despite some ugly collisions and damage, 'the seamanship displayed was really magnificent' and mass embarkation got under way. It was only after Vice Admiral Abrial and General Falgalde had departed for Dover that it was realized Abrial's embarkation figures had been a ghastly underestimate.

War correspondent Christoph von Imhoff, interviewing two rescued German prisoners, wrote about the chaotic scenes for German domestic home consumption. 'The English all fled, with no consideration for each other', the prisoners predictably claimed. The harbour was packed, 'everyone wanted to be first', they explained, just the sort of atmospheric propaganda von Imhoff sought: 'In between were sirens, sounding out blasts on ship's horns, as nervous ships announced they were about to cast off. Then German shells burst in the middle of the harbour.'

Some of these scenes were not totally divorced from the truth, because the underestimation of embarkation numbers heralded a final Allied tragedy at Dunkirk. Jacques Mordal with the French Dunkirk naval headquarters monitored General Barthélémy's weary SFF rearguards tramping past Malo-les-Bains, heading for the sanctuary of the port and rescue. He then saw:

> A vast crowd of soldiers, whose existence became apparent, as news spread of the final departures. From every cellar, from every hole in the ground, unarmed men emerged... Naturally enough, none of the stout fellows who for days had not come out of their shelters were prepared to leave room for those who had done the fighting for them. Marking time, Barthélémy's column waited, while across their front passed these men from the ordinance depots, these truck drivers, these representatives of all the rear echelons.

Only a ruthless police operation could have cleared the way for the rearguards coming directly from the front. Mordal legitimately asked: 'Anyone who recalls the appalling confusion of St Malo and the approaches to the East Mole must agree, that the job could only have been done with machine guns. What commander would willingly have done that?'[33]

At 3.18 in the morning the destroyer *Express* backed out of the harbour with 611 troops and the British Royal Navy pier party on board. General Barthélémy managed to embark on the old destroyer *Shikari* with 383 of his men from the East Mole. Finally, 27,000 French soldiers and six British stragglers were lifted off during the final night before the 687-ton block ship *Pacifico* was sunk to block the harbour entrance. The evacuation was over; 40,000 French troops remained, including the valiant rearguards of the SFF, 68th and 12th Divisions in their entirety.

As the embarkations reached their height, at 11pm the 208th Division's 337th Regiment conducted a night raid to occupy the forward Zouave positions alongside the beach at Bray Dunes. This foray by its 2nd Battalion opened up the way into the Dunes frontier line. Following a fierce firefight in the dark its 6th Company managed to gain a foothold in the bunker line, which was secured when the whole battalion followed up with a night attack.

Zouave Willy Hertzog had been warned off to depart five hours before, and recalled 'we marched all night and waited for the boats that never came'. His despair was echoed by Jean Contanceau, caught up in the debacle at the jetties. 'Everything was so shocking,' he remembered, with defeat staring him in the face; 'we were just not used to it'. 'Personally I remained confident. I knew that whatever happened I wasn't going to be evacuated, so I knew it was going to be death or captivity.' It was to be the latter.[34]

The 208th German Division was at last moving in strength along the dune road from the east towards Dunkirk. *Hauptmann* Pöthko's 3rd Battalion penetrated the still-contested bunker line, but by dawn had fought its way into the southern outskirts of Zuydcoote village. The 2nd Battalion bypassed Bray Dunes along the beach, and despite being engaged by six medium tanks approached Zuydcote and the Dunes fort.

Dawn emerged on 4 June through a light mist, presaging another clear and stifling hot day. *Oberleutnant* Richtsteig, an artillery battery commander with 18th Division to the south of Dunkirk, set up his scissors spotting scope in the roof of the barn that adjoined his headquarters. Straw was brushed aside to create clear observation to Dunkirk. 'The houses and towers of the city rose in the morning mist,' he remembered, 'an unusual stillness lay over the battlefield'.[35] Von Altenstadt, with division headquarters, recalled 'until the unforgettable early morning of 4 June, the enemy had demonstrated with strong artillery and mortar fire that he was determined to resist to the utmost'. But then, 'At a stroke, fire slackened off and an unusual silence reigned. Our soldiers, engineers, artillery crews and signals men dead beat from all their efforts, slept like the dead in their foxholes.'[36]

The only soldiers awake were sentries and reconnaissance patrols and they had not noticed anything untoward. *Major* Chrobek, the 1st Battalion commander, sensed something was different. Von Altenstadt recalled 'the sudden stillness spoke volumes more than the thunder of artillery and hammering machine gun fire'. Chrobek's early morning patrols came back through gently rising mist to report the enemy had withdrawn from the city's outskirts. An advance guard was immediately dispatched with Graf von Nayhaus's 4th Company into the town, in two abandoned lorries they had managed to start. They drove off fast, heading for the port area and sea.[37]

To their left the 61st Division had sent recce patrols forward after a quiet night and found the north bank of the contested Dunkirk-Furnes canal clear. When they penetrated further large numbers of French soldiers came out, with their hands raised. The 161st and 151st Infantry Regiments were quickly ordered to advance, a movement branded 'the race to the sea'. The 151st Regiment entered the port area where collapsed housing blocks had been reduced to huge piles of rubble. They later reported:

It was still burning at many places and the entry roads to the harbour and moles were stuffed full with abandoned English vehicle columns of every conceivable type. In the harbour basins and channels lay sunken merchant ships and destroyers. A dark smoke cloud lay over the city, great thick black palls of smoke from burning harbour oil tanks. Tanks were stuck in the white sand dunes. The sea lay immobile, with dead English soldiers wearing life jackets floating on its oily surface. The air still tasted like burnt ash, the noise of battle had ceased and a weak sun hung over the city. The soldiers glanced at the chaos, countless prisoners and war booty, not without a certain measure of satisfaction. All their efforts and suffering had not been in vain.[38]

'We're off,' declared *Unteroffizier* Järisch, with 18th Division's Pioneer Battalion, 'along the canal to the great cloud of smoke'. They marched on the port area from the south: 'An infantry assault group is just ahead of us in shouting distance. Then us engineers, and behind us, another handful of infantry.'

They approached the two final bridges crossing the canal, both standing, with some trepidation; 'would they go sky high?' they wondered. Checking for demolition charges and finding none, they advanced. 'It was stiflingly hot. The air tasted of smoke, destruction and death. The flamethrower men [with heavy loads] had sweat running down their faces.'

As they made their way past countless abandoned and destroyed vehicles, heading for the sea, tensions rose. 'Keep your distance,' instructed the officers. Men were on the lookout for potential cover, convinced at any moment they would hear the strike and whistle of a bullet. 'It was diabolically quiet,' Järisch recalled, 'just our steps on the surface of the road of a dead city.' The assault group leader had received no situation brief: 'Since the beginning of this advance there had been no report of a capitulation or of the escape of the Franco-British army; no white flags or surrender negotiation parties.'

House after house proved empty on checking. They were suspicious. All too often surrender negotiations had previously been a ruse for a bridge demolition or the blowing up of an ammunition dump. Meanwhile, the infantry assault group up ahead had disappeared from view. Why was there no enemy reaction? 'Perhaps,' he thought, 'the lead group had requisitioned vehicles and was "motorized", maybe they had already reached the sea.' Bridges they passed were not wired for demolition. Soon 30, 40, 60 men appeared, moving in three ranks: 'all Frenchmen; the fellows gave a friendly grin'. They were sent back to the rear. Thick clouds of smoke from the burning oil refineries and factories started enveloping the street. Houses around them were missing roofs. Taking a deep breath, they plunged through the smoke and emerged on a small rise, and, as Järisch recalled, 'we were standing on the sea, staring like children'.[39]

In depth to this advance was *Oberleutnant* Richtsteig's 18th Artillery Regiment battery in support. Mysteriously, enemy counter-fire had waned and ceased during the morning. 'What did this mean,' he recalled, 'the calm before the storm?' He could see the houses and towers of the city through the rising morning mist from his barn roof position. The battery was ordered to fire a single round to establish the basic direction of fire:

Everyone is convinced that enemy counter-battery fire would start again. Minutes and hours went by with no shooting, a peaceful stillness reigned. The only activity was around us, feverish anticipation … all appreciated the situation was hanging somewhat in the air. Nobody could put it in words. Then suddenly it was clear, Dunkirk had fallen, the enemy has laid down his weapons!

It was difficult to encompass what had happened. 'It was self-evident to us that each day brought a new mission or fight, as it had been so for the past three weeks.' Now it was over.

Richtsteig drove into the destroyed town, where he was accosted by an emotional French policeman who demanded to know, 'why have you shot up the city so much?' The sweet-sour smell of death permeated the air as the battery commander drove on:

> Thousands of prisoners, some drunk, came out of the cellars of shot-up houses. The dead were taken out of piles of rubble by men wearing gasmasks. At the beach French soldiers buried their fallen comrades in the sand. The rubble all around was witness to the huge defeat.

Looking out to sea, Richtsteig saw a destroyer, likely the French *Adroit*, cut in two by a Stuka bomb. One of his officers took down a flag flying from its mast as booty.[40]

Hauptmann Pöthko's 3rd Battalion with the 208th Division's 337th Regiment forced a passage past the Zuydcoote red-brick sanatorium and the Fort des Dunes to Rosendaël. By 7am he had reached the easternmost Dunkirk bridge on the Champs de Mauveuvres. Progress had been swift, driving captured vehicles, which towed three of his anti-tank guns. Securing the bridge, Pöthko pushed on with an advance guard and drove into the Place de la Republique 15 minutes later, the centre of Dunkirk. Artillery fire was still intermittently exploding inside the city, but as Pöthko recalled, 'whether it was our own or enemy artillery was not discernible'.

> During the entire advance of the 3rd Battalion, Frenchmen left their positions and assembled in great numbers on the streets, throwing down weapons and giving up without fighting. The streets were filled with countless quantities of equipment and material.[41]

'I am standing in front of an elegant English car', *Oberleutnant* Heinrich Braumann, with *Sturmgeshütze Abteilung* 210, later wrote. He had reached Bray Dunes:

> It had undoubtedly belonged to a very high-ranking English staff officer, because it still contained maps of Belgium and France, as well

as recently written orders. In a hurried escape, the vehicle had been deserted by its passengers; scattered clothes and equipment stand witness to that – especially the uniform of the driver left behind in all haste, which still contained his wallet with military pass and the worn-out picture of a woman and a little girl, which under different circumstances, he would certainly never have left behind. I wonder if he ever made it to the English coast?[42]

Pöthko ordered his companies to assemble in the harbour district on arrival. Very lights were fired up to indicate their positions to the other German units penetrating the city.

Generalleutnant Cranz arrived at the beaches shortly after his infantry vanguard. *Major* von Altenstadt patriotically recalled the inspiring moment: 'the sea, the sea!' he exclaimed. It was still a volatile situation; 'the first shot broke through the stillness, then a second!' he recalled. Soldiers were mopping up a house directly on the beach, shooting inside:

Five, ten, twenty, one hundred, three hundred Frenchmen came out with their hands up ... now already a thousand. Where were the British? There was no sign of life to be seen. Had the enemy escaped last night? Was it correct for us not to lay down harassing fire on the beach in order to save the ammunition for identified targets?[43]

Oberleutnant Lachenwitz from the 54th Regiment raised the blood-red *Hakenkreuz* (swastika) flag over the town hall, the highest point in the city.

Isolated shooting rang out, indicating continued French resistance. *Unteroffizier* Järisch took no chances; 'hard determination does not recognize chivalrous rules,' he determined, so out came the hand grenades. 'Whoever doesn't come out immediately,' they threatened, stick grenades poised aloft, would suffer the consequences. The Baron family sheltering in the Vanoorenberghe Brewery cellars in Coudekerque-Branche heard Germans approaching through their ventilators. A head garnished with camouflage leaves suddenly appeared at their entrance. The Germans spotted two French soldiers among the civilians and tossed in a hand grenade, injuring several people. They were removed to hospital following the intervention of a German officer. Järisch remembered a similar incident, defiance from 'six to eight courageous

Frenchmen'. A prisoner was instructed to tell them that 'if you don't come out immediately, you are finished!' *Pas tuer!* – came the plaintive response, 'please don't kill us'.

In the 61st Division sector, 151st Regiment reported 'here and there, there was some shooting'. 'While combing the summer holiday colony at St Pol sur Mer,' its after-action account reported, 'two soldiers from the 3rd Company were killed.' An old French World War I veteran had shot a German warrant officer when he approached his house in the railway workers' housing estate. He was taken out and shot, as was his 19-year-old son, who tried to intervene with a whip.[44]

General Herman Geyer commanding IX Corps had been concerned that the loss of their heavy artillery would hinder his attack from the east along the dune road. So he was sceptical when *Oberleutnant* Arndt from 337th Regiment radioed 'the enemy appears to have given up resistance'. Aware of the blood it had cost his 56th Division to force the dune line, he immediately drove forward to verify the claim, ordering a general advance, 'which was hardly necessary', he remembered, because 'the vanguards of the 208th, 216th, 253rd, 18th and perhaps even more divisions were entering the fallen town from all sides'. He drove 'peacefully' past hordes of French soldiers mixed up with civilian refugees coming from the opposite direction. At the Zuydcoote sanatorium he stopped his *Kubelwagen* jeep to confer with the 208th Division staff and the commander of the 156th Artillery Regiment, the only 56th Division officer present. 208th Division had in effect stolen the march on a triumphant entry by 56th Division, when it folded in a welter of casualties and exhaustion in the soft dune sand of the French line. Within 24 hours, *Hauptmann* Pöthko's 337th Regiment had led the dash from the east, winning the race to the harbour waterfront. Geyer felt impelled to sympathize, confiding to the 56th Division artillery commander that: 'It is regrettable that the 56th Division, that had achieved so much, could not experience this day. I am, however pleased that at least the artillery were a part of this, and congratulate you.'

Geyer glanced along the beach, 'with French soldiers pressed up against the edge of the sea, who would no longer be embarked – the English had rescued themselves'. With that, Geyer continued 'a triumphant drive' towards Malo-les-Bains.[45]

As German infantrymen combed through the wreckage littering the beaches, an exhausted airman waved and stumbled towards them. It was *Leutnant* Joachim von Oelhaven, the squadron commander of 6 *Lehrgeschwader* 1 whose Junkers Ju 88 had belly-landed on the beach at Nieuport after it had been shot down by a Hurricane. He had been hiding for 36 hours beneath the planking of one of the improvised lorry piers, grimly holding on as the tide ebbed and flowed. By evading capture until his countrymen appeared, he avoided nearly five years in captivity. Two of his crew had not survived; it was a victory of sorts.

French civilians knew it was all over by the early morning hours. Abbot Lecointe, the vicar of St Martin's, came across a German machine gun nest next to a large swastika flag that had been draped on the pavement in front of his church. Inside a German soldier was playing the organ. At 6.30am the inhabitants on the Rue Lion d'Or saw German soldiers heading for the Quai des Hollandais, weapons pointing up at the windows of any houses that were still standing. Ten minutes after, Fernand Polle spotted another machine gun nest, this time set up at the Place Jean Bart, near the statue of the corsair with sword in hand, surrounded by wrecked buildings. Robert Bethagries had seen the Germans on the beach at Malo-les-Bains at 7.30am; departure from the port was no longer tenable. By 9am three German divisions had entered the town in strength. 208th Division gathered in the Malo-les-Bains area while the 18th and 254th Divisions were coming together in the port and harbour area. The 18th Division vanguards had motored across the Canal des Moëres, driving directly to the East Mole, getting there at 9.30am. There were so many French troops crowded on the Mole and quayside that it was difficult to round them up quickly.

'As if from a whistle, hundreds and hundreds of unarmed Frenchmen came out of all the houses and streets,' recalled one soldier, 'worn out, desiring only to be taken prisoner.' On reaching the East Mole, 'thousands and thousands emerged from the casemates'; the 1st Battalion rounded up 11,000, having taken 700 in the town centre. The 2nd Battalion took near 12,000 so that the 54th Regiment total approached 30,000, including three generals and several hundred officers. The assault into the town had, however, been costly for the regiment, losing 53 of its 'best' men and 142 wounded.

It was a humiliating and emotional experience for the French rearguards, pushed aside by the deserters and stragglers in the final chaotic rush for the boats. They had no option but to await the outcome. 'I was fully aware of everything and afraid,' admitted Jean Contanceau, a Seventh Army survivor: 'There was a real hammering in my chest. Almost impossible to describe, but I didn't cry. Still I had tears in my eyes when I gave myself up.'

'We were all taken prisoner on 4th June,' Zouave Corporal Arsène Lebrun with the 8th remembered. They had fought four days along the dune line to keep the port and beaches secure, to the east of the perimeter. 'It was all over for us. We went to Greater Germany via Holland by train and boat, where we arrived at *Stalag VI D* on 18th July.'[46]

Unteroffizier Järisch's 2nd Pioneer Company was engaged in the monumental task of rounding up prisoners. His gaze took in the mile-wide bushy sand dune beach area, 'teeming and crawling like a huge ant's nest': 'For hours we had nothing else to do but organize these thousands upon thousands of Frenchmen, previously awaiting flight, into three ranks and set them off in a new march direction.'

Best of all was the booty, Järisch recalled, which they turned over with relish: 'The enemy had left behind overstocked canteens. They didn't dip into a shared officers and men pot like us, but had ham, lobster, pineapple and hundreds of fine things.'

When a well-respected *Major*, 'with whom we had hauled the devil out of hell,' turned up, he simply said with a wink: 'carry on boys – you've earned it!'[47] When *Major* von Altenstadt with the 18th Division arrived in the port he was confronted by an 'overwhelming' spectacle:

Thousands, ten thousand French soldiers stood with raised hands so far as the eye could see. Placid and downcast, they gave themselves up to the few German soldiers, who first reached the beach. In endless columns, still with their hands up, they marched to the collection points, which were soon filled with masses disappearing into the distance.[48]

Prisoners were gathered at the Place Vauban, in the centre of Dunkirk, the shooting range, glacis, the Ste-Ursule Institution at Malo, a field at Rexpoede and even the underground cellars of the arsenal at Gravelines. There were probably 40,000, vastly more than expected. *Oberleutnant* Heinrich Braumann with *Sturmgeschütze Abteilung* 210 passed a prison pen at Bray Dunes and commented: 'It is incomprehensible how the watch post can bear the overwhelming cadaver stench, because the whole street is covered with dead bodies of the enemy.'

He drove into the eastern suburbs of Dunkirk. The street was blocked with corpses, so much so, 'to move forward we must drive over the dead bodies', he admitted. The prisoners passing by reflected the totality of their defeat: 'uniforms torn to pieces, covered in dirt. Their faces look pale, tired from lack of sleep, their eyes seem dead and their mouths are shut in silence'.[49]

Shortly before 10am *Generalleutnant* Cranz commanding the 18th Division drove up to the red-brick *Hôtel de Ville*, General Beaufrère's final headquarters, to take the surrender. 'Where are the English?' Cranz enquired; 'Not here,' Beaufrère replied, 'they are in England.' Where indeed were they?

The Germans combed the beach areas where fugitives were still trying to make it back to Britain. One German soldier remembered coming across a large motorboat with a covered cabin, which 'looked very suspicious to me'. He boarded the boat, with a covering force and yanked open the cabin door, pistol in hand:

I found myself facing a bunch of Tommies, who must have thought I was the devil incarnate. Disturbed while taking a nap, they woke up with a start and stared at me in fright. They put their hands up straight away. At first, I thought I was only dealing with five or six men. But more and more emerged from a cabin to the rear, and in the end I counted 15 of them.

After they were disarmed another seven British soldiers were found in the boatman's hut nearby. They had been waiting for the tide to turn and lift them off. 'Once again,' the soldier jibed, 'the Tommies had missed the bus.'[50]

This may well have been the case, but 221,504 British and 122,000 French troops had not. Another 144,171 British soldiers were lifted south of the Somme, mainly BEF logistics rear area personnel, but also men from the 1st Armoured, 52 Lowland and 1st Canadian Divisions. The 51st (Highland) Division was captured in its entirety at St Valery en Caux eight days later, awaiting evacuation. The German 18th Division, whose infantry were at the heart of the Dunkirk pocket fighting, took only 325 British soldiers. Its tally of prisoners for the western campaign was 52,143 French, 3,404 Belgian and 185 Dutch troops.

German officer Eberhard Dennerlein perused the abandoned Dunkirk beaches after the battle:

> The beach was littered with equipment and vehicles and a torpedo was washed ashore. There was a deathly silence, no soldiers could be seen – a British army that vanishes into thin air, even though it had been fighting extremely hard beforehand. They were the bravest compared to the others we were up against. They had retreated step by step until the moment that they suddenly vanished into thin air.

The battle for Flanders and Dunkirk had been an overwhelming success, but some of the gloss of victory was tarnished by the escape of the British. Dennerlein mused:

> After so many successes in such a short time you say 'how much does the world cost?' [laughing]. It was an indescribable atmosphere, euphoric perhaps, because we thought that we were bound to win the war in the near future. The only one in our way was England.[51]

Postscript

Dünkirchen

During the evening conference at the *Felsennest* headquarters on 2 June, von Brauchitsch the Army chief reported formally to Hitler: 'My *Führer*, I report that this campaign is won.' *Oberst* Liss, listening in, remembered, 'this evening conference was the high point of my 12 years on the General Staff, despite the fact the encirclement did not bring the hoped-for total result'. He saw also 'the feeling of disappointment that lingered with those there', reflecting 'they knew what was ahead'.[1]

Liss worked the intelligence estimates for enemy forces at OKH, calculating the French now had 69 divisions remaining, plus 14 fortress garrisons to face 136 German divisions. Flanders had been an important victory; 62 Dutch, Belgian and French divisions had been knocked from the Allied order of battle, with 17 more badly mauled. This amounted to a two-fold strength advantage at the outset of the coming battle for the rest of France. Liss assessed 28 French divisions and three fortress garrisons had been destroyed in the Dunkirk encirclement. Despite the BEF getting away, it was by any account a stunning outcome. He managed to secure a three-day furlough to drive along the victorious front with *Oberstleutnant* Winter from OKH operations. During the drive, Liss convinced himself 'I was driving through the last ever French-German war, there would never be another one'.[2]

Hitler moved his headquarters away from the *Felsennest* the following day to a new site in the small village of Bruly de Pêche in southern Belgium to oversee Operation *Röt*. His *Luftwaffe* adjutant Nicolaus von Below remembered he was confident of success, envisioning a swift drive towards southern France:

> The elite of the French divisions had been knocked out here: the British divisions, in a state of exhaustion, decamped to England, leaving their equipment behind. Fifty per cent of our divisions saw no action at all. The *Führer* himself is very stirred by this great success.

'The British had no relevance for him'; they had been the smallest opposing contingent in any case.[3]

Hitler, according to *Oberst* Warlimont, was sentimental on leaving the *Felsennest* headquarters, a place of high drama, tense expectancy and symbolic achievement. 'Before leaving Hitler ordered that the entire area should be preserved as a "national monument"; every room was to be kept unchanged, every nameplate was to remain upon its door.'[4]

Warlimont 'had certain qualms' whether the *Felsennest* warranted such an exalted status. 'Could we be certain and all that sure that the part played by Hitler and his military staff in the great victory in France merited it?' *General* von Manstein, the plan author, had been side-stepped into an uneventful corps command, 'fated to be little more than an onlooker for most of the first phase of the campaign in the west'. Corrosive OKW versus OKH politics at the time of the Halt Order had distracted from the fundamental aim, which was to destroy all the Allied armies. Hitler's preservation order did not predictably include the OKH 'hunting lodge', which Warlimont maintained contained 'the architects of the victory'.[5]

There was disappointment that the BEF had evaded capture at Dunkirk, but it was fleeting. *Feldpost* letters from soldiers reveal no such introspection at this time. Hans S. with the 12th Infantry Division wrote to his parents four days before the fall of Dunkirk that 'the drive continues onward, who knows where, London or Paris?' 'Dunkirk fell today,' wrote an *Oberjäger* (NCO), 'truly opening a new phase.' 'In the next week we could be in Paris,' he continued, 'In general, it certainly cannot last much longer. The high point of this war is clearly already here.'[6]

Thirty per cent of the French Army had been taken prisoner, he pointed out, 'and they were the elite, positioned in the north'. As such, 'France has suffered an awful reverse'. Another infantry anti-tank *Gefreiter* wrote 'any further progression of the war would likely be played out in England'. 'Who would have thought,' he maintained, 'that the proud *Wehrmacht* could have destroyed the Maginot Line and partly rolled it up in such a short time?' Another *Oberleutnant* simply summed it up: 'a great moment here,' he wrote, 'the north front has been rolled up'.[7]

Hitler was a World War I *Frontkämpfer* (front veteran), wounded three times and decorated with the Iron Cross 1st Class. He had endured four years as a headquarters runner with the 16th Bavarian Reserve Infantry Regiment, a dangerous assignment, and survived the 'massacre of the innocents' during the first 1914 battle of Ypres. His victory over the same ground in fewer weeks than the years it had taken the Kaiser's army to fail resonated hugely with him, as it did with his soldiers. World War I veterans were still prominent in the ranks, primarily officers and senior NCOs. One *Hauptmann* with the 73rd Infantry Division wrote 'our companies are lying in almost the same area I lay during World War I... I was there during the first war when we lost it, and there again as we won it in an unprecedentedly quick way!'[8]

If they were not veterans, they were the sons of veterans. *Unteroffizier* Järisch, who entered Dunkirk with the 18th Division, heard one of his men whimsically remark,'I wish I had the power for a brief hour, to open all the German [World War I] graves in Flanders, and lead the dead army down here – just once – to see this!'[9]

Panzer *Aufklärungs Abteilung* commander Hans von Luck with Rommel's 7th Panzer Division admitted 'we could not understand why we let so many get away'.[10] Likewise, *SS-Hauptsturmführer* Kurt Meyer with the LAH was equally frustrated. 'We had to watch the English evacuating Dunkirk and see them vanish across the Channel,' suggesting halting the panzers adversely affected the outcome.[11] Most of these dissenting voices are heard later, with hindsight, in post-war publications. SS Infantry Battalion commander Otto Kumm with the *SS-Der Führer-Regiment* offered a more credible commentary in a later post-war interview:

> Sure, we had some second thoughts at the end of the western campaign in 1940, when we let the British get away, but these didn't last long. They were superficial and didn't cause us to question Hitler or his genius. The real doubts only came much later, at the end of the war, but then they came in force.[12]

The majority of German soldiers who converged on the Dunkirk pocket on 4 June were vaguely regretful but mostly indifferent at the British escape. An engineer *Unteroffizier* summed up prevailing opinion by writing home that 'strong trust in God and our fine leadership precludes the emergence of doubts'. They were probably relieved not to have to overcome a 'last ditch' resistance. Viewing the vast quantities of abandoned and destroyed equipment, discarded bodies and sunken ships suggested the BEF had taken a considerable beating, and that they would sue for an armistice soon in Britain in any case.[13]

Josef Goebbels back home in the *Reich* was exuberant. When Hitler corresponded with him again on 29 May, as he did regularly, to monitor home morale, he was able to assure him the mood was 'ecstatic'. When the perimeter collapsed on 4 June Goebbels ridiculed claims of dubious British success saving their army, confiding to his diary:

> Their victory is in fact the most catastrophic defeat in their history. I have made greater efforts with all our [propaganda] resources to make this abundantly clear to the public.[14]

'The English', he claimed, 'must have lost 100,000 men alone from their transport fleet'. Popular acclaim was also observed by the *SS-Sicherheitsdienst* secret reports on the German home front. Victory at Dunkirk was viewed by the German public as a clear sign that the war in the west would not last long, 'with trust in the *Führer* and *Wehrmacht* to optimistically view future events'. The 6 June commentary noted: 'With the victorious outcome of the heavy fighting in Flanders, much of the population feels *the worst is over*, with increasing expectation that the war will end soon.'[15]

Fighter pilot Ulrich Steinhilper's squadron *Jagdgeschwader* 52 returned to the Channel coast and was to later participate in the Battle of Britain. He found 'Calais and Dunkirk were rather like vast military supermarkets. Virtually anything you wanted could be found in or around the harbours or on the beaches.' Visiting the evacuation beaches became a form of military tourism for German soldiers. 'Our first real foray into the giant supply dump,' he recalled, was 'spectacularly successful'. Several barrels of untainted red wine were found floating in the harbour, and every unit technician managed to supplement vehicle holdings. Steinhilper's unit found 'a large pantechnicon' that was laboriously hauled out of the Dunkirk sands and converted into a mobile tool-truck and parts store. That and a host of other vehicles 'were to follow the squadron across many borders and do sterling service'.[16]

Fall Röt, the final offensive in the west, was launched on 5 June. Like phase one, differences of opinion emerged very quickly between Hitler and the Army chiefs. The army staff looked for the destruction of the remaining enemy forces as the key objective, while Hitler wanted to secure the Lorraine iron ore basin first, to deprive France of her armaments industry. 'As it turned out,' *Oberst* Warlimont observed, 'victory was so complete that both Halder's and Hitler's objectives were attained simultaneously.' Ten days later Paris fell and the Germans reached a line from Bordeaux to the Swiss frontier when the Armistice came into effect at 1.35am on 25 June 1940.

Of the 122,000 French troops evacuated to Britain, most were quickly returned to France to continue the fight, apart from 2,000 or so wounded who remained. They arrived in the region between Caen and the Seine and were re-formed into divisions. Despite being rearmed, they were in terrible shape and hopelessly mixed in units from 17 different divisions. They were overrun in the ensuing collapse and fewer than half saw combat against the Germans again. Ironically, the fighting post-Dunkirk proved tougher for the Germans. Despite low overall casualties for the campaign, 27,074 killed, 111,034 wounded and 18,384 missing, average casualties for this second phase were higher. During the attack to the sea from 10 May to 3 June the *Wehrmacht* lost on average 2,500 casualties per day. This doubled between 4 June and 18 June to over 5,000 each day. Like the Belgians, the French found an outraged capacity for self-sacrifice when they realized all was lost.[17]

Assault pioneer Wolfgang Döring reflected typical commentary in German *Feldpost* letters at this time when he referred to the *Wunder* or 'miracle' that was achieved. 'Our troops are already in Paris,' he wrote home on 14 June, and how 'unbelievable all this was, truly a miracle that one cannot comprehend'.[18] The 'miracle of Dunkirk' for the average German soldier was about achievement. They had poured through France and swiftly reached the sea, eclipsing the failure of their fathers in World War I. The miracle for the British soldier was 'deliverance'; against all the odds they had escaped. The difference in perspective and shared experience could not be greater. British soldiers had to destroy all their vehicles and guns as they passed through 'immobilization areas,' before moving down to designated corps evacuation beaches. The sight of all this smashed and abandoned equipment demonstrated to German soldiers the extent of their overwhelming victory, because much of the discarded material was superior to their own.

Only a small proportion of the BEF fought in the two to three-day desperate rearguard actions often lauded in British Dunkirk accounts before hurriedly retiring to the harbour and beaches. The battle was then taken up by the French, who fought alone for three days. The British had run a 16-day exhausting gauntlet of rearguard drives and marches under constant air attack. The German experience was a steady plod forward, hindered by countless waterways – primarily an engineer problem – then occupying defensive positions to contain the perimeter. Local attacks kept them penned inside. This was static warfare, conducted across flat open flooded terrain with a high water table preventing digging in, with repeated reliefs in place before the final attacks to secure Dunkirk. Not a remarkable experience in infantry operation terms.

The British and French were subjected to terrifying air attacks on vulnerable beaches and shipping. Many were exhausted and often shell-shocked by the time they boarded boats. German soldiers were tired, but able to watch this unfolding catastrophe reduce their opponents from afar, as they watched their own *Luftwaffe* attacks going in. The *Landser* were well satisfied with their military leaders, directed by a hypnotic *Führer*, who had led them to unparalleled success. British soldiers suspected they had been led by 'Colonel Blimps', who had already mismanaged the Norwegian campaign, with a new prime minister who had just emerged when *Blitzkrieg* was already under way. The *Führer* enjoyed the unmitigated trust and confidence of his soldiers. This then resulted in largely indifference at soldier level to the Panzer Halt Order, which achieved less than *total* victory. They were untroubled by this; 'the *Führer* knew best', he had his reasons. How was it then that the British escaped?

How indeed? Hitler, with no formal high-level military training, a junior NCO from the trenches of World War I, seemed to lose control of the *Blitzkrieg* momentum streaming across France and Belgium. Creative tactical thinking by the leaders of the mobile panzer vanguards outpaced the traditional views of senior staff officers at OKW and

OKH. Both they, and Hitler, who had spent four years manning static positions on the Western Front between 1914 and 1918, could not encompass what was being accomplished. The instinctive reaction was to rein in the panzers and impose control. *Auftragstaktik* or initiative-driven mission-control tactics had got Hitler's commanders to the Atlantic coast, but there was not an immediate plan about what to do next, having achieved this Shangri-La outcome. The very corps commanders who had exercised such initiative to get there were not centrally directed to achieve a new aim. There was insufficient space for two Army Groups – A and B – converging on Flanders and Dunkirk to effectively coordinate movement. The consequence was time lost disentangling units and formations instead of attacking. There was no credible von Manstein figure (as he proved by 1943) sufficiently experienced in large-scale mobile operations to creatively assume command. The BEF was able to reach the Channel coast amid the confusion of a German command vacuum menacing them.[19]

Most historical accounts rationalizing less than total German victory at Dunkirk dwell on the German Panzer Halt Order of 24 May. Its main impact was less failure to immediately drive on Dunkirk and deny it to the BEF and more that German troops were prevented from advancing north, across suitable panzer terrain, to seriously impede the British withdrawal. Dunkirk, surrounded by a concentric canal system, enabled the 1st Panzer Division assault to be fought off by the French 68th Division before the Halt Order was imposed. A more rewarding area of research is to ask why it was that the BEF could, over nine days – only one of which included the Halt Order – evacuate its core fighting divisions. These units represented the seed corn of future armies that would return to fight back. The true 'miracle' of Dunkirk was the crucial four-day period between 29 May and 1 June when the bulk of these quality divisions were lifted from the port and beaches. These days represent the climax of the battle for Dunkirk.

The battles for the Channel ports at Boulogne and Calais, and the failure of the Dunkirk panzer attack on 24 May, revealed the shortcomings of tanks fighting in built-up areas. The panzer divisions had insufficient *panzergrenadier* infantry to fight through. Boulogne and Calais demonstrated how difficult and casualty intensive it was to fight through dense housing districts, commercial areas and dockside installations. There was little option except to wait for the slow-moving foot infantry divisions with their horse-drawn artillery to close up. This delayed the final result at Dunkirk.

Soon after it was set up, the Dunkirk perimeter was relegated to the status of a subordinate front by the German high command. Even as the perimeter formed, German panzer and mobile units were being siphoned off, alongside heavy artillery, to occupy assembly areas further south in preparation for Operation *Röt*. After 1 June, a day of maximum *Luftwaffe* effort with fine weather, air attacks levelled off. Severe losses to the evacuation fleet meant daylight embarkation became impractical. This was also the point at which the main *Luftwaffe* effort became subordinated to Operation *Paula*, large-scale air attacks around Paris, another digression of effort.

With only ten divisions manning this subsidiary front, little was subsequently written about it by veterans. As a consequence, it is necessary to intensively trawl surviving corps and division post-action operation accounts to gain a clear picture of the chronology of the battle from the German perspective. As *Oberst* Liss calculated in his analysis of enemy forces, 11 Dutch, 22 Belgian and 29 French divisions were destroyed in the Flanders pocket, with 17 others badly mauled. The escape therefore of some ten British divisions, three of which were equipped for only line-of-communication duties, was small fry indeed. Regrettable they should escape, but having lost all their tanks, guns and vehicles, they were effectively neutered.[20]

One of the difficulties researching Dunkirk from the German perspective is that, like another iconic British defeat at Arnhem, in September 1944, Dunkirk was viewed as a 'sideshow' in relation to what else was going on. The main German imperative once the perimeter had been surrounded was to defeat the remaining 69 divisions south of the Somme and around Paris. Both Dunkirk and Arnhem were catastrophes, celebrated in British military history and folklore as examples of outstanding human endeavour. For the Germans, they were militarily insignificant.

Inspirational battles against the odds attract heroic myths, and the battles for the Dunkirk perimeter are no exception. The RAF for example, despite veteran views to the contrary, even today, played an important role in the rescue of the BEF. High above the battle, visible only as vapour trails to watching troops below, they managed to hold their own and caused unexpected losses to a depleted and tired *Luftwaffe*. Moreover, and less well known, exhaustive trawling of surviving veteran and unit post-action accounts reveals the extent to which German troops were highly sensitive to enemy air attack. RAF bombing and strafing runs on German ground columns caused casualties, harassed headquarters and troop movement, and above all caused anxiety to soldiers. For the first time in this campaign, German soldiers complained about a hostile air environment.

The Belgians fought harder than anyone had previously assessed, including post-war historians. Von Bock's Army Group B infantry divisions regarded them with wary respect. They inflicted heavy casualties on the pursuing Germans at canal and river lines. The best chance, and second opportunity after the failed panzer attack to take Dunkirk, before the BEF were evacuated was offered by the Belgian capitulation on 28 May. It was not a surprise to the Allies, who were given due warning, but it was, inexplicably, for the Germans. The sheer mass of surrendering Belgian troops and the refugee flow prevented the Germans from exploiting this windfall on the east side of the perimeter. By the time the German vanguards got themselves motorized and moving, they were screened off by the skilful retirement conducted by the British II Corps, which kept the Belgian beaches at La Panne and Bray open until the mass of the BEF was embarked.

French resistance was decisive on both the west and east side of the perimeter at crisis moments, enabling the British to thin out from the perimeter and embark. This coincided with German complacency at the extent of their success and the ongoing more urgent distraction of feeding units south to the Somme, for the forthcoming *Röt* offensive. Aggressive action against the perimeter was sidelined as panzer and motorized units were relieved in the line by the follow-up foot-marching German infantry divisions. This occurred even as the BEF was being embarked, to the extent that, by 30 May, Allied troops bottled up in the perimeter outnumbered their German attackers. Ironically, as German ground coordination improved and the Eighteenth Army was put in overall control of operations against the perimeter, the number of besieging divisions and supporting artillery was reduced. The French held the majority of the reduced perimeter by the end of May, and all of it from 2 June, while the vital element of the BEF's fighting capacity was embarked. The French fought on tenaciously for a further three days after the British had gone.

The real 'miracle' of Dunkirk was the confluence of climate and geography that allowed the British to be safely embarked from the beaches and East Mole. Concentric lines of canal obstacles surrounded Dunkirk. Four covered the western approach, seven from the south and six in the east. Opening sea defences also inundated low-lying areas with floodwater. These expanses of water denied potential German dry land avenue approaches, which meant the Allies had only to defend a half to two-thirds of the surrounding perimeter. Channel weather, usually notoriously unpredictable, held for nearly nine days, the time it took to embark the mass of the encircled BEF and a sizable number of French forces. The difficulty re-crossing the same stretch of water four years later for D-Day in June 1944, with all its postponements and vagaries of weather, is a telling case in point.

A key failure of German operations was the inability of the *Luftwaffe* and *Kriegsmarine* to meaningfully reduce the carrying capacity of the Allied evacuation fleet. The sinking of the passenger liner *Lancastria* by a Ju 88 bomber off St Nazaire on 17 June is alleged to have resulted in losses of between 3,000 and 5,800. The death toll represented about one-third of the fatalities suffered by the BEF in France and is an indication of what might have been achieved. *Luftwaffe* attacks were effective for only two and a half days of the nine it took to embark the force, due to vagaries of weather. Also, the 'Brylcreem Boys' of the RAF were more successful than they have previously been given credit for. They withdrew from mainland France on 21 May, abandoning some 200 Hurricanes, only 75 of which were destroyed or written off in air combat. Examination of unit reports and records reveals the RAF destroyed 42 bombers and 36 fighters over Dunkirk, with six other aircraft downed by anti-aircraft fire. Air Vice-Marshall Park's UK-based 11 Group lost 84 fighters to *Luftwaffe* action. German soldiers on the ground also became acutely sensitive to RAF air attack, which certainly impeded troop moves around Nieuport and the vulnerable east Belgian side of the perimeter.[21]

German casualties around the Dunkirk perimeter were comparatively light. Unit records are sketchy about losses because, being a subsidiary action, casualties were expressed as outcomes for one or other of the two separate phases of the western campaign: *Fall Gelb* (Case Yellow), the *Blitzkrieg* to the coast, 10 May–3 June, and *Fall Röt*, 3 June–18 June, Paris and beyond. A rough estimate can be gauged from the daily average of 2,500 lost per day in the first phase. Perhaps one-third of this total might represent Dunkirk at 800 casualties per day, shared by ten divisions securing the perimeter at the end. Because of obstacles imposed by flooding, many approaches to Dunkirk were untenable. Of the ten divisions, six – the 18th, 254th, 56th, 61st, 208th and 14th – were more active, using ribbons and areas of dry ground to reach the port. The 56th Division lost 50% of its officers, 24.3% of its NCOs and 21.7% in the ranks in the period leading up to and including Dunkirk. Overall German casualties were likely to be in the region of 5,000 to 7,500. The 18th Division lost 608 dead and 1,990 wounded in this first phase of the campaign. Its 54th Infantry Regiment suffered just under 200 casualties in the final fight for Dunkirk. Extrapolating this figure to six to ten divisions involved, at three regiments per division, suggests losses of between 3,600 and 6,000 for the perimeter battles.[22]

Many of the German voices at Dunkirk were lost to posterity due to later appalling losses in Russia. All ten of the divisions that fought around the Dunkirk perimeter were in Russia by 1941, eight directed against Moscow and two against Leningrad. By the summer of 1941, when a plethora of war correspondent and popular unit accounts of the victorious French campaign were published, it had already been eclipsed by the drama being played out on the Russian front, where many of the soldiers had perished. By the end of September, the *Ostheer* (Eastern Army) in Russia had lost half a million men; this represented the equivalent of 30 divisions and enough officers and NCO casualties to man 37 others. The seed corn of future leadership and possible future written accounts had gone. It was as if the entire strength of von Bock's Army Group B that had advanced through Belgium and France to Dunkirk had gone.

Generalleutnant Cranz, who commanded the 18th Division and was awarded the Knight's Cross for his division's accomplishments, was killed in a friendly fire artillery accident on a German training area in March 1941, even before the launch of Operation *Barbarossa* three months later. Two of the ten divisions at Dunkirk (the 18th and 20th) lasted until the final battle for Berlin in 1945. Two others (the 56th and 256th) were wiped out with Army Group Centre in the summer of 1944; the 9th Panzer Division was badly mauled during the titanic tank battle at Kursk in 1943. Small wonder that so few personal accounts of German soldiers at Dunkirk have survived. *Unteroffizier* Järisch, an assault pioneer with the 18th Division, recalled, during the pause after fighting for Dunkirk ended:

> Someone began to talk about our fallen friends as though they were still alive. What they used to do and what fun they had, which we all laughed about. We elbowed each other in this evening circle: 'Ho ho, Lümmels! we're still here with you'.[23]

The war started and ended for Dunkirk with a siege. Bypassed after the June 1944 D-Day landings in Normandy, 'Fortress Dunkirk' was cut off by British, Canadian, French and Czech troops in September 1944, with about 25,000 civilians initially trapped in the town. Strongly supported by artillery and AA guns with plenty of ammunition, 10,000 Wehrmacht and SS troops aggressively held out until one day after the official ending of the war in Europe.

The town was reduced to 95% ruins and rubble by war's end. The siege cost the Allies some 800 casualties and the Germans over 1,000 dead. The port was left inoperable. Demolitions and mining had begun in the town and quays even before D-Day to prevent any Allied landings there. Its fairways, channels, locks and basins were jammed with 110 sunken wrecks, most from the fighting and evacuation during May and June 1940. Dünkirchen did not really become Dunkerque again until the quaysides were cleared of mines by March 1946. Its crisis began in May 1940 and ended in May 1945, the last town in France to be liberated.

Notes

PROLOGUE: DÜNKIRCHEN 1940

1 Oddone, *Dunkirk 1940*, p.8.
2 Percentage figures IFOP Survey, quoted in Zylberman, Zadig, *France 1939: One Last Summer*, French TV, 2019.
3 Interview, www.angelfire.com/ct/ww2europe/, 2004.
4 Oddone, p.14.
5 Heikel III incident, Oddone, p.31. Vancoille, interview, Lawrence, *The Other Side of Dunkirk*, BBC TV, 2004.

CHAPTER 1: *FÜHRER* WEATHER

1 Schroeder, *Er War Mein Chef*, p.101.
2 Below, *At Hitler's Side*, p.57. Warlimont, *Inside Hitler's Headquarters 1939–45*, pp.85 and 95.
3 Schroeder, *Er War Mein Chef*, p.102.
4 Ibid.
5 Below, *At Hitler's Side*, p.58.
6 Schroeder, *Er War Mein Chef*, p.102.
7 Below, *At Hitler's Side*, p.58.
8 Schroeder, *Er War Mein Chef*, p.102. Jacobsen, *Dokumente zum Westfeldzug 1940*, pp.3–4.
9 Berndt, *Tanks Break Through!*, p.27.
10 Ibid., pp.27–8 and 34. Liss, *Westfront 1939–40*, p.128.
11 Force comparisons, Jacobsen, *Dünkirchen*, pp.15–16.
12 Altenstadt, *Unser Weg zum Meer*, p.10.
13 Ibid., pp.10–11. *SS-LAH*, winter and training, Lehman, *The Leibstandarte*, Vol. 1, pp.125 and 123.
14 Berndt, *Tanks Break Through!*, pp.34–5.
15 Ibid., pp.34–5 and 37.
16 Altenstadt, *Unser Weg zum Meer*, p.13.
17 *Luftwaffe* figures, Hooten, *Luftwaffe at War*, p.47.
18 Bock, *Diary*, 10 May 1940, pp.134–5.
19 Altenstadt, *Unser Weg zum Meer*, pp.14–15.
20 Haakert, Altenstadt, *Unser Weg zum Meer*, pp.16, 17 and 15.

21 Schonfeldt, *Diary*, 13 May, ed. Dollinger, *Kain, wo ist dein Bruder?* p.49. *Gefreiter* H., 35 Inf Div, Field Post letter 10 May, ed. Buchbender and Sterz, *Das Andere Gesicht des Krieges*, p.53.
22 Tonry and Bradley, interviews, *Dunkirk the Soldiers' Story*, BBC TV, 2004.
23 Weeks, interview, ibid.
24 Messerschmidt, German SWF TV interview, *Die Deutschen im Zweitenweltkrieg*, p.55.
25 'Blitzkrieg', *Time* magazine, 25 Sep 1939. Figures, Kershaw, *Tankmen*, p.96.
26 Ahlschwede, interview, *The Other Side of Dunkirk*, BBC TV, 2004. Reinhardt, Frieser, *Blitzkrieg Legende*, p.114.
27 Carganico, *Blitzkrieg in their own Words*, p.70. Christophé and Steinbecher, *Wir Stossen mit Panzern zum Meer*, pp.23 and 153.
28 Luxembourg Police, Blumentritt, *Von Rundstedt*, p.66. Hans P., *Diary*, 12 May 1940, ed. Hammer and Zur Nieden, *Sehr Selten Habe Ich Geweint*, pp.39–40.
29 Kuby, *Mein Krieg*, pp.34–6.
30 Kielmansegg, Frieser, *Blitzkrieg Legende*, p.118.
31 Ahlschwede and Becker, interview, *The Other Side of Dunkirk*, BBC TV, 2004.
32 Novak and Michard, Frieser, *Blitzkrieg Legende*, p.160.
33 Ahlschwede, ibid.
34 Nehring, *Amiens to Dunkirk: A Personal Impression*, Purnell's History of the Second World War, p.225. Balck, *Order in Chaos*, p.172.
35 Signals *Unteroffizier* AR, *Feldpost* letter 12 May, ed. Buchbender and Sterz, *Das Andere Gesicht des Krieges*, p.54.
36 Luck, *Panzer Commander*, p.39.
37 Möllmann, *Blitzkrieg in their own Words*, p.76.
38 Luck, *Panzer Commander*, p.41. Möllmann, *Blitzkrieg in their own Words*, P.76.
39 Böll, *Briefe aus dem Krieg 1939–45*, and Ohler, *Blitzed*, pp.49 and 51.
40 Pervitin detail, Ohler, *Blitzed: Drugs in Nazi Germany*, pp.73, 78–9, 87 and 109–10. Sleepless veterans, Hoggard, TV Documentary *World War Speed*, interview Dr Steinkamp, Medical historian, Ulm University, 2018.
41 Ahlschwede, BBC interview 2004.
42 Meyer, *Grenadiers*, pp.14–16.
43 Pohl, interview, *Die Deutschen im Zweiten Weltkrieg*, German SWF TV. Rymer, interview, *Dunkirk: The Soldiers' Story*, BBC TV, 2004.
44 Interview, www.angelfire.com/ct/ww2europe/, 2004.
45 Béthegrues, *Le Sacrifice de Dunkerque*, 1947.
46 Schroeder, *Er War Mein Chef*, p.102. Below, *At Hitler's Side*, p.39.
47 Below, *At Hitler's Side*, pp.39 and 44. Halder, *Diary*, 25 May 1940, p.166.
48 Warlimont, *Inside Hitler's Headquarters 1939–45*, p.88.
49 Ibid., pp.87–90.
50 Halder, *Diary*, 16 May 1940, p.145, 17 May, pp.148–9.
51 Jodl, *Diary*, 18 May 1940, Jacobsen, *Dokumente zum Westfeldzug 1940*, p.44. Halder, *Diary*, 18 May, p.149.
52 Guderian, *Panzer Leader*, pp.109–10.
53 Guderian row, Nehring, *Amiens to Dunkirk*, p.225. Guderian, *Panzer Leader*, pp.109–10. Balck, interview, *Conversations with General Hermann Balck*, Battelle Columbus Laboratories USA, January 1979, p.30.
54 Luck, *Panzer Commander*, pp.39 and 41. Balck, *Order in Chaos*, pp.viii and 175.
55 Christophé, *Wir Stossen mit Panzern zum Meer*, pp.41–2. Steinbrecher, *Diary*, 13–15 May 1940, ibid., pp.158–9.

56 Officer, 75th Pz Regt, *France 1940*, captured German document, *The Tank Magazine*, December 1957, pp.85–6.

57 Ibid.

58 Richthofen, Log 18 May 1940, *VIII Fliegerkorps im Frankreich-Feldzug*, Bundesarchiv BA R2 8/43, p.32. Nehring, *Amiens to Dunkirk*, p.226.

59 Dietz, *Blitzkrieg in their own Words*, p.137. Christophé, *Wir Stossen mit Panzern zum Meer*, p.159.

60 Waite, interview, *Dunkirk: The Forgotten Heroes*, BBC TV, 2010.

61 Weeks, interview, *Dunkirk: The Soldiers' Story*, BBC TV, 2004.

62 Waite, interview, *Dunkirk: The Forgotten Heroes*, BBC TV, 2010.

63 Jodl, *Diary*, 20 May 1940, Jacobsen, *Dokumente*, p.53.

64 Hill, interview, *Dunkirk: The Soldiers' Story*, BBC TV, 2004.

65 Hans P., *Diary*, 13 May 1940, ed. Hammer and zur Nieden, *Sehr Selten Habe Ich Geweint*, p.41.

66 Feldwebel, *Die Deutschen im Zweiten Weltkrieg*, German SWF TV.

CHAPTER 2: *LANDSER*

1 Kleist, letter 14 May 1940 on the march through Belgium, ed. Kaufmann, *Botschaft der Gefallenen*, p.120.

2 Schönfeld, *Diary*, 15 May, Ed. Dollinger, *Kain, wo ist dein Bruder?* p.50.

3 Jodl, *Diary*, 21 May, Jacobsen, *Dokumente*, p.57.

4 Klaus, *Unser Weg zum Meer*, p.25.

5 Knappe, *Soldat*, p.166.

6 Neu, Gareis, *Kampf und Ende 98 Division*, p.22.

7 Klaus, *Unser Weg zum Meer*, pp.104–5.

8 Bönsch, *Unser Weg zum Meer*, p.38.

9 Klaus, *Unser Weg zum Meer*, p.105.

10 Bönsch, Klaus, Knappe, *Unser Weg zum Meer*, pp.38, 105 and 166–7.

11 Wied, *Unser Weg zum Meer*, p.48. Kleist, 14 May 1940, Kaufmann, *Botschaft de Gefallenen*, p.120. Kleist was killed at Chateaubriand in France on 21 June 1940.

12 Cranz, *Erfahrungsbericht der 18. Division* 18.740, Bundesarchiv, BA RH 26-18119.

13 Frey, *Kampfbericht der 7. KP. IR.192, 30 Jul. 40.* Bundesarchiv, BA RH 26-5C/75.

14 Ibid.

15 Ibid.

16 Leixner, *Signal* Magazine, Heft 6, 1 July 1940.

17 Ibid. Also Time/Life, *Lightning War*, pp.92–5.

18 Frey, *Kampfbericht der 7. KP. IR.192, 30 Jul. 40.* Bundesarchiv, BA RH 26-5C/75.

19 Ibid.

20 Hans P., *Diary*, 18 May 1940, ed. Hammer and zur Nieden, *Sehr Selten Habe Ich Geweint*, pp.42–6.

21 Ibid.

22 *Gefreiter* LM, letter 14 May 1940, ed. Buchbender and Sterz, *Das Andere Gesicht des Krieges*, p.54.

23 Hans P., ed. Hammer and zur Nieden, *Sehr Selten Habe Ich Geweint*, p.36.

24 Spanocchi and Müllender, interviews, *Die Deutschen Im Zweiten Weltkrieg*, German SWF TV, p.50.

25 Division 216 example, *Mitteilungsblatt No 5 Der Niedersächsischen 216/272 Inf Div*, Hannover, July 1967.

26 Otto W., letter, Moutier, *Liebste Schwester*, p.41. 'Like God in France', Gockel, *Das Tor Zur Hölle*, p.46.

27 Heck, *A Child of Hitler*, p.41.

28 *Wehrmacht* Magazine, No. 20, 24 September 1941.

29 Döring, 28 May 1940, Ed. Bahr, Meyer and Orthbandt, *Kriegsbriefer Gefallener Studenten*, p.17. Gschöpf, *Mein Weg mit der 45.Infanterie Division*, p.127. Werner L., 24 May 1940, Moutier, *Liebste Schwester*, p.66. Niethammer, Latzel, *Deutsche Soldaten – Nationalsozialistischer Krieg?* p.138.

30 Mansfeld, from Hesse, *Über Schlachtfelder Vorwarts!*. The article by Hesse is a typical example of a National Socialist sponsored publication covering personalized campaign episodes and highlights, pp.128 and 130.

31 *Gefreiter* A.M., letter 24 May 1940, *Das Andere Gesicht des Krieges*, p.55. *Gefreiter* H.B., Ibid. Müllender, interview, *Die Deutschen im Zweiten Weltkrieg*, German SWF TV, p.50.

32 Döring, *Kriegsbriefer Gefallener Studenten*, p.18. Kuby, *Diary*, 18 May 1940, *Mein Krieg*, p.38.

33 Heck, *A Child of Hitler*, pp.2 and 32.

34 Köppen, Damaske and Heisig interviews, P.Hartl, *Hitler's Children*, German ZDF TV. Metelmann, *Through Hell for Hitler*, p.19.

35 Kiemig, interview *Mein Krieg*, Eder and Kufus, German WDR TV 1991. Becker, *Devil on My Shoulder*, pp.16–17.

36 NS slogan, Stöhr, 'Wie War das mit der Tapferkeit?', *Der II Weltkrie, Tief im Feindesland, Band 1*, Jahr Verlag 1976. Olte, Latzel, *Deutsche Soldaten, Nationalsozialstche Krieg?* Letters, 1 April, 16 May, 20 May 1940, pp.40 and 42.

37 Stöhr, 'Wie War das mit der Tapferkeit?', *Der II Weltkrie, Tief im Feindesland, Band 1*, Jahr Verlag 1976.

38 Cranz, *Erfarhrungsbericht der 18.Div 18 Jul 40. II Taktik 1)-2)* pp.2–3, Bundesarchiv BA RH 26-18119. Kuby, *Diary*, 11 May 1940, *Mein Krieg*, pp.35–6.

39 Liss, *Westfront 1939–40*, pp.62–3. Werner L., letter 24 May 1940, Moutier, *Liebste Schwester*, p.66.

40 Schönfeld, ed. Dollinger, *Kain Wo ist dein Bruder?* pp.48–9.

41 Belgians, Liss, *Westfront*, pp.45 and 61.

42 Berndt, *Tanks Break Through*, pp.154, 104–5 and 134. Neelsen, letter, May 1940, *Kriegsbriefer Gefallener Studenten*, p.22.

43 Dittert, *Unser Weg zum Meer*, p.97.

44 Knappe, *Soldat*, pp.164–5.

45 Lachner, interview, *Die Deutschen im Zweiten Weltkrieg*, German SWF TV.

46 Heck, *A Child of Hitler*, p.37.

47 Roux, *Diary*, 11 May 1940, ed. Dollinger, *Kain Wo ist dein Bruder?* p.48. Grady, *Gardens of Stone*, pp.40–1.

48 Liss, *Westfront*, pp.24, 33, 45, 46 and 47–8.

49 Balck, *Order in Chaos*, pp.174, 175 and 192–3.

50 Meyer, *Grenadiers*, p.17.

51 Balck, *Order in Chaos*, p.174.

52 Liss, view of French, *Westfront*, pp.24, 33, 45, 46, 47–8. Vancoille, interview, *The Other Side of Dunkirk*, BBC TV, 2004. Habe, *A Thousand Shall Fall*, p.16.

53 Sgt Roux, ed. Dollinger, *Kain Wo ist dein Bruder?* p.50.

54 Grady, *Gardens of Stone*, p.49.

55 Murray, *Images of War 1939–45*, Marshall Cavendish, p.20.

56 Cranz, and 54 Regt Dr, Altenstadt, *Unser Weg zum Meer*, pp.47 and 78.

57 Liss, view of the English, *Westfront*, pp.53 and 55–6.

58 Fane, interview, *Dunkirk: The Forgotten Heroes*, Testimony Films TV, 2010.

59 Weeks, Saunders, Bradley and Tonry, interviews, *Dunkirk: The Soldiers' Story*, BBC TV, 2004.

60 Waite, interview, *Dunkirk: The Forgotten Heroes*, 2010. Hill, interview, *The Soldiers' Story*, BBC TV, 2004. Scannell, Holden, *Shell Shock*, p.75.

61 David RAF, Gelb, *Scramble*, p.16. Refugee figures, Diamond, *Fleeing Hitler*, p.5. Rymer, interview, *The Soldiers' Story*, BBC TV, 2004.

62 Steinhoff, Pechel and Showalter, *Deutsche im Zweiten Weltkrieg*, pp.45–6.

63 David RAF, *Scramble*, p.17.

64 German pilot, Poland, Tapes of German POWs, Neitzel and Welzer, *Soldaten*, p.45. Küster, ibid., pp.57–8.

65 Hill, interview, *The Soldiers' Story*, BBC TV, 2004.

66 Heinkel bomber crew and 5th Pz Court Martial, de Zayas, *Die Wehrmacht-Untersuchungsstelle*, pp.180–1. French refugee, Diamond, *Fleeing Hitler*, p.71.

67 Thalmaier, Dollinger, *Kain Wo ist dein Bruder? p.51.

68 Knappe, *Soldat*, p.170.

69 Gschöpf, *Mein Weg mit der 45. Infanterie Division*, p.132.

70 Adrey, Diamond, *Fleeing Hitler*, pp.32–3. Hans S., letter 30 May 1940, Moutier, *Liebste Schwester*, p.71.

71 Knappe, *Soldat*, p.170. Hans P., *Diary*, 24 May 1940, Hammer and zur Nieden, *Sehr Selten Habe Ich Geweint*, pp.49–50. Kuby, *Diary*, 18 May 1940, *Mein Krieg*, p.39.

72 Berndt, *Tanks Break Through*, p.137.

73 Becker, interview, *The Other Side of Dunkirk*, BBC TV, 2004.

74 Edge RAF, *Scramble*, p.17.

CHAPTER 3: THE SEA

1 Guderian, *Panzer Leader*, p.113.

2 Nehring, *Amiens to Dunkirk*, p.226.

3 Guderian, *Panzer Leader*, p.113.

4 Nehring, *Amiens to Dunkirk*, p.226.

5 Guderian, *Panzer Leader*, p.113. Nehring, *Amiens to Dunkirk*, p.226. Balck, interview, Battelle Columbus Laboratories, January 1979.

6 Guderian, *Panzer Leader*, p.113. Directive, War Diary AGp A, 21 May 1940, Jacobsen, *Dokumente*, pp.59–60.

7 Interview, https://www.angelfire.com/ct/ww2europe/, 2004.

8 Allied counter offensives, Coyle and Rowland, *A Preliminary Analysis of Counter-Offensive Battles in World War II*, Def Op. Analysis Working Paper 670-2, November 1986.

9 Regiment 6 Message, Frieser, *Blitzkrieg Legende*, p.346. Div Log, Annex E to 4th Armd Div *Arras Battlefield Guide*, 31 January 1985. Rommel, Liddell-Hart, *The Rommel Papers*, pp.31–2. Div report 21 May, ibid.

10 Vaux, Kershaw, *Tankmen*, pp.119–20.

11 Becker, interview, *The Other Side of Dunkirk*, BBC TV, 2004.

12 Figures, 7 Pz Div log 21 May and Bond, *Arras 21 May 1940. A Case Study in the Counter Offensive*, pp.9–10.

13 Div 12 War Diary, Tesky, *Fuhrungsprobleme einer Infanterie Division im Westfeldzug 1940*, pp.44–5. Agp A War Diary, 01.30, 22 May 1940, Jacobsen, *Dokumente*, p.65.

14 Kielmansegg, *Panzer Zwischen Warschau und Atlantik*, pp.145–8.

15 Guderian, *Panzer Leader*, p.114. Nehring, *Amiens to Dunkirk*, p.226.

16 *Luftwaffe* Reports, *Berichte des Oberbefehlshaber der Luftwaffe Fuhrungstab Ic*, 22 and 23 May 1940, Bundesarchiv BA R12II/ 206, 207 and 208.

17 Official Hist 10 Pz, Schick, *The Combat History of the 10th Panzer Division 1939–1943*, pp.113–16.

18 Kielmansegg, *Panzer Zwischen Warschau und Atlantik*, pp.148–9.

19 Susskind-Schwendi, Strauss, *Geschichte der 2(Wiener) Panzer Division*, pp.47–8.

20 Dietz, *Blitzkrieg in their own Words*, p.138.

21 Spaeter, *History of the Panzerkorps Grossdeutschland*, p.102.

22 VIII *Fliegerkorps*, 28 May, BA RL8/43.

23 Kielmansegg, *Panzer Zwischen Warschau und Atlantik*, p.150.

24 Halder, *Diary*, 24 May 1940, Jacobsen, *Dokumente*, P.74. Aircraft figures, Dildy, *Dunkirk 1940*, p.18.

25 Behr, *Blitzkrieg in their own Words*, pp.143–5.

26 Ibid.

27 Guderian, *Panzer Leader*, p.116.

28 Kielmansegg, *Panzer Zwischen Warschau und Atlantik*, p.151. Reeves, Cooksey, *Calais*, p.69.

29 Evans, Cooksey, *Boulogne 1940*, p.69.

30 Behr, *Blitzkrieg in Their Own Words*, p.145.

31 Künzler and Evans, Cooksey, pp.71–2.

32 Dietz, *Blitzkrieg in their own Words*, p.138. Dürkes, Strauss, *Geschichte der 2. (Wiener) Panzer Division*, pp.48–9.

33 Dwinger, *Panzerführer*, p.3.

34 Kp briefing, *Kradschutzen Vor! Frankreich Tagebuch 7. Kompanie*, original document 1940.

35 Dwinger, *Panzerführer*, p.4.

36 Dürkes, Strauss, *Geschichte der 2. (Wiener) Panzerdivision*, p.49.

37 Stanier, Cooksey, *Boulogne 1940*, p.87.

38 Ibid.

39 Davis, ibid., p.92.

40 Christophé, *Wir Stossen mit Panzern zum Meer*, p.131.

41 Künzel, Cooksey, *Boulogne 1940*, p.105.

42 Leslie, Cooksey, pp.106–7.

43 Stoner, Cooksey, p.109.

44 Dürkes, Strauss, *Geschichte der 2. (Wiener) Panzerdivision*, pp.49–51.

45 Dietz, *Blitzkrieg in their own Words*, p.139. XIX Armeekorps report 14.45 hours, quoted in Cooksey, p.111.

46 Fox Pitt, Levine, *Forgotten Voices of Dunkirk*, p.102. Sutton, Cooksey, *Boulogne 1940*, p.73.

47 Propaganda, Hubert Borchert, *Panzerkampf im Westen*, Wehrmacht publication. Dürkes, Strauss, *Geschichte der 2. (Wiener) Panzerdivision*, p.52.

48 Lumsden, Cooksey, *Boulogne 1940*, pp.115–16. Harris, ibid., p.120–1.

49 Dietz, *Blitzkrieg*, p.139. Lumsden, Cooksey, *Boulogne 1940*, p.119.

50 Dietz, *Blitzkrieg*, p.139.

51 Sqn Int Report, Parry and Postlethwaite, *Dunkirk. Air Combat Archive*, p.52.

52 Langhammer, *Blitzkrieg*, pp.146–8, and Steinzer, *Die Friedens und Kriegsjahre der 2. (Wiener) Panzerdivision in Wort und Bild*, pp.58–9.

53 Stanier, Cooksey, *Boulogne 1940*, p.133.

54 Dietz, *Blitzkrieg*, p.140. Evacuation figures, Ed. Gardner, *The Evacuation from Dunkirk*, p.10. Battalion figs, Cooksey, *Boulogne 1940*, p.139. Fox Pitt, Levine, *Forgotten Voices of Dunkirk*, p.102.

CHAPTER 4: 24 MAY, THE DAY OF THE HALT ORDER

1 Brauchitsch quote, Frieser, *Blitzkrieg Legende*, p.368.

2 Halder, *Diary*, 25 May 1940, p.165. Schmundt, quoted in Frieser, *Blitzkrieg Legende*, p.370.

3 Kleist, Reinhardt and 3rd Pz Div report, Jacobsen, *Dünkirchen*, pp.96, 97 and 98.

4 Halder on Brauchitsch, Halder, *Diary*, 24 May 1940. Warlimont at *Felsennest* and on Göring, *Inside Hitler's Headquarters 1939–45*, p.98. Richthofen, Jodl and Halder on Hitler, Frieser, *Blitzkrieg Legende*, pp.387 and 392.

5 Heck, *A Child of Hitler*, p.19. Goebbels, *Diary*, 15 May 1940, p.1421 and 18 May, p.1423.

6 Goebbels, *Diary*, ibid., p.1423. Kunze, interview, Knopp and Hartl, *Hitler's Children*, German ZDF TV.

7 SS/SD Reports, Ed. Boberach, *Meldungen aus dem Reich*, 16 May, p.1139; 20 May, p.1140; 23 May, pp.1163 and 1167; 6 June, p.1223; all 1940.

8 British Home Intelligence Reports, Addison and Crang, *Listening to Britain*, 19–20 May 1940, pp.14–15 and 46; 24 May, pp.24, 34 and 47. Knight, Levine, *Forgotten Voices of Dunkirk*, p.118.

9 Knight, Levine, *Forgotten Voices of Dunkirk*, p.118.

10 BBC, Stourton, *Auntie's War*, pp.107 and 115. Goebbels, *Diary*, 23 May, pp.1425–6.

11 Kielmansegg, *Panzer Zwischen Warschau und Atlantik*, p.152.

12 Balck, interview, Battelle Columbus Laboratories, January 1979.

13 Kielmansegg, *Panzer Zwischen Warschau und Atlantik*, p.152.

14 Ibid.

15 Balck, *Order in Chaos*, p.179.

16 Soldier, *Grossdeutschland*, Spaeter, *History of the Panzercorps Grossdeutschland*, p.101.

17 Morel, Murland, *The Canal Line*, pp.24–6.

18 Timerman, Murland, *The Canal Line*, pp.24–6.

19 Kielmansegg, *Panzer Zwischen Warschau und Atlantik*, pp.152–3.

20 Nehring, *Amiens to Dunkirk*, p.226. Panzer 2 losses, Deutsche Dienstelle Berlin, letter Herr Betten to author 22 April 2005.

21 Vancoille, interview, *The Other Side of Dunkirk*, BBC TV, 2004.

22 'GD' report, Spaeter, *History of the Panzerkorps Grossdeutschland*, p.102.

23 Balck and Balck's son, *Order in Chaos*, p.182

24 Kielmansegg, *Panzer Zwischen Warschau und Atlantik*, p.154. 'GD' report, Spaeter, *History of the Panzerkorps Grossdeutschland*, p.102.

25 Neumann, *Boulogne 1940* p.105.

26 Balck, *Order in Chaos*, p.180. Kielmansegg, *Panzer Zwischen Warschau und Atlantik*, p.154. Nehring, *Amiens to Dunkirk*, p.227.

27 Guderian's son, interview, Harman, *Dunkirk: The Story Behind the Legend*, BBC TV, 1980.

28 Warlimont, *Inside Hitler's Headquarters 1939–45*, p.99.

29 Ahlswede, interview, *The Other Side of Dunkirk*, BBC TV, 2004.
30 Müller, Spaeter, *History of the Panzerkorps Grossdeutschland*, p.105–6.
31 Kleist quote, Army Gp A War Diary, Frieser, *Blitzkrieg Legende*, p.366.
32 Casualty figure discrepancies, see Frieser, *Blitzkrieg Legende*, pp.366 and 399; supported by analysis, Schick letter to author 9 March 2005. Hoth figures, *XXXIX AK KTB 24 May.* S.48. Bundesarchiv BA RH 24-3917. Recent assessment, Battistelli, *Panzer Divisions: The Blitzkrieg Years 1939–40*.
33 Rundstedt and Bock, *Von Bock's Diary*, 29 May 1940, pp.157–8. Fourth Army Officer, Jacobsen, *Dünkirchen*, p.101.
34 Filor, interview, C Frey and G Knopp, *The SS*, German ZDF TV 2002.
35 Meyer and Dietrich, *Grenadiers*, p.18. Filor, interview, Frey and Knopp, *The SS*, German ZDF TV, 2002.
36 Ritgen, *Gefechtsbericht KTB II/Panzerregiment 11, Anlage 10*, from *Westfront 1944*, p.15.
37 Young and Shaw, *We Remember Dunkirk*, p.49. Kanzler, *Images of War*, Marshall Cavendish, pp.20–1.
38 Panzer 3 artillery officer, Anon, *France 1940*, *The Tank* Magazine, December 1957 Vol. 40, p.86.
39 Guderian, *Panzer Leader*, p.120.
40 Kuby, 24 May 1940, *Mein Krieg*, p.41.
41 Schönfeld, ed. Dollinger, *Kain, Wo ist dein Bruder?* pp.51–2.
42 Walter, Bähr, Meyer and Orthbandt, *Kriegsbriefe Gefallener Studenten 1939–45*, p.25.
43 Hans P., *Diary*, 24 May 1940, ed. Hammer and zur Nieden, *Sehr Selten Habe Ich Geweint*, p.50.
44 Div Lys crossing, Jenner, Die 216/272 Niedersachsische Inf Div, Podzun-Pallas 1964. *Mitteilungsblatt Nr 6, Der 216/272 Inf Div*, April 1971, p.8. *Gefechtsbericht IV Art Regt 216 Mai/Juni 1940*, Bundesarchiv BA RH 41/406 and Gen Kdo IX AK 24 May, *Feldzug in Frankreich*, RH 24-9/17.
45 Neelsen, *Kriegsbriefe Gefallener Studenten 1939–45*, pp.22–3.
46 /56 Div figs, *Feldzug in Frankreich*, IX AK, 24 May, RH 24-9/17. Schimpf, *Kriegstagebuch I/192*, 25 May, p.15, RH 37/2799. Geyer, IX Corps, ibid.

CHAPTER 5: PANZERS AGAINST PORTS

 1 Kunzel, Cooksey, *Boulogne*, p.147.
 2 Christophé, *Wir Stossen mit Panzern zum Meer*, p.145.
 3 Panzer-Division 2 casualties were a total of 214 all ranks between 22 and 24 May. Letter Betten/Kershaw, Berlin Dienstelle 22 April 2005. Dietz, *Blitzkrieg in their own Words*, pp.140–1.
 4 Christophé, p.146.
 5 Guderian, *Panzer Leader*, p.116. Dietz, *Blitzkrieg*, p.116.
 6 Davis, Cooksey, *Boulogne 1940*, p.158.
 7 Borchert, Cooksey, *Calais*, p.93.
 8 Dwinger, *Panzerführer*, p.21.
 9 Borchert, Cooksey, *Calais*, p.93.
10 Otto W., letter home 31 May 1940, Moutier, *Liebste Schwester*, p.74.
11 Neave, *The Flames of Calais*, p.9.
12 Dwinger, *Panzerführer*, p.11. Air attack detail, *Kriegstagebuch der 10. Pz. Div. 9.5.–29.6.40.* 15.00 24 May, Bundesarchiv BA RH 27-10/9. (Thereafter 10.Pz Log).
13 Doe, Levine, *Forgotten Voices of Dunkirk*, p.122.

0

14 Ibid., pp.118 and 119.

15 Davies-Scourfield, Cooksey, *Calais*, p.131.

16 Neave, *The Flames of Calais*, pp.131–2.

17 König, *Zweieinhalbtausand kilometer durch Frankreich, Kampf um Calais!* März 1941, Heft 30/1941.

18 Ibid.

19 Motorcycle Kompanie 7, *Kradschützen Vor! Frankreich Tagebuch 7. Kompanie (86 Regt)*, p.30.

20 Ibid.

21 Guderian, 10th Pz Log, 17.00, 24 May 1940.

22 Konig, *Der Zweite Tag!* Article *Zweieinhalbtausand Kilometer durch Frankreich, 1941*.

23 . Pz Strength Return, Div log, 19.00, 24 May. Pz ban, ibid., 03.00 25 May 1940.

24 Motorcycle Kompanie 7, *Kradschützen Vor!*, p.31.

25 Reports, Div Log, 15.35–16.00 hours 25 May 1940.

26 Stuka pilot, Weal, *Junkers Ju 87*, p.50.

27 Dinort, Bekker, *The Luftwaffe War Diaries*, pp.123–4.

28 Sqn RAF report, Parry and Postlethwaite, *Dunkirk Air Combat Archive*, pp.72–3.

29 Borchert, Cooksey, *Calais*, p.118.

30 Pardoe, Levine, *Forgotten Voices of Dunkirk*, p.119.

31 Borchert, Cooksey, *Calais*, p.120.

32 Doe, Levine, *Forgotten Voices of Dunkirk*, p.120.

33 Watson, Levine, *Forgotten Voices of Dunkirk*, p.123.

34 Division Log, 23.00 and 23.45 25 May 1940.

35 Stuka attack, Kageneck, Bekker, *The Luftwaffe War Diaries*, p.125.

36 Dwinger, *Panzerführer*, p.16.

37 Fischer, *Blitzkrieg*, p.161.

38 Dwinger, *Panzerführer*, p.16. Pardoe, Levine, *Forgotten Voices of Dunkirk*, p.120.

39 Fischer, *Blitzkrieg*, p.161,

40 Watson, Levine, *Forgotten Voices of Dunkirk*, p.121.

41 Fischer, *Blitzkrieg*, p.161.

42 Chambers, Cooksey, *Calais*, p.128.

43 Churchill, Jackson, *Dunkirk*, p.54.

44 Churchill, Jackson, *Dunkirk*, p.60.

45 Division log, 11.45 26 May 1940. Fischer, *Blitzkrieg*, p.161.

46 Konig, *Der Zweite Tag!* Article *Zweieinhalbtausand Kilometer durch Frankreich, 1941*.

47 Kompanie 7, *Kradschützen Vor!* pp.32–4.

48 Fischer, *Blitzkrieg*, p.162.

49 Evitts, Cooksey, *Calais*, p.133.

50 Fischer, *Blitzkrieg*, p.162.

51 Pardoe, Doe and Watson, Levine, *Forgotten Voices of Dunkirk*, p.124.

52 Kidd, Cooksey, *Calais*, p.133.

53 POW numbers, Cooksey, *Calais*, p.140.

54 Dwinger, *Panzerführer*, pp.19–20.

55 König, article, *Ruhe nach den Sturm!* March 1941.

56 Fischer, division log, 17.30 26 May 1940 and interview conducted by Schick, *The Combat History of the 10th Panzer Division 1939–1943*, p.132.

57 Declared tank losses were often inaccurate because of varying rates of repair. Panzer crew casualties, Betten letter to author, Deutsche Dienststelle Berlin, 22 April 2005.

58 Otto W., Letter 31 May 1940, Moutier, *Liebste Schwester*, p.73.
59 König, article, *Ruhe nach den Sturm!* Division log, 20.10, 27 May 1940.
60 White, Levine, *Forgotten Voices of Dunkirk*, p.130.
61 Stanton, interview, *Dunkirk: The Forgotten Heroes*, Testimony Films, 2010.
62 Weeks, interview, *Dunkirk: The Soldiers' Story*, BBC TV, 2004.
63 Division 3, Drewienkiewicz, RCDS thesis on the TA in 1940, p.92, 1992. Trinder, interview, *Dunkirk: The Forgotten Heroes*, Testimony Films 2010.
64 Geyer, *Gen Kdo IX AK Feldzug in Frankreich*, p.31, 23 May 1940, BA RH 24-9/17.
65 Bradley, interview, *Dunkirk: The Soldiers' Story*, BBC TV, 2004.
66 Bloch, *Strange Defeat*, pp.xv and 31.
67 Weeks and Bradley, interviews, *Dunkirk: The Soldiers' Story*, BBC TV, 2004.
68 Crockitt, interview, *The Other Side of Dunkirk*, BBC TV, 2004.
69 *Luftwaffe* Reports, Oberbefehlshaber der Luftwaffe. Führungsstab Ic. Lagebericht Nr 263, finalized 10.00, 26 May 1940. Ibid. *Lagebericht Nr 259*, 22 May 1940 and *Lagebericht Nr 265*, 26 May 1940. Liss, *Westfront*, pp.209 and 201.
70 Steinhilper, *Spitfire On My Tail*, p.254.
71 Kreipe, Bekker, *The Luftwaffe War Diaries*, pp.127–8.
72 Destruction of Dunkirk, Blanckaert, *Dunkirk 1939–45*, pp.39–41. Oddone, *Dunkirk 1940*, pp.88–90.
73 Rhodes, Harman, *Dunkirk: The Patriotic Myth*, p.124.
74 Tennant, Official Report 26–27 May, Mace, *The Royal Navy at Dunkirk*, p.367.
75 Ibid. Göring, Harman, *Dunkirk: The Patriotic Myth*, p.115.

CHAPTER 6: RUNNING THE GAUNTLET

1 Halder, *Diary*, 26 May 1940, p.167. Brennecke, Jacobsen, *Decisive Battles of World War II: The German View, Dunkirk 1940*, pp.64–5.
2 Ritgen, *Westfront 1944*, p.17. Imhoff, *Stürm durch Frankreich*, pp.134–5.
3 Young, Shaw and Shaw, *We Remember Dunkirk*, p.49.
4 Imhoff, *Stürm durch Frankreich*, pp.134–5. Fane, interview, *Dunkirk: The Soldiers' Story*, BBC TV, 2004.
5 Ritgen, *The 6th Panzer Division 1937–45*, pp.14–15.
6 Munn, Dildy, *Dunkirk 1940*, p.48.
7 Ritgen, *The 6th Panzer Division 1937–45*, pp.14–15.
8 Hoss, Lane, *Last Stand at Le Paradis*, p.108. Bock, Knopp, *The SS: A Warning from History*, p.237.
9 Farrow, Hart, *Britain at War* magazine, May 2015, p.37.
10 Stürzbecher, Lane, *Last Stand at Le Paradis*, pp.134–5.
11 Leitl, ibid., p.138.
12 Stürzbecher, Lane, ibid., pp.134–5.
13 Brown, Hart, *Britain at War* Magazine, May 2015, p.41.
14 Brunnegger, *The War Years*, Marshal Cavendish, p.50.
15 Farrow, Hart, *Britain at War* Magazine, May 2015, p.40–41.
16 Brunnegger, *The War Years*, p.50.
17 Paar, *Diary*, 28 May 1940, ed. Dollinger, *Kain, wo ist dein Bruder?* pp.53–4. Knöchlein was indicted by a war crimes court and hanged at Hamburg in January 1949.
18 Brunnegger, *The War Years*, p.50.
19 Ibid. Manstein, Knopp, *The SS*, p.237.
20 Kanzler, *Images of War*, Marshal Cavendish, p.21.

21 Regt Officer, Anon from 8 Bty 75 Pz Arty Regt 75, *France 1940*, p.87, *The Tank Magazine*, December 1957.
22 Ritgen, *Westfront*, p.17.
23 Fane, interviews, *Dunkirk: The Forgotten Heroes*, Testimony Films, 2010 and *The Other Side of Dunkirk*, BBC TV, 2004.
24 Ritgen, *Westfront*, p.17. 6 Pz Report, 28 May 1940, p.163, KTB XIX Corps, RH 21-2/V 41. Fane, interviews, *Dunkirk: The Forgotten Heroes*, Testimony Films, 2010 and *The Other Side of Dunkirk*, BBC TV, 2004.
25 Stanton, interview, *Dunkirk: The Forgotten Heroes*, Testimony Films, 2010.
26 Meyer, *Grenadiers*, p.21.
27 Maas, Aitken, *Massacre on the Road to Dunkirk*, p.62.
28 Sametreiter, interview, Frey and Knopp, *The SS*, German ZDF TV, 2002. Nobody was ever indicted for the massacre at Wormhoudt.
29 Official history, Lehmann, *The Leibstandarte*, p.149. Guderian, *Panzer Leader*, p.118.
30 Kielmansegg, *Panzer Zwischen Warschau und Atlantik*, p.155.
31 Imhoff, *Sturm durch Frankreich*, p.127.
32 Guderian, *KTB Nr 3. Schlacht in Frankreich*, 28 May 1940: 08.40, 15.05, 20.30 and *Abend Zusammenfassung*. 29 May, 19.40, BA RH 21-2/V 41.
33 Hans P., *Diary*, 27 May 1940, Ed. Hammer and zur Nieden, *Sehr Selten Habe Ich Geweint*, p.57. Imhoff, *Landser*, p.134.
34 Regt, anon officer, 'France 1940', *The Tank* Magazine, December 1957, p.87,.
35 Geyer, Gen Kdo IX AK. 24–27 May 1940, *Feldzug in Frankreich*, BA RH 24-9/17. Otte and Lormes, *Warschau-Dunkirchen. Kriegselebnisse einer Batterie* 1939/40, pp.314–15.
36 Brooke, *War Diaries 1939–1945*, 13 May 1940, p.62, 25 May, p.69, 27 May, p.71.
37 Westphal, Taylor, *The March of Conquest*, p.252.
38 Geyer, Gen Kdo IX AK, 28–29 May 1940.
39 Clapham and Shaw, *We Remember Dunkirk*, p.137–8. Brooke, *War Diaries*, 27 May 1940, p.71.
40 Kleist, letter near Ypres, 28 May 1940, ed. Bähr, Meyer and Orthbandt, *Kriegsbriefe Gefallener Studenten*, p.27.
41 Sandau, Altenstadt, *Unser Weg zum Meer*, pp.122–3.
42 Ibid.
43 Berndt, *Tanks Break Through!* pp.114–15.
44 Ibid.
45 Werner L., letter 24 May 1940, Moutier, *Liebste Schwester*, p.67.
46 Kleist, 28 May 1940, p.27 and 12 June 1940, p.28, *Kriegsbriefe Gefallener Studenten*.
47 Schimpf, *Kriegstagebuch I/192*, 27–29 May 1940. BA RH 37/2799.
48 Bock, *The War Diary*, 27 and 28 May 1940, pp.155–6.
49 *Gefreiter* Regiment 77, letter 28 May 1940, ed. Buchbender and Sterz, *Das Andere Gesicht des Krieges*, p.56. Berndt, *Tanks Break Through!* pp.150 and 152. Signals *Leutnant*, Buchbender and Sterz, *Das Andere Gesicht des Krieges*, p.56.
50 Geyer, *Gen Kdo IX AK*, 28–29 May 1940, pp.34–8.
51 Ibid.
52 BA RH 24-9/17. Berndt, *Tanks Break Through!* p.155.
53 *Inf Div Ia Kriegstagebuch*, 28/29 May 1940, BA RH 26-208/10. X Corps, *Kriegstagebuch des X AK Westfeldzug*, 03.45, 28 May 1940, BA RH 24-10/42.
54 Geyer, 29 May 1940. Division 56 on march, *Kriegstagebuch Nr 3. Die Schlacht in Flandern und im Artois bei 18.Armee. 56 Infanterie Division Unterstand, 28 May 1940*, (hereafter Div 56 Log). BA RH 26-56/6a.

55 Guderian, Taylor, *The March of Conquest*, pp.267–8.
56 Division 61, Hubatsch, *Die Deutsche Divisionen 1939–45, 61 Infanterie Division*, p.22. Guderian, Taylor, *The March of Conquest*, pp.267–8.
57 Halder, *Diary*, 30 and 31 May 1940, pp.172–3.
58 Bombardment, KTB A, 30 May 1940, Jacobsen, *Dokumente*, p.96.
59 Kompanie 8 soldier, Spaeter, *History of the Panzerkorps Grossdeutschland*, pp.107–8.
60 Martin, *Blitzkrieg in their own Words*, p.168.
61 'GD' Coys, Spaeter, *History of the Panzerkorps Grossdeutschland*, p.108.
62 Liss, *Westfront*, pp.55 and 53.
63 Ibid. Wake-Walker, ed. Mace, *The Royal Navy at Dunkirk*, p.340–1. Evacuation figures, British Admiralty Historical Section.

CHAPTER 7: SEA, AIR AND LAND

1 Sprang, Heft 14, *Die Kriegsmarine 1940*, p.105, Band 1 1940.
2 Interview, BBC Radio 4, 20 May 1980.
3 Wake-Walker, Mace, *The Royal Navy at Dunkirk*, p.342.
4 Sprang, Heft 14, *Die Kriegsmarine 1940*, p.105, Band 1 1940.
5 Ibid.
6 Ibid. Fisher, Mace, pp.91–2.
7 Ibid.
8 Spears, Taylor, *The March of Conquest*, p.264. Lantenois, interview based on diary account *De la Bataille du Nord aux Stalags 1940*.
9 Coutanceau, interview, *The Other Side of Dunkirk*, BBC TV, 2004. *Wehrmacht Bulletin*, 27 May 1940, *Die Wehrmachtberichte 1939–1945*, Band 1, GLB Koln 1989.
10 Richthofen, *VIII Fliegerkorps im Frankreich Feldzug*, Log, 29 May 1940, BA RL 8/43.
11 Kesselring, *The Memoirs of Field Marshal Kesselring*, p.59.
12 Steinhilper, *Spitfire on my Tail*, pp.257–8.
13 Richthofen, Log, 29 May 1940.
14 Tennant report, Mace, p.369.
15 Mahlke, *Memoires of a Stuka Pilot*, p.99. Anon Kettenführer, Weal, *Junkers Ju 87*, p.87. Peltz, Grabler, 'Stukas am Feind', *Der Adler* Magazine, Heft 13, 1940.
16 Merle, *Weekend at Dunkirk*, novel, p.60.
17 Mahlke, *Memoires of a Stuka Pilot*, pp.55 and 99. Photo study, *Signal* Magazine, *Das Gesicht des Stuka-Fliegers*, Heft 10, August 1940.
18 Merle, *Weekend at Dunkirk*, novel, p.60.
19 Peltz, Grabler, 'Stukas am Feind', *Der Adler* Magazine, Heft 13 1940.
20 Merle, *Weekend at Dunkirk*, p.90.
21 Pattrick, Plummer, *The Ships that Saved an Army*, p.206–7. Merle, *Weekend at Dunkirk*, p.90.
22 Ships lost, Ed. Gardner, Naval Staff History, *The Evacuation from Dunkirk*, pp.54–5 and Table 1, pp.212–13.
23 Dinort, Collier, *The Sands of Dunkirk*, p.145. Richthofen, Log, 29 and 30 May 1940, *VIII Fliegerkorps*, BA RL/8/43. *Daily Gen Staff Ic – Situation Reports Luftwaffe High Command (OKL)*, 31 May 1940, Jacobsen, *Dünkirchen*, pp.188–9.
24 Kingcome, Gelb, *Scramble*, pp.24–5.
25 Richthofen, Log, 31 May 1940.
26 Hansen, 29 and 30 May 1940, *KTB des X AK, Westfeldzug*, BA RH 24-10/42.
27 Imhoff, *Sturm durch Frankreich*, pp.131 and 132.

28 *Grossdeutschland*, Spaeter, *History of the Panzerkorps Grossdeutschland*, pp.110–11.
29 Dennis, Wilson, *Dunkirk*, p.103.
30 Schimpf, 30 May 1940, KTB 1/192, BA RH 37/2799. Jones, Wilson, p.100–1.
31 Schimpf, 30 May 1940, KTB 1/192, BA RH 37/2799.
32 Halder, *Diary*, 31 May 1940, pp.172–3.
33 Geyer, 31 May 1940, *Gen Kdo IX AK*, BA RH 24-9/17.
34 Geyer, ibid., and 29 May. Halder, *Diary*, 3 June 1940, p.164. Kesseling, *Memoires*, pp.59–60.
35 Schimpf, 30 May 1940, KTB 1/192, BA RH 37/2799.
36 Ibid.
37 Sprenger, *KTB 56 Infanterie Division, Die Sclacht in Flandern und im Artois bei 18.Armee*, 30 May 1940. BA RH 26-56/6a.
38 Schimpf's company commanders, *KTB 56 Div*, 30 May 1940.
39 Jones received an MC for this action, Wilson, *Dunkirk*, p.105.
40 Schimpf's company commanders, *KTB 56 Div*, 30 May 1940.
41 Div 56 log, 31 May 1940, BA RH 37/2799.
42 Ibid.
43 Montgomery, Hamilton, *Monty: The Making of a General*, p.392.
44 Oelhaven, Bekker, *The Luftwaffe War Diaries*, p.130 and Cornwell, *The Battle of France: Then and Now*, p.393.
45 Green, Levine, *Forgotten Voices of Dunkirk*, p.175.
46 Div 56 log, 31 May 1940.

CHAPTER 8: THE GREAT ESCAPE, 1 JUNE

1   Groth and Mölders, Vascoe and Cornwall, *Zerstörer*, pp.51 and 48–9.
2   Ibid. Richthofen, Log, 1.6. 1940. BA RL 8/43.
3   He 111 pilot, OKW Publication, *Sieg Über Frankreich*, p.88. Vonier, Collier, *The Sands of Dunkirk*, pp.223–4.
4   *Oberbefehlshaber der Luftwaffe Fuhrungstab Ic Lagerbericht* Nr 270. 2 June 1940.
5   BA RL 2II/208.
6   Lantenois, *De la Bataille du Nord aux Stalags 1940*, Diary, 29 May 1940, pp.45–6.
7   Interview, https://www.angelfire.com/ct/ww2europe/, 2004.
8   Lantenois, Diary, 29 May 1940, p.51.
9   Interview, https://www.angelfire.com/ct/ww2europe/, 2004.
10 Mahlke, *Memoirs of a Stuka Pilot*, pp.99–100.
11 Richthofen, Log, 1 June 1940.
12 Wake-Walker, Mace, *The Royal Navy at Dunkirk*, pp.377–8.
13 Ibid., p.378. *Wochenschau* Nr 510, 12.06.40. Mahlke, *Memoires of a Stuka Pilot*, pp.100–01. Lantenois, *Diary*, 1 June 1940, pp.51–2.
14 Mahlke, *Memoires of a Stuka Pilot*, pp.100–01.
15 Shipping losses and totals, Gardner, Admiralty account, *The Evacuation from Dunkirk*, p.158 and Table 3, p.174.
16 Peltz, Grabler, 'Stukas am Feind', *Der Adler* Magazine, Heft 13, 1940. Temme, Ed. McManus, Time/Life *Lightning War*, p.87. Bennett and Avon, interviews, Dimbleby, *Dunkirk: The Final Tribute*, BBC TV, 2000.
17 Corbishley, interview, Harman, *Dunkirk: The Story Behind the Legend*, BBC TV, 1980.
18 Bredin, Levine, *Forgotten Voices of Dunkirk*, p.190.
19 Corbishley, interview, Harman, *Dunkirk: The Story Behind the Legend*, BBC TV, 1980.
20 MacDonald, Mace, *The Royal Navy at Dunkirk*, p.39.

21 Aircraft figures, Dildy, *Dunkirk 1940*, p.74.
22 Crockitt, interview, *The Other Side of Dunkirk*, BBC TV, 2004.
23 Bartley, Brown, *Spitfire Summer*, p.55.
24 Ramsay Signal, Dildy, *Dunkirk 1940*, p.77.
25 Storrar, Franks, *Air Battle Over Dunkirk*, p.139.
26 Steinhilper, *Spitfire on My Tail*, pp.264–5.
27 Imhoff, *Sturm durch Frankreich*, pp.145–6.
28 Regiment 234, Div 56 log, 1 June 1940. BA RH 26-56/6b. Geyer, *Gen Kdo IX AK Feldzug in Frankreich*, 1 June 1940, BA RH 24-9/17.
29 Sprenger, Div 56 log, 1 June 1940.
30 Dehay, Eloi and Marquis, *Operation Dynamo*, p.111.
31 Sprenger, Div 56 log, 1 June 1940.
32 Div Ops Officer, Div 56 log, 1 June 1940.
33 Plan and intelligence, *KTB X AK Westfeldzug*, 1 June 1940, 11.00–18.00 Uhr. BA RH24-10/42.
34 Altenstadt, *Unser Weg zum Meer*, pp.141–2.
35 Lachmann, ibid., pp.146–7.
36 Altenstadt, *Unser Weg Zum Meer*, p.143.
37 Storz, Hesse, *Über Schlachtfelder Vorwärts!* pp.135–6.
38 Wilson, *Dunkirk*, p.90
39 Langley, interview, Harman, *Dunkirk: The Story Behind the Legend*, BBC TV, 1980.
40 Curry, Levine, *Forgotten Voices of Dunkirk*, p.169.
41 Regiment 454 account, *Grenadier Regiment 454*, 1 June 1940. BA RH 37/3098. Ervine-Andrews, Mace, *The Dunkirk Evacuation in 100 Objects*, p.115. Storz, *Über Schlachtfelder Vorwärts!* pp.138 and 140.
42 Regiment 454, RH 37/3098.
43 Langley, interview, Harman, *Dunkirk: The Story Behind the Legend*, BBC TV, 1980.
44 Ibid.
45 Ibid.
46 Ibid. 454 Regiment, RH 37/3098.
47 Contanceau, interview, *The Other Side of Dunkirk*, BBC TV, 2004.
48 Crockitt, interview, ibid.

CHAPTER 9: ELUSIVE VICTORY

1 Richsteig, Otte and Lormes, *Warschau-Dünkirchen, Kriegserlebnisse einer Batterie 1939/40*, p.343.
2 Altenstadt, *Unser Weg Zum Meer*, p.162.
3 Heck, *A Child of Hitler*, p.40. Regiment 77 *Gefreiter*, letter 28 May 1940, Buchbender and Sterz, *Das Andere Gesicht des Krieges*, p.56. Division 44 gunner, ibid., 30 May 1940, p.57.
4 SS Secret Reports, ed. Boberach, *Meldungen aus dem Reich*, Nr 91, 27 May 1940, p.1175. Nr 92 30 Mai, p.1189 and Nr 93, 3 June 1940, p.1205. Hans S., letter 30 May, Moutier, *Liebste Schwester*, p.71.
5 Zouaves Dehay and Weber, Eloi and Marquis, *Operation Dynamo*, p.113.
6 Sprenger, Ops Officer Div 56 log, 2 June 1940.
7 Sprenger, Ops Officer and Kriebel, Div 56 log, 2 June 1940.
8 Figures, *171 Regiment Erfahrungsbericht*, St Quentin, 23.7.40 and Div 56 log, 3 June 1940.
9 Vater, *Unser Weg zum Meer*, p.144.

10 Richtsteig, Otte and Lormes, *Warschau-Dünkirchen, Kriegserlebnisse einer Batterie 1939/40*, pp.329–30.
11 X Corps report, *KTB X AK*, 2.6.40. BA RH 24-10/42. Oblt Otte, *Warschau-Dünkirchen*, p.335.
12 Voigt action, *Unser Weg zum Meer*, p.143.
13 Vater, ibid., pp.144–6.
14 Division 61 action, Hubatsch, *Die Deutschen Divisionen: 61 Infanterie Division*, pp.25–6. Borbe, *Das Infanterie Regiment 151 1939–42, Heisse Tage vor Dünkirchen*, pp.125–8. BA H20-151/1.
15 Küchler, Stasi, *Dunkirk 1940: Operation Dynamo*, p.56.
16 Coutanceau, interview, *The Other Side of Dunkirk*, BBC TV, 2004.
17 Vancoille, interview, ibid.
18 French soldier diary, Stasi, *Dunkirk 1940: Operation Dynamo*, p.59.
19 Tennant and boat details, Mace, *The Royal Navy at Dunkirk*, p.377. Lantenois, *Diary*, 2 June 1940, *De la Bataille du Nord aux Stalags* 1940, p.56. Vancoille, interview, BBC TV .
20 Wilson-Haffenden, Levine, *Forgotten Voices of Dunkirk*, p.234.
21 Vancoille, interview, BBC TV.
22 Wake-Walker, Mace, p.362.
23 Richthofen, Log, 1 and 2 June 1940, BA RL 8/43.
24 Kesselring, *The Memoirs of Field Marshal Kesselring*, p.61. Geyer, *Gen Kdo IX AK* 2.6.40, BA RH 24-9/17.
25 Järisch and Altenstadt, *Unser Weg zum Meer*, pp.166 and 156.
26 Division 18 action, *Unser Weg zum Meer*, p.163.
27 Artillery observer, *Warschau-Dünkirchen*, p.351.
28 Järisch, *Unser Weg zum Meer*, p.166.
29 Division 61, *Das Infanterie Regiment 151, 13.Abschnitt, Heisse Tage vor Dünkirchen*, p.131, BA H 20-151/1.
30 Regiment 337 report, *Inf Regt 337 Ia, Bericht uber die Einnahme von Dünkirchen*, 3 June 1940, p.7. BA RH-26-208/10.
31 Zouave Hertzog, Eloi and Marquis, *Operation Dynamo*, p.113.
32 Wake-Walker report, Mace, p.363.
33 Imhoff, *Sturm durch Frankreich*, p.152. Mordal (pen name), Harman, *Dunkirk the Patriotic Myth*, pp.219–20.
34 Hertzog, *Operation Dynamo*, p.113. Contanceau, interview, *The Other Side of Dunkirk*, BBC TV, 2004.
35 Richtsteig, *Warschau-Dünkirchen*, pp.355–6.
36 Altenstadt, *Unser Weg zum Meer*, pp.157–8.
37 Ibid.
38 Division 61, Hubatsch, p.27. Regiment 151 report, *Das Infanterie Regiment 151, Heisse Tage vor Dünkirchen*, pp.132–3, BA H20-151/1.
39 Järisch, *Unser Weg zum Meer*, pp.168 and 171.
40 Richtsteig, *Warschau-Dunkirchen*, pp.355–7.
41 Pöthko, *337 Regt Bericht uber die Einnahme von Dünkirchen*, p.9.
42 BA RH26-208/10. Braumann, Mace, *The Dunkirk Evacuation in 100 Objects*, p.198. IWM doc ref 9144.
43 Altenstadt, *Unser Weg zum Meer*, p.158.
44 Järisch, ibid., p.170. Baron family, Blankaert, *Dunkirk 1939–45*, pp.58–9. Division 61 sector report, *Das Infanterie Regiment 151*, p.132, BA H20-151/1 and Blanckaert, *Dunkirk 1939–45*, p.60.

45 Geyer, Gen Kdo IX AK, 4 June 1940, BA RH 24-9/17 and Div 56 log, 4 June 1940, BA RH 26 56/6b.

46 Timings of entry and French civilians, Blanckaert, p.59. Soldier and Regiment 54 casualties, *Unser Weg zum Meer*, p.165. Contanceau, interview, *The Other Side of Dunkirk*, BBC TV, 2004. Lebrun, Eloi and Marquis, *Operation Dynamo*, p.113.

47 Järisch, *Unser Weg zum Meer*, pp.170–1.

48 Altenstadt, ibid., pp.158–9.

49 Braumann, Mace, *The Dunkirk Evacuation in 100 Objects*, p.197.

50 Cranz, surrender conversation, Dildy, *Dunkirk 1940*, p.85. Tommies and boat, *Blitzkrieg in their own Words*, p.166. Division 18 POW figures, *Unser Weg zum Meer*, p.181.

51 Dennerlein, interview, *Hitler and the Invasion of Britain*, BBC TV, Timewatch, 1998.

POSTSCRIPT: DÜNKIRCHEN

1 Liss, *Westfront*, pp.212–13.

2 Ibid. and p.215.

3 Below, *At Hitler's Side*, p.61.

4 Warlimont, *Inside Hitler's Headquarters 1939–45*, p.101.

5 Ibid.

6 *Feldpost* letters, Hans S., 30 May 1940, Moutier, *Liebste Schwester*, p.70. Oberjäger, 4 June 1940, Buchbender and Sterz, *Das Andere Gesicht des Krieges*, p.58.

7 Atk *Gefreiter*, Infanterie-Division 44, 30 May 1940, ibid., p.57. Oberleutnant, KS Korps Kdo VAK, 30 May 1940, ibid., p.57.

8 Hauptmann 73 Div, Buchbender and Sterz, *Das Andere Gesicht des Krieges*, pp.58–9.

9 Järisch, *Unser Weg Zum Meer*, pp.170–1.

10 Luck, *Panzer Commander*, p.42.

11 Meyer, *Grenadiers*, p.22.

12 Kumm, Steinhoff, Pechel and Showalter, *Voices from the Third Reich*, p.56.

13 Unteroffizier, 4 June 1940, Buchbender and Sterz, *Das Andere Gesicht des Krieges*, pp.58–9.

14 Goebbels, Diary, ed. Reuth, *Joseph Goebbels Tagebücher, Band 4, 1940–1942*, 29 May 1940, p.1426–7 and 4 June, p.1428.

15 SS Reports, ed. Boberach, *Meldungen aus dem Reich*, Nr 94, 6 June 1940, p.1218.

16 Steinhilper, *Spitfire on my Tail*, pp.283–5.

17 Warlimont, p.100. Casualty figures, Ed. Bond and Taylor, *The Battle for France and Flanders Sixty Years On*, p.49.

18 Döring, letter 14 June 1940, ed. Bähr, Meyer and Orthbandt, *Kriegsbriefe Gefallener Studenten 1939–45*, p.18.

19 Ibid.

20 Liss, *Westfront*, p.21.

21 Air Combat losses, Dildy, *Dunkirk 1940*, p.89.

22 Casualties, Division 56, Div 56 log, 4 June 1940. Division 18, *Unser Weg zum Meer*, p.184. Regiment 54, ibid., p.165.

23 Järisch, *Unser Weg Zum Meer*, p.172.

Bibliography

GENERAL

Addison, P. and Calder, A., *Time to Kill*, Pimlico, 1997.
————ed., *Listening to Britain*, Vintage, 2011.
Aitken, L., *Massacre on the Road to Dunkirk*, Purnell, 1977.
Benoist-Méchin, J., *Sixty Days that Shook the West*, Jonathan Cape, 1963.
Blanckaert, S., *Dunkirk 1939–1945*, Editions des Beffrois, 1990.
Blumentritt, G., *Von Rundstedt*, Odhams Press, 1952.
Bond, B. and Taylor, M., *The Battle of France and Flanders Sixty Years On*, Leo Cooper, 2001.
British Army, *Royal Engineers Battlefield Tour. The Seine to the Rhine*. Vol 1, 1947, The Naval & Military Press, 2020.
Brown, M., *Spitfire Summer*, Carlton Books, 2000.
Collier, R., *The Sands of Dunkirk*, Fontana, 1963.
Cooksey, J., *Boulogne: 20 Guards Brigade's Fighting Defence, May 1940*, Pen & Sword, 2002.
————*Calais: A Fight to the Finish, May 1940*, Leo Cooper, 2000.
Cornwell, P.D., *The Battle of France Then and Now*, After The Battle, 2007.
Diamond, H., *Fleeing Hitler: France 1940*, Oxford University Press, 2007.
Dildy, D.C., *Dunkirk 1940*, Osprey, 2010.
ed. Various, *Der II Weltkrieg*, Band 3, *Tief im Feindesland*, Jahr Verlag, 1976.
Ellis, L.F., *The War in France and Flanders, 1939–1940*, HMSO, 1953.
Eloi, S. and Marquis, D., *Operation Dynamo*, A l'Assaut des Mémoires, 2018.
Franks, N., *Air Battle for Dunkirk: 26 May–3 Jun 1940*, Grub Street, 2000.
Frieser, K-H., *Blitzkrieg-Legende*, R. Oldenbourg Verlag, 1996.
Gelb, N., *Scramble. A Narrative History of the Battle of Britain*, Pan, 1986.
Greentree, D., *German Infantryman Versus British Infantryman*, Osprey, 2015.
Hamilton, N., *Monty. The Making of a General 1887–1942*, Hamlyn, 1981.
Harman, N., *Dunkirk: The Patriotic Myth*, Simon & Schuster, 1980.
Holland, J., *The Battle of Britain*, Bantum Press, 2010.
Jacobsen, H-A., *Dünkirchen*, Neckargemünd, 1958.
————ed., *Decisive Battles of World War II The German View*, André Deutsch, 1965.
————ed., *Dokumente zum Westfeldzug 1940*, Musterschmidt Verlag Band 2b, 1960.

Jackson, R., *Dunkirk The British Evacuation 1940*, Cassell, 2002.

————*Air War Over France, 1939–40*, Ian Allan, 1974.

Kershaw, R.J., *Tankmen*, Hodder & Stoughton, 2008

————*Never Surrender*, Hodder & Stoughton, 2009.

Knopp, G., *The SS: A Warning from History*, Sutton, 2002.

————*Hiter's Children*, Sutton, 2000.

Lane, R., *Last Stand at Le Paradis*, Pen & Sword, 2009.

Lantenois, M., *De la Bataille du Nord aux Stalags 1940*, Ysec Editions, 2004.

Latzel, K., *Deutscher Soldaten – Nationalsozialischer Krieg?* Ferdinand Schöningh, 1998.

Levine, J., *Forgotten Voices of Dunkirk*, Ebury Press, 2010.

Liss, U., *Westfront 1939–40*, K. Vowinckel Verlag, 1959.

Mace, M., ed., *The Royal Navy at Dunkirk*, Frontline Books, 2017.

————*The Dunkirk Evacuation in 100 Objects*, Pen & Sword, 2017.

Marshall Cavendish, *Images of War* series.

————*The War Years 1939–45*.

Mayer. S.L. and Tokoi, Masami, *Der Adler: The Luftwaffe Magazine*, Arms & Armour Press, 1977.

Mcmanus, J., ed., *Lightning War*, Third Reich Series, Time-Life, 1989.

Murland, J., *The Canal Line France and Flanders Campaign 1940*, Pen & Sword, 2018.

————*The Dunkirk Perimeter Evacuation 1940*, Pen & Sword, 2019.

Neave, A., *The Flames of Calais*, Coronet Hodder, 1974.

Neitzel, S. and Welzer, H., *Soldaten*, Simon & Schuster, 2011.

Oddone, P., *Dunkirk 1940*, Tempus, 2000.

Ohler, N., *Blitzed. Drugs in Nazi Germany*, Penguin, 2017.

Parry, S. and Postlethwaite, M., *Dunkirk Air Combat Archive*, Red Kite, 2017.

Plummer, R., *The Ships that Saved an Army*, Patrick Stephens, 1990.

Shulman, M., *Defeat in the West*, Coronet, 1973.

Shaw, F. and J., *We Remember Dunkirk*, Echo Press, 1983.

Stasi, J-C., *Dunkirk 1940 Operation Dynamo*, Heimdal, 2018.

Stourton, E., *Auntie's War*, Transworld, 2018.

Taylor, T., *The March of Conquest*, Edward Hulton, 1959.

Wilson, P., *Dunkirk From Disaster to Deliverance*, Pen & Sword, 1999.

Zayas de, A.M., *Die Wehrmacht Untersuchungs-Stelle*, Heyne Bücher, 1981.

UNPUBLISHED GENERAL ACCOUNTS

Coyle, J.M. and Rowland, D., *A Preliminary Analysis of Counter-Offensive Battles in World War II*, Nov 1986, British Army TDRC Index 7827.

Bond, B., *Arras 21 May 1940*, Research Paper, British Army TDRC Index 7030.

British Army, *Arras 21 May 1940*, 20 Armd Bde HQ, 4th Armd Div Study Period 31 Jan 1985.

————*Calais Battlefield Tour*, British Army TRDC Index 12118.

————*France 1940*, Tank Magazine Vol 40 1957.

Drewienkiewicz, *Early Training and Employment of TA build Up and Early Days of World War II*, RCDS MA Thesis 1992.

GERMAN BIOGRAPHIES, PERSONAL ACCOUNTS, DIARIES AND LETTERS

Bähr, H.W., *Die Stimme des Menschen*, Piper & Co Verlag, 1961.

————Bähr H.W., Meyer H., Orthbandt E., *Kriegsbriefe Gefallener*

————*Studenten 1939–45*, R. Wunderlich Verlag, 1952.

Balck, *Order in Chaos*, Univerity Press.

————*Conversation with General Hermann Balck*, Battelle Columbus Laboratories, Jan 1979.

Becker, H., *Devil On My Shoulder*, Jarrolds, 1955.

von Below, N., *At Hitler's Side*, Greenhill Books, 2004.

Berndt, A-I., *Tanks Break Through!* SF Tafel Pub, 2016.

Bloch, M., *Strange Defeat*, Folio, 2015.

Boberach, H., ed., *Meldungen Aus dem Reich*, Band 4, Pawlak Verlag, 1984.

von Bock, F., *Generalfeldmarschall Fedor von Bock. The War Diary 1939–45*, ed. Gerbet K., Schiffer, 1996.

Buchbender, O. and Sterz, R., *Das Andere Gesicht des Krieges, Deutsche Feldpostbriefe 1939–1945*, Verlag CH Beck, 1982.

Dollinger, H., *Kain, Wo ist dein Bruder?* Fischer Verlag, 1987.

Goebbels, J., *Tagebücher*, Band 4 1940–42, ed. R.G. Reuth, Piper, 1999.

Grady, S., *Gardens of Stone*, Hodder, 2013.

Guderian, H., *Panzer Leader*, Michael Joseph, 1970.

————Fwd Guderian, *Blitzkrieg in Their Own Words*, Amber Books 2005.

Habe, H., *A Thousand Shall Fall*, Mayflower, 1970.

Halder, F., *The Halder War Diary 1939–1942*, ed. Burdick C. and Jacobsen H-A., Greenhill Books, 1988.

Hammer, I. and Nieden zur S., *Sehr Selten Habe Ich Geweint*, Schweizer Verlaghaus, 1992.

Heck, A., *A Child of Hitler*, Renaissance House, 1985.

Kaufmann, G., *Botschaft der Gefallenen. Briefe aus dem II Weltkrieg*, VGB Verlag, 1996.

Kesselring, A., *The Memoirs of Field Marshal Kesselring*, Greenhill 1988.

Knappe, S., *Soldat*, Dell, 1992.

Kuby, E., *Mein Krieg*, Deutscher Taschenbuch Verlag, 1977.

von Luck, H., *Panzer Commander*, Dell, 1989.

Moutier, M., *Lieber Schwester, wir müssen hier sterben oder siegen, Briefe deutscher Wehrmachtssoldaten 1939–45*, Blessing, 2015.

Schroeder, C., *Er War Mein Chef*, Herbig, 1985.

Steinhilper, U., *Spitfire on my Tail*, Independent Books, 1989.

Steinhoff, J., Pechel, P. and Showalter, D., *Deutsche im Zweiten Weltkrieg*, Bastei-Lübbe, 1989.

Mahlke, H., *Memoires of a Stuka Pilot*, Frontline Books, 2013.

Merle, R., *Weekend at Dunkirk*, Signet, 1965.

Meyer, K., *Grenadiers*, Stackpole, 2005.

Nehring, W.K., *Amiens to Dunkirk: A Personal Impression*, Purnell's History of the Second World War, Vol 1.

Ritgen, H., *Westfront 1944*, Motor Buch Verlag, 2004.

Warlimont, W., *Inside Hitler's Headquarters 1939–45*, Presidio, 1964.

GERMAN UNIT ACCOUNTS

Published Luftwaffe

Bekker, C., *The Luftwaffe War Diaries*, Macdonald, 1966.
Brütting, G., *Das Waren die deutschen Kampfflieger Asse 1939–45*, Motorbuch, 1993.
Caldwell, D.L., *JG 26 Top Guns of the Luftwaffe*, Orion, 1991.
Dierich, W., *Kampfgeschwader 55 'Greif'*, Motorbuch, 1994.
Hooten, E.R., *Luftwaffe at War, Blitzkrieg in the West 1939–40*, Ian Allen, 2007.
Mackay, R., *Heinkel III*, Crowood Press, 2003.
Musciano, W.A., *Die Berühmten Me 109 und ihre Piloten 1939–45*, Weltbild, 1995.
Priller, J., *Geschichte Eines Jagdgeschwaders Das JG26 von 1937 bis 1945*, Kurt Vowinckel, 1956.
Smith, P.C., *Stuka*, Motorbuch, 1993.
Vasco, J.J. and Cornwell, P.D., *Zerstörer. The Messerschmitt 110 and its Units in 1940*, JAC Pub, 1995.
Weal, J., *Junkers Ju 87 Stukageschwader 1937–41*, Osprey, 1997.
Winter, F.F., *Die Deutschen Jagdflieger*, Universitas München, 2001.

Unpublished Luftwaffe, Bundesarchiv

Berichte des Oberbefehlshaber der Luftwaffe Führungstab Ic, 22.5.1940–3.6.1940 R12II/206, 207 & 208.
VIII Fliegerkorps in Frankreich Feldzug, (Richthofen), RL8/43.
Kriegstagebuch JG 77 9 Mai 1940 bis 21 Juli 1940, RL10/301.

Published Army

Bernage, G. and Mary, J-Y., *Les Panzers France 1940*, Heimdal, 2020.
Buchner, A., *Das Handbuch der Deutschen Infanterie 1939–45*, Podzun Pallas, 1987.
Engelmann, J., *Die 18. Infanterie und Panzergrenadier Division 1934–1945*, Podzun-Pallas, 1984.
Gareis, M., *Kampf und Ende Der Frankisch Sudetendeutschen 98. Division*, Podzun-Pallas, 1956.
Gshöpf, R., *Mein Weg mit der 45.Infanterie Division*, Buchdienst Südtirol, 2002.
Haupt, W., *Die 8. Panzer Division im Zweiten Weltkrieg*, Podzun-Pallas, 1987.
Hubatsch, W., *61 Infanterie Division*, Hans Henning Podzun, 1952.
Jenner, M., *Die Niedersächsische 216/272 Infanterie Division 1939–45*, Podzun-Pallas Verlag, 1964.
——*Mitteilungsblatt Nr 5*, Hannover, Jul 1967.
Lehmann, R., *Die Leibstandarte Band I*, J.J. Fedorowicz, 1987.
Lefèvre, E., *SS Totenkopf France 1940*, Histoire & Collections, 2010.
Lucas, J. and Cooper, M., *Hitler's Elite Leibstandarte SS*, Macdonald & Jane's, 1975.
von Manteuffel, H.E., *Die 7. Panzer Division im Zweiten Weltkrieg*, Podzun-Pallas, 1986.
Ritgen, H., *The 6th Panzer Division 1937–35*, Osprey, 1982.
Schick, A., *Combat History of the 10th Panzer Division 1939–43*, J.J. Fedorowicz, 2013.

Spaeter, H., *The History of the Panzerkorps Grossdeutschland*, Vol 1, J.J. Fedorowicz, 1992.

Steiner, F., *Die Friedens und Kriegsjahre der 2. (Wiener) Panzer Division in Wort und Bild*, Eigen Verlag, 1990.

Steinzer, F., *Die 2. Panzer Division*, Dorfler Zeitgeschichte.

Strauss, F-J., *Geschichte der 2. (Wiener) Panzer Division*, Podzun-Pallas, 1987.

Stoves, R.O.G., *1 Panzer Division 1935–45*, Hans-Henning Podzun, 1962.

Ullrich, K., *Wie Ein Fels Im Meer. Kriegsgeschichte der 3.SS Panzer Division Totenkopf*, Munin Verlag, 1987.

Unpublished Army, Bundesarchiv

18 Armee Oberkommando Kriegstagebuch des Westfeldzuges, a) Niederlande-Flandern - Dunkirchen, 9.5. - 4.6. 40. RH20-18/35.

Armee Kdo 18. Meldungen der 18. Armee an die Heeresgruppe B während des Frankreichfeldzuges. RH20-18/29.

XXXIX AK Kriegstagebuch 17.5 - 31.5. 40, (Gruppe Hoth, Fourth Army). RH24-3917.

Generalkommando IX AK Feldzug in Frankreich. Der Feldzug des IX AK von der Maas bis Dunkirchen 10.5.- 4.6.1940. (Gen Hermann Geyer). RH24-9/17.

Kriegstagebuch Nr 3 der Gruppe Guderian XIX AK Uber die Sclacht in Frankreich 9.5. - 24.6.40. RH21-2/V 41.

Kriegstagebuch des Gen Kdo XXXXI AK 2.2.40 - 8.7.40. (Gruppe Reinhardt) RH24-41/2

Kriegstagebuch des X AK Westfeldzug. 1.5. - 31. 7. 40. RH24-10/42.

Kriegstagebuch Nr 2 IX AK - Ia vom 9.5.40 - 7.6.40. RH24/9 12.

Kriegstagebuch 5 Pz Div. Einsatz im Westen 10.5.40 - 12.7. 40. RH27-5179.

Kriegstagebuch der 10. Pz Div vom 9.5. - 29.6.40. RH27-10/9.

18.Div Kriegstagebuch 1.2.40 - 2.8. 40. RH26-18/5.

Erfahrungsbericht der 18. Division. RH26-18/19.

18.Inf Div Ia Kartenanlagen zum KTB nr 2 17.10.39 - 5.6. 40.(Situation Map)

Kriegstagebuch 56 Infanterie Division. Die Schlacht in Flandern und in Artois bei 18.Armee:
Teil 1. 9.5.1940 - 19.5. 1940. RH26-56/5
Teil 2. 20.5.1940 - 4.6.1940. RH26-56/6a-6b

56 Infanterie Division Erfahrungsbericht 171 Inf Regt St Qu. 23.7.1940.

Kriegstagebuch I/192 (with 56 Div Hpt Schimpf) RH37/2799.

208 Inf Division Ia Kriegstagebuch 22.5.40-10.6.40. RH26-208/10.

Das Infanterie Regiment 151 1939-1942, H20-151/1. (with 61 Div).

Schicksale und Kämpfe des II Gren Regt 454 1939–45, (with 254 Inf Div). 1951. RH37/3098

Kriegstagebuch des Art Regt 156 vom 10.5. - 4.6.Flandernschlacht 1940.

Gefechtsberichte der IV/Art Rgt 216 Mai/Juni 1940. (216 Inf Div) *Kämpfe an der Lys 24.26.5.1940. Kämpfe vor Dünkirchen 29.5 - 4.6.1940*

Kampfbericht der 7. Kompanie Belgien 1940. (Inf Regt 192 with 56 Div). RH26-56/75.

GERMAN LANGUAGE WARTIME ACCOUNTS

von Altenstadt, H-G., *Unser Weg Zum Meer*, Wehrmacht Verlag, 1940.

Der Adler, Luftwaffe wartime magazine, Issue 13, 1940 copies.

DÜNKIRCHEN 1940

Christophé, C.C., *Wir Stossen mit Panzern zum Meer*, Steiniger Verlag Berlin, 1941.

Dwinger, E., *Panzer Führer*, Eugen Diedrichs Verlag Jena, 1941.

Hesse, K., *Über Schlachtfelder Vorwärts!* Wilhelm-Limpert Verlag Berlin, 1940.

von Imhoff, C. Freiherr, *Sturm Durch Frankreich*, Hans von Hugo Verlag Berlin, 1941.

von Kielmansegg, Graf, *Panzer Zwischen Warschau und Atlantik*, Wehrmacht Verlag, 1941.

———Schick, A., donation, *Kradschützen Vor! Frankreich Tagebuch 7. Kompanie*, 1940.

———Schick, A., donation, König B, *Zweieinhalbtausand Kilometer durch Frankreich*, magazine article, Heft 30/1941.

Otte and Lormes, *Warschau-Dunkirchen Kriegserlebnisse einer Batterie 1939–40*, Wagner Liegnitz, 1942.

Sieg Über Frankreich, Wilhelm Andermann OKW publication, 1940.

Signal, German wartime magazine, 1940 copies.

Die Wehrmacht 1940, Die Wehrmacht Verlag, 1940.

TV & MEDIA INTERVIEWS

Eder, H. and Kufus, T., *Mein Krieg*, German WDR TV.

Dimbleby, R., *Dunkirk. The Final Tribute*, BBC TV, 2000.

Fey, C. and Knopp, G., *The SS*, German ZDF TV, 2002.

Gorden, P., *Dunkirk. The Soldier's Story*, BBC 2 TV, 2004.

Harman, N., *Dunkirk. The Story Behind the Legend*, Prod Hastings, BBC TV, 1980.

Hartl, P. and Knopp, G., *Hitler's Children*, ZDF TV.

Hess, J. and Wuermeling, *Die Deutschem im Zweiten Weltkrieg*, German TV BR/SWF/ORF Filmserie, 1985.

Hoggard, S., *World War Speed*, Brave Planet & Thirteen Productions, 2018.

Holmes, R., *War Walks, Dunkirk*, BBC TV, 1997.

Laurence, A., *The Other Side of Dunkirk*, BBC TV Bristol, 2004.

Maddocks, N., *Dunkirk. The Forgotten Heroes*, Testimony Films, 2010.

Rogalin, P., *Interview*, Mémoires Internet.

Snow, D. and Sands, L., *Little Ships*, BBC NI TV, 2010.

Zylberman, R., *France 1939 One Last Summer*, Zadig TV Production, 2019.

Index

Page numbers in **bold** refer to maps